BUSINESS ANALYSIS & VALUATION

USING FINANCIAL STATEMENTS

Fourth Edition

Krishna G. Palepu, PhD

Ross Graham Walker Professor of Business Administration
Harvard University

Paul M. Healy, PhD, ACA

James R. Williston Professor of Business Administration
Harvard University

THOMSON
TM
SOUTH-WESTERN

Australia · Canada · Mexico · Singapore · Spain · United Kingdom · United States

THOMSON

™

SOUTH-WESTERN

Business Analysis & Valuation: Using Financial Statements, 4th edition
Krishna G. Palepu, Paul M. Healy

VP/Editorial Director:
Jack W. Calhoun

VP/Editor-in-Chief:
Rob Dewey

Acquisitions Editor:
Matt Filimonov

Developmental Editor:
Craig Avery

Marketing Manager:
Kristen Hurd

Content Project Manager:
Diane Bowdler

Manager of Technology, Editorial:
Matt McKinney

Technology Project Manager:
Robin Browning

Website Project Manager:
Brian Courter

Manufacturing Coordinator:
Doug Wilke

Production House:
Integra Software Services Pvt. Ltd.

Printer:
Transcontinental Gagne
Louiseville, QC

Art Director:
Linda Helcher

Internal Designer:
Ke Design

Cover Designer:
Paul Neff

Cover Image:
Jerry Alexander/Stone/
© Getty Images

Library of Congress Control Number: 2007924489

For more information about our products, contact us at:

Thomson Learning
Academic Resource Center

1-800-423-0563

Thomson Higher Education
5191 Natorp Boulevard
Mason, OH 45040
USA

PREFACE

Financial statements are the basis for a wide range of business analysis. Managers use them to monitor and judge their firms' performance relative to competitors, to communicate with external investors, to help judge what financial policies they should pursue, and to evaluate potential new businesses to acquire as part of their investment strategy. Securities analysts use financial statements to rate and value companies they recommend to clients. Bankers use them in deciding whether to extend a loan to a client and to determine the loan's terms. Investment bankers use them as a basis for valuing and analyzing prospective buyouts, mergers, and acquisitions. And consultants use them as a basis for competitive analysis for their clients. Not surprisingly, therefore, we find that there is a strong demand among business students for a course that provides a framework for using financial statement data in a variety of business analysis and valuation contexts. The purpose of this book is to provide such a framework for business students and practitioners. The first three editions of this book have succeeded far beyond our expectations in equipping readers with this useful framework, and the book has gained proponents in accounting and finance departments in business schools in the U.S. and around the world.

CHANGES FROM THE THIRD EDITION

Colleagues and reviewers have made suggestions and comments that led us to incorporate the following changes in the fourth edition:

- Data, analyses, and issues have been thoroughly updated in the fourth edition.
- The financial analysis and valuation chapters (chapters 6–8) have been updated with a focus on firms in the U.S. discount retail sector, primarily Wal-Mart and Dell.
- Chapter 6 on forecasting has been enhanced with an expanded discussion of business strategy analysis.
- We have increased conciseness by incorporating key elements of the chapter in the third edition on debt financing into this edition's chapters on credit analysis (Chapter 10) and corporate governance (Chapter 12).
- In our Text and Cases edition, we have included new and updated Harvard Business School cases, both to accompany the individual chapters as well as in Section 4 containing additional cases. In all, we include 29 cases in the fourth edition.
- We have enhanced the usability of the BAV software tool, including, most importantly, the ability to automatically download data from the Compustat database of the Wharton Research Data Services. This comprehensive software model, the **BAV Tool**, implements the analytical framework and techniques discussed in this book. BAV allows students to import a company's reported financial statements from any source, as long as they are in a Microsoft Excel spreadsheet format, and analyze them. The tool allows the analyst to import financial statements of a company from any database into an excel-based workbook, create a set of financial statements in a standardized format to facilitate analysis, and implement the key steps of analysis

discussed in the book – accounting adjustments, ratio and cash flow analysis, preparation of pro forma financial statements for a chosen forecast horizon (up to fifteen years), and estimate the intrinsic value of the company using a variety of valuation techniques. User-friendly interface and drop down menus allow the analyst to navigate through the tool with ease. Built-in databases of historical financial ratios allow students to compare their forecasting assumptions with historical trends.

The tool facilitates the following activities: (1) recasting the reported financial statements in a standard format for analysis; (2) performing accounting analysis as discussed in Chapters 3 and 4, making desired accounting adjustments, and producing restated financials; (3) computing ratios and free cash flows presented in Chapter 5; (4) producing forecasted income statement, balance sheet, and cash flow statements for as many as 15 years into the future, using the approach discussed in Chapter 6; and (5) valuing a company (either assets or equity) from these forecasts and preparing a terminal value forecast using the abnormal earnings, the abnormal returns, and discounted cash flow methods discussed in Chapters 7 and 8. The tool also allows students to graph their assumptions and compare them with the historical performance of a large group of U.S. companies that are in the same performance range at the beginning of the forecasting period. This comparison is facilitated by a database consisting of key ratios for a comprehensive set of U.S. public companies listed on Standard & Poor's Compustat. We think that the BAV Tool will make it significantly easier for students to apply the framework and techniques discussed in the book in a real-world context.

KEY FEATURES

This book differs from other texts in business and financial analysis in a number of important ways. We introduce and develop a **four-part framework for business analysis and valuation** using financial statement data. We then show how this framework can be applied to a variety of decision contexts.

Framework for Analysis

We begin the book with a discussion of the role of accounting information and intermediaries in the economy, and how financial analysis can create value in well functioning markets (Chapter 1). We identify four key components, or steps, of effective financial statement analysis:

- Business strategy analysis
- Accounting analysis
- Financial analysis
- Prospective analysis

The first step, **business strategy analysis** (Chapter 2), involves developing an understanding of the business and competitive strategy of the firm being analyzed. Incorporating business strategy into financial statement analysis is one of the distinctive features of this book. Traditionally, this step has been ignored by other financial statement analysis books. However, we believe that it is critical to begin financial statement analysis with a company's strategy because it provides an important foundation for the subsequent analysis. The strategy analysis section discusses contemporary tools for analyzing a company's industry, its competitive position and sustainability within an industry, and the company's corporate strategy.

Accounting analysis (Chapters 3 and 4) involves examining how accounting rules and conventions represent a firm's business economics and strategy in its financial statements, and, if necessary, developing adjusted accounting measures of performance. In the accounting analysis section, we do not emphasize accounting rules. Instead we develop general approaches to analyzing assets, liabilities, entities, revenues, and expenses. We believe that such an approach enables students to effectively evaluate a company's accounting choices and accrual estimates, even if students have only a basic knowledge of accounting rules and standards. The material is also designed to allow students to make accounting adjustments rather than merely identify questionable accounting practices.

Financial analysis (Chapter 5) involves analyzing financial ratio and cash flow measures of the operating, financing, and investing performance of a company relative to either key competitors or historical performance. Our distinctive approach focuses on using financial analysis to evaluate the effectiveness of a company's strategy and to make sound financial forecasts.

Finally, in **prospective analysis** (Chapters 6–8) we show how to develop forecasted financial statements and how to use these to make estimates of a firm's value. Our discussion of valuation includes traditional discounted cash flow models as well as techniques that link value directly to accounting numbers. In discussing accounting-based valuation models, we integrate the latest academic research with traditional approaches such as earnings and book value multiples that are widely used in practice.

Although we cover all four steps of business analysis and valuation in the book, we recognize that the extent of their use depends on the user's decision context. For example, bankers are likely to use business strategy analysis, accounting analysis, financial analysis, and the forecasting portion of prospective analysis. They are less likely to be interested in formally valuing a prospective client.

Application of the Framework to Decision Contexts

The next section of the book shows how our business analysis and valuation framework can be applied to a variety of decision contexts:

- Equity securities analysis (Chapter 9)
- Credit analysis and distress prediction (Chapter 10)
- Merger and acquisition analysis (Chapter 11)
- Communication and governance (Chapter 12)

For each of these topics we present an overview to provide a foundation for the class discussions. Where possible we discuss relevant institutional details and the results of academic research that are useful in applying the analysis concepts developed earlier in the book. For example, the chapter on credit analysis shows how banks and rating agencies use financial statement data to develop analysis for lending decisions and to rate public debt issues. This chapter also presents academic research on how to determine whether a company is financially distressed.

USING THE BOOK

We designed the book so that it is flexible for courses in financial statement analysis for a variety of student audiences—MBA students, master's in accounting students, executive program participants, and undergraduates in accounting or finance. Depending upon the audience, the instructor can vary the manner in which the conceptual materials in the chapters and end-of-chapter questions are used. To get the most out of the book, students should have completed basic courses in financial accounting, finance, and either business strategy or business economics. The text provides a concise overview of some of these topics. But it would probably be difficult for students with no prior knowledge in these fields to use the chapters as stand-alone coverage of them.

If the book is used for students with prior working experience or for executives, the instructor can use almost a pure case approach, adding relevant lecture sections as needed. When teaching students with little work experience, a lecture class can be presented first, followed by an appropriate case or other assignment material. Alternatively, lectures can be used as a follow-up to cases to more clearly lay out the conceptual issues raised in the case discussions. This may be appropriate when the book is used in undergraduate capstone courses. In such a context, cases can be used in course projects that can be assigned to student teams.

ACKNOWLEDGMENTS

The first edition of this book was co-authored with our colleague and friend, Victor Bernard. Vic was the Price Waterhouse Professor of Accounting and Director of the Paton Accounting Center at the University of Michigan. He passed away unexpectedly on November 14, 1995. We are indebted to Vic for his contributions to the ideas reflected in the book. Over the years, we have continued to include Vic as a co-author since the initial project was such a team effort and many of his early contributions continued to be reflected in the text. We wish to acknowledge Vic's enduring contributions to our own views on financial analysis and valuation. However, we have decided that in the twelve years since Vic's passing, it is time to recognize the sad reality that almost all of Vic's material has been updated to reflect the changes that have occurred in the field.

We also wish to thank Arjuna Costa for his tireless research assistance in the revision of the text chapters; Jonathan Barnett for his work as a research assistant on prior editions of the book and especially for his help in developing the BAV Model; Keith MacKay (Village Software) and HBS Publishing for building and enhancing the BAV Model; Chris Allen for assistance with data on financial ratios for U.S. companies; the Division of Research at the Harvard Business School for assistance in developing materials for this book; and our past and present MBA students for stimulating our thinking and challenging us to continually improve our ideas and presentation.

We especially thank the following colleagues who gave us feedback as we wrote this edition: Randolph Coyner (Florida Atlantic University), John Hand (University of North Carolina, Chapel Hill), Mary Fox Luquette (University of Louisiana at Lafayette), Amin Mawani (York University), Laurel Bond Mitchell (University of Redlands and Pomona College), Partha Mohanram (Columbia University), Jay Rich (Illinois State University), Michael Sandretto (University of Illinois, Urbana-Champaign), William Salatka (Wilfred Laurier University), and Linda Thorne (York University).

We are also very grateful to Laurie Palepu and Deborah Marlino for their help and assistance throughout this project. Special gratitude goes to Rob Dewey and Matt

Filimonov for their publishing leadership on this edition, to our colleagues, and to Craig Avery, Kristen Hurd, and Diane Bowdler for their developmental, marketing, and production help. Michael Sandretto deserves great credit for his careful reading of each chapter in page proof and for his numerous insights. We would like to thank our parents and families for their strong support and encouragement throughout this project.

Krishna G. Palepu
Paul M. Healy

AUTHORS

Krishna G. Palepu is the Ross Graham Walker Professor of Business Administration and Senior Associate Dean for International Development, at the Harvard Business School, Harvard University. Prior to assuming his current administrative position, Professor Palepu held other positions at the School, including Senior Associate Dean, Director of Research, and Chair, Accounting and Control Unit.

Professor Palepu's current research and teaching activities focus on strategy and governance. In the area of strategy, his recent focus has been on the globalization of emerging markets. In the area of corporate governance, Professor Palepu's work focuses on how to make corporate boards more effective, and on improving corporate disclosure. Professor Palepu teaches these topics in several HBS programs aimed at members of corporate boards: "How to make corporate boards more effective," "Audit Committees in the new era of governance, "Compensation Committees: Preparing the challenges ahead." He also co-led Harvard Business School's Corporate Governance, Leadership, and Values initiative, launched in response to the recent wave of corporate scandals and governance failures.

Professor Palepu serves on a number of public company and non-profit Boards. He has been on the Editorial Boards of leading academic journals, and has served as a consultant to a wide variety of businesses. He is also a frequent commentator in the news media on issues related to emerging markets and corporate governance. Professor Palepu has a doctorate from the Massachusetts Institute of Technology, and an Honorary Doctorate from the Helsinki School of Economics and Business Administration.

Paul M. Healy is James R. Williston Professor of Business Administration and Chair of the Accounting and Management Unit at Harvard Business School, Harvard University. Professor Healy joined Harvard Business School as a Professor of Business Administration in 1997. His primary teaching and research interests include corporate financial reporting, financial analysis, corporate governance, and corporate finance. Professor Healy received his B.C.A. Honors (1st Class) in Accounting and Finance from Victoria University, New Zealand in 1977, his M.S. in Economics from the University of Rochester in 1981, his Ph.D. in Business from the University of Rochester in 1983, and is a New Zealand CPA. In New Zealand, Professor Healy worked for Arthur Young and ICI. Prior to joining Harvard, Professor Healy spent fourteen years on the faculty at the M.I.T. Sloan School of Management, where he received awards for teaching excellence in 1991, 1992, and

1997. In 1993–94 he served as Deputy Dean at the Sloan School, and in 1994–95 he visited London Business School and Harvard Business School.

Professor Healy's research has focused on the performance of financial analysts, the effectiveness of management disclosure strategies, post-merger performance, and earnings management. His work has been published in leading journals in accounting and finance. In 1990, his article 'The Effect of Bonus Schemes on Accounting Decisions,' published in *Journal of Accounting and Economics*, was awarded the AICPA/AAA Notable Contribution Award. His text *Business Analysis and Valuation* was awarded the AICPA/AAA's Wildman Medal for contributions to the practice in 1997, and the AICPA/AAA Notable Contribution Award in 1998.

CONTENTS

3: Overview of Accounting Analysis   *3-1*

4: Implementing Accounting Analysis   *4-1*

PART THREE
BUSINESS ANALYSIS AND VALUATION APPLICATIONS

PART ONE

FRAMEWORK

Chapter 1

A Framework for Business Analysis and Valuation Using Financial Statements

This chapter outlines a comprehensive framework for financial statement analysis. Because financial statements provide the most widely available data on public corporations' economic activities, investors and other stakeholders rely on financial reports to assess the plans and performance of firms and corporate managers.

A variety of questions can be addressed by business analysis using financial statements, as shown in the following examples:

- A security analyst may be interested in asking: "How well is the firm I am following performing? Did the firm meet my performance expectations? If not, why not? What is the value of the firm's stock given my assessment of the firm's current and future performance?"
- A loan officer may need to ask: "What is the credit risk involved in lending a certain amount of money to this firm? How well is the firm managing its liquidity and solvency? What is the firm's business risk? What is the additional risk created by the firm's financing and dividend policies?"
- A management consultant might ask: "What is the structure of the industry in which the firm is operating? What are the strategies pursued by various players in the industry? What is the relative performance of different firms in the industry?"
- A corporate manager may ask: "Is my firm properly valued by investors? Is our investor communication program adequate to facilitate this process?" or "Is this firm a potential takeover target? How much value can be added if we acquire this firm? How can we finance the acquisition?"
- An independent auditor would want to ask: "Are the accounting policies and accrual estimates in this company's financial statements consistent with my understanding of this business and its recent performance? Do these financial reports communicate the current status and significant risks of the business?"

The industrial age has been dominated by two distinct and broad ideologies for channeling savings into business investments—capitalism and central planning. The capitalist market model broadly relies on the market mechanism to govern economic activity, and decisions regarding investments are made privately. Centrally planned economies have used central planning and government agencies to pool national savings and to direct investments in business enterprises. The failure of this model is evident from the fact that most of these economies have abandoned it in favor of the market model. In almost all countries in the world today, capital markets play an important role in channeling financial resources from savers to business enterprises that need capital.

Financial statement analysis is a valuable activity when managers have in-depth information on a firm's strategies and performance and a variety of institutional factors make it unlikely that they fully disclose this information. In this setting, outside analysts attempt to create "inside information" from analyzing financial statement data, thereby gaining valuable insights about the firm's current performance and future prospects.

To understand the contribution that financial statement analysis can make, it is important to understand the role of financial reporting in the functioning of capital markets and the institutional forces that shape financial statements. Therefore, we first present a brief description of these forces followed by a discussion of the steps that an analyst must perform to extract information from financial statements and provide valuable forecasts.

THE ROLE OF FINANCIAL REPORTING IN CAPITAL MARKETS

A critical challenge for any economy is the allocation of savings to investment opportunities. Economies that do this well can exploit new business ideas to spur innovation and create jobs and wealth at a rapid pace. In contrast, economies that manage this process poorly tend to dissipate their wealth and fail to support business opportunities.

Figure 1-1 provides a schematic representation of how capital markets typically work. Savings in any economy are widely distributed among households. There are usually many new entrepreneurs and existing companies that would like to attract these savings to fund their business ideas. While both savers and entrepreneurs would like to do business with each other, matching savings to business investment opportunities is complicated for at least three reasons. First, entrepreneurs typically have better information than savers on the value of business investment opportunities. Second, communication by entrepreneurs to investors is not completely credible because investors know entrepreneurs have an incentive to inflate the value of their ideas. Third, savers generally lack the financial sophistication needed to analyze and differentiate between the various business opportunities.

The information and incentive problems lead to what economists call the "lemons" problem, which can potentially break down the functioning of capital markets.[1] It works like this: Consider a situation where half the business ideas are "good" and the other half are "bad." If investors cannot distinguish between the two types of business ideas, entrepreneurs with bad ideas will try to claim that their ideas are as valuable as the

| FIGURE 1-1 | Capital Markets |

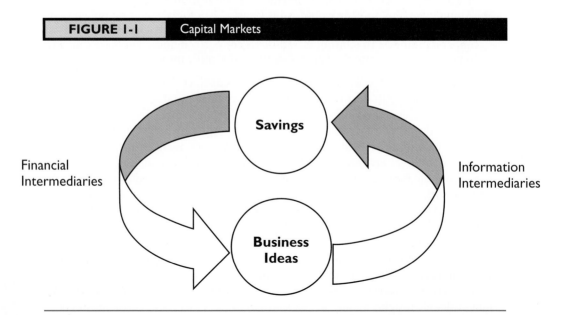

good ideas. Realizing this possibility, investors value both good and bad ideas at an average level. Unfortunately, this penalizes good ideas, and entrepreneurs with good ideas find the terms on which they can get financing to be unattractive. As these entrepreneurs leave the capital market, the proportion of bad ideas in the market increases. Over time, bad ideas "crowd out" good ideas, and investors lose confidence in this market.

The emergence of intermediaries can prevent such a market breakdown. Intermediaries are like a car mechanic who provides an independent certification of a used car's quality to help a buyer and seller agree on a price. There are two types of intermediaries in the capital markets. Financial intermediaries, such as venture capital firms, banks, mutual funds, and insurance companies, focus on aggregating funds from individual investors and analyzing different investment alternatives to make investment decisions. Information intermediaries, such as auditors, financial analysts, bond-rating agencies, and the financial press, focus on providing information to investors (and to the financial intermediaries who represent them) on the quality of various business investment opportunities. Both these types of intermediaries add value by helping investors distinguish good investment opportunities from the bad ones.

Financial reporting plays a critical role in the functioning of both the information intermediaries and financial intermediaries. Information intermediaries add value by either enhancing the credibility of financial reports (as auditors do), or by analyzing the information in financial statements (as analysts and the rating agencies do). Financial intermediaries rely on the information in financial statements to analyze investment opportunities, and they supplement this with information from other sources.

Ideally, the different intermediaries serve as a system of checks and balances to ensure the efficient functioning of the capital markets system. However, this is not always the case as on occasion the intermediaries tend to mutually reinforce rather than counterbalance each other. A number of problems can arise as a result of incentive issues, governance issues within the intermediary organizations themselves, and conflicts of interest, as evidenced by the spectacular failures of companies such as Enron and WorldCom.[2] However, in general this market mechanism functions efficiently and prices reflect all available information on a particular investment. Despite this overall market efficiency, individual securities may still be mispriced, thereby justifying the need for financial statement analysis.

In the following section, we discuss key aspects of the financial reporting system design that enable it to effectively play this vital role in the functioning of the capital markets.

FROM BUSINESS ACTIVITIES TO FINANCIAL STATEMENTS

Corporate managers are responsible for acquiring physical and financial resources from the firm's environment and using them to create value for the firm's investors. Value is created when the firm earns a return on its investment in excess of the cost of capital. Managers formulate business strategies to achieve this goal, and they implement them through business activities. A firm's business activities are influenced by its economic environment and its own business strategy. The economic environment includes the firm's industry, its input and output markets, and the regulations under which the firm operates. The firm's business strategy determines how firm positions itself in its environment to achieve a competitive advantage.

As shown in Figure 1-2, a firm's financial statements summarize the economic consequences of its business activities. The firm's business activities in any time period are

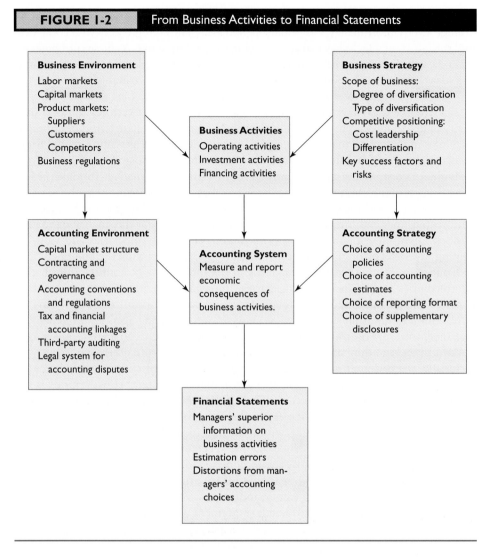

FIGURE I-2   From Business Activities to Financial Statements

too numerous to be reported individually to outsiders. Further, some of the activities undertaken by the firm are proprietary in nature, and disclosing these activities in detail could be a detriment to the firm's competitive position. The firm's accounting system provides a mechanism through which business activities are selected, measured, and aggregated into financial statement data.

INFLUENCES OF THE ACCOUNTING SYSTEM ON INFORMATION QUALITY

Intermediaries using financial statement data to do business analysis have to be aware that financial reports are influenced both by the firm's business activities and by its accounting system. A key aspect of financial statement analysis, therefore, involves understanding the influence of the accounting system on the quality of the financial statement data being used in the analysis. The institutional features of accounting systems discussed below determine the extent of that influence.

Feature 1: Accrual Accounting

One of the fundamental features of corporate financial reports is that they are prepared using accrual rather than cash accounting. Unlike cash accounting, accrual accounting distinguishes between the recording of costs and benefits associated with economic activities and the actual payment and receipt of cash. Net income is the primary periodic performance index under accrual accounting. To compute net income, the effects of economic transactions are recorded on the basis of *expected*, not necessarily *actual*, cash receipts and payments. Expected cash receipts from the delivery of products or services are recognized as revenues, and expected cash outflows associated with these revenues are recognized as expenses.

The need for accrual accounting arises from investors' demand for financial reports on a periodic basis. Because firms undertake economic transactions on a continual basis, the arbitrary closing of accounting books at the end of a reporting period leads to a fundamental measurement problem. Since cash accounting does not report the full economic consequence of the transactions undertaken in a given period, accrual accounting is designed to provide more complete information on a firm's periodic performance.

Feature 2: Accounting Conventions and Standards

The use of accrual accounting lies at the center of many important complexities in corporate financial reporting. Because accrual accounting deals with *expectations* of future cash consequences of current events, it is subjective and relies on a variety of assumptions. Who should be charged with the primary responsibility of making these assumptions? In the current system, a firm's managers are entrusted with the task of making the appropriate estimates and assumptions to prepare the financial statements because they have intimate knowledge of their firm's business.

The accounting discretion granted to managers is potentially valuable because it allows them to reflect inside information in reported financial statements. However, since investors view profits as a measure of managers' performance, managers have incentives to use their accounting discretion to distort reported profits by making biased assumptions. Further, the use of accounting numbers in contracts between the firm and outsiders provides another motivation for management manipulation of accounting numbers. Income management distorts financial accounting data, making them less valuable to external users of financial statements. Therefore, the delegation of financial reporting decisions to corporate managers has both costs and benefits.

A number of accounting conventions have evolved to ensure that managers use their accounting flexibility to summarize their knowledge of the firm's business activities and not disguise reality for self-serving purposes. For example, the measurability and conservatism conventions are accounting responses to concerns about distortions from managers' potentially optimistic bias. Both these conventions attempt to limit managers' optimistic bias by imposing their own pessimistic bias.

Accounting standards, promulgated by the Financial Accounting Standards Board (FASB) in the U.S. and similar standard-setting bodies in other countries, also limit potential distortions that managers can introduce into reported numbers. These uniform standards, such as the Generally Accepted Accounting Principles (GAAP) in the U.S. and the International Financial Reporting Standards (IFRS) internationally, attempt to reduce managers' ability to record similar economic transactions in dissimilar ways, either over time or across firms.

Increased uniformity from accounting standards, however, comes at the expense of reduced flexibility for managers to reflect genuine business differences in their firms' financial statements. Rigid accounting standards work best for economic transactions whose accounting treatment is not predicated on managers' proprietary information. However, when there is significant business judgment involved in assessing a transaction's economic consequences, rigid standards which prevent managers from using their superior business knowledge would be counterproductive. Further, if accounting standards are too rigid, they may induce managers to expend economic resources to restructure business transactions to achieve a desired accounting result.

Feature 3: Managers' Reporting Strategy

Because the mechanisms that limit managers' ability to distort accounting data add noise, it is not optimal to use accounting regulation to eliminate managerial flexibility completely. Therefore, real-world accounting systems leave considerable room for managers to influence financial statement data. A firm's reporting strategy, i.e., the manner in which managers use their accounting discretion, has an important influence on the firm's financial statements.

Corporate managers can choose accounting and disclosure policies that make it more or less difficult for external users of financial reports to understand the true economic picture of their businesses. Accounting rules often provide a broad set of alternatives from which managers can choose. Further, managers are entrusted with making a range of estimates in implementing these accounting policies. Accounting regulations usually prescribe *minimum* disclosure requirements, but they do not restrict managers from *voluntarily* providing additional disclosures.

A superior disclosure strategy will enable managers to communicate the underlying business reality to outside investors. One important constraint on a firm's disclosure strategy is the competitive dynamics in product markets. Disclosure of proprietary information about business strategies and their expected economic consequences may hurt the firm's competitive position. Subject to this constraint, managers can use financial statements to provide information useful to investors in assessing their firm's true economic performance.

Managers can also use financial reporting strategies to manipulate investors' perceptions. Using the discretion granted to them, managers can make it difficult for investors to identify poor performance on a timely basis. For example, managers can choose accounting policies and estimates to provide an optimistic assessment of the firm's true performance. They can also make it costly for investors to understand the true performance by controlling the extent of information that is disclosed voluntarily.

The extent to which financial statements reveal the underlying business reality varies across firms and across time for a given firm. This variation in accounting quality provides both an important opportunity and a challenge in doing business analysis. The process through which analysts can separate noise from information in financial statements, and gain valuable business insights from financial statement analysis, is discussed in the following section.

Feature 4: Auditing

Auditing, broadly defined as a verification of the integrity of the reported financial statements by someone other than the preparer, ensures that managers use accounting rules and conventions consistently over time, and that their accounting estimates are reasonable. Therefore, auditing improves the quality of accounting data.

Third-party auditing may also reduce the quality of financial reporting because it constrains the kind of accounting rules and conventions that evolve over time. For example, the FASB considers the views of auditors in the standard-setting process. Auditors are likely to argue against accounting standards producing numbers that are difficult to audit, even if the proposed rules produce relevant information for investors.

The legal environment in which accounting disputes between managers, auditors, and investors are adjudicated can also have a significant effect on the quality of reported numbers. The threat of lawsuits and resulting penalties has the beneficial effect of improving the accuracy of disclosure. However, the potential for a significant legal liability might also discourage managers and auditors from supporting accounting proposals requiring risky forecasts, such as forward-looking disclosures.

The governance structure of firms includes an audit committee of the board of directors. The audit committee is expected to be independent of management and its key roles include overseeing the work of the auditor and ensuring that financial statements are properly prepared. This governance mechanism further serves to enhance the quality and accountability of financial reporting.

The Impact of the Sarbanes-Oxley Act on Financial Reporting and Auditing

In the aftermath of the collapse of the dot-com bubble and high-profile accounting scandals such as Enron and WorldCom, the U.S. Congress passed the bipartisan Sarbanes-Oxley Act (the Act) in July 2002. The margin by which the bill was enacted—it passed by a vote of 424 to 3 in the House of Representatives and a vote of 99 to 0 in the Senate—and the far-reaching nature of the reforms reflected the degree to which the public's confidence in the quality of corporate financial reporting had been undermined.

The Act mandated certain fundamental changes to corporate governance as related to financial reporting and altered the relationship between a firm and its auditor. Some of the highlights of the Act include

- Creating a not-for-profit accounting oversight board, the Public Company Accounting Oversight Board (PCAOB), to ensure standards for auditing and the ethics and independence of public accounting firms;
- Mandating stricter guidelines for the composition and role of the audit committee of the Board of Directors, including director independence and financial expertise;
- Enhancing corporate responsibility for financial reporting by requiring the CEO and CFO to personally certify the appropriateness of periodic reports;
- Requiring management to assess and report on the adequacy of internal controls, which then needs to be certified by the auditor;
- Providing greater whistleblower protection;
- Allowing for the imposition of stiffer penalties, including prison terms and fines, for securities fraud;
- Prohibiting accounting firms from providing certain non-audit services contemporaneously with an audit and mandating audit partner rotation;
- Prescribing conflict of interest rules for equity research analysts; and
- Increasing the funding available to the Securities and Exchange Commission to ensure compliance.

While the Act does improve the quality of financial reporting and create a stronger regulatory environment, its detractors argue that in attempting to reduce information risk, the Act could have unintended consequences such as higher business costs (arising from higher audit fees, greater compliance costs, and potential litigation) and a disincentive for firms to take on business activities that entail complex or ambiguous accounting issues. Empirical evidence shows that the cost of compliance with the Act has had an impact on the decision of public companies to go private, perhaps in an attempt to avoid these costs.[3]

FROM FINANCIAL STATEMENTS TO BUSINESS ANALYSIS

Because managers' insider knowledge is a source of both value and distortion in accounting data, it is difficult for outside users of financial statements to separate true information from distortion and noise. Not being able to undo accounting distortions completely, investors "discount" a firm's reported accounting performance. In doing so, they make a probabilistic assessment of the extent to which a firm's reported numbers reflect economic reality. As a result, investors can have only an imprecise assessment of an individual firm's performance. Financial and information intermediaries can add value by improving investors' understanding of a firm's current performance and its future prospects.

Effective financial statement analysis is valuable because it attempts to get at managers' inside information from public financial statement data. Since intermediaries do not have direct or complete access to this inside information, they rely on their knowledge of the firm's industry and its competitive strategies to interpret financial statements. Successful intermediaries have at least as good an understanding of the industry economics as the firm's managers do, as well as a reasonably good understanding of the firm's competitive strategy. Although outside analysts have an information disadvantage relative to the firm's managers, they are more objective in evaluating the economic consequences of the firm's investment and operating decisions. Figure 1-3 provides a schematic overview of how business intermediaries use financial statements to accomplish four key steps: (1) business strategy analysis, (2) accounting analysis, (3) financial analysis, and (4) prospective analysis.

Analysis Step 1: Business Strategy Analysis

The purpose of business strategy analysis is to identify key profit drivers and business risks, and to assess the company's profit potential at a qualitative level. Business strategy analysis involves analyzing a firm's industry and its strategy to create a sustainable competitive advantage. This qualitative analysis is an essential first step because it enables the analyst to frame the subsequent accounting and financial analysis better. For example, identifying the key success factors and key business risks allows the identification of key accounting policies. Assessment of a firm's competitive strategy facilitates evaluating whether current profitability is sustainable. Finally, business analysis enables the analyst to make sound assumptions in forecasting a firm's future performance.

Analysis Step 2: Accounting Analysis

The purpose of accounting analysis is to evaluate the degree to which a firm's accounting captures the underlying business reality. By identifying places where there

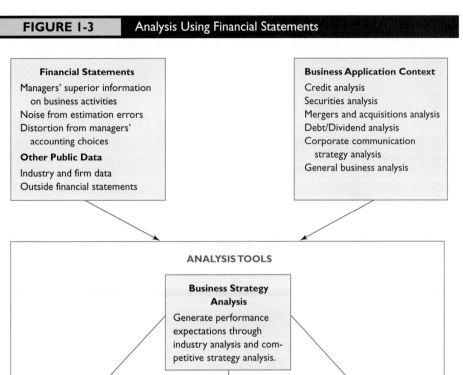

FIGURE 1-3   Analysis Using Financial Statements

Financial Statements

Managers' superior information on business activities
Noise from estimation errors
Distortion from managers' accounting choices

Other Public Data

Industry and firm data
Outside financial statements

Business Application Context

Credit analysis
Securities analysis
Mergers and acquisitions analysis
Debt/Dividend analysis
Corporate communication strategy analysis
General business analysis

ANALYSIS TOOLS

Business Strategy Analysis

Generate performance expectations through industry analysis and competitive strategy analysis.

Accounting Analysis

Evaluate accounting quality by assessing accounting policies and estimates.

Financial Analysis

Evaluate performance using ratios and cash flow analysis.

Prospective Analysis

Make forecasts and value business.

is accounting flexibility, and by evaluating the appropriateness of the firm's accounting policies and estimates, analysts can assess the degree of distortion in a firm's reported numbers. Another important step in accounting analysis is to "undo" any distortions by recasting a firm's accounting numbers to create unbiased accounting data. Sound accounting analysis improves the reliability of conclusions from financial analysis, the next step in financial statement analysis.

Analysis Step 3: Financial Analysis

The goal of financial analysis is to use financial data to evaluate the current and past performance of a firm and to assess its sustainability. There are two important skills related to financial analysis. First, the analysis should be systematic and efficient. Second, the analysis should allow the analyst to use financial data to explore business issues. Ratio analysis and cash flow analysis are the two most commonly used financial tools. Ratio analysis focuses on evaluating a firm's product market performance and financial policies while cash flow analysis focuses on a firm's liquidity and financial flexibility.

Analysis Step 4: Prospective Analysis

Prospective analysis, which focuses on forecasting a firm's future, is the final step in business analysis. Two commonly used techniques in prospective analysis are financial statement forecasting and valuation. Both these tools allow the synthesis of the insights from business analysis, accounting analysis, and financial analysis in order to make predictions about a firm's future.

While the intrinsic value of a firm is a function of its future cash flow performance, it is also possible to assess a firm's value based on the firm's current book value of equity and its future return on equity (ROE) and growth. Strategy analysis, accounting analysis, and financial analysis, the first three steps in the framework discussed above, provide an excellent foundation for estimating a firm's intrinsic value. Strategy analysis, in addition to enabling sound accounting and financial analysis, also helps in assessing potential changes in a firm's competitive advantage and their implications for the firm's future ROE and growth. Accounting analysis provides an unbiased estimate of a firm's current book value and ROE. Financial analysis allows you to gain an in-depth understanding of what drives the firm's current ROE.

The predictions from a sound business analysis are useful to a variety of parties and can be applied in various contexts. The exact nature of the analysis will depend on the context. The contexts that we will examine include securities analysis, credit evaluation, mergers and acquisitions, and the assessment of corporate communication strategies. The four analytical steps described above are useful in each of these contexts. Appropriate use of these tools, however, requires a familiarity with the economic theories and institutional factors relevant to the context.

There are several ways in which financial statement analysis can add value, even when capital markets are reasonably efficient. First, there are many applications of financial statement analysis whose focus is outside the capital market context—credit analysis, competitive benchmarking, and analysis of mergers and acquisitions, to name a few. Second, markets become efficient precisely because some market participants rely on analytical tools such as the ones we discuss in this book to analyze information and make investment decisions. This in turn imposes greater discipline on corporate managers to develop an appropriate disclosure and communication strategy.

SUMMARY

Financial statements provide the most widely available data on public corporations' economic activities; investors and other stakeholders rely on them to assess the plans and performance of firms and corporate managers. Accrual accounting data in financial statements are noisy, and unsophisticated investors can assess firms' performance only imprecisely. Financial analysts who understand managers' disclosure strategies have an opportunity to create inside information from public data, and they play a valuable role in enabling outside parties to evaluate a firm's current and prospective performance.

This chapter has outlined the framework for business analysis with financial statements, using four key steps: business strategy analysis, accounting analysis, financial analysis, and prospective analysis. The remaining chapters in this book describe these steps in greater detail and discuss how they can be used in a variety of business contexts.

DISCUSSION QUESTIONS

1. John, who has just completed his first finance course, is unsure whether he should take a course in business analysis and valuation using financial statements since he believes that financial analysis adds little value, given the efficiency of capital markets. Explain to John when financial analysis can add value, even if capital markets are efficient.

2. Accounting statements rarely report financial performance without error. List three types of errors that can arise in financial reporting.

3. Joe Smith argues that "learning how to do business analysis and valuation using financial statements is not very useful, unless you are interested in becoming a financial analyst." Comment.

4. Four steps for business analysis are discussed in the chapter (strategy analysis, accounting analysis, financial analysis, and prospective analysis). As a financial analyst, explain why each of these steps is a critical part of your job and how they relate to one another.

NOTES

1. See G. Akerlof, "The Market for 'Lemons': Quality Uncertainty and the Market Mechanism," *Quarterly Journal of Economics* (August 1970): 488–500. Akerlof recognized that the seller of a used car knew more about the car's value than the buyer. This meant that the buyer was likely to end up overpaying, since the seller would accept any offer that exceeded the car's true value and reject any lower offer. Car buyers recognized this problem and would respond by only making low-ball offers for used cars, leading sellers with high quality cars to exit the market. As a result, only the lowest quality cars (the "lemons") would remain in the market. Akerlof pointed out that qualified independent mechanics could correct this market breakdown by providing buyers with reliable information on a used car's true value.

2. See P. Healy and K. Palepu, "How the Quest for Efficiency Undermined the Market," *Harvard Business Review* (July 2003): 76–85.

3. See, for example, E. Engel, R. Hayes, and X. Wang, "The Sarbanes-Oxley Act and Firms' Going-Private Decisions" (working paper, University of Chicago, 2004). Research evidence also points to the impact of Sarbanes-Oxley on firms' decision to "go dark" (cease filing with the SEC by deregistering their securities without changing shareholders). See, for example, A. Marosi and N. Massoud, "Why Do Firms Go Dark?" (working paper, University of Alberta, 2004); and C. Leuz, A. Triantis, and T. Wang, "Why Do Firms Go Dark? Causes and Economic Consequences of Voluntary SEC Deregistrations," (working paper, University of Pennsylvania, 2004).

PART TWO

BUSINESS ANALYSIS AND VALUATION TOOLS

Chapter 2
Strategy Analysis

S trategy analysis is an important starting point for the analysis of financial statements. Strategy analysis allows the analyst to probe the economics of a firm at a qualitative level so that the subsequent accounting and financial analysis is grounded in business reality. Strategy analysis also allows the identification of the firm's profit drivers and key risks. This in turn enables the analyst to assess the sustainability of the firm's current performance and make realistic forecasts of future performance.

A firm's value is determined by its ability to earn a return on its capital in excess of the cost of capital. What determines whether or not a firm is able to accomplish this goal? While a firm's cost of capital is determined by the capital markets, its profit potential is determined by its own strategic choices: (1) the choice of an industry or a set of industries in which the firm operates (industry choice), (2) the manner in which the firm intends to compete with other firms in its chosen industry or industries (competitive positioning), and (3) the way in which the firm expects to create and exploit synergies across the range of businesses in which it operates (corporate strategy). Strategy analysis, therefore, involves industry analysis, competitive strategy analysis, and corporate strategy analysis.[1] In this chapter, we will briefly discuss these three steps and use the personal computer industry, Dell Inc., and General Electric, respectively, to illustrate the application of the steps.

INDUSTRY ANALYSIS

In analyzing a firm's profit potential, an analyst has to first assess the profit potential of each of the industries in which the firm is competing because the profitability of various industries differs systematically and predictably over time. For example, the ratio of earnings before interest and taxes to the book value of assets for all U.S. companies between 1981 and 1997 was 8.8 percent. However, the average returns varied widely across specific industries: for the bakery products industry, the profitability ratio was 43 percentage points greater than the population average, and for the silver ore mining industry it was 23 percentage points less than the population average.[2] What causes these profitability differences?

There is a vast body of research in industrial organization on the influence of industry structure on profitability.[3] Relying on this research, strategy literature suggests that the average profitability of an industry is influenced by the "five forces" shown in Figure 2-1.[4] According to this framework, the intensity of competition determines the potential for creating abnormal profits by the firms in an industry. Whether or not the potential profits are kept by the industry is determined by the relative bargaining power of the firms in the industry and their customers and suppliers. We will discuss each of these industry profit drivers in more detail below.

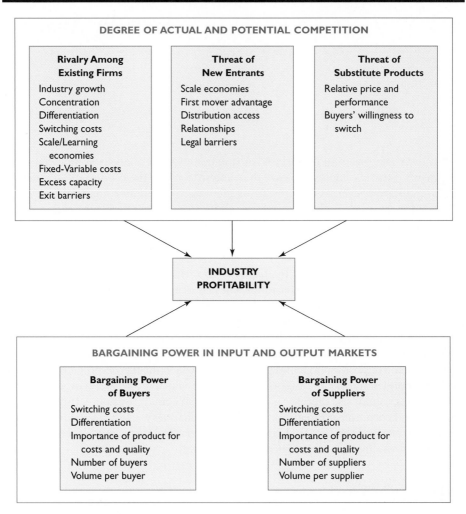

FIGURE 2-1   Industry Structure and Profitability

DEGREE OF ACTUAL AND POTENTIAL COMPETITION

Rivalry Among Existing Firms

Industry growth
Concentration
Differentiation
Switching costs
Scale/Learning economies
Fixed-Variable costs
Excess capacity
Exit barriers

Threat of New Entrants

Scale economies
First mover advantage
Distribution access
Relationships
Legal barriers

Threat of Substitute Products

Relative price and performance
Buyers' willingness to switch

INDUSTRY PROFITABILITY

BARGAINING POWER IN INPUT AND OUTPUT MARKETS

Bargaining Power of Buyers

Switching costs
Differentiation
Importance of product for costs and quality
Number of buyers
Volume per buyer

Bargaining Power of Suppliers

Switching costs
Differentiation
Importance of product for costs and quality
Number of suppliers
Volume per supplier

Degree of Actual and Potential Competition

At the most basic level, the profits in an industry are a function of the maximum price that customers are willing to pay for the industry's product or service. One of the key determinants of the price is the degree to which there is competition among suppliers of the same or similar products. At one extreme, if there is a state of perfect competition in the industry, micro-economic theory predicts that prices will be equal to marginal cost, and there will be few opportunities to earn supernormal profits. At the other extreme, if the industry is dominated by a single firm, there will be potential to earn monopoly profits. In reality, the degree of competition in most industries is somewhere in between perfect competition and monopoly.

There are three potential sources of competition in an industry: (1) rivalry between existing firms, (2) threat of entry of new firms, and (3) threat of substitute products or services. We discuss each of these competitive forces in the following paragraphs.

Competitive Force 1: Rivalry Among Existing Firms

In most industries the average level of profitability is primarily influenced by the nature of rivalry among existing firms in the industry. In some industries firms compete aggressively, pushing prices close to (and sometimes below) the marginal cost. In other industries firms do not compete aggressively on price. Instead, they find ways to coordinate their pricing, or compete on non-price dimensions such as innovation or brand image. Several factors determine the intensity of competition between existing players in an industry:

Industry Growth Rate If an industry is growing very rapidly, incumbent firms need not grab market share from each other to grow. In contrast, in stagnant industries the only way existing firms can grow is by taking share away from the other players. In this situation one can expect price wars among firms in the industry.

Concentration and Balance of Competitors The number of firms in an industry and their relative sizes determine the degree of concentration in an industry.[5] The degree of concentration influences the extent to which firms in an industry can coordinate their pricing and other competitive moves. For example, if there is one dominant firm in an industry (such as IBM in the mainframe computer industry in the 1970s), it can set and enforce the rules of competition. Similarly, if there are only two or three equal-sized players (such as Coca-Cola and Pepsi in the U.S. soft drink industry), they can implicitly cooperate with each other to avoid destructive price competition. If an industry is fragmented, price competition is likely to be severe.

Degree of Differentiation and Switching Costs The extent to which firms in an industry can avoid head-on competition depends on the extent to which they can differentiate their products and services. If the products in an industry are very similar, customers are ready to switch from one competitor to another purely on the basis of price. Switching costs also determine customers' propensity to move from one product to another. When switching costs are low, there is a greater incentive for firms in an industry to engage in price competition. The PC industry, where the standardization of the software and microprocessor has led to relatively low switching costs, is extremely price competitive.

Scale/Learning Economies and the Ratio of Fixed to Variable Costs If there is a steep learning curve or there are other types of scale economies in an industry, size becomes an important factor for firms in the industry. In such situations, there are incentives to engage in aggressive competition for market share. Similarly, if the ratio of fixed to variable costs is high, firms have an incentive to reduce prices to utilize installed capacity. The airline industry, where price wars are quite common, is an example of this type of situation.

Excess Capacity and Exit Barriers If capacity in an industry is larger than customer demand, there is a strong incentive for firms to cut prices to fill capacity. The problem of excess capacity is likely to be exacerbated if there are significant barriers for firms to exit the industry. Exit barriers are high when the assets are specialized or if there are regulations which make exit costly. The competitive dynamics of the steel industry demonstrates these forces at play.

Competitive Force 2: Threat of New Entrants

The potential for earning abnormal profits will attract new entrants to an industry. The very threat of new firms entering an industry potentially constrains the pricing of existing firms within it. Therefore, the ease with which new firms can enter an industry is a key determinant of its profitability. Several factors determine the height of barriers to entry in an industry:

Economies of Scale When there are large economies of scale, new entrants face the choice of having either to invest in large capacity which might not be utilized right away or to enter with less than the optimum capacity. Either way, new entrants will at least initially suffer from a cost disadvantage in competing with existing firms. Economies of scale might arise from large investments in research and development (the pharmaceutical or jet engine industries), in brand advertising (soft drink industry), or in physical plant and equipment (telecommunications industry).

First Mover Advantage Early entrants in an industry may deter future entrants if there are first mover advantages. For example, first movers might be able to set industry standards, or enter into exclusive arrangements with suppliers of cheap raw materials. They may also acquire scarce government licenses to operate in regulated industries. Finally, if there are learning economies, early firms will have an absolute cost advantage over new entrants. First mover advantages are also likely to be large when there are significant switching costs for customers once they start using existing products. For example, switching costs faced by the users of Microsoft's Windows operating system make it difficult for software companies to market a new operating system.

Access to Channels of Distribution and Relationships Limited capacity in the existing distribution channels and high costs of developing new channels can act as powerful barriers to entry. For example, a new entrant into the domestic auto industry in the U.S. is likely to face formidable barriers because of the difficulty of developing a dealer network. Similarly, new consumer goods manufacturers find it difficult to obtain supermarket shelf space for their products. Existing relationships between firms and customers in an industry also make it difficult for new firms to enter an industry. Industry examples of this include auditing and investment banking.

Legal Barriers There are many industries in which legal barriers such as patents and copyrights in research-intensive industries limit entry. Similarly, licensing regulations limit entry into taxi services, medical services, broadcasting, and telecommunications industries.

Competitive Force 3: Threat of Substitute Products

The third dimension of competition in an industry is the threat of substitute products or services. Relevant substitutes are not necessarily those that have the same form as the existing products but those that perform the same function. For example, airlines and car rental services might be substitutes for each other when it comes to travel over medium distances. Similarly, plastic bottles and metal cans substitute for each other as packaging in the beverage industry. In some cases, threat of substitution comes not from customers' switching to another product but from utilizing technologies that allow them to do without, or use less of, the existing products. For example, energy-conserving technologies allow customers to reduce their consumption of electricity and fossil fuels.

The threat of substitutes depends on the relative price and performance of the competing products or services and on customers' willingness to substitute. Customers' perception of whether two products are substitutes depends to some extent on whether they perform the same function for a similar price. If two products perform an identical function, then it would be difficult for them to differ from each other in price. However, customers' willingness to switch is often the critical factor in making this competitive dynamic work. For example, even when tap water and bottled water serve the same function, many customers may be unwilling to substitute the former for the latter, enabling bottlers to charge a price premium. Similarly, designer label clothing commands a price premium even if it is not superior in terms of basic functionality because customers place a value on the image or style offered by designer labels.

Bargaining Power in Input and Output Markets

While the degree of competition in an industry determines whether there is *potential* to earn abnormal profits, the *actual profits* are influenced by the industry's bargaining power with its suppliers and customers. On the input side, firms enter into transactions with suppliers of labor, raw materials and components, and finances. On the output side, firms either sell directly to the final customers or enter into contracts with intermediaries in the distribution chain. In all these transactions, the relative economic power of the two sides is important to the overall profitability of the industry firms.

Competitive Force 4: Bargaining Power of Buyers

Two factors determine the power of buyers: price sensitivity and relative bargaining power. Price sensitivity determines the extent to which buyers care to bargain on price; relative bargaining power determines the extent to which they will succeed in forcing the price down.[6]

Price Sensitivity Buyers are more price sensitive when the product is undifferentiated and there are few switching costs. The sensitivity of buyers to price also depends on the importance of the product to their own cost structure. When the product represents a large fraction of the buyers' cost (for example, the packaging material for soft drink producers), the buyer is likely to expend the resources necessary to shop for a lower cost alternative. In contrast, if the product is a small fraction of the buyers' cost (for example, windshield wipers for automobile manufacturers), it may not pay to expend resources to search for lower-cost alternatives. Further, the importance of the product to the buyers' own product quality also determines whether or not price becomes the most important determinant of the buying decision.

Relative Bargaining Power Even if buyers are price sensitive, they may not be able to achieve low prices unless they have a strong bargaining position. Relative bargaining power in a transaction depends, ultimately, on the cost to each party of not doing business with the other party. The buyers' bargaining power is determined by the number of buyers relative to the number of suppliers, volume of purchases by a single buyer, number of alternative products available to the buyer, buyers' costs of switching from one product to another, and the threat of backward integration by the buyers. For example, in the automobile industry, car manufacturers have considerable power over component manufacturers because auto companies are large buyers with several alternative suppliers to choose from, and switching costs are relatively low. In contrast, in the personal computer industry, computer makers have low bargaining power relative to the operating system software producers because of high switching costs.

Competitive Force 5: Bargaining Power of Suppliers

The analysis of the relative power of suppliers is a mirror image of the analysis of the buyer's power in an industry. Suppliers are powerful when there are only a few companies and few substitutes available to their customers. For example, in the soft drink industry, Coke and Pepsi are very powerful relative to the bottlers. In contrast, metal can suppliers to the soft drink industry are not very powerful because of intense competition among can producers and the threat of substitution by plastic bottles. Suppliers also have a lot of power over buyers when the suppliers' product or service is critical to buyers' business. For example, airline pilots have a strong bargaining power in the airline industry. Suppliers also tend to be powerful when they pose a credible threat of forward integration. For example, IBM is powerful relative to mainframe computer leasing companies because of its unique position as a mainframe supplier and its own presence in the computer leasing business.

APPLYING INDUSTRY ANALYSIS: THE PERSONAL COMPUTER INDUSTRY

Let us consider the above concepts of industry analysis in the context of the personal computer (PC) industry.[7] The industry began in 1981 when IBM announced its PC with Intel's microprocessor and Microsoft's DOS operating system, and it has seen spectacular growth since then. Now personal computers are almost ubiquitous—an estimated 208 million units were shipped worldwide in 2005 alone. Despite this growth in the sales volume, the industry is characterized by low profitability. The largest and best known companies in the industry, including IBM, Compaq, Dell and Hewlett-Packard, have been trying to improve performance since the early 1990s through internal restructuring and mergers. What accounts for this low profitability? What is the computer industry's future profit potential?

Competition in the Personal Computer Industry

Competition continues to be very intense for a number of reasons:

- The industry is fragmented, with many firms producing virtually identical products. Even though the computer market continues to become increasingly concentrated with a series of high-profile transactions, such as the mergers of Compaq with Hewlett-Packard and Gateway with eMachines and the sale of IBM's PC business to Lenovo, competition is intense—there are routine price cuts on a monthly basis. The top five vendors in 2005 controlled less than 50 percent of worldwide PC sales.
- Component costs account for more than 60 percent of total hardware costs of a personal computer, and volume purchases of components reduce these costs. While prices for critical components such as microprocessors and disk drives continue to decline, customers in turn expect lower prices, contributing to the increasing reliance on volume growth. Therefore, there is intense competition for market share among competing manufacturers.
- PCs produced by different firms in the industry are virtually identical, and there are few opportunities to differentiate the products. While brand name and service were dimensions that customers valued in the early years of the industry, they have become less important as PC buyers are more informed about the technology. Companies are attempting to differentiate themselves through innovative design and high-end performance, but this remains a small niche in the industry.
- Switching costs across different brands of PCs are relatively low because a vast majority of PCs use Intel microprocessors and Microsoft Windows operating systems.
- Access to distribution has not been a significant barrier, as demonstrated by Dell, which distributed its computers by direct mail through the 1980s and introduced Internet-based sales in the mid-1990s. In recent years, all the major PC manufacturers have adopted some elements of Dell's direct sales model, a

process that has accelerated with the popularity of Internet commerce. The advent of computer superstores like CompUSA also mitigated this constraint, since these stores were willing to carry several brands.

- Since virtually all the components needed to produce a personal computer were available for purchase, there were very few barriers to entering the industry. In fact, Michael Dell started Dell Computer Company in the early 1980s by assembling PCs in his University of Texas dormitory room.

- Apple's line of computers continues to offer competition as a substitute product. Workstations produced by Sun and other vendors are also potential substitutes at the higher end of the personal computer market though most PC manufacturers now offer more powerful machines as well.

The Power of Suppliers and Buyers

Suppliers and buyers have significant power over firms in the industry for these reasons:

- Essential hardware and software components for PCs are controlled by firms with a virtual monopoly and consequently manufacturers return a large portion of their net profits to the component makers. Intel continues to dominate microprocessor production for the personal computer industry with market share of close to 80 percent, though smaller rival AMD has made inroads on Intel's dominance, which could lead to greater price competition in the near future. Microsoft's control over the operating system market with its DOS and Windows operating systems persists, with between 85 and 90 percent of PCs worldwide using its software. While open source alternatives such as Linux remain a threat to Microsoft's dominance of the PC industry, pirated software in emerging economies is the real threat to Microsoft's revenue model. Software piracy is likely to lead to two simultaneous responses—low-cost versions of Windows in the emerging markets because of lower purchasing power, and price increases in the developed markets, neither of which will alleviate the margin pressure on PC manufacturers.[8]

- Buyers have gained more and more power as the PC industry has matured over the last two decades. Corporate buyers, who represent a significant portion of the customer base, are highly price sensitive since the expenditure on PCs represents a significant cost to their operations. Further, as penetration of the home market has increased, customers are less influenced by brand name. Except for a small, high-end market niche, buyers increasingly view PCs as commodities and use price as the most important consideration in their purchase decisions.

As a result of the intense rivalry and low barriers to entry in the personal computer industry, there is severe price competition among different manufacturers. Further, there is tremendous pressure on firms to spend large sums of money to introduce new products rapidly, maintain high quality, and provide excellent customer support. Both these factors have led to a low profit potential in the industry. The power of suppliers and buyers has reduced profit potential further. Thus, while the personal computer industry represents a technologically dynamic industry, its profit potential continues to be poor.

There are few indications of change in the basic structure of the personal computer industry, and there is little likelihood in the near term of viable competition emerging to unseat the domination of Microsoft and Intel in the input markets. Attempts by industry leaders like IBM to create alternative proprietary technologies have not succeeded. Desktop replacement cycles are lengthening, slowing demand. The PC industry is under further threat from the mobile device market. Although at an early stage, advanced mobile communication, Internet access, and multimedia entertainment technologies could replace the PC for some users. While many in the industry pin their hopes on the digital home with a media-centric PC to drive sales growth and improve margins, experience in the U.S. market to date has fallen short of expectations.[9] As a result, the profitability of the PC industry may not improve significantly any time in the near future.

Limitations of Industry Analysis

A potential limitation of the industry analysis framework discussed in this chapter is the assumption that industries have clear boundaries. In reality, it is often not easy to demarcate industry boundaries. For example, in analyzing Dell's industry, should one focus on the IBM-compatible personal computer industry or the personal computer industry as a whole? Should one include workstations in the industry definition? Should one consider only the domestic manufacturers of personal computers or also manufacturers abroad? Inappropriate industry definition will result in incomplete analysis and inaccurate forecasts.

COMPETITIVE STRATEGY ANALYSIS

The profitability of a firm is influenced not only by its industry structure but also by the strategic choices it makes in positioning itself in the industry. While there are many ways to characterize a firm's business strategy, as Figure 2-2 shows, there are two generic competitive strategies: (1) cost leadership and (2) differentiation.[10] Both these strategies can potentially allow a firm to build a sustainable competitive

FIGURE 2-2	Strategies for Creating Competitive Advantage

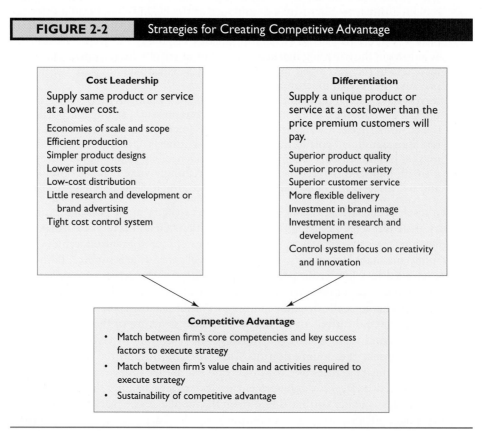

advantage. Strategy researchers have traditionally viewed cost leadership and differentiation as mutually exclusive strategies. Firms that straddle the two strategies are considered to be "stuck in the middle" and are expected to earn low profitability.[11] These firms run the risk of not being able to attract price conscious customers because their costs are too high; they are also unable to provide adequate differentiation to attract premium price customers.[12]

Sources of Competitive Advantage

Cost leadership enables a firm to supply the same product or service offered by its competitors at a lower cost. Differentiation strategy involves providing a product or service that is distinct in some important respect valued by the customer. As an example in retailing, Nordstrom has succeeded on the basis of differentiation by emphasizing exceptionally high customer service. In contrast, Filene's Basement is a discount retailer competing purely on a low-cost basis.

Competitive Strategy 1: Cost Leadership

Cost leadership is often the clearest way to achieve competitive advantage. In industries where the basic product or service is a commodity, cost leadership might be the only way to achieve superior performance. There are many ways to achieve cost leadership, including economies of scale and scope, economies of learning, efficient production, simpler product design, better sourcing and lower input costs, and efficient organizational processes. If a firm can achieve cost leadership, then it will be able to earn above-average profitability by merely charging the same price as its rivals. Conversely, a cost leader can force its competitors to cut prices and accept lower returns or to exit the industry.

Firms that achieve cost leadership focus on tight cost controls. They make investments in efficient scale plants, focus on product designs that reduce manufacturing costs, minimize overhead costs, capitalize on global sourcing opportunities, make little investment in risky research and development, and avoid serving marginal customers. They have organizational structures and control systems that focus on cost control.

Competitive Strategy 2: Differentiation

A firm following the differentiation strategy seeks to be unique in its industry along some dimension that is highly valued by customers. For differentiation to be successful, the firm has to accomplish three things. First, it needs to identify one or more attributes of a product or service that customers value. Second, it has to position itself to meet the chosen customer need in a unique manner. Finally, the firm has to achieve differentiation at a cost that is lower than the price the customer is willing to pay for the differentiated product or service.

Drivers of differentiation include providing superior intrinsic value via product quality, product variety, bundled services, or delivery timing. Differentiation can also be achieved by investing in signals of value such as brand image, product appearance, or reputation. Differentiated strategies require investments in research and development, engineering skills, and marketing capabilities. The organizational structures and control systems in firms with differentiation strategies need to foster creativity and innovation.

While successful firms choose between cost leadership and differentiation, they cannot completely ignore the dimension on which they are not primarily competing. Firms that target differentiation still need to focus on costs so that the differentiation can be achieved at an acceptable cost. Similarly, cost leaders cannot compete unless they achieve at least a minimum level on key dimensions on which competitors might differentiate, such as quality and service.

Achieving and Sustaining Competitive Advantage

The choice of competitive strategy does not automatically lead to the achievement of competitive advantage. To achieve competitive advantage, the firm has to have the capabilities needed to implement and sustain the chosen strategy. Both cost leadership and differentiation strategy require that the firm make the necessary commitments to acquire the core competencies needed and structure its value chain in an appropriate way. Core competencies are the economic assets that the firm possesses, whereas the value chain is the set of activities that the firm performs to convert inputs into outputs. The uniqueness of a firm's core competencies and its value chain and the extent to which it is difficult for competitors to imitate them determine the sustainability of a firm's competitive advantage.[13]

To evaluate whether a firm is likely to achieve its intended competitive advantage, the analyst should ask the following questions:

- What are the key success factors and risks associated with the firm's chosen competitive strategy?
- Does the firm currently have the resources and capabilities to deal with the key success factors and risks?
- Has the firm made irreversible commitments to bridge the gap between its current capabilities and the requirements to achieve its competitive advantage?
- Has the firm structured its activities (such as research and development, design, manufacturing, marketing and distribution, and support activities) in a way that is consistent with its competitive strategy?
- Is the company's competitive advantage sustainable? Are there any barriers that make imitation of the firm's strategy difficult?
- Are there any potential changes in the firm's industry structure (such as new technologies, foreign competition, changes in regulation, changes in customer requirements) that might dissipate the firm's competitive advantage? Is the company flexible enough to address these changes?

Applying Competitive Strategy Analysis

Let's consider the concepts of competitive strategy analysis in the context of Dell Inc., based in Round Rock, Texas. The company, founded by Michael Dell in his University of Texas dorm room, started selling "IBM clone" personal computers in 1984. From the beginning Dell sold its machines directly to end users rather than through retail outlets, at a significantly lower price than its competitors.

After rapid growth and some management hiccups, Dell firmly established itself in the PC industry by following a low-cost strategy. Within ten years of its founding, Dell was among the five largest PC vendors, and by 1999 Dell was the leading seller of PCs in the U.S. For the fiscal year ending February 3, 2006, Dell achieved $55.9 billion in revenues and $3.6 billion in net income, up from $49.2 billion and $3.0 billion, respectively, for the prior year. Dell's growth rates continue to outpace the market, and in 2005 it increased its market share in every region around the world. Dell's stellar performance over its first two decades made it one of the most profitable personal computer makers in a highly competitive industry. How did Dell achieve such performance?

Dell's superior performance was based on a low-cost competitive strategy that consisted of the following key elements:

- *Direct selling.* Dell sold most of its computers directly to its customers, thus saving on retail markups. As computer users become sophisticated, and as computers become standardized on the Windows-Intel platform, the value of distribution through retailers declined. Dell was the first company to capitalize on this trend. In 1996 Dell began selling computers through its Internet web site. In 2005 the company was generating a significant amount of its sales through on-line orders.
- *Made-to-order manufacturing.* Dell developed a system of flexible manufacturing that allowed the company to assemble and ship computers very quickly, usually within five days of receiving an order. This allowed the company to avoid large inventories of parts and assembled computers. Low inventories allowed Dell to save on working capital costs and also reduced costly write-offs of obsolete inventories, a significant risk in the fast-changing computer industry.
- *Third-party service.* Dell used two low-cost approaches to after-sales service: telephone-based service and third-party maintenance service. Dell had several hundred technical support representatives accessible to customers by phone any time of the day. Using a comprehensive electronic maintenance system, the service representatives could diagnose problems and help customers to resolve them in the vast majority of cases. In the rare instance where on-site maintenance was required, Dell used third-party maintenance contracts with office equipment companies such as Xerox. Through this service strategy, Dell was able to avoid investing in an expensive field service network without compromising on service quality.
- *Low accounts receivable.* Dell was able to reduce its accounts receivable days to an industry minimum by encouraging its customers to pay by credit card at the time of the purchase or through electronic payment immediately after the purchase.
- *Focused investment in R&D.* Dell recognized that most of the basic innovations in the personal computer industry were led by the component suppliers and software producers. For example, two key suppliers, Intel and Microsoft, invested billions of dollars in developing new generation processors and software, respectively. Dell's innovations were primarily in creating a low-cost, high velocity organization that could respond quickly to these changes. By focusing its R&D innovations, Dell was able to minimize these costs and get high returns on its investments.

As a result of the above strategy, Dell achieved a significant cost advantage over its competitors in the PC industry. This advantage resulted in a consistent pattern of rapid growth, increasing market share, and very high profitability in an industry that is characterized by rapid technological changes, significant supplier and buyer power, and intense competition. Further, because the strategy involved activities that are highly interrelated and involved continuous organizational innovations, Dell's business model was difficult to replicate.

However, there are signs that Dell's dominance is being challenged. The company missed its profit estimates and saw quarter over quarter profit declines in 2005 and 2006. On the commoditized PC front, competitors such as Hewlett-Packard have narrowed the productivity and price gap with Dell, further driving down profit margins. With the proliferation of new digital gear, consumers are increasingly seeking unique design features, which requires innovation, greater R&D spending, and often a retail presence. Dell's stock, which once traded at extraordinarily high earnings and book value multiples, has underperformed competitors such as Apple and Hewlett-Packard.

Dell's management has responded to the challenges of slowing growth. Dell is focusing on growing its international sales, especially in fast-growing consumer markets in China and India. To ensure that its direct model will work in these new geographies, Dell is shifting manufacturing overseas to be closer to its customers. Dell is also increasing its focus on the consumer market in the U.S. To help consumer market penetration, the firm is showing a willingness to break with its traditional direct-sales model and opened its first full store in Dallas in July 2006. It also announced plans to simplify its current pricing and rebate structure for consumers. In a departure from its belief in stressing internal growth, in May 2006 Dell acquired Alienware, a high-end PC manufacturer that offers Dell stronger branding and more stylish design in the niche gaming market. It will be interesting to see whether Dell's plans, dubbed Dell 2.0, are able to sustain the competitive advantage that led to its dominance as the PC industry continues to evolve.

CORPORATE STRATEGY ANALYSIS

So far in this chapter we have focused on strategies at the individual business level. While some companies focus on only one business, many companies operate in multiple businesses. For example, the average number of business segments operated by the top 500 U.S. companies in 1992 was eleven industries.[14] In recent years, there has been an attempt by U.S. companies to reduce the diversity of their operations and focus on a relatively few "core" businesses. However, multi-business organizations continue to dominate the economic activity in most countries in the world.

When analyzing a multi-business organization, an analyst has to evaluate not only the industries and strategies of the individual business units but also the economic consequences—either positive or negative—of managing all the different businesses under one corporate umbrella. For example, General Electric has been very successful in creating significant value by managing a highly diversified set of businesses ranging from aircraft engines to light bulbs. In contrast, Sears has not been very successful in managing retailing together with financial services, divesting itself of Allstate Insurance, Dean Witter, Coldwell Banker Residential Services, and its credit card business in the past 15 years to focus on retailing activities.

Sources of Value Creation at the Corporate Level

Economists and strategy researchers have identified several factors that influence an organization's ability to create value through a broad corporate scope. Economic theory suggests that the optimal scope of activity of a firm depends on the relative transaction cost of performing a set of activities inside the firm versus using the market mechanism.[15] Transaction cost economics implies that the multi-product firm is an efficient choice of organizational form when coordination among independent, focused firms is costly due to market transaction costs.

Transaction costs can arise out of several sources. They may arise if the production process involves specialized assets such as human capital skills, proprietary technology, or other organizational know-how that is not easily available in the marketplace. Transaction costs also may arise from market imperfections such as information and incentive problems. If buyers and sellers cannot solve these problems through standard mechanisms such as enforceable contracts, it will be costly to conduct transactions through market mechanisms.

For example, as discussed in Chapter 1, public capital markets may not work well when there are significant information and incentive problems, making it difficult for entrepreneurs to raise capital from investors. Similarly, if buyers cannot ascertain the quality of products being sold because of lack of information, or cannot enforce warranties because of poor legal infrastructure, entrepreneurs will find it difficult to break into new markets. Finally, if employers cannot assess the quality of applicants for new positions, they will have to rely more on internal promotions rather than external recruiting to fill higher positions in an organization. Emerging economies often suffer from these types of transaction costs because of poorly developed intermediation infrastructure.[16] Even in many advanced economies, examples of high transaction costs can be found. For example, in most countries other than the U.S., the venture capital industry is not highly developed, making it costly for new businesses in high technology industries to attract financing. Even in the U.S., transaction costs may vary across economic sectors. For example, until recently, electronic commerce was hampered by consumer concerns regarding the security of credit card information sent over the Internet.

Transactions inside an organization may be less costly than market-based transactions for several reasons. First, communication costs inside an organization are reduced because confidentiality can be protected and credibility can be assured through internal mechanisms. Second, the head office can play a critical role in reducing costs of enforcing agreements between organizational subunits. Third, organizational subunits can share valuable nontradable assets (such as organizational skills, systems, and processes) or nondivisible assets (such as brand names, distribution channels, and reputation).

There are also forces that increase transaction costs inside organizations. Top management of an organization may lack the specialized information and skills necessary to manage businesses across several different industries. This lack of expertise reduces the possibility of actually realizing economies of scope, even when there is potential for such economies. This problem can be remedied by creating a decentralized organization, hiring specialist managers to run each business unit, and providing these managers with proper incentives. However, decentralization will also potentially decrease goal congruence among subunit managers, making it difficult to realize economies of scope.

Whether or not a multi-business organization creates more value than a comparable collection of focused firms is, therefore, context dependent.[17] Analysts should ask the following questions to assess whether an organization's corporate strategy has the potential to create value:

- Are there significant imperfections in the product, labor, or financial markets in the industries (or countries) in which a company is operating? Is it likely that transaction costs in these markets are higher than the costs of similar activities inside a well managed organization?
- Does the organization have special resources such as brand names, proprietary know-how, access to scarce distribution channels, and special organizational processes that have the potential to create economies of scope?
- Is there a good fit between the company's specialized resources and the portfolio of businesses in which the company is operating?
- Does the company allocate decision rights between the headquarters office and the business units optimally to realize all the potential economies of scope?
- Does the company have internal measurement, information, and incentive systems to reduce agency costs and increase coordination across business units?

Empirical evidence suggests that creating value through a multi-business corporate strategy is difficult in practice. Several researchers have documented that diversified U.S. companies trade at a discount in the stock market relative to a comparable portfolio of focused companies.[18] Studies also show that acquisitions of one company by another, especially when the two are in unrelated businesses, often fail to create value for the acquiring companies.[19] Finally, there is considerable evidence that value is created when multi-business companies increase corporate focus through divisional spin-offs and asset sales.[20]

There are several potential explanations for this diversification discount. First, managers' decisions to diversify and expand are frequently driven by a desire to maximize the size of their organization rather than to maximize shareholder value. Second, diversified companies often suffer from incentive misalignment problems leading to suboptimal investment decisions and poor operating performance. Third, capital markets find it difficult to monitor and value multi-business organizations because of inadequate disclosure about the performance of individual business segments.

In summary, while companies can theoretically create value through innovative corporate strategies, there are many ways in which this potential fails to get realized in practice. Therefore, it pays to be skeptical when evaluating companies' corporate strategies.

Applying Corporate Strategy Analysis

Let's apply the concepts of corporate strategy analysis to General Electric (GE), one of the world's leading diversified businesses. GE has had a storied history since it was founded by Thomas Edison in 1878, and it is consistently one of the world's most admired companies. In May 2006, GE was the second largest corporation in the world as measured by its market capitalization, and it consistently ranks in the top ten in *Fortune* magazine's Global 500 rankings. GE has a portfolio of world class businesses that dominate their respective industries. GE sees itself not as a conglomerate built through a series of add-on acquisitions but as a group of diverse businesses that are closely integrated through a tradition of sharing talent and best practices and a culture of unwavering integrity.[21] The GE business mix, which management believes to be aligned with the prevailing demographic trends, is managed along six broad segments:

- *Infrastructure:* In 2005 Infrastructure represented about 35 percent of GE's profits. GE competes in all the major infrastructure markets including energy, aviation, rail, oil and gas, and water. GE generates more than 60 percent of its orders from outside the U.S. and is well positioned to benefit from the significant investments in infrastructure that is expected in the developing world. Long-term service agreements and the financial services components of the aviation and energy businesses provide a high-margin and diversified source of revenue.
- *Commercial Finance:* Commercial Finance contributes about 20 percent of the firm's profits. GE's franchise includes an extremely profitable real estate business and a variety of high-margin lending businesses in industry verticals such as healthcare and entertainment. Commercial Finance leverages a combination of strong origination, low cost of funds, and prudent risk management to deliver strong earnings growth.
- *Consumer Finance:* Consumer Finance produced approximately 15 percent of the profits, with over 70 percent of the earnings in this business unit coming from outside the U.S. GE has built significant capability in the developing

markets and is benefiting from rising incomes in these geographies. GE offers a wide suite of products ranging from personal and auto loans to mortgages and private-label credit cards.

- *Healthcare:* The Healthcare business represents about 10 percent of profits and its strong performance has been driven by favorable demographic trends, strong growth in service revenue, and a successful acquisition strategy. GE's diagnostic imaging equipment and patient monitoring systems are used in hospitals worldwide. Bio-sciences and drug discovery systems are a growing source of revenue within the Healthcare unit. GE is also using partnerships with firms such as Eli Lilly and Roche to expand its product development capabilities.

- *NBC Universal:* NBC Universal was created through the merger of the NBC network with Vivendi Universal's entertainment assets. Its television assets include NBC network, Spanish language network Telemundo, and cable channels such as Bravo and USA Network. Other properties include the Universal Pictures movie studio and Universal Parks and Resorts. While the segment contributed to 10 percent of earnings and includes stellar brands, the unit's performance has lagged as the NBC network has struggled of late.

- *Industrial:* Industrial encompasses a broad range of products and services that includes the pioneering lighting division, home appliances, residential security systems, and high-performance polymers used by electronics and automotive manufacturers. Industrial represents about 10 percent of the profits at GE. Industrial has capitalized on outsourcing trends and is cost competitive due to a strategy of sourcing products from China and Mexico.

Given the breadth of its business interests and the sheer size of the company, GE is able to enjoy tremendous benefits from common sourcing, consolidated IT platforms, and research synergies. The firm is able to scale ideas quickly and impose GE competencies such as process discipline, global distribution, and customer relationships on new ideas and acquisitions. In addition, there are certain core, overarching themes that influence the way GE is run that have contributed to its superior performance over a prolonged period:

- GE has been able to attract and develop talent on a sustained basis. Senior executives have spent time at multiple business units, have a first-hand knowledge of the drivers of the different businesses, and are positioned to identify synergies between them. Throughout its history, GE's top leaders have come from within the firm's executive ranks and personify the GE culture and values.

- GE is constantly optimizing the mix of businesses to exploit new growth opportunities. Since Jeff Immelt took over as CEO from Jack Welch in 2001, GE has divested $30 billion of slow-growth divisions and spent $65 billion on acquisitions to push into high-growth areas such as healthcare.

- GE is willing to continually reinvent itself to align better with the evolving needs of its customers and markets. This relentless push for re-evaluation and improvement is not limited to its business portfolio but extends to its processes, management capabilities, focus on innovation, and measures of success as well.

- GE has embraced globalization, and hence each of its businesses is focused on diversifying the geographic sources of revenues. GE's breadth of offerings allows the firm to adopt a "company to country" approach to business development in many emerging economies by providing infrastructure, financing, and partnership.[22]

However, GE's stock price has languished in recent times relative to the major U.S. market indices. Over the five-year period through the end of 2006, GE's stock has significantly underperformed the S&P 500 Index. While the Index has gained 24 percent, GE stock lost almost 8 percent of its value. Though some fund managers claim that they prefer to allocate assets among sectors themselves rather than leave it to the management of diversified companies, GE management has repeatedly stressed that it is not going to break up the business. It will be interesting to see whether GE can deliver stellar returns for its shareholders in the near and medium term or whether activist investors, who have successfully pushed companies such as Tyco and Cendant to break up, will seek to break up the company.

SUMMARY

Strategy analysis is an important starting point for the analysis of financial statements because it allows the analyst to probe the economics of the firm at a qualitative level. Strategy analysis also allows the identification of the firm's profit drivers and key risks, enabling the analyst to assess the sustainability of the firm's performance and make realistic forecasts of future performance.

Whether a firm is able to earn a return on its capital in excess of its cost of capital is determined by its own strategic choices: (1) the choice of an industry or a set of industries in which the firm operates (industry choice), (2) the manner in which the firm intends to compete with other firms in its chosen industry or industries (competitive positioning), and (3) the way in which the firm expects to create and exploit synergies across the range of businesses in which it operates (corporate strategy). Strategy analysis involves analyzing all three choices.

Industry analysis consists of identifying the economic factors which drive industry profitability. In general, an industry's average profit potential is influenced by the degree of rivalry among existing competitors, the ease with which new firms can enter the industry, the availability of substitute products, the power of buyers, and the power of suppliers. To perform industry analysis, the analyst has to assess the current strength of each of these forces in an industry and make forecasts of any likely future changes.

Competitive strategy analysis involves identifying the basis on which the firm intends to compete in its industry. In general, there are two potential strategies that could provide a firm with a competitive advantage: cost leadership and differentiation. Cost leadership involves offering at a lower cost the same product or service that other firms offer. Differentiation involves satisfying a chosen dimension of customer need better than the competition, at an incremental cost that is less than the price premium that customers are willing to pay. To perform strategy analysis, the analyst has to identify the firm's intended strategy, assess whether the firm possesses the competencies required to execute the strategy, and recognize the key risks that the firm has to guard against. The analyst also has to evaluate the sustainability of the firm's strategy.

Corporate strategy analysis involves examining whether a company is able to create value by being in multiple businesses at the same time. A well crafted corporate strategy reduces costs or increases revenues from running several businesses in one firm relative to the same businesses operating independently and transacting with each other in the marketplace. These cost savings or revenue increases come from specialized resources that the firm has to exploit synergies across these businesses. For these resources to be valuable, they must be nontradable, not easily imitated by competition, and nondivisible. Even when a firm has such resources, it can create value through a multi-business organization only when it is managed so that the information and agency costs inside the organization are smaller than the market transaction costs.

The insights gained from strategy analysis can be useful in performing the remainder of the financial statement analysis. In accounting analysis, the analyst can examine whether a firm's accounting policies and estimates are consistent with its stated strategy. For example, a firm's choice of functional currency in accounting for its international operations should be consistent with the level of integration between domestic and international operations that the business strategy calls for. Similarly, a firm that mainly sells housing to high-risk customers should have higher than average bad debts expenses and a higher than average allowance for loan losses.

Strategy analysis is also useful in guiding financial analysis. For example, in a cross-sectional analysis, the analyst should expect firms with cost leadership strategy to have lower gross margins and higher asset turnover than firms that follow differentiated strategies. In a time series analysis, the analyst should closely monitor any increases in expense ratios and asset turnover ratios for low-cost firms, and any decreases in investments critical to differentiation for firms that follow differentiation strategy.

Business strategy analysis also helps in prospective analysis and valuation. First, it allows the analyst to assess whether, and for how long, differences between the firm's performance and its industry's (or industries') performance are likely to persist. Second, strategy analysis facilitates forecasting investment outlays the firm has to make to maintain its competitive advantage.

DISCUSSION QUESTIONS

1. Judith, an accounting major, states, "Strategy analysis seems to be an unnecessary detour in doing financial statement analysis. Why can't we just get straight to the accounting issues?" Explain to Judith why she might be wrong.

2. What are the critical drivers of industry profitability?

3. One of the fastest growing industries in the last twenty years is the memory chip industry, which supplies memory chips for personal computers and other electronic devices. Yet the average profitability for this industry has been very low. Using the industry analysis framework, list all the potential factors that might explain this apparent contradiction.

4. Rate the pharmaceutical and lumber industries as high, medium, or low on the following dimensions of industry structure:

	Pharmaceutical Industry	Lumber Industry
Rivalry		
Threat of new entrants		
Threat of substitute products		
Bargaining power of buyers		
Bargaining power of suppliers		
Given your ratings, which industry would you expect to earn the highest returns?		

5. Joe Smith argues, "Your analysis of the five forces that affect industry profitability is incomplete. For example, in the banking industry, I can think of at least three other factors

that are also important; namely, government regulation, demographic trends, and cultural factors." His classmate Jane Brown disagrees and says, "These three factors are important only to the extent that they influence one of the five forces." Explain how, if at all, the three factors discussed by Joe affect the five forces in the banking industry.

6. Coca-Cola and Pepsi are both very profitable soft drinks. Inputs for these products include corn syrup bottles/cans, and soft drink syrup. Coca-Cola and Pepsi produce the syrup themselves and purchase the other inputs. They then enter into exclusive contracts with independent bottlers to produce their products. Use the five forces framework and your knowledge of the soft drink industry to explain how Coca-Cola and Pepsi are able to retain most of the profits in this industry.

7. In the early 1980s, United, Delta, and American Airlines each started frequent flier programs as a way to differentiate themselves in response to excess capacity in the industry. Many industry analysts, however, believe that this move had only mixed success. Use the competitive advantage concepts to explain why.

8. What are the ways that a firm can create barriers to entry to deter competition in its business? What factors determine whether these barriers are likely to be enduring?

9. Explain why you agree or disagree with each of the following statements:
   a. It's better to be a differentiator than a cost leader, since you can then charge premium prices.
   b. It's more profitable to be in a high technology industry than a low technology one.
   c. The reason why industries with large investments have high barriers to entry is because it is costly to raise capital.

10. There are very few companies that are able to be both cost leaders and differentiators. Why? Can you think of a company that has been successful at both?

11. Many consultants are advising diversified companies in emerging markets such as India, South Korea, Mexico, and Turkey to adopt corporate strategies proven to be of value in advanced economies such as the U.S. and the U.K. What are the pros and cons of this advice?

NOTES

1. The discussion presented here is intended to provide a basic background in strategy analysis. For a more complete discussion of the strategy concepts, see, for example, *Contemporary Strategy Analysis* by Robert M. Grant (Cambridge, MA: Blackwell Publishers, 1991); *Economics of Strategy* by David Besanko, David Dranove, and Mark Shanley (New York: John Wiley & Sons, 1996); *Strategy and the Business Landscape* by Pankaj Ghemawat (Reading, MA: Addison Wesley Longman, 1999); and *Corporate Strategy: Resources and the Scope of the Firm* by David J. Collis and Cynthia Montgomery (Burr Ridge, IL: Irwin/McGraw-Hill, 1997).

2. These data are taken from "Do Competitors Perform Better When They Pursue Different Strategies?" by Anita M. McGahan (working paper, Harvard Business School, May 12, 1999).

3. For a summary of this research, see *Industrial Market Structure and Economic Performance,* second edition, by F. M. Scherer (Chicago: Rand McNally College Publishing Co., 1980).

4. See *Competitive Strategy* by Michael E. Porter (New York: The Free Press, 1980).

5. The U.S. Department of Justice and the Federal Trade Commission use the Herfindahl-Hirschman Index (HHI) to measure concentration when evaluating horizontal mergers. The HHI is calculated by summing the squares of the individual market shares of all the participants. The Department of Justice considers a market with a result of less than 1,000 to be a competitive marketplace; a result of 1,000 to 1,800 to be a moderately concentrated marketplace; and a result of 1,800 or greater to be a highly concentrated marketplace. The four-firm concentration ratio is another commonly used measure of industry concentration; it refers to the market share of the four largest firms in an industry.

6. While the discussion here uses *buyer* to connote industrial buyers, the same concepts also apply to buyers of consumer products. Throughout this chapter we use the terms *buyers* and *customers* interchangeably.

7. The data on Dell and the PC industry discussed here and elsewhere in this chapter were primarily drawn from "Dell Computer Corporation" by Das Narayandas and V. Kasturi Rangan, Harvard Business School Publishing Division, Case 9-596-058, and "Dell Online" by V. Kasturi Rangan and Marie Bell, Harvard Business School Publishing Division, Case 9-598-116, updated as appropriate for recent changes in the firm and industry.

8. Brian Gammage, Charles Smulders, and Martin Reynolds, "PC Market Realities Will Force Changes on Intel and Microsoft," Gartner, Inc., September 20, 2005.

9. Mikako Kitagawa, "Digital Home is Not a Mass PC Market," Gartner, Inc., May 10, 2005.

10. For a more detailed discussion of these two sources of competitive advantage, see Michael E. Porter, *Competitive Advantage: Creating and Sustaining Superior Performance* (New York: The Free Press, 1985).

11. Ibid.

12. In recent years one of the strategic challenges faced by corporations is having to deal with competitors who achieve differentiation with low cost. For example, Japanese auto manufacturers have successfully demonstrated that there is no necessary trade-off between quality and cost. Similarly, in recent years several highly successful retailers like Wal-Mart and Home Depot have been able to combine high quality, high service, and low prices. These examples suggest that combining low cost and differentiation strategies is possible when a firm introduces a significant technical or business innovation. However, such cost advantage and differentiation will be sustainable only if there are significant barriers to imitation by competitors.

13. See *Competing for the Future* by Gary Hamel and C. K. Prahalad (Boston: Harvard Business School Press, 1994) for a more detailed discussion of the concept of core competencies and their critical role in corporate strategy.

14. C. Montgomery, "Corporate Diversification," *Journal of Economic Perspectives,* Summer 1994.

15. The following works are seminal to transaction cost economics: R. Coase, "The Nature of the Firm," *Economica* 4 (1937): 386–405; *Markets and Hierarchies: Analysis and Antitrust Implications* by Oliver Williamson (New York: The Free Press, 1975); and D. Teece, "Toward an Economic Theory of the Multi-product Firm," *Journal of Economic Behavior and Organization* 3 (1982): 39–63.

16. For a more complete discussion of these issues, see T. Khanna and K. Palepu, "Building Institutional Infrastructure in Emerging Markets," *Brown Journal of World Affairs,* Winter/Spring 1998, and T. Khanna and K. Palepu, "Why Focused Strategies May Be Wrong for Emerging Markets," *Harvard Business Review,* July/August 1997.

17. For an empirical study which illustrates this point, see T. Khanna and K. Palepu, "Is Group Affiliation Profitable in Emerging Markets? An Analysis of Diversified Indian Business Groups," *Journal of Finance* (April 2000): 867–91.

18. See L. Lang and R. Stulz, "Tobin's q, diversification, and firm performance," *Journal of Political Economy* 102 (1994): 1248–80, and P. Berger and E. Ofek, "Diversification's Effect on Firm Value," *Journal of Financial Economics* 37 (1994): 39–65.

19. See P. Healy, K. Palepu, and R. Ruback, "Which Takeovers Are Profitable: Strategic or Financial?" *Sloan Management Review* 38 (Summer 1997): 45–57.

20. See K. Schipper and A. Smith, "Effects of Recontracting on Shareholder Wealth: The Case of Voluntary Spinoffs," *Journal of Financial Economics* 12 (December 1983): 437–67, and L. Lang, A. Poulsen, and R. Stulz, "Asset Sales, Firm Performance, and the Agency Costs of Managerial Discretion," *Journal of Financial Economics* 37 (January 1995): 3–37.

21. General Electric Company, 2001 Annual Report (Fairfield, CT, 2002), p. 6.

22. General Electric Company, 2005 Annual Report (Fairfield, CT, 2006), p. 10.

Chapter 3
Overview of Accounting Analysis

The purpose of accounting analysis is to evaluate the degree to which a firm's accounting captures its underlying business reality.[1] By identifying places where there is accounting flexibility, and by evaluating the appropriateness of the firm's accounting policies and estimates, analysts can assess the degree of distortion in a firm's accounting numbers. Having identified accounting distortions, analysts can then adjust a firm's accounting numbers using cash flow and footnote information to "undo" the distortions. Sound accounting analysis improves the reliability of conclusions from financial analysis, the next step in financial statement analysis.

THE INSTITUTIONAL FRAMEWORK FOR FINANCIAL REPORTING

There is typically a separation between ownership and management in public corporations. Financial statements serve as the vehicle through which owners keep track of their firms' financial situation. On a periodic basis, firms typically produce three primary financial reports: (1) an income statement that describes the operating performance during a time period, (2) a balance sheet that states the firm's assets and how they are financed, and (3) a cash flow statement (or in some countries, a funds flow statement) that summarizes the cash (or fund) flows of the firm. These statements are accompanied by footnotes that provide additional details on the financial statement line items, as well as by management's narrative discussion of the firm's performance in the Management Discussion and Analysis section.

To evaluate effectively the quality of a firm's financial statement data, the analyst needs to first understand the basic features of financial reporting and the institutional framework that governs them, as discussed in the following sections.

Accrual Accounting

One of the fundamental features of corporate financial reports is that they are prepared using accrual rather than cash accounting. Unlike cash accounting, accrual accounting distinguishes between the recording of costs and benefits associated with economic activities and the actual payment and receipt of cash. Net income is the primary periodic performance index under accrual accounting. To compute net income, the effects of economic transactions are recorded on the basis of *expected*, not necessarily *actual*, cash receipts and payments. Expected cash receipts from the delivery of products or services are recognized as revenues, and expected cash outflows associated with these revenues are recognized as expenses.

While there are many rules and conventions that govern a firm's preparation of financial statements, there are only a few conceptual building blocks that form the foundation of accrual accounting. The following definitions are critical to the income statement, which summarizes a firm's revenues and expenses[2]:

- **Revenues** are economic resources earned during a time period. Revenue recognition is governed by the realization principle, which proposes that revenues should be recognized when (a) the firm has provided all, or substantially all, the goods or services to be delivered to the customer and (b) the customer has paid cash or is expected to pay cash with a reasonable degree of certainty.[3]
- **Expenses** are economic resources used up in a time period. Expense recognition is governed by the matching and the conservatism principles. Under these principles, expenses are resource costs (a) directly associated with revenues recognized in the same period, (b) associated with benefits that are consumed in this time period, or (c) whose future benefits are not reasonably certain.
- **Profit** is the difference between a firm's revenues and expenses in a time period.[4]

The following fundamental relationship is therefore reflected in a firm's income statement:

$$Profit = Revenues - Expenses$$

In contrast, the balance sheet is a summary at one point in time. The principles that define a firm's assets, liabilities, and equity are as follows:

- **Assets** are economic resources owned by a firm that are (a) likely to produce future economic benefits and (b) measurable with a reasonable degree of certainty.
- **Liabilities** are economic obligations of a firm arising from benefits received in the past that (a) are required to be met with a reasonable degree of certainty and (b) whose timing is reasonably well defined.
- **Equity** is the difference between a firm's assets and its liabilities.

The definitions of assets, liabilities, and equity lead to the fundamental relationship that governs a firm's balance sheet:

$$Assets = Liabilities + Equity$$

Delegation of Reporting to Management

While the basic definitions of the elements of a firm's financial statements are simple, their application in practice often involves complex judgments. For example, how should revenues be recognized when a firm sells land to customers and also provides customer financing? If revenue is recognized before cash is collected, how should potential defaults be estimated? Are the outlays associated with research and development activities, whose payoffs are uncertain, assets or expenses when incurred? Are contractual commitments under lease arrangements or post-retirement plans liabilities? If so, how should they be valued?

Because corporate managers have intimate knowledge of their firms' businesses, they are entrusted with the primary task of making the appropriate judgments in portraying myriad business transactions using the basic accrual accounting framework. The accounting discretion granted to managers is potentially valuable because it allows them to reflect inside information in reported financial statements. However, since investors view profits as a measure of managers' performance, managers have an incentive to use their accounting discretion to distort reported profits by making biased assumptions. Further, the use of accounting numbers in contracts between the firm and outsiders provides a motivation for management manipulation of accounting numbers.

This earnings management distorts financial accounting data, making it less valuable to external users of financial statements. Therefore, the delegation of financial reporting decisions to managers has both costs and benefits. Accounting rules and auditing are mechanisms designed to reduce the cost and preserve the benefit of delegating financial reporting to corporate managers. The Sarbanes-Oxley Act increased the involvement of the audit committee of a firm's board of directors and required the personal certification of the CEO and CFO as to the appropriateness of financial reports as a way of reducing the costs of this delegation. The legal system is used to adjudicate disputes between managers, auditors, and investors.

Generally Accepted Accounting Principles

Given that it is difficult for outside investors to determine whether managers have used accounting flexibility to signal their proprietary information or merely to disguise reality, a number of accounting conventions have evolved to mitigate the problem. For example, in most countries financial statements are prepared using the historical cost convention, where assets and liabilities are recorded at historical exchange prices rather than fair values, replacement values, or values in use. This reduces managers' ability to overstate the value of the assets that they have acquired or developed, or to understate the value of liabilities. Of course, historical cost also limits the information that is available to investors about the potential of the firm's assets, since exchange prices are usually different from fair values or values in use.[5]

Accounting standards and rules also limit management's ability to misuse accounting judgment by regulating how particular types of transactions are recorded. For example, accounting standards for leases stipulate how firms are to record contractual arrangements to lease resources. Similarly, pension and other post-employment benefit standards describe how firms are to record commitments to provide pensions and other retirement benefits for employees. These accounting standards, which are designed to convey quantitative information on a firm's performance, are complemented by a set of disclosure principles. The disclosure principles guide the amount and kinds of information that is disclosed and require a firm to provide qualitative information related to the assumptions, policies, and uncertainties that underlie the quantitative data presented.

In the United States, the Securities and Exchange Commission (SEC) has the legal authority to set accounting standards. The SEC typically relies on private sector accounting bodies to undertake this task. Since 1973 accounting standards in the United States have been set by the Financial Accounting Standards Board (FASB); and Generally Accepted Accounting Principles (GAAP) denotes the standards, conventions, rules, and procedures that FASB requires firms to apply in preparing their financial statements. There are similar private sector or public sector accounting standard-setting bodies in many other countries. More recently, the International Accounting Standards Board (IASB) and its predecessor, the International Accounting Standards Committee (IASC), have been attempting to set worldwide accounting standards. Those standards, the International Financial Reporting Standards (IFRS), are gaining increasing acceptance throughout Europe and in many developed and emerging markets across the globe. While IFRS is not applicable to U.S. companies, experts anticipate that GAAP and IFRS are likely to ultimately converge. At present, foreign companies registered with the SEC have to file a Form 20-F, which shows a reconciliation between the company's IFRS or local accounts and U.S. GAAP.

Uniform accounting standards attempt to reduce managers' ability to record similar economic transactions in dissimilar ways, either over time or across firms. Thus they create a uniform accounting language and increase the credibility of financial statements by limiting a firm's ability to distort them. Increased uniformity from accounting standards, however, comes at the expense of reduced flexibility for managers to reflect genuine business differences in a firm's accounting decisions. Rigid accounting standards work best for economic transactions whose accounting treatment is not predicated on managers' proprietary information. However, when there is significant business judgment involved in assessing a transaction's economic consequences, rigid standards are likely to be dysfunctional for some companies because they prevent managers from using their superior knowledge of the business to determine how best to report the economics of key business events. Further, if accounting standards are too rigid, they may induce managers to expend economic resources to restructure business transactions to achieve a desired accounting result or to forego transactions that may be difficult to report on.

External Auditing

External auditing, broadly defined as a verification of the integrity of the reported financial statements by someone other than the preparer, ensures that managers use accounting rules and conventions consistently over time, and that their accounting estimates are reasonable. In the U.S., all listed companies are required to have their financial statements audited by an independent public accountant. The standards and procedures to be followed by independent auditors are known as Generally Accepted Auditing Standards (GAAS). Under the Sarbanes-Oxley Act, the responsibility for overseeing audit firms and for ensuring that they are complying with GAAS resides with the Public Company Accounting Oversight Board (PCAOB), a new U.S. regulatory body. All public accounting firms are required to register with the PCAOB, which has the power to inspect and investigate audit work, and if needed to discipline auditors.

The Sarbanes-Oxley Act also specifies the relationship between a company and its external auditor, requiring auditors to report to, and be overseen by, a company's audit committee rather than its management. In addition, the Act prohibits public accounting firms from providing non-audit services, such as bookkeeping, information systems design and implementation, valuation and a range of other consulting services, to a company that it audits. Finally, the Act requires that audit firms rotate the lead and reviewing audit partner every five years. These changes are expected to affect the economics of audit firms and to increase the cost of audits.

While auditors issue an opinion on published financial statements, it is important to remember that the primary responsibility for the statements still rests with corporate managers. Auditing improves the quality and credibility of accounting data by limiting a firm's ability to distort financial statements to suit its own purposes. However, as recent audit failures at companies such as Enron and WorldCom show, auditing is imperfect. Audits cannot review all of a firm's transactions. They can also fail because of lapses in quality, or because of lapses in judgment by auditors who fail to challenge management for fear of losing future business.

Third-party auditing may also reduce the quality of financial reporting because it constrains the kind of accounting rules and conventions that evolve over time. For example, the FASB considers the views of auditors in the standard-setting process. Auditors are likely to argue against accounting standards that produce numbers which are difficult to audit, even if the proposed rules produce relevant information for investors.

Legal Liability

The legal environment in which accounting disputes between managers, auditors, and investors are adjudicated can also have a significant effect on the quality of reported numbers. The threat of lawsuits and resulting penalties has the beneficial effect of improving the accuracy of disclosure. However, the potential for significant legal liability might also discourage managers and auditors from supporting accounting proposals requiring risky forecasts, for example, forward-looking disclosures. The U.S. auditing community often expresses this type of concern.

FACTORS INFLUENCING ACCOUNTING QUALITY

Because the mechanisms that limit managers' ability to distort accounting data themselves add noise, it is not optimal to use accounting regulation to completely eliminate managerial flexibility. Therefore, real-world accounting systems leave considerable room for managers to influence financial statement data. The net result is that information in corporate financial reports is noisy and biased, even in the presence of accounting regulation and external auditing.[6] The objective of accounting analysis is to evaluate the degree to which a firm's accounting captures its underlying business reality and to "undo" any accounting distortions. When potential distortions are large, accounting analysis can add considerable value.[7]

There are three potential sources of noise and bias in accounting data: (1) that introduced by rigidity in accounting rules, (2) random forecast errors, and (3) systematic reporting choices made by corporate managers to achieve specific objectives. Each of these factors is discussed below.

Noise from Accounting Rules

Accounting rules introduce noise and bias because it is often difficult to restrict management discretion without reducing the information content of accounting data. For example, the Statement of Financial Accounting Standards (SFAS) No. 2 issued by the FASB requires firms to expense research outlays when they are incurred. Clearly, some research expenditures have future value while others do not. However, because SFAS 2 does not allow firms to distinguish between the two types of expenditures, it leads to a systematic distortion of reported accounting numbers. Broadly speaking, the degree of distortion introduced by accounting standards depends on how well uniform accounting standards capture the nature of a firm's transactions.

Forecast Errors

Another source of noise in accounting data arises from pure forecast error, because managers cannot predict future consequences of current transactions perfectly. For example, when a firm sells products on credit, accrual accounting requires managers to make a judgment about the probability of collecting payments from customers. If payments are deemed "reasonably certain," the firm treats the transactions as sales, creating accounts receivable on its balance sheet. Managers then make an estimate of the proportion of receivables that will not be collected. Because managers do not have perfect foresight, actual customer defaults are likely to be different from estimated defaults, leading to a forecast error. The extent of errors in managers' accounting forecasts depends on a variety of factors including the complexity of the business transactions, the predictability of the firm's environment, and unforeseen economy-wide changes.

Managers' Accounting Choices

Corporate managers also introduce noise and bias into accounting data through their own accounting decisions. Managers have a variety of incentives to exercise their accounting discretion to achieve certain objectives[8]:

- *Accounting-based debt covenants.* Managers may make accounting decisions to meet certain contractual obligations in their debt covenants. For example, firms' lending agreements with banks and other debt holders require them to meet covenants related to interest coverage, working capital ratios, and net worth, all defined in terms of accounting numbers. Violation of these agreements may be costly because lenders can trigger penalties including demanding immediate repayment of their loans. Managers of firms close to violating debt covenants have an incentive to select accounting policies and estimates to reduce the probability of covenant violation. The debt covenant motivation for managers' accounting decisions has been analyzed by a number of accounting researchers.[9]

- *Management compensation.* Another motivation for managers' accounting choice comes from the fact that their compensation and job security are often tied to reported profits. For example, many top managers receive bonus compensation if they exceed certain prespecified profit targets. This provides motivation for managers to choose accounting policies and estimates to maximize their expected compensation.[10] Stock option awards can also potentially induce managers to manage earnings. Options provide managers with incentives to understate earnings prior to option grants to lower the firm's current stock price and hence the option exercise price, and to inflate earnings and stock prices at the time of option exercise.[11]

- *Corporate control contests.* In corporate control contests, including hostile takeovers and proxy fights, competing management groups attempt to win over the firm's shareholders. Accounting numbers are used extensively in debating managers' performance in these contests. Therefore, managers may make accounting decisions to influence investor perceptions in corporate control contests.[12]

- *Tax considerations.* Managers may also make reporting choices to trade off between financial reporting and tax considerations. For example, U.S. firms are required to use LIFO inventory accounting for shareholder reporting in order to use it for tax reporting. Under LIFO, when prices are rising, firms report lower profits, thereby reducing tax payments. Some firms may forgo the tax reduction in order to report higher profits in their financial statements.[13]

- *Regulatory considerations.* Since accounting numbers are used by regulators in a variety of contexts, managers of some firms may make accounting decisions to influence regulatory outcomes. Examples of regulatory situations where accounting numbers are used include antitrust actions, import tariffs to protect domestic industries, and tax policies.[14]

- *Capital market considerations.* Managers may make accounting decisions to influence the perceptions of capital markets. When there are information asymmetries between managers and outsiders, this strategy may succeed in influencing investor perceptions, at least temporarily.[15]

- *Stakeholder considerations.* Managers may also make accounting decisions to influence the perception of important stakeholders in the firm. For example, since labor unions can use healthy profits as a basis for demanding wage increases, managers may make accounting decisions to decrease income when they are facing union contract negotiations. In countries like Germany, where labor unions are strong, these considerations appear to play an important role in firms' accounting policy. Other important stakeholders that firms may wish to influence through their financial reports include suppliers and customers.[16]

- *Competitive considerations.* The dynamics of competition in an industry might also influence a firm's reporting choices. For example, a firm's segment disclosure decisions may be influenced by its concern that disaggregated disclosure may help competitors in their business decisions. Similarly, firms may not disclose data on their margins by product line for fear of giving away proprietary information. Finally, firms may discourage new entrants by making income-decreasing accounting choices.

In addition to accounting policy choices and estimates, the level of disclosure is also an important determinant of a firm's accounting quality. Corporate managers can choose disclosure policies that make it more or less costly for external users of financial reports to understand the true economic picture of their businesses. Accounting regulations usually prescribe minimum disclosure requirements, but they do not restrict managers from voluntarily providing additional disclosures. Managers can use various parts of the financial reports, including the Letter to the Shareholders, Management Discussion and Analysis, and footnotes, to describe the company's strategy, its accounting policies, and its current performance. There is wide variation across firms in how managers use their disclosure flexibility.[17]

STEPS IN PERFORMING ACCOUNTING ANALYSIS

In this section we discuss a series of steps that an analyst can follow to evaluate a firm's accounting quality.

Step 1: Identify Principal Accounting Policies

As discussed in the chapter on business strategy analysis, a firm's industry characteristics and its own competitive strategy determine its key success factors and risks. One of the goals of financial statement analysis is to evaluate how well these success factors and risks are being managed by the firm. In accounting analysis, therefore, the analyst should identify and evaluate the policies and the estimates the firm uses to measure its critical factors and risks.

Key success factors in the banking industry include interest rate and credit risk management; in the retail industry, inventory management is important; and for a manufacturer competing on product quality and innovation, research and development, and product defects after sale are major areas of concern. A significant success factor in the leasing business is to make accurate forecasts of residual values of the leased equipment at the end of the lease terms. In each of these cases, the analyst has to identify the accounting measures the firm uses to capture these business constructs, the policies that determine how the measures are implemented, and the important estimates embedded in these policies. For example, the accounting measure a bank uses to capture credit risk is its loan loss reserves, and the accounting measure that captures product quality for a manufacturer is its warranty expenses and reserves. For a firm in the equipment leasing industry, one of the most important accounting policies is the way residual values are recorded. Residual values influence the company's reported profits and its asset base. If residual values are overestimated, the firm runs the risk of having to take large write-offs in the future.

Step 2: Assess Accounting Flexibility

Not all firms have equal flexibility in choosing their accounting policies and estimates. Some firms' accounting choice is severely constrained by accounting standards and conventions. For example, even though research and development is a key success factor for biotechnology companies, managers have no accounting discretion in reporting on this activity. Similarly, even though marketing and brand building are essential to the success of consumer goods firms, they are required to expense all their marketing outlays. In contrast, managing credit risk is one of the critical success factors for banks, and bank managers have the freedom to estimate expected defaults on their loans. Similarly, software developers have the flexibility to decide at what points in their development cycles the outlays can be capitalized.

If managers have little flexibility in choosing accounting policies and estimates related to their key success factors (as in the case of biotechnology firms), accounting data are likely to be less informative for understanding the firm's economics. In contrast, if managers have considerable flexibility in choosing the policies and estimates (as in the case of software developers), accounting numbers have the potential to be informative, depending upon how managers exercise this flexibility.

Regardless of the degree of accounting flexibility a firm's managers have in measuring their key success factors and risks, they have some flexibility with respect to several other accounting policies. For example, all firms have to make choices with respect to depreciation policy (straight-line or accelerated methods), inventory accounting policy (LIFO, FIFO, or Average Cost), and policies regarding the estimation of pension and other post-employment benefits (expected return on plan assets, discount rate for liabilities, and rate of increase in wages and health care costs). Since all these policy choices can have a significant impact on the reported performance of a firm, they offer an opportunity for the firm to manage its reported numbers and should be the focus of analysis in this step.

Step 3: Evaluate Accounting Strategy

When managers have accounting flexibility, they can use it either to communicate their firm's economic situation or to hide true performance. Some of the strategy questions one could ask in examining how managers exercise their accounting flexibility include the following:

- How do the firm's accounting policies compare to the norms in the industry? If they are dissimilar, is it because the firm's competitive strategy is unique? For example, consider a firm that reports a lower warranty allowance than the industry average. One explanation is that the firm competes on the basis of high quality and has invested considerable resources to reduce the rate of product failure. An alternative explanation is that the firm is merely understating its warranty liabilities.
- Do managers face strong incentives to use accounting discretion to manage earnings? For example, is the firm close to violating bond covenants? Or are the managers having difficulty meeting accounting-based bonus targets? Does management own significant stock? Is the firm in the middle of a proxy fight or union negotiations? Managers may also make accounting decisions to reduce tax payments or to influence the perceptions of the firm's competitors.
- Has the firm changed any of its policies or estimates? What is the justification? What is the impact of these changes? For example, if warranty expenses decreased, is it because the firm made significant investments to improve quality?
- Have the company's policies and estimates been realistic in the past? For example, firms may overstate their revenues and understate their expenses during the year

by manipulating quarterly reports, which are not subject to a full-blown external audit. However, the auditing process at the end of the fiscal year forces such companies to make large fourth-quarter adjustments, providing an opportunity for the analyst to assess the quality of the firm's interim reporting. Similarly, firms that depreciate fixed assets too slowly will be forced to take a large write-off later. A history of write-offs may be, therefore, a sign of prior earnings management.

- Does the firm structure any significant business transactions so that it can achieve certain accounting objectives? For example, leasing firms can alter lease terms (the length of the lease or the bargain purchase option at the end of the lease term) so that the transactions qualify as sales-type leases for the lessors. Enron structured acquisitions of joint venture interests and hedging transactions with special purpose entities to avoid having to show joint venture liabilities, and to avoid reporting investment losses in its financial statements.[18] Such behavior may suggest that the firm's managers are willing to expend economic resources merely to achieve an accounting objective.

Step 4: Evaluate the Quality of Disclosure

Managers can make it more or less easy for an analyst to assess the firm's accounting quality and to use its financial statements to understand business reality. While accounting rules require a certain amount of minimum disclosure, managers have considerable choice in the matter. Disclosure quality, therefore, is an important dimension of a firm's accounting quality.

In assessing a firm's disclosure quality, an analyst could ask the following questions:

- Does the company provide adequate disclosures to assess the firm's business strategy and its economic consequences? For example, some firms use the Letter to the Shareholders in their annual report to clearly lay out the firm's industry conditions, its competitive position, and management's plans for the future. Others use the letter to puff up the firm's financial performance and gloss over any competitive difficulties the firm might be facing.
- Do the footnotes adequately explain the key accounting policies and assumptions and their logic? For example, if a firm's revenue and expense recognition policies differ from industry norms, the firm can explain its choices in a footnote. Similarly, when there are significant changes in a firm's policies, footnotes can be used to disclose the reasons.
- Does the firm adequately explain its current performance? The Management Discussion and Analysis (MD&A) section of the annual report provides an opportunity to help analysts understand the reasons behind a firm's performance changes. Some firms use this section to link financial performance to business conditions. For example, if profit margins went down in a period, was it because of price competition or because of increases in manufacturing costs? If the selling and general administrative expenses went up, was it because the firm is investing in a differentiation strategy, or because unproductive overhead expenses were creeping up? Based on a review of the Fortune 500 companies, the SEC released in 2003 a circular indicating that companies should provide more discussion in MD&A about their critical accounting policies.[19] Companies were encouraged to disclose the most difficult and judgmental estimates and accounting policies they used, among other guidance.
- If accounting rules and conventions restrict the firm from measuring its key success factors appropriately, does the firm provide adequate additional disclosure to help outsiders understand how these factors are being managed? For example, if a firm invests in product quality and customer service, accounting rules do not allow the management to capitalize these outlays, even when the future benefits are certain. The firm's MD&A can be used to highlight how

these outlays are being managed and their performance consequences. For example, the firm can disclose physical indexes of defect rates and customer satisfaction so that outsiders can assess the progress being made in these areas and the future cash flow consequences of these actions.

- If a firm is in multiple business segments, what is the quality of segment disclosure? Some firms provide excellent discussion of their performance by product segments and geographic segments. Others lump many different businesses into one broad segment. The level of competition in an industry and management's willingness to share desegregated performance data influence a firm's quality of segment disclosure.

- How forthcoming is the management with respect to bad news? A firm's disclosure quality is most clearly revealed by the way management deals with bad news. Does it adequately explain the reasons for poor performance? Does the company clearly articulate its strategy, if any, to address the company's performance problems?

- How good is the firm's investor relations program? Does the firm provide fact books with detailed data on the firm's business and performance? Is management accessible to analysts?

Step 5: Identify Potential Red Flags

In addition to the preceding steps, a common approach to accounting quality analysis is to look for "red flags" pointing to questionable accounting. These indicators suggest that the analyst should examine certain items more closely or gather more information on them. Some common red flags are the following:

- *Unexplained changes in accounting, especially when performance is poor.* This may suggest that managers are using their accounting discretion to "dress up" their financial statements.[20]

- *Unexplained transactions that boost profits.* For example, firms might undertake balance sheet transactions, such as asset sales or debt for equity swaps, to realize gains in periods when operating performance is poor.[21]

- *Unusual increases in accounts receivable in relation to sales increases.* This may suggest that the company is relaxing its credit policies or artificially loading up its distribution channels to record revenues during the current period, a practice commonly referred to as "channel stuffing." If credit policies are relaxed unduly, the firm may face receivable write-offs in subsequent periods as a result of customer defaults. If the firm accelerates shipments to its distributors, it may face either product returns or reduced shipments in subsequent periods.

- *Unusual increases in inventories in relation to sales increases.* If the inventory build-up is due to an increase in finished goods inventory, it could be a sign that demand for the firm's products is slowing down, suggesting that the firm may be forced to cut prices (and hence earn lower margins) or write down its inventory. A build-up in work-in-progress inventory tends to be good news on average, probably signaling that managers expect an increase in sales. If the build-up is in raw materials, it could suggest manufacturing or procurement inefficiencies, leading to an increase in cost of goods sold (and hence lower margins).[22]

- *An increasing gap between a firm's reported income and its cash flow from operating activities.* While it is legitimate for accrual accounting numbers to differ from cash flows, there is usually a steady relationship between the two if the company's accounting policies remain the same. Therefore, any *change* in the relationship between reported profits and operating cash flows might indicate subtle changes in the firm's accrual estimates. For example, a firm undertaking large construction contracts might use the percentage-of-completion method to record revenues. While earnings and operating cash flows are likely to differ for such a firm, they should bear a steady relationship to each other. Now suppose the firm increases revenues in a period through an aggressive application of the percentage-of-completion method. Then its earnings will go up, but its cash flow remains unaffected. This change in the firm's accounting quality will be manifested by a *change* in the relationship between the firm's earnings and cash flows.

- *An increasing gap between a firm's reported income and its tax income.* Once again, it is quite legitimate for a firm to follow different accounting policies for financial reporting and tax accounting as long as the tax law allows it.[23] However, the relationship between a firm's book and tax accounting is likely to remain stable over time unless there are significant changes in tax rules or accounting standards. Thus, an increasing gap between a firm's reported income and its tax income may indicate that financial reporting to shareholders has become more aggressive. For example, warranty expenses are estimated on an accrual basis for financial reporting, but they are recorded on a cash basis for tax reporting. Unless there is a big change in the firm's product quality, these two numbers bear a consistent relationship to each other. Therefore, a change in this relationship can be an indication either that product quality is changing significantly or that financial reporting estimates are changing.
- *A tendency to use financing mechanisms such as research and development partnerships, special-purpose entities, and the sale of receivables with recourse.* While these arrangements may have a sound business logic, they can also provide management with an opportunity to understate the firm's liabilities and/or overstate its assets.[24]
- *Unexpected large asset write-offs.* This may suggest that management is slow to incorporate changing business circumstances into its accounting estimates. Asset write-offs may also be a result of unexpected changes in business circumstances.[25]
- *Large fourth-quarter adjustments.* A firm's annual reports are audited by the external auditors, but its interim financial statements are usually only reviewed. If a firm's management is reluctant to make appropriate accounting estimates (such as provisions for uncollectible receivables) in its interim statements, it could be forced to make adjustments at the end of the year as a result of pressure from its external auditors. A consistent pattern of fourth-quarter adjustments, therefore, may indicate aggressive management of interim reporting.[26]
- *Qualified audit opinions or changes in independent auditors that are not well justified.* These may indicate a firm's aggressive attitude or a tendency to "opinion shop."
- *Related-party transactions or transactions between related entities.* These transactions may lack the objectivity of the marketplace, and managers' accounting estimates related to these transactions are likely to be more subjective and potentially self-serving.[27]

While the preceding list provides a number of red flags for potentially poor accounting quality, it is important to do further analysis before reaching final conclusions. Each of the red flags has multiple interpretations; some interpretations are based on sound business reasons, and others indicate questionable accounting. It is, therefore, best to use the red flag analysis as a starting point for further probing, not as an end point in itself.[28]

Step 6: Undo Accounting Distortions

If the accounting analysis suggests that the firm's reported numbers are misleading, analysts should attempt to restate the reported numbers to reduce the distortion to the extent possible. It is, of course, virtually impossible to perfectly undo the distortion using outside information alone. However, some progress can be made in this direction by using the cash flow statement and the financial statement footnotes.

A firm's cash flow statement provides a reconciliation of its performance based on accrual accounting and cash accounting. If the analyst is unsure of the quality of the firm's accrual accounting, the cash flow statement provides an alternative benchmark of its performance. The cash flow statement also provides information on how individual line items in the income statement diverge from the underlying cash flows. For example, if an analyst is concerned that the firm is aggressively capitalizing certain costs that should be expensed, the information in the cash flow statement provides a basis to make the necessary adjustment.

Financial statement footnotes also provide information that is potentially useful in restating reported accounting numbers. For example, when a firm changes its accounting policies, it provides a footnote indicating the effect of that change if it is material. Similarly, some firms provide information on the details of accrual estimates such as the allowance for bad debts. The tax footnote usually provides information on the differences between a firm's accounting policies for shareholder reporting and tax reporting. Since tax reporting is often more conservative than shareholder reporting, the information in the tax footnote can be used to estimate what the earnings reported to shareholders would be under more conservative policies.

In Chapter 4, we show how to make accounting adjustments for some of the most common types of accounting distortions.

ACCOUNTING ANALYSIS PITFALLS

There are several potential pitfalls and common misconceptions in accounting analysis that an analyst should avoid.

1. Conservative accounting is not "good" accounting.

Some firms take the approach that it pays to be conservative in financial reporting and to set aside as much as possible for contingencies. This logic is commonly used to justify the expensing of R&D and advertising, and the rapid write-down of intangible assets. It is also used to support large loss reserves for insurance companies, for merger expenses, and for restructuring charges.

From the standpoint of a financial statement user, it is important to recognize that conservative accounting is not the same as "good" accounting. Financial statement users want to evaluate how well a firm's accounting captures business reality in an unbiased manner, and conservative accounting can be as misleading as aggressive accounting in this respect.

It is certainly true that it can be difficult to estimate the economic benefits from many intangibles. However, the intangible nature of some assets does not mean that they do not have value. Indeed, for many firms these types of assets are their most valued. For example, the two most valued assets for the pharmaceutical company Pfizer are its research capabilities that permit it to generate new drugs, and its sales force that enables it to sell those drugs to doctors. Yet neither is recorded on Pfizer's balance sheet. From the investors' point of view, accountants' reluctance to value intangible assets does not diminish their importance. If they are not included in financial statements, investors must look to alternative sources of information on these assets.

Further, conservative accounting often provides managers with opportunities for "income smoothing," which may prevent analysts from recognizing poor performance in a timely fashion. Finally, over time investors are likely to figure out which firms are conservative and may discount their management's disclosures and communications.

2. Not all unusual accounting is questionable.

It is easy to confuse unusual accounting with questionable accounting. While unusual accounting choices might make a firm's performance difficult to compare with other firms' performance, such an accounting choice might be justified if the company's business is unusual. For example, firms that follow differentiated strategies or firms that structure their business in an innovative manner to take advantage of particular market situations may make unusual accounting choices to properly reflect their business. Therefore, it is important to evaluate a company's accounting choices in the context of its business strategy.

Similarly, it is important not to automatically attribute all changes in a firm's accounting policies and accruals to earnings management motives.[29] Accounting changes can also reflect changed business circumstances. For example, as already discussed, a firm that shows unusual increases in its inventory might be preparing for a new product introduction. Similarly, unusual increases in receivables might merely be due to changes in a firm's sales strategy. Unusual decreases in the allowance for uncollectible receivables might reflect a firm's changed customer focus. It is therefore important for an analyst to consider all possible explanations for accounting changes and investigate them using the qualitative information available in a firm's financial statements.

VALUE OF ACCOUNTING DATA AND ACCOUNTING ANALYSIS

What is the value of accounting information and accounting analysis? Given the incentives and opportunities for managers to affect their firms' reported accounting numbers, some have argued that accounting data and accounting analysis are not likely to be useful for investors.

Researchers have examined the value of earnings and return on equity (ROE) by comparing stock returns that could be earned by a hypothetical investor who has perfect foresight of firms' earnings, return on equity (ROE), and cash flows for the following year.[30] To assess the importance of earnings, the hypothetical investor is assumed to buy stocks of firms that have earnings increases for the subsequent year and to sell stocks of firms with subsequent earnings decreases. If this strategy is followed each year during the period 1954 to 1996, the hypothetical investor would have earned an average return of 37.5 percent per year. If a similar investment strategy is followed using ROE, buying stocks with subsequent increases in ROE and selling stocks with ROE decreases, an even higher annual return, 43 percent, would be earned. In contrast, cash flow data appear to be considerably less valuable than earnings or ROE information. Annual returns generated from buying stocks with increased subsequent cash flows from operations and selling stocks with cash flow decreases would be only 9 percent. This suggests that next period's earnings and ROE performance are more relevant information for investors than cash flow performance.

Overall, this research suggests that the institutional arrangements and conventions created to mitigate potential misuse of accounting by managers are effective in providing assurance to investors. The research indicates that investors do not view earnings management as so pervasive as to make earnings data unreliable.

A number of research studies have examined whether accounting analysis is a valuable activity. By and large, this evidence indicates that there are opportunities for superior analysts to earn positive stock returns. Studies show that companies criticized in the financial press for misleading financial reporting subsequently suffered an average stock price drop of 8 percent.[31] Firms where managers appeared to inflate reported earnings prior to an equity issue and subsequently reported poor earnings performance had more negative stock performance after the offer than firms with no apparent earnings management.[32] Finally, firms subject to SEC investigation for earnings management showed an average stock price decline of 9 percent when the earnings management was first announced, and they continued to have poor stock performance for up to two years.[33]

These findings imply that analysts who are able to identify firms with misleading accounting are able to create value for investors. The findings also indicate that the stock market ultimately sees through earnings management. In most cases, earnings management is eventually uncovered and the stock price responds negatively to evidence that firms have inflated prior earnings through misleading accounting.

SUMMARY

In summary, accounting analysis is an important step in the process of analyzing corporate financial reports. The purpose of accounting analysis is to evaluate the degree to which a firm's accounting captures the underlying business reality. Sound accounting analysis improves the reliability of conclusions from financial analysis, the next step in financial statement analysis.

There are six principal steps in accounting analysis. The analyst begins by identifying the key accounting policies and estimates, given the firm's industry and its business strategy. The second step is to evaluate the degree of flexibility available to managers, given the accounting rules and conventions. Next, the analyst evaluates how managers exercise their accounting flexibility and the likely motivations behind managers' accounting strategy. The fourth step involves assessing the depth and quality of a firm's disclosures. The analyst should next identify any red flags needing further investigation. The final step in accounting analysis is to restate accounting numbers to remove any noise and bias introduced by the accounting rules and management decisions.

The next chapter discusses how to implement these concepts and shows how to make some of the most common types of adjustments.

DISCUSSION QUESTIONS

1. A finance student states, "I don't understand why anyone pays any attention to accounting earnings numbers, given that a 'clean' number like cash from operations is readily available." Do you agree? Why or why not?

2. Fred argues, "The standards that I like most are the ones that eliminate all management discretion in reporting—that way I get uniform numbers across all companies and don't have to worry about doing accounting analysis." Do you agree? Why or why not?

3. Bill Simon says, "We should get rid of the FASB and SEC since free market forces will make sure that companies report reliable information." Do you agree? Why or why not?

4. Many firms recognize revenues at the point of shipment. This provides an incentive to accelerate revenues by shipping goods at the end of the quarter. Consider two

companies, one of which ships its product evenly throughout the quarter, and the second which ships all its products in the last two weeks of the quarter. Each company's customers pay thirty days after receiving shipment. Using accounting ratios, how can you distinguish these companies?

5. a. If management reports truthfully, what economic events are likely to prompt the following accounting changes?
    - Increase in the estimated life of depreciable assets
    - Decrease in the uncollectible allowance as a percentage of gross receivables
    - Recognition of revenues at the point of delivery rather than at the point cash is received
    - Capitalization of a higher proportion of software R&D costs

    b. What features of accounting, if any, would make it costly for dishonest managers to make the same changes without any corresponding economic changes?

6. The conservatism principle arises because of concerns about management's incentives to overstate the firm's performance. Joe Banks argues, "We could get rid of conservatism and make accounting numbers more useful if we delegated financial reporting to independent auditors rather than to corporate managers." Do you agree? Why or why not?

7. A fund manager states, "I refuse to buy any company that makes a voluntary accounting change, since it's certainly a case of management trying to hide bad news." Can you think of any alternative interpretation?

NOTES

1. Accounting analysis is sometimes also called "quality of earnings analysis." We prefer to use the term *accounting analysis* since we are discussing a broader concept than merely a firm's earnings quality.

2. These definitions paraphrase those of the Financial Accounting Standards Board (FASB), Statement of Financial Accounting Concepts No. 6, "Elements of Financial Statements" (1985). Our intent is to present the definitions at a conceptual, not technical, level. For more complete discussion of these and related concepts, see the FASB's Statements of Financial Accounting Concepts.

3. SEC rules state that these criteria are satisfied when (i) there is persuasive evidence that an arrangement exists, (ii) delivery has occurred or services have been rendered, (iii) the selling price is fixed or determinable, and (iv) collectibility is reasonably assured. (see SAB 104).

4. Strictly speaking, the comprehensive net income of a firm also includes gains and losses from increases and decreases in equity from nonoperating activities or extraordinary items.

5. Both U.S. and international standard setters are placing increased emphasis on fair value as a basis for accounting valuation. See for example recent U.S. standards on derivatives and most marketable securities.

6. Thus, although accrual accounting is theoretically superior to cash accounting in measuring a firm's periodic performance, the distortions it introduces can make accounting data less valuable to users. If these distortions are large enough, current cash flows may measure a firm's periodic performance better than accounting profits. The relative usefulness of cash flows and accounting profits in measuring performance, therefore, varies from firm to firm. For empirical evidence on this issue, see P. Dechow, "Accounting Earnings and Cash Flows as Measures of Firm Performance: The Role of Accounting Accruals," *Journal of Accounting and Economics* 18 (July 1994): 3–42.

7. For example, Abraham Briloff wrote a series of accounting analyses of public companies in *Barron's* over several years. On average, the stock prices of the analyzed companies changed by about 8 percent on the day these articles were published, indicating the potential value of performing such analysis. For a more complete discussion of this evidence, see G. Foster, "Briloff and the Capital Market," *Journal of Accounting Research* 17 (Spring 1979): 262–74.

8. For a complete discussion of these motivations, see *Positive Accounting Theory*, by R. Watts and J. Zimmerman, (Englewood Cliffs, NJ: Prentice-Hall, 1986). A summary of this research is provided by T. Fields, T. Lys, and L. Vincent in "Empirical Research on Accounting Choice," *Journal of Accounting & Economics* 31 (September 2001): 255–307.

9. The most convincing evidence supporting the covenant hypothesis is reported in a study of the accounting decisions by firms in financial distress: A. Sweeney, "Debt-Covenant Violations and Managers' Accounting Responses," *Journal of Accounting and Economics* 17 (May 1994): 281–308.

10. Studies that examine the bonus hypothesis generally report evidence supporting the view that managers' accounting decisions are influenced by compensation considerations. See, for example, P. Healy, "The Effect of Bonus Schemes on Accounting Decisions," *Journal of Accounting and Economics* 7 (April 1985): 85–107; R. Holthausen, D. Larcker, and R. Sloan, "Annual Bonus Schemes and the Manipulation of Earnings," *Journal of Accounting and Economics* 19 (February 1995): 29–74; and F. Guidry, A. Leone, and S. Rock, "Earnings-Based Bonus Plans and Earnings Management by Business Unit Managers," *Journal of Accounting and Economics* 26 (January 1999): 113–42.

11. For empirical evidence that CEOs of firms with scheduled awards make opportunistic voluntary disclosures to maximize stock award compensation, see D. Aboody and R. Kasznik, "CEO Stock Option Awards and the timing of corporate voluntary disclosures, *Journal of Accounting and Economics* 29 (February 2000): 73–100.

12. L. DeAngelo, "Managerial Competition, Information Costs, and Corporate Governance: The Use of Accounting Performance Measures in Proxy Contests," *Journal of Accounting and Economics* 10 (January 1988): 3–36.

13. The trade-off between taxes and financial reporting in the context of managers' accounting decisions is discussed in detail in *Taxes and Business Strategy* by M. Scholes and M. Wolfson (Englewood Cliffs, NJ: Prentice-Hall, 1992). Many empirical studies have examined firms' LIFO/FIFO choices.

14. Several researchers have documented that firms affected by such situations have a motivation to influence regulators' perceptions through accounting decisions. For example, J. Jones documents that firms seeking import protections make income-decreasing accounting decisions in "Earnings Management During Import Relief Investigations," *Journal of Accounting Research* 29, no. 2 (Autumn 1991): 193–228. A number of studies find that banks that are close to minimum capital requirements overstate loan loss provisions, understate loan write-offs, and recognize abnormal realized gains on securities portfolios. See S. Moyer, "Capital Adequacy Ratio Regulations and Accounting Choices in Commercial Banks," *Journal of Accounting and Economics* 12 (July 1990): 123–54; M. Scholes, G. P. Wilson, and M. Wolfson, "Tax Planning, Regulatory Capital Planning, and Financial Reporting Strategy for Commercial Banks," *Review of Financial Studies* 3 (1990): 625–50; A. Beatty, S. Chamberlain, and J. Magliolo, "Managing Financial Reports of Commercial Banks: The Influence of Taxes, Regulatory Capital and Earnings," *Journal of Accounting Research* 33, no. 2 (1995): 231–61; and J. Collins, D. Shackelford, and J. Wahlen, "Bank Differences in the Coordination of Regulatory Capital, Earnings and Taxes," *Journal of Accounting Research* 33, no. 2 (Autumn 1995): 263–91. Finally, Kathy Petroni finds that financially weak property-casualty insurers that risk regulatory attention understate claim loss reserves: K. Petroni, "Optimistic Reporting in the Property Casualty Insurance Industry," *Journal of Accounting and Economics* 15 (December 1992): 485–508.

15. P. Healy and K. Palepu, "The Effect of Firms' Financial Disclosure Strategies on Stock Prices," *Accounting Horizons* 7 (March 1993): 1–11. For a summary of the empirical evidence, see P. Healy and J. Wahlen, "A Review of the Earnings Management Literature and Its Implications for Standard Setting," *Accounting Horizons* 13 (December 1999): 365–84.

16. R. Bowen, L. DuCharme, and D. Shores, "Stakeholders' Implicit Claims and Accounting Method Choice," *Journal of Accounting and Economics* 20 (December 1995): 255–295, argue that, based on theory and anecdotal evidence, managers choose long-run income-increasing accounting methods as a result of ongoing implicit claims between a firm and its customers, suppliers, employees, and short-term creditors.

17. Financial analysts pay close attention to managers' disclosure strategies; the Association for Investment Management and Research publishes an annual report evaluating them for U.S. firms. For a discussion of these ratings, see M. Lang and R. Lundholm, "Cross-sectional Determinants of Analysts' Ratings of Corporate Disclosures," *Journal of Accounting Research* 31 (Autumn 1993): 246–71.

18. See P. Healy and K. Palepu, "The Fall of Enron," *Journal of Economic Perspectives* 17, no. 2 (Spring 2003): 3–26.

19. Securities and Exchange Commission, "Summary by the Division of Corporation Finance of Significant Issues Addressed in the Review of the Periodic Reports of the Fortune 500 Companies," SEC Web site (accessed May 8, 2006).

20. For a detailed analysis of a company that made such changes, see "Anatomy of an Accounting Change" by K. Palepu in *Accounting & Management: Field Study Perspectives*, edited by W. Bruns, Jr. and R. Kaplan (Boston: Harvard Business School Press, 1987).

21. An example of this type of behavior is documented by John Hand in his study, "Did Firms Undertake Debt-Equity Swaps for an Accounting Paper Profit or True Financial Gain?" *The Accounting Review* 64 (October 1989): 587–623.

22. For an empirical analysis of inventory build-ups, see V. Bernard and J. Noel, "Do Inventory Disclosures Predict Sales and Earnings?" *Journal of Accounting, Auditing, and Finance* (Fall 1991).

23. This is true by and large in the United States and in several other countries. However, in some countries such as Germany and Japan, tax accounting and financial reporting have historically been closely tied together, so this particular red flag has not been very meaningful. With the adoption of international accounting standards and the development of public capital markets, financial reporting and tax accounting in these countries have begun to diverge.

24. For research on accounting and economic incentives in the formation of R&D partnerships, see A. Beatty, P. Berger, and J. Magliolo, "Motives for Forming Research and Development Financing Organizations," *Journal of Accounting and Economics* 19 (April 1995): 411–42. An overview of Enron's use of special purpose entities to manage earnings and window-dress its balance sheet is provided by P. Healy and K. Palepu, "The Fall of Enron," *Journal of Economic Perspectives* 17, no. 2 (Spring 2003): 3–26.

25. For an empirical examination of asset write-offs, see J. Elliott and W. Shaw, "Write-offs as Accounting Procedures to Manage Perceptions," *Journal of Accounting Research* 26, 1988: 91–119.

26. R. Mendenhall and W. Nichols report evidence consistent with managers taking advantage of their discretion to postpone reporting bad news until the fourth quarter. See R. Mendenhall and W. Nichols, "Bad News and Differential Market Reactions to Announcements of Earlier-Quarter versus Fourth-Quarter Earnings," *Journal of Accounting Research*, Supplement (1988): 63–86.

27. The role of insider transactions in the collapse of Enron are discussed by P. Healy and K. Palepu, "The Fall of Enron," *Journal of Economic Perspectives* 17, no. 2 (Spring 2003): 3–26.

28. This type of analysis is presented in the context of provisions for bad debts by M. McNichols and P. Wilson in their study, "Evidence of Earnings Management from the Provisions for Bad Debts," *Journal of Accounting Research*, Supplement (1988): 1–31.

29. This point has been made by several accounting researchers. For a summary of research on earnings management, see K. Schipper, "Earnings Management," *Accounting Horizons* (December 1989): 91–102.

30. See J. Chang, "The Decline in Value Relevance of Earnings and Book Values" (dissertation, Harvard University, 1998). Evidence is also reported by J. Francis and K. Schipper, "Have Financial Statements Lost Their Relevance?" *Journal of Accounting Research* 37, no. 2 (Autumn 1999): 319–52, and W. E. Collins, E. Maydew, and I. Weiss, "Changes in the Value-Relevance of Earnings and Book Value over the Past Forty Years, *Journal of Accounting and Economics* 24 (1997): 39–67.

31. See G. Foster, "Briloff and the Capital Market," *Journal of Accounting Research* 17, no. 1 (Spring 1979): 262–74.

32. See S. H. Teoh, I. Welch, and T. J. Wong, "Earnings Management and the Long-Run Market Performance of Initial Public Offerings," *Journal of Finance* 53 (December 1998a): 1935–74; S. H. Teoh, I. Welch, and T. J. Wong, "Earnings Management and the Post-Issue Underperformance of Seasoned Equity Offerings," *Journal of Financial Economics* 50 (October 1998): 63–99; and S. Teoh, T. Wong, and G. Rao, "Are Accruals During Initial Public Offerings Opportunistic?" *Review of Accounting Studies* 3, no. 1–2 (1998): 175–208.

33. See P. Dechow, R. Sloan, and A. Sweeney, "Causes and Consequences of Earnings Manipulation: An Analysis of Firms Subject to Enforcement Actions by the SEC," *Contemporary Accounting Research* 13, no. 1 (1996): 1–36, and M. D. Beneish, "Detecting GAAP Violation: Implications for Assessing Earnings Management among Firms with Extreme Financial Performance," *Journal of Accounting and Public Policy* 16 (1997): 271–309.

Chapter 4
Implementing Accounting Analysis

We learned in Chapter 3 that accounting analysis requires the analyst to adjust a firm's accounting numbers using cash flow and footnote information to "undo" any accounting distortions. This entails recasting a firm's financial statements using standard reporting nomenclature and formats. Firms frequently use somewhat different formats and terminology for presenting their financial results. Recasting the financial statements using a standard template, therefore, helps ensure that performance metrics used for financial analysis are calculated using comparable definitions across companies and over time.

Once the financial statements have been standardized, the analyst is ready to identify any distortions in financial statements. The analyst's primary focus should be on those accounting estimates and methods that the firm uses to measure its key success factors and risks. If there are differences in estimates and methods between firms or for the same firm over time, the analyst's job is to assess whether they reflect legitimate business differences or differences in managerial judgment or bias. Differences arising from managerial bias will require adjustment. In addition, even if accounting rules are adhered to consistently, accounting distortions can arise because accounting rules themselves do a poor job of capturing firm economics, creating opportunities for the analyst to adjust a firm's financials in a way that presents a more realistic picture of its performance.

This chapter shows how to recast the firm's financial statements into a template that uses standard terminology and classifications, discusses the most common types of accounting distortions that can arise, and shows how to make adjustments to the standardized financial statements to undo these distortions.

A balance sheet approach is used to identify whether there have been any distortions to assets, liabilities, or owners' equity. Once an asset and liability misstatement has been identified, the analyst can make adjustments to the balance sheet at the beginning and/or end of the current year, as well as any needed adjustments to revenues and expenses in the latest income statement. This approach ensures that the financial ratios used to evaluate a firm's most recent results and forecast its future performance are based on financial data that appropriately reflect its business economics.

In some instances, information taken from a firm's footnotes and cash flow statement enables the analyst to make a precise adjustment for an accounting distortion. However, for many types of accounting adjustments, the company does not disclose all of the information needed to perfectly undo the distortion, requiring the analyst to make an approximate adjustment to the financial statements.

RECASTING FINANCIAL STATEMENTS

Firms sometimes use different nomenclature and formats to present their financial results. For example, the asset goodwill can be reported separately using such titles as Goodwill, Excess of Cost Over Net Assets of Acquired Companies, and Cost in Excess of Fair Value, or it can be included in the line item Other Intangible Assets. Interest Income can be reported either as a subcategory of Revenues, shown lower down the income statement as part of Other Income and Expenses, or sometimes as Interest Expense, Net of Interest Income.

These differences in financial statement terminology, classifications, and formats can make it difficult to compare performance across firms, and sometimes to compare performance for the same firm over time. The first task for the analyst in accounting analysis is, therefore, to recast the financial statements into a common format. This involves designing a template for the balance sheet, income statement, and cash flow statement that can be used to standardize financial statements for any company. Tables 4-1, 4-2, and 4-3 present the format used throughout the book to standardize the income statement, balance sheet, and cash flow statement, respectively.

To create standardized financials for a particular company, the analyst classifies each line item in that firm's financial statements using the appropriate account name from

TABLE 4-1	Standardized Income Statement Format
Standard Income Statement Accounts	**Sample Line Items in Reported Accounts**
Sales	Revenues Membership fees Commissions Licenses
Cost of Sales	Cost of merchandise sold Cost of products sold Cost of revenues Cost of services Depreciation on manufacturing facilities
SG&A	General and administrative Marketing & sales Salaries and benefits Servicing and maintenance Depreciation on selling and administrative facilities
Other Operating Expense	Amortization of intangibles Product development Research & development Provision for losses on credit sales Pre-opening costs Special charges

Net Interest Expense (Income)
  Interest Income
  Interest Expense
	
	Interest income
	Interest expense

(continued)

Standard Income Statement Accounts	Sample Line Items in Reported Accounts
Investment Income	Equity income (from associates) Dividend income Rental income[1]
Other Income	Gains on sale of investments/long-term assets Foreign exchange gains Pre-tax gains from accounting changes
Other Expense	Losses on sale of investments/long-term assets Foreign exchange losses Pre-tax losses from accounting changes Restructuring charges Merger expenses Asset impairments
Minority Interest	Minority interest
Tax Expense	Provision for taxes
Unusual Items (after tax)	Any gains or losses reported on an after-tax basis, such as Extraordinary items Non-recurring charges Effect of accounting changes

the above templates. This may require using information from the footnotes to ensure that accounts are classified appropriately. An example, applying the above template to standardize the financial statements for the year ending January 2006 for discount retailer Wal-Mart Stores, Inc., is shown in the appendix at the end of this chapter.

Once the financials have been standardized, the analyst can evaluate whether accounting adjustments are needed to correct any distortions in assets, liabilities, or equity, as discussed below.

ASSET DISTORTIONS

Accountants define assets as resources that a firm owns or controls as a result of past business transactions, and which are expected to produce future economic benefits that can be measured with a reasonable degree of certainty. Assets can take a variety of forms, including cash, marketable securities, receivables from customers, inventory, fixed assets, long-term investments in other companies, and intangibles.

Distortions in asset values generally arise because there is ambiguity about whether

- The firm owns or controls the economic resources in question,
- The economic resources are likely to provide future economic benefits that can be measured with reasonable certainty, or
- The fair values of assets are lower or higher than their book values.

TABLE 4-2 Standardized Balance Sheet Format

Standard Balance Sheet Accounts	Sample Line Items in Reported Accounts	Standard Balance Sheet Accounts	Sample Line Items in Reported Accounts
Assets		**Liabilities and Equity**	
Cash and Marketable Securities	Cash Short-term investments Time deposits	Short-Term Debt	Notes payable Current portion of long-term debt Current portion of capital lease obligation
Accounts Receivable	Accounts/trade receivables (net) Trade debtors	Accounts Payable	Accounts/trade payables Trade creditors
Inventory	Inventory Finished goods Raw materials Work-in-process Stocks	Other Current Liabilities	Accrued expenses Accrued liabilities Taxes payable Dividends payable Deferred (unearned) revenue Customer advances
Deferred Taxes – Current Asset	Deferred income taxes – current	Deferred Taxes – Current Liability	Deferred income taxes – current
Other Current Assets	Prepaid expenses Taxes refundable Current assets of discontinued operations Due from affiliates Due from employees	Long-Term Debt	Long-term debt Senior term notes Subordinated debt Capital lease obligations Convertible debt Pension/post-retirement benefit obligation
Long-Term Tangible Assets	Plant, property & equipment Land Non-current assets of discontinued operations	Deferred Taxes – Long-Term Liability	Deferred income taxes – long-term

(continued)

Standard Balance Sheet Accounts	Sample Line Items in Reported Accounts
Long-Term Intangible Assets	Goodwill Software development costs Deferred financing costs Deferred subscriber acquisition costs Deferred charges Trademarks License rights
Deferred Taxes – LT Asset	Deferred income taxes – long-term
Other Long-Term Assets	Long-term investments Long-term receivables Investment in sales-type or direct-financing leases

Standard Balance Sheet Accounts	Sample Line Items in Reported Accounts
Other Long-Term Liabilities (non-interest bearing)	Non-current deferred (unearned) revenues Other non-current liabilities
Minority Interest	Minority interest
Preferred Stock	Preferred stock Preferred convertible stock
Common Shareholders' Equity	Common stock Additional paid-in capital Capital in excess of par Treasury stock Retained earnings Cumulative foreign currency gains and losses Accumulated other comprehensive income

TABLE 4-3	Standardized Cash Flow Statement Format

Standard Cash Flow Statement Accounts	Sample Line Items in Reported Accounts
Net Income	
Non-operating Gains (Losses)	Gain (loss) on sale of investments/non-current assets Cumulative effect of accounting changes Gain (loss) on foreign exchange Extraordinary gains (losses)
Long-Term Operating Accruals	Depreciation and amortization Deferred revenues/costs Deferred income taxes Impairment of non-current assets Other non-cash charges to operations Equity earnings of affiliates/unconsolidated subs, net of cash received Minority interest Stock bonus awards
Net (Investments in) or Liquidation of Operating Working Capital	Changes in: Trade accounts receivable Other receivables Prepaid expenses Trade accounts payable Accrued expenses (liabilities) Due from affiliates Accounts payable and accrued expenses Refundable/payable income taxes Inventories Provision for doubtful accounts and bad debts Other current liabilities Other current assets
Net (Investment in) or Liquidation of Operating Long-Term Assets	Purchase/sale of non-current assets Acquisition of research and development Acquisition/sale of business Capital expenditures Equity investments Acquisition of subsidiary stock Capitalization of computer software development costs Cost in excess of the fair value of net assets acquired Investment in sales-type and direct financing leases
Net Debt (Repayment) or Issuance	Principal payments on debt Borrowings (repayments) under credit facility Issuance (repayment) of long-term debt Net increase (decrease) in short-term borrowings Notes payable

(continued)

Standard Cash Flow Statement Accounts	Sample Line Items in Reported Accounts
Dividend (Payments)	Cash dividends paid on common stock
	Cash dividends paid on preferred stock
	Distributions
Net Stock (Repurchase) or Issuance	Proceeds from issuance of common stock
	Issue of common stock for services
	Issue (redemption) of preferred securities
	Issue of subsidiary equity
	Purchase (issue) of treasury stock

Who owns or controls resources?

For most resources used by a firm, ownership or control is relatively straightforward—the firm using the resource owns the asset. However, some types of transactions make it difficult to assess who owns a resource. For example, does the lessor or the lessee own or control a resource that has been leased? Or consider a firm that discounts a customer receivable with a bank. If the bank has recourse against the firm should the customer default, is the real owner of the receivable the bank or the company?

Accountants frequently use mechanical rules to determine whether a company owns or controls an asset. While these rules make it easy for accountants to implement accounting standards, they also permit managers to "groom" transactions to satisfy their own financial reporting objectives. For example, U.S. rules on lease accounting permit essentially the same lease transaction to be structured in such a way that the leased asset is reported on the balance sheet of the lessee, the lessor, or on neither party's balance sheet. Accounting analysis, therefore, involves assessing whether a firm's reported assets adequately reflect the key resources that are under its control, and whether adjustments are required to compare its performance with that of competitors.

Asset ownership issues also arise indirectly from the application of rules for revenue recognition. Firms are permitted to recognize revenues only when their product has been shipped or their service has been provided to the customer. Revenues are then considered "earned," and the customer has a legal commitment to pay for the product or service. As a result, for the seller, recognition of revenue frequently coincides with "ownership" of a receivable that is shown as an asset on its balance sheet. Therefore, accounting analysis that raises questions about whether or not revenues have been earned often affects the valuation of assets.

Ambiguity over whether a company owns an asset creates a number of opportunities for accounting analysis:

- Despite management's best intentions, financial statements sometimes do a poor job of reflecting the firm's economic assets since it is difficult for accounting rules to capture all of the subtleties associated with ownership and control.
- Because accounting rules on ownership and control permit managers to groom transactions such that essentially similar transactions are reported in very different ways, important assets may be omitted from the balance sheet even though the firm bears many of the economic risks of ownership.
- There may be legitimate differences in opinion between managers and analysts over residual ownership risks borne by the company, leading to differences in opinion over reporting for these assets.
- Aggressive revenue recognition, which boosts reported earnings, is likely to affect asset values.

Can economic benefits be measured with reasonable certainty?

It is almost always difficult to accurately forecast the future benefits associated with capital outlays because the world is uncertain. A company does not know whether a competitor will offer a new product or service that makes its own offering obsolete. It does not know whether the products manufactured at a new plant will be the type that customers want to buy. A company does not know whether changes in oil prices will make the oil drilling equipment that it manufactures less valuable.

Accounting rules deal with these challenges by stipulating the types of resources that can be recorded as assets and those that cannot. For example, the economic benefits from research and development (R&D) are generally considered highly uncertain—research projects may never deliver promised new products, the products they generate may not be economically viable, or products may be made obsolete by competitors' research. Accounting rules in most countries, therefore, require that R&D outlays be expensed.[2] In contrast, the economic benefits from plant acquisitions are considered less uncertain and are required to be capitalized.

Rules that require the immediate expensing of outlays for some key resources may be good accounting, but they create a challenge for the analyst—they make it more difficult to infer financial performance from the financial statements. If all firms expense R&D, financial statements will reflect differences in R&D success only when new products are commercialized rather than during the development process. The analyst may attempt to correct for this distortion by capitalizing key R&D outlays and adjusting the value of the intangible asset based on R&D updates.[3]

Have fair values of assets declined below book value?

An asset is impaired when its fair value falls below its book value. Of course, markets for many long-term operating assets are illiquid and incomplete, making it highly subjective to infer their fair values. Consequently, considerable management judgment is involved in deciding whether an asset is impaired and determining the value of any impairment loss.

For the analyst, this raises the possibility that asset values are misstated. In most countries, accounting rules require that a loss be recorded for permanent asset impairments. However, U.S. accounting rules (SFAS 144) permit a certain amount of asset overstatement since the test for asset impairment compares the asset's book value to the expected value of *undiscounted* (rather than *discounted*) future cash flows expected to be generated from future use and sale of the asset. This can create situations where no financial statement loss is reported for an asset that is economically impaired.

In addition, the task of determining whether there has been an asset impairment and valuing the impairment is delegated to management, with oversight by the firm's auditors. This leaves opportunities for potential management bias in valuing assets and for legitimate differences in opinion between managers and analysts over asset valuations. In most cases, management bias will lead to overstated assets since managers will prefer not to recognize an impairment. However, managers can also bias asset values downward by overstating the current level of impairment, thereby reducing future expenses and increasing future earnings.

Opportunities for accounting adjustments can therefore arise in the situations discussed above if
- Accounting rules do not do a good job of capturing the firm's economics,
- Managers use their discretion to distort the firm's performance, or
- There are legitimate differences in opinion between managers and analysts about economic uncertainties facing the firm that are reflected in asset values.

OVERSTATED ASSETS

Asset overstatements are likely to arise when managers have incentives to increase reported earnings. Thus, adjustments to assets also typically require adjustments to the income statement in the form of either increased expenses or reduced revenues. The most common forms of asset (and earnings) overstatement are the following:

1. *Delayed write-downs of current assets.* If current assets become impaired, that is, their realizable values fall below their book values, accounting rules generally require that they be written down to their fair values. Current asset impairments also affect earnings since write-offs are charged directly to earnings. Deferring current asset write-downs is, therefore, one way for managers to boost reported profits.[4] Analysts that cover firms where management of inventories and receivables is a key success factor (e.g., the fashion retail and consumer electronics industries) need to be particularly cognizant of this form of earnings management. If managers over-buy or over-produce in the current period, they are likely to have to offer customers discounts to get rid of surplus inventories. In addition, providing customers with credit carries risks of default. Warning signs for delays in current asset write-downs include growing days' inventory and days' receivable, write-downs by competitors, and business downturns for a firm's major customers.

2. *Underestimated reserves (e.g., allowances for bad debts or loan losses).* Managers make estimates of expected customer defaults on accounts receivable and loans and create reserves to cover these anticipated costs. If managers underestimate the value of these reserves, assets and earnings will be overstated. Warning signs of inadequate allowances include growing days' receivable, business downturns for a firm's major clients, and growing loan delinquencies.

3. *Accelerated recognition of revenues (increasing receivables).* Managers typically have the best information on the uncertainties governing revenue recognition—whether a product or service has been provided to customers and whether cash collection is reasonably likely. However, managers may also have incentives to accelerate the recognition of revenues, boosting reported earnings for the period. Accounts receivable and earnings will then be overstated. Aggressive revenue recognition is one of the most popular forms of earnings management cited by the SEC. Warning signs include growth in receivables outpacing sales growth, and increasing days' receivable.

4. *Delayed write-downs of long-term assets.* Deteriorating industry or firm economic conditions can affect the value of long-term assets as well as current assets. Firms are required to recognize impairments in the values of long-term assets when they arise. However, since second-hand markets for long-term assets are typically illiquid and incomplete, estimates of asset valuations and impairment are inherently subjective. This is particularly true for intangible assets such as goodwill. As a result, managers can use their reporting judgment to delay write-downs on the balance sheet and avoid showing impairment charges in the income statement.[5] This issue is likely to be particularly critical for asset-intensive firms in volatile markets (e.g., airlines) or for firms that follow a strategy of aggressive growth through acquisitions.[6] Warning signs of impairments in long-term assets include declining long-term asset turnover, declines in return on assets to levels lower than the weighted average cost of capital, write-downs by other firms in the same industry that have also suffered deteriorating asset use, and overpayment for or unsuccessful integration of key acquisitions.

5. *Understated depreciation/amortization on long-term assets.* Managers make estimates of asset lives, salvage values, and amortization schedules for depreciable

long-term assets. If these estimates are optimistic, long-term assets and earnings will be overstated. This issue is likely to be most pertinent for firms in asset-intensive businesses (e.g., airlines, utilities). A comparison of the firm's policies to those of its industry competitors with a similar asset base and strategy will help an analyst identify potential overstatements.

Examples of How to Correct for Asset Overstatement

We illustrate some of the distortions that lead to overstated assets and the types of corrections that the analyst can make to reduce bias in the financial statements.

Delayed Write-Downs of Current Assets

In recent years, the popularity of portable MP3 players has increased tremendously. Apple has dominated the market with its iPod player and managed to maintain a U.S. market share of over 75 percent. Rivals such as Creative Technology, Sony, Microsoft, and Samsung have entered the market aggressively in an attempt to grab a share of the market. Key risks facing these firms include rapid changes in MP3 player technology and inventory management in the face of both relentless competition and potential technological obsolescence.

Singapore-based Creative Technology posted impressive revenue growth from the second half of 2003 through the first quarter of 2005, with predictable spikes in holiday season sales in both 2003 and 2004. However, gross margins steadily declined from 35 percent to 23 percent over this period. A more worrying trend was the firm's inventory management. Growth in inventory far outpaced growth in sales, leading to a 58 percent increase in days' inventory, from 100 days for the quarter ending September 30, 2003, to 158 days for the quarter ending March 31, 2005. Inventory at the end of March 2006 was valued at $451.2 million, up from $183.9 million nine months prior. This increase in inventory raises questions for analysts about Creative Technology's inventory value and potential obsolescence.

An analyst can assess whether inventory is impaired by talking with suppliers and customers, observing the speed of new product launches for MP3 players and the performance of other firms in the industry, and understanding the general sentiment about expected market growth. Based on this research, an analyst can judge whether Creative Technology's slowdown in inventory turnover is likely to persist, whether there are serious technological risks for the current inventory and, if so, whether and how large an impairment charge is appropriate. Prior to the release of earnings for the June 31, 2005, quarter, several analysts raised questions about the growth in Creative Technology's inventory and anticipated that the company would be forced to record future inventory impairment charges.

Once an analyst concludes that inventory is overstated, the challenge is to estimate the magnitude of the write-down. For Creative Technology, this depends on the price discounts that are required to move slow-moving products. The after-tax cost of the impairment will reduce current and retained earnings. In addition, the tax effect of the impairment will lower the Tax Expense and reduce the Deferred Tax Liability since the inventory write-down is not recorded for tax purposes until the inventory is subsequently sold. Creative Technology enjoys a special status in Singapore that exempts certain elements of revenues from income tax. However, for illustrative purposes, using the local statutory tax rate of 20 percent, the financial statements could be modified as follows for an assumed inventory overstatement of $25 million:

	Adjustment	
($ Millions)	Assets	Liabilities & Equity
Balance Sheet		
Inventory	−25.0	
Deferred Tax Liability		−8.8
Common Shareholders' Equity		−16.2
Income Statement		
Cost of Sales		+25.0
Tax Expense		−8.8
Net Income		−16.2

In August 2005, Creative Technology announced that it would take a $20 million charge against inventory to reflect a decline in prices of certain components used to manufacture MP3 players. In the quarter ending March 31, 2006, the company took another inventory write-down due to a steep drop in the price of components such as flash memory and hard drives. Not surprisingly, Creative Technology's share price tumbled in response to news of the write-downs—from a high of close to $17 per share in early 2005, the stock traded down to below $5 per share in mid-2006.

Underestimated Reserves

In late 2006, Community Health Systems (CHS) was the leading operator of general and acute care hospitals in nonurban communities in the U.S. The company owned 77 hospitals in 22 states, had a dominant market share in more than 85 percent of the markets it served, and in fiscal 2005 generated $3.7 billion in revenues.

CHS received payments for its services from governmental agencies, private insurers, and directly from the patients it served. Medicare was the single largest revenue provider, accounting for approximately 33 percent of net operating revenue in the quarter ended June 30, 2006. Managed care provided a further 25 percent of revenues, 10 percent came from Medicaid, and 13 percent was from self-pay sources (uninsured patients, patient deductibles, co-insurance payments not covered by the insurer, and patients whose insurance providers had failed to pay).

To estimate receivable allowances, CHS used an aging analysis which did not differentiate between risk characteristics of different classes of patients. For example, it failed to reflect that collection rates were lowest for self-pay accounts. As a result, in the 12-month period from June 2005 to June 2006, the company held the allowance for doubtful accounts as a percentage of gross receivables steady at 33 percent, even though there was an increase in the proportion of revenues and receivables from self-pay patients.

If an analyst decides that receivable allowances are understated, balance sheet adjustments are made to Accounts Receivable (for the gross change in reserve), to the Deferred Tax Liability (for the tax impact of the increased expense), and to Retained Earnings (for the net effect). For example, if an analyst decided that allowances for doubtful accounts for Community Health should be 36 percent rather than 33 percent, Accounts Receivable would have to be reduced by $37.5 million. Given the company's effective tax rate of 39 percent, this would reduce earnings and equity by $22.9 million and the Deferred Tax Liability by 14.6 million. The adjustment to the June 30, 2006, financial statements would, therefore, be as follows:

	Adjustment	
($ Millions)	Assets	Liabilities & Equity
Balance Sheet		
Accounts Receivable	−37.5	
Deferred Tax Liability		−14.6
Common Shareholders' Equity		−22.9
Income Statement		
Provision for Doubtful Accounts		+37.5
Tax Expense		−14.6
Net Income		−22.9

At the end of October 2006, CHS announced its results for the quarter ending September 30, 2006. The financial results included a $65 million increase in the allowance for bad debts and a change in methodology for estimating the allowance. Under the new method, CHS reserved a percentage of all self-pay accounts receivable based on their collection history. The company reported that the new methodology would better reflect changes in payor mix and historical collection patterns and allow it to respond to changes in trends. The share price declined 10 percent on the day the earnings were announced.

Accelerated Recognition of Revenues

In November 1999 and January 2000, analysts at the Center for Financial Research and Analysis (CFRA) raised questions about the propriety of revenue recognition for MicroStrategy, a software company. MicroStrategy recognized revenues from the sale of licenses "after execution of a licensing agreement and shipment of the product, provided that no significant Company obligations remain and the resulting receivable is deemed collectible by management."[7] CFRA analysts were concerned about MicroStrategy's booking two contracts worth $27 million as quarterly revenues when the contracts were not announced until several days after the quarter's end. If the analysts decided to adjust for these distortions, the following changes would have to be made to MicroStrategy's financial reports:
1. In the quarter that the contracts were booked, Sales and Accounts Receivable would both decline by $27 million.
2. Cost of Sales would decline and Inventory would increase to reflect the reduction in sales. The value of the Cost of Sales/Inventory adjustment can be estimated by multiplying the sales adjustment by the ratio of cost of sales to sales. For MicroStrategy, cost of license revenues is only 3 percent of license revenues, indicating that the adjustment would be modest ($0.8 m). Also, since MicroStrategy does not report any inventory, the balance sheet adjustment would be to prepaid expenses, which are included in Other Current Assets on the standardized balance sheet.

3. The decline in pretax income would result in a lower Tax Expense in the company's financial reporting books (but presumably not in its tax books). Consequently, the Deferred Tax Liability would have to be reduced. MicroStrategy's marginal tax rate was 35 percent, implying that the decline in the Tax Expense and Deferred Tax Liability would be $9.2 million [($27 − 0.8) × .35].

The full effect of the adjustment on the quarterly financial statements would therefore be as follows:

($ millions)	Adjustment	
	Assets	Liabilities & Equity
Balance Sheet		
Accounts Receivable	−27.0	
Other Current Assets	+0.8	
Deferred Tax Liability		−9.2
Common Shareholders' Equity		−17.0
Income Statement		
Sales		−27.0
Cost of Sales		−0.8
Tax Expense		−9.2
Net Income		−17.0

Of course, provided the contracts were legitimate transactions, the above adjustments imply that forecasts of next quarter's revenues should include the $27 million worth of contracts.

In March 2000, MicroStrategy confirmed that the CFRA analysts' suspicions about aggressive revenue recognition were legitimate. The company announced that it had "recorded revenue on certain contracts in one reporting period where customer signature and delivery had been completed, but where the contract may not have been fully executed by the Company in that reporting period."[8] After reviewing all licensing contracts near the end of the prior three years, MicroStrategy was forced to restate its financial statements to correct for the improprieties. The outcome was that accounts receivable for 1999 were reduced from $61.1 million to $37.6 million, leading to a dramatic drop in the company's stock price.

Delayed Write-Downs of Long-Term Assets

Consider the widely acclaimed merger between AOL and Time Warner. The combination of the two companies was justified as enabling AOL to cross-sell Time Warner's content (film, news, etc.) to its large subscriber base, a win for both companies. Careful strategic analysis, however, would raise some questions about the merits of the deal. Earlier combinations of content providers and distributors in the entertainment industry (e.g., Disney's acquisition of ABC) had faced difficulties in realizing their potential. Why would the outcome of an AOL–Time Warner merger be any different? Also, it was not clear why AOL had to buy Time Warner to access its content. Why couldn't AOL simply sign a long-term licensing agreement for content with Time Warner? Finally, the merger raised questions about the relationships AOL and Time Warner had with existing customers and suppliers. For example, would Time Warner still be able to sell its content to AOL's competitors (e.g., Microsoft), or would its own market be narrowed? Would AOL still be able to negotiate content deals with Time Warner's competitors? If Time Warner's content became stale, would AOL be committed to continue supplying it to its subscribers, leading to a decline in the value of both firms?

The questions about the economic benefits from the merger were quickly answered when Internet sector stocks crashed in mid-2000. AOL subsequently struggled to retain and grow its subscriber base and encountered more difficulty than expected in developing a successful business model to take advantage of Time Warner's content. As a result, in its December 31, 2001, report, the new company was forced to recognize that the $128 billion of goodwill recorded under the merger was impaired and would have to be written down by $54 billion at the end of the following quarter (March 2002).

This raised several issues for analyzing AOL Time Warner. First, given the questionable strategic rationale for the merger in the first place, did the initial $128 billion of goodwill ever represent a true economic asset? If not, when would it make sense to recognize the impairment of goodwill—prior to December 31, 2001, in the December 31 financials, or when the company subsequently reported the decline in value (March 2002)? Second, was the $54 billion write-down adequate given the magnitude of the Internet stock market crash, which indicated that investors as a whole had radically lowered their expectations for Internet stocks such as AOL?

If an analyst decided to record the $54 billion write-down in the December 2001 financials, it would be necessary to make the following balance sheet adjustments:

1. Reduce Long-term Intangible Assets by $54 billion.
2. Reduce the Deferred Tax Liability for the tax effect of the write-down. Assuming a 35 percent tax rate, this amounts to $19 billion.
3. Reduce Common Shareholders' Equity for the after-tax effect of the write-down ($35 billion).

($ billions)	Adjustment	
	Assets	Liabilities & Equity
Balance Sheet		
Long-Term Intangible Assets	−54	
Deferred Tax Liability		−19
Common Shareholders' Equity		−35
Income Statement		
Other Expenses		+54
Tax Expense		−19
Net Income		−35

Note that the write-down of depreciable assets at the beginning of the year requires the analyst to also estimate the write-down's impact on depreciation and amortization expense for the year, impacting net income. For AOL Time Warner, since the asset was goodwill, which was no longer amortized (see SFAS 142), no such expense adjustment was required.

At the end of 2002, AOL announced the write-down of a further $45.5 billion of goodwill, and many of the top AOL managers that had advocated the merger in the first place were no longer with the company.

UNDERSTATED ASSETS

Asset understatements typically arise when managers have incentives to deflate reported earnings. This may occur when the firm is performing exceptionally well and managers decide to store away some of the current strong earnings for a rainy day. Income smoothing, as it has come to be known, can be implemented by overstating current period expenses (and understating the value of assets) during good times. Asset (and expense) understatements can also arise in a particularly bad year, when managers decide to "take a bath" by understating current period earnings to create the appearance of a turnaround in following years. Accounting analysis involves judging whether managers have understated assets (and also income) and, if necessary, adjusting the balance sheet and income statement accordingly.

Asset understatements can also arise because of accounting rules themselves. In many countries, accounting standards require firms to expense outlays for R&D and advertising because, even though they may create future value for owners, their outcomes are highly uncertain. Asset understatements can also arise when managers have incentives to understate liabilities. For example, if a firm records lease transactions as operating leases or if it discounts receivables with recourse, neither the assets nor the accompanying obligations are shown on its balance sheet. Yet, in some instances, this accounting treatment does not reflect the underlying economics of the transactions—the lessee may effectively own the leased assets, and the firm that sells receivables may still bear all of the risks associated with ownership. The analyst will then want to adjust the balance sheet (and also the income statement) for these effects.

The most common forms of asset (and earnings) understatement arise when there are the following:

1. *Overstated write-downs of current assets.* Managers potentially have an incentive to overstate current asset write-downs either during years of exceptionally strong performance, or when the firm is financially distressed. By overstating current asset impairments and overstating expenses in the current period, managers can show lower future expenses, boosting earnings in years of sub-par performance or when a turnaround is needed. Overstated current asset write-downs can also arise when managers are less optimistic about the firm's future prospects than the analyst.

2. *Overestimated reserves (e.g., allowances for bad debts or loan losses).* If managers overestimate reserves for bad debts or loan losses, accounts receivable and loans will be understated.

3. *Overstated write-downs of long-term assets.* Overly pessimistic management estimates of long-term asset impairments reduce current period earnings and boost earnings in future periods.

4. *Overstated depreciation/amortization on long-term assets.* Firms that use tax depreciation estimates of asset lives, salvage values, or amortization rates are likely to amortize assets more rapidly than justifiable given the assets' economic usefulness, leading to long-term asset understatements.

5. *Lease assets off balance sheet.* Assessing whether a lease arrangement should be considered a rental contract (and hence recorded using the operating method) or equivalent to a purchase (and hence shown as a capital lease) is subjective. It depends on whether the lessee has effectively accepted most of the risks of ownership, such as obsolescence and physical deterioration. To standardize the reporting of lease transactions, U.S. accounting standards have created clear criteria for distinguishing between the two types. Under SFAS 13, a lease

transaction is equivalent to an asset purchase if any of the following conditions hold: (1) ownership of the asset is transferred to the lessee at the end of the lease term, (2) the lessee has the option to purchase the asset for a bargain price at the end of the lease term, (3) the lease term is 75 percent or more of the asset's expected useful life, and (4) the present value of the lease payments is 90 percent or more of the fair value of the asset. However, although the criteria for reporting leases are objective, they create opportunities for management to circumvent the spirit of the distinction between capital and operating leases, potentially leading to the understatement of lease assets.[9] This is likely to be an important issue for the analysis of asset-intensive industries where there are options for leasing (e.g., airlines and retail chains).[10]

6. *Discounted receivables off balance sheet even though the firm still retains considerable collection risk.* Under current U.S. accounting rules (SFAS 140), receivables that are discounted with a financial institution are considered "sold" if the "seller" cedes control over the receivables to the financier. Control is surrendered if the receivables are beyond the reach of the seller's creditors should the seller file for bankruptcy, if the financier has the right to pledge or sell the receivables, and if the seller has no commitment to repurchase the receivables. The seller can then record the discount transaction as an asset sale. Otherwise it is viewed as a financing transaction that generates a liability for the seller. However, just because a firm has "sold" receivables for financial reporting purposes does not necessarily mean that it is off the hook for credit risks. Financial institutions that discount receivables often have recourse against the seller, requiring the seller to continue to estimate bad debt losses. In this event, U.S. rules permit the transaction to be reported as an asset sale only when the seller satisfies the above conditions for surrendering control of the receivables and has experience in estimating the value of the recourse liability (i.e., allowances for credit and refinancing risks). In extreme cases, where there is significant uncertainty about the value of the recourse liability, the analyst has to decide whether to restate the firm's financial statements by returning the "sold" receivables to the balance sheet. As discussed later in this chapter, this will also increase the firm's liabilities, and it will affect its income statement since any gains and losses on the sale need to be excluded, and interest income on the notes receivables and interest expense on the loan need to be recorded each year.

7. *Key intangible assets, such as R&D and trademarked brands, not reported on the balance sheet.* Some firms' most important assets are excluded from the balance sheet. Examples include investments in R&D, software development outlays, and brands and membership bases that are created through advertising and promotions. Accounting rules in most countries specifically prohibit the capitalization of R&D outlays and membership acquisition costs, primarily because it is believed that the benefits associated with such outlays are too uncertain.[11] New products may never reach the market due to technological infeasibility or to the introduction of superior products by competitors; and new members that sign up for a service as a result of a promotions campaign may subsequently quit. Expensing the cost of intangibles has two implications for analysts. First, the omission of intangible assets from the balance sheet inflates measured rates of return on capital (either return on assets or return on equity).[12] For firms with key omitted intangible assets, this omission has important implications for forecasting long-term performance; unlike firms with no intangibles, competitive forces will not cause their rates of return to fully revert to the cost of capital over time. For example, pharmaceutical firms have shown very high rates of return over many decades, in part because of the impact of R&D accounting. A second effect of expensing outlays for intangibles is that it makes it more difficult for the analyst to assess whether the firm's

business model works. Under the matching concept, operating profit is a meaningful indicator of the success of a firm's business model since it compares revenues and the expenses required to generate them. Immediately expensing outlays for intangible assets runs counter to matching and, therefore, makes it more difficult to judge a firm's operating performance. Consistent with this, research shows that investors view R&D and advertising outlays as assets rather than expenses.[13] Understated intangible assets are likely to be important for firms in pharmaceutical, software, branded consumer products, and subscription businesses.

Examples of How to Correct for Asset Understatement

We illustrate some of the types of distortions that understate assets, and show corrections that the analyst can make to ensure that assets are reflected appropriately.

Overstated Depreciation for Long-Term Assets

In 2005 Lufthansa, the German national airline, reported that it depreciated its aircraft over 12 years on a straight-line basis, with an estimated residual value of 15 percent of initial cost. Air France-KLM, an airline formed by the merger of the French airline Air France and the Dutch airline KLM, is one of Lufthansa's main competitors. In contrast to Lufthansa, Air France-KLM reported that its aircraft depreciation was also estimated using the straight-line method but assuming an average life of 20 years and no salvage value.[14]

For the analyst, these differences raise several questions. Do Lufthansa and Air France-KLM fly different types of routes, potentially explaining the differences in their depreciation policies? Alternatively, do they have different asset management strategies? For example, does Lufthansa use newer planes to attract more business travelers, to lower maintenance costs, or to lower fuel costs? If there do not appear to be operating differences that explain the differences in the two firms' depreciation rates, the analyst may well decide that it is necessary to adjust the depreciation rates for one or both firms to ensure that their performance is comparable.

To adjust for this effect, the analyst could choose to decrease Lufthansa's depreciation rates to match those of Air France-KLM. The following financial statement adjustments would then be required in Lufthansa's financial statements:

1. Increase the book value of the fleet at the beginning of the year to adjust for the relatively high depreciation rates that had been used in the past. This will also require an offsetting increase in equity (retained earnings) and in the deferred tax liability.
2. Reduce the depreciation expense (and increase the book value of the fleet) to reflect the lower depreciation for the current year, and increase the tax expense (in 2005, Lufthansa's marginal tax rate was 35 percent.) On the balance sheet, show an increase in equity and deferred tax liability.

Note that these changes are designed to show Lufthansa's results as if it had always used the same depreciation assumptions as Air France-KLM rather than to reflect a change in the assumptions for the current year going forward. This enables the analyst to compare ratios that use assets (e.g., return on assets) for the two companies.

At the beginning of 2005, Lufthansa reported in its footnotes that its fleet of aircraft had originally cost €15,350 m, and that accumulated depreciation was €8,399 m. This implies that the average life of Lufthansa's fleet was 7.72 years, calculated as follows:

€ Millions (unless otherwise noted)		
Aircraft cost, 01/01/05	15,350	Reported
Depreciable cost	13,048	Cost × (1 − .15)
Accumulated depreciation, 01/01/05	8,399	Reported
Accumulated depreciation/Depreciable cost	64.4%	
Depreciable life	12 years	Reported
Average age of aircraft	7.72	12 × .644 years

If Lufthansa used the same useful life and salvage estimates as Air France-KLM, Accumulated Depreciation would have been only €5,929 m, thereby increasing the company's Long-term Tangible Assets by €2,470 m and Common Shareholders' Equity by €1,606 m.

€ Millions (unless otherwise noted)		
Aircraft cost, 01/01/05 date	15,350	Reported
Depreciable cost	15,350	No residual value
Depreciable life	20 years	Air France-KLM
Accumulated depreciation, 01/01/05	5,929	Over 7.72 years
Increase in Long-Term Tangible Assets	2,470	
Marginal Tax Rate	35.0%	Reported
Increase in Deferred Tax Liability	864	
Increase in Common Shareholders Equity	1,606	

Since Lufthansa made a net investment of €657 m in new aircraft in 2005, the depreciation expense for 2005 (included in Cost of Sales) would have been €784 m [(15,350 − 657/2)/20] versus the €871 m reported by the company.[15] Thus, Cost of Sales would decline by €87 m, increasing the Tax Expense for the year by €30 m. On the balance sheet, these changes would increase Long-Term Tangible Assets by €87 m, increase Deferred Tax Liability by €30 m, and increase Common Shareholders' Equity by €57 m.

In summary, if Lufthansa were using the same depreciation method as Air France-KLM, its financial statements for the years ended December 31, 2000 and 2001, would have to be modified as follows:

(€ Millions)	Adjustment December 31, 2005		Adjustment December 31, 2004	
	Assets	Liabilities & Equity	Assets	Liabilities & Equity
Balance Sheet				
Long-Term Tangible Assets	+2,470 + 87		+2,470	

(continued)

(€ Millions)	Adjustment December 31, 2005		Adjustment December 31, 2004	
	Assets	Liabilities & Equity	Assets	Liabilities & Equity
Deferred Tax Liability		+864 + 30		+864
Common Shareholders' Equity		+1,606 + 57		+1,606
Total Impact	+2,557	+2,557	+2,470	+2,470
Income Statement				
Cost of Sales		−87		
Tax Expense		+30		
Net Income		+57		

Lease Assets Off Balance Sheet

Japan Airlines (JAL) leases part of its flight equipment and reports for these transactions using the operating method. These leased resources are therefore excluded from JAL's balance sheet, making it difficult for an analyst to compare JAL's financial performance to that of other airlines that either own their equipment or record leased resources using the capital method, and hence show their value on their balance sheet.

JAL discloses that, even though it uses the operating method to report for leases, its leases actually qualify as capital leases.[16] To correct this accounting, the analyst can use information on lease commitments presented in JAL's lease footnote to estimate the value of the assets and liabilities that are omitted from the balance sheet. The leased equipment is then depreciated over the life of the lease, and the lease payments are treated as interest and debt repayment. JAL estimates the present value of its future lease commitments for the years ended March 31, 2005 and 2006, as follows[17]:

(¥ Millions)	March 31, 2006	March 31, 2005
Within 1 year	51,839	51,004
Over 1 year	347,488	345,002
	399,327	396,006

In addition, JAL reported a lease expense of ¥58,155 million in 2006, and the average interest rate on its outstanding debt was 1.7 percent. The weighted-average lease term is estimated to be 8 years. Given this information, the analyst can make the following adjustments to JAL's beginning and ending balance sheets, and to its income statement for the year ended March 31, 2006:

1. Capitalize the present value of the lease commitments for March 31, 2005, increasing Long-Term Tangible Assets and Long-Term Debt by ¥396,006 million.[18]
2. Calculate the value of any change in lease assets and lease liabilities during the year from new lease transactions or the return of leased equipment prior to the end of the contracted lease term. On March 31, 2005, JAL's liability for lease commitments in 2007 and beyond was ¥345,002 million. If there had been no changes in these commitments, one year later (on March 31, 2006)

they would have been valued at ¥350,867 million (¥345,002 m × 1.017). Yet JAL's actual lease commitment on March 31, 2006, was ¥399,327 million, indicating that the company increased its leased aircraft equipment capacity by ¥48,398 million. JAL's Long-Term Tangible Assets and Long-Term Debt therefore increased by ¥48,460 million during 2006 as a result of new lease commitments.

3. Reflect the change in lease asset value and expense from the depreciation during the year. The depreciation expense for 2006 (included in Cost of Sales) is the depreciation rate (1/8) multiplied by the beginning cost of leased equipment (¥396,006 million) plus depreciation on new lease commitments (¥48,460 million), prorated throughout the year. The depreciation expense for 2006 is therefore ¥52,530 million {[¥396,006 m + (¥48,460 m/2)]/8}.

4. Add back the lease expense in the income statement, included in Cost of Sales, and apportion the payment between Interest Expense and repayment of Long-Term Debt. As previously mentioned, the lease expense is ¥58,155 million. The portion of this that is shown as Interest Expense is calculated as follows:

Interest on beginning lease obligation (.017 × 396,006)	¥6,803
Plus: interest on 2006 net new lease commitments (.017 × 48,460/2)	412
Interest expense on lease debt	¥7,215

The Long-Term Debt repayment portion is then the remainder of the total lease payment, ¥50,940 million.

5. Make any needed changes to the Deferred Tax Liability to reflect differences in earnings under the capital and operating methods. JAL's expenses under the capital lease method are ¥59,745 million (¥52,940 million depreciation expense plus ¥7,215 million interest expense) versus ¥58,155 million under the operating method. JAL will not change its tax books, but for financial reporting purposes it will show higher earnings before tax and thus a higher Tax Expense through deferred taxes. In fiscal year 2006, JAL lost money as a result of which it paid no taxes. However, the statutory tax rate for the year was 40.7 percent. Given this tax rate, the Tax Expense will decrease by ¥647 million [0.407 × (¥59,745 m − ¥58,155 m)] and the Deferred Tax Liability will decrease by the same amount.

In summary, the adjustments to JAL's financial statements on March 31, 2005 and 2006 are as follows:

	Adjustment March 31, 2006		Adjustment March 31, 2005	
(¥ Millions)	Assets	Liabilities & Equity	Assets	Liabilities & Equity
Balance Sheet				
Long-Term Tangible Assets				
(1) Beginning capitalization	+396,006		+396,006	
(2) Net new lease commitments	+48,460			
(3) Annual depreciation	−52,530			

(continued)

(¥ Millions)	Adjustment March 31, 2006		Adjustment March 31, 2005	
	Assets	Liabilities & Equity	Assets	Liabilities & Equity
Long-Term Debt				
(1) Beginning debt		+396,006		+396,006
(2) Net new lease commitments		+48,460		
(4) Debt Repayment		−50,940		
(5) Deferred Tax Liability		−647		
Common Shareholders' Equity		−943		
Income Statement				
Cost of Sales				
(4) Lease expense		−58,155		
(3) Depreciation expense		+52,530		
(4) Interest Expense		+7,215		
(5) Tax Expense		−647		
Total Expenses		+943		
Net Income		−943		

These adjustments increase JAL's fixed assets by 18 percent in 2005 and 19 percent in 2006, reducing the company's asset turnover (sales/assets) from the reported value of 0.98 to 0.83 in 2005, and from 1.02 to 0.86 in 2006.

Key Intangible Assets Off Balance Sheet

How should the analyst approach the omission of intangibles? One way is to leave the accounting as is but to recognize that forecasts of long-term rates of return will have to reflect the inherent biases that arise from this accounting method. A second approach is to capitalize intangibles and amortize them over their expected lives.

For example, consider the case of Microsoft, the most valuable software company in the world. Microsoft capitalizes only a small portion of its software R&D costs, arguing that most of the costs are incurred before technological feasibility is reached, as required under U.S. standards. What adjustment would be required if the analyst decided to capitalize all of Microsoft's software R&D and to amortize the intangible asset using the straight-line method over the expected life of software (approximately three years)? Assume that R&D spending occurs evenly throughout the year and that only half a year's amortization is taken on the latest year's spending. Given R&D outlays for the years 2003 to 2006, the R&D asset at the end of fiscal year 2006 is $9.9 billion, calculated as follows:

Year	R&D Outlay	Proportion Capitalized 06/30/06	Asset 06/30/06	Proportion Capitalized 06/30/05	Asset 06/30/05
2006	$6.6 b	(1 − .33/2)	$5.5 b		
2005	6.1	(1 − .33/2 − .33)	3.1	(1 − .33/2)	$5.1 b
2004	7.7	(1 − .33/2 − .67)	1.3	(1 − .33/2 − .33)	3.9
2003	6.6			(1 − .33/2 − .67)	1.0
Total			$9.9 b		$10.0 b

The R&D amortization expense (included in Other Operating Expenses) for 2005 and 2006 are $6.7 billion and $6.8 billion, respectively, and are calculated as follows:

Year	R&D Outlay	Proportion Amortized 06/30/06	Expense 06/30/06	Proportion Amortized 06/30/05	Expense 06/30/05
2006	$6.6 b	.33/2	$1.1 b		
2005	6.1	.33	2.0	.33/2	$1.0 b
2004	7.7	.33	2.6	.33	2.6
2003	6.6	.33/2	1.1	.33	2.2
2002	6.3			.33/2	1.0
Total			$6.7 b		$6.8 b

Since Microsoft will continue to expense software R&D immediately for tax purposes, the change in reporting method will give rise to a Deferred Tax Liability. Given a marginal tax rate of 35 percent, this liability will equal 35 percent of the value of the Long-Term Intangible Assets reported, with the balance increasing Common Shareholders' Equity.

In summary, the adjustments required to capitalize software R&D for Microsoft for the years 2005 and 2006 are as follows:

($ Billions)	Adjustment June 30, 2006 Assets	Adjustment June 30, 2006 Liabilities & Equity	Adjustment June 30, 2005 Assets	Adjustment June 30, 2005 Liabilities & Equity
Balance Sheet				
Long-Term Intangible Assets	+9.9		+10.0	
Deferred Tax Liability		+3.4		+3.5
Common Shareholders' Equity		+6.5		+6.5
Income Statement				
Research and Development		−6.6		−6.1
Other Operating Expenses		+6.7		+6.8
Tax Expense		−0.1		−0.2
Total Expenses		0.0		+0.5
Net Income		0.0		−0.5

LIABILITY DISTORTIONS

Liabilities are defined as economic obligations arising from benefits received in the past, and for which the amount and timing is known with reasonable certainty. Liabilities include obligations to customers that have paid in advance for products or services; commitments to public and private providers of debt financing; obligations to federal and local governments for taxes; commitments to employees for unpaid wages, pensions, and other retirement benefits; and obligations from court or government fines or environmental cleanup orders.

Distortions in liabilities generally arise because there is ambiguity about whether (1) an obligation has really been incurred and/or (2) the obligation can be measured.

Has an obligation been incurred?

For most liabilities there is little ambiguity about whether an obligation has been incurred. For example, when a firm buys supplies on credit, it has incurred an obligation to the supplier. However, for some transactions it is more difficult to decide whether there is any such obligation. For example, if a firm announces a plan to restructure its business by laying off employees, has it made a commitment that would justify recording a liability? Or, if a software firm receives cash from its customers for a five-year software license, should the firm report the full cash inflow as revenues, or should some of it represent the ongoing commitment to the customer for servicing and supporting the license agreement?

Can the obligation be measured?

Many liabilities specify the amount and timing of obligations precisely. For example, a 20-year, $100 million bond issue with an 8 percent coupon payable semi-annually specifies that the issuer will pay the holders $100 million in 20 years, and it will pay out interest of $4 million every six months for the duration of the loan. However, for some liabilities it is difficult to estimate the amount of the obligation. For example, a firm that is responsible for an environmental cleanup clearly has incurred an obligation, but the amount is highly uncertain.[19] Similarly, firms that provide pension and post-retirement benefits for employees have incurred commitments that depend on uncertain future events, such as employee mortality rates and future inflation rates, making valuation of the obligation subjective. Future warranty and insurance claim obligations fall into the same category—the commitment is clear but the amount depends on uncertain future events.

Accounting rules frequently specify when a commitment has been incurred and how to measure the amount of the commitment. However, as discussed earlier, accounting rules are imperfect—they cannot cover all contractual possibilities and reflect all of the complexities of a firm's business relationships. They also require managers to make subjective estimates of future events to value the firm's commitments. Thus the analyst may decide that some important obligations are omitted from the financial statements or, if included, are understated, either because of management bias or because there are legitimate differences in opinion between managers and analysts over future risks and commitments. As a result, analysis of liabilities is usually with an eye to assessing whether the firm's financial commitments and risks are understated and/or its earnings overstated.

UNDERSTATED LIABILITIES

Liabilities are likely to be understated when the firm has key commitments that are difficult to value and therefore not considered liabilities for financial reporting purposes. Understatements are also likely to occur when managers have strong incentives to overstate the soundness of the firm's financial position or to boost reported earnings. By understating leverage, managers present investors with a rosy picture of the firm's financial risks. Earnings management also understates liabilities (namely deferred or unearned revenues) when revenues are recognized upon receipt of cash, even though not all services have been provided.

The most common forms of liabilities understatements arise when the following conditions exist:

1. *Unearned revenues are understated through aggressive revenue recognition.* If cash has already been received but the product or service has yet to be provided, unearned or deferred revenues are created. This liability reflects the company's

commitment to provide the service or product to the customer and is extinguished once that is accomplished. Firms that recognize revenues prematurely—after the receipt of cash but prior to fulfilling their product or service commitments to customers—understate deferred revenue liabilities and overstate earnings. Firms that bundle service contracts with the sale of a product are particularly prone to deferred revenue liability understatement since separating the price of the product from the price of the service is subjective.

2. *Loans from discounted receivables are off balance sheet*. As discussed earlier, receivables that are discounted with a financial institution are considered "sold" if the "seller" cedes control over the receivables to the financier. Yet if the sale permits the buyer to have recourse against the seller in the event of default, the seller continues to face collection risk. Given the management judgment involved in forecasting default and refinancing costs, as well as the incentives faced by managers to keep debt off the balance sheet, it is important for the analyst to evaluate the firm's estimates for default as well as the inherent commitments that it has for discounted receivables. Are the firm's estimates reasonable? Is it straightforward to forecast the costs of the default and prepayment risks? If not, does the analyst need to increase the value of the recourse liability? Or, in the extreme, does the analyst need to undo the sale and recognize a loan from the financial institution for the discounted value of the receivables.

3. *Long-term liabilities for leases are off balance sheet*. As discussed earlier in the chapter, key lease assets and liabilities can be excluded from the balance sheet if the company structures lease transactions to fit the accounting definition of an operating lease. Firms that groom transactions to avoid showing lease assets and obligations will have very different balance sheets from firms with virtually identical economics but which either use capital leases or borrow from the bank to actually purchase the equivalent resources. For firms that choose to structure lease transactions to fit the definition of an operating lease, the analyst can restate the leases as capital leases, as discussed in the Asset Understatement section. This will ensure that the firm's true financial commitments and risks will be reflected on its balance sheet, enabling comparison with peer firms.

4. *Pension and post-retirement obligations are not fully recorded*. Many firms make commitments to their employees under defined benefit pension plans and post-retirement benefit plans. Accounting rules require managers to estimate and report the present value of the commitments that have been earned by employees over their years of working for the firm. This obligation is offset by any assets that the firm has committed to pension/retirement plans to fund future plan benefits. If the funds set aside in the retirement plan are greater (less) than the plan commitments, the plan is overfunded (underfunded). Several important issues arise for analyzing pension/post-retirement plan obligations. First, estimating the obligations themselves is subjective—managers have to make forecasts of future wage and benefit rates, worker attrition rates, the expected lives of retirees, and the discount rate.[20] If these forecasts are too low, the firm's benefit obligations (as well as the annual expenses for benefits reported in the income statement) will be understated.[21] Second, accounting rules require that incremental benefit commitments that arise from changes to a plan, and changes in plan funding status that arise from abnormal investment returns on plan assets, are smoothed over time rather than reflected immediately. As a result, for labor-intensive firms that offer attractive retirement benefits to employees, it is important that the analyst assess whether reported pension and retirement plan liabilities reflect the firms' true commitments.

Examples of How to Correct for Liability Understatement

We illustrate some of these types of liability understatements and the corrections that the analyst can make to reduce bias in the financial statements.

Unearned Revenues Understated

Consider the case of MicroStrategy, the software company discussed earlier, which bundles customer support and software updates with its initial licensing agreements. This raises questions about how much of the contract price should be allocated to the initial license versus the company's future commitments. In March 2000, MicroStrategy conceded that it had incorrectly overstated revenues on contracts that involved significant future customization and consulting by $54.5 million. As a result, it would have to restate its financial statements for 1999 as well as for several earlier years. To undo the distortion to 1999 financials, the following adjustments would have to be made:

1. In the quarter that the contracts were booked by the company, Sales would decline and unearned revenues (included in Other Current Liabilities) would increase by $54.5 million.
2. Cost of Sales would decline and prepaid expenses (inventory for companies selling physical products) would increase to reflect the lower sales. As noted earlier, MicroStrategy's cost of license revenues is only 3 percent of license revenues, implying that the adjustment to prepaid expenses (included in Other Current Assets) and Cost of Sales is modest ($1.6 m).
3. The decline in pretax income would result in a lower Tax Expense in the company's financial reporting books (but presumably not in its tax books). Given MicroStrategy's marginal tax rate of 35 percent, the decline in the Tax Expense as well as in the Deferred Tax Liability is $18.5 million [($54.5 − 1.6) · .35].

The full effect of the adjustment on the quarterly financial statements would therefore be as follows:

($ millions)	Adjustment	
	Assets	Liabilities & Equity
Balance Sheet		
Other Current Assets	+1.6	
Other Current Liabilities		+54.5
Deferred Tax Liability		−18.5
Common Shareholders' Equity		−34.4
Income Statement		
Sales		−54.5
Cost of Sales		−1.6
Tax Expense		−18.5
Net Income		−34.4

MicroStrategy's announcement on March 10, 2000, that it had overstated revenues prompted the SEC to investigate the company. In the period when it announced its overstatements, MicroStrategy's stock price plummeted 94 percent, compared to the 37 percent drop by the NASDAQ in the same period.

Discounted Receivables Off Balance Sheet

Prior to 2000, Computer Associates (CA) discounted notes receivable from its long-term licensing contracts. In 2002 it reported a contingent liability of $218 million for receivables that had been discounted with recourse. The company did not provide information on the value of the recourse liability for these notes receivable, making it difficult to judge the adequacy of the allowance for credit and refinancing losses that potentially could arise on the discounted receivables. One way for the analyst to assess the impact of the financing is to reverse the sale and include a liability for the full $218 million on CA's balance sheet. This would require the following adjustments:

1. CA's Other Long-Term Assets would be increased by the receivable commitment ($218 million). In turn, Long-Term Debt would be recorded to reflect the value of the cash advanced to CA under the discount transaction. CA appears to charge its customers an annual interest rate of roughly 9 percent. Assuming customers repay the receivables in equal monthly installments over the next four years and the bank charges a 10 percent interest rate, the receivable loan would be valued at $214.1 million.

2. The after-tax difference between the face value of the receivables and the loan, which would have been shown as a loss on sale under the reported accounting, needs to be reversed, increasing equity. Given the above assumptions and CA's 35 percent marginal tax rate, the adjustment would increase Common Shareholders' Equity by $2.5 million [3.9 · (1 − .35)].

3. The impact of the tax deduction from reporting a loss on sale, which would have reduced the Deferred Tax Liability, needs to be reversed. For CA this amount would have resulted in a roughly $1.4 million (3.9 · .35) increase in the Deferred Tax Liability.

4. During the year ended March 31, 2003, customers are scheduled to make monthly payments on the discounted receivables, reducing the value of notes receivable under the adjusted accounting. For CA these amounted to $54.5 million ($218 million · .25). Notes receivable would increase if any additional notes were discounted during the year. For CA no new receivable discounts were undertaken since the company changed its sales strategy.

5. For 2003 CA's income statement would include Interest Income from notes receivable for $17.2 million {(218.0 · .09) − [(54.5 · .09) · .5]} and Interest Expense from the loan for roughly $18.7 million {(214.0 · .10) − [(54.5 · .10) · .5]} along with any tax effects.[22] The loan would decline by a smaller amount, since $1.6 million of the receivable repayments are allocated to covering the higher interest charged on the loan (exactly offsetting the spread between the Interest Income and the Interest Expense for the year).

6. The value of the loan increases by the amount of any additional discounts undertaken during the year ($0) and declines by the value of receivable repayments by customers ($54.5 million) net of the portion of the repayment that represents incremental interest charged by the bank relative to the rate CA charged its customers ($1.5 million, or $18.7 million − $17.2 million).

The overall effect of these adjustments on CA's financial statements would therefore be as follows:

($ millions)	Adjustment for March 31, 2002		Adjustment for March 31, 2003	
	Assets	Liabilities & Equity	Assets	Liabilities & Equity
Balance Sheet				
Other Long-Term Assets	+218.0		+218.0 −54.5	
Long-Term Debt		+214.1		+214.1 −54.5 +1.5
Balance Sheet				
Deferred Tax Liability		+1.4		+1.4 −0.5
Common Shareholders' Equity		+2.5		+2.5 −1.0
Income Statement				
Interest Income				+17.2
Interest Expense				+18.7
Tax Expense				−0.5
Net Income				−1.0

Pension/Post-Retirement Obligations Not Fully Recorded

Accounting rules require that firms estimate the value of defined benefit pension and post-retirement commitments as the present value of future expected payouts under the plans. The obligation under defined benefit pension plans is referred to as the Projected Benefit Obligation, and is the present value of plan commitments factoring in the impact of future increases in wage rates on projected payouts.[23] For post-retirement benefits such as health care costs and health insurance premiums, the firm's obligation is called the Projected Post-Retirement Benefit Obligation and is calculated as the present value of expected future benefits for employees and their beneficiaries.

Each year the firm's pension and post-retirement obligations are adjusted to reflect the following factors:

- *Service Cost:* Defined benefit plans typically provide additional benefits for each additional year of service with the company. The present value of incremental benefits earned from another year of service is called the service cost, and it increases the firm's obligation each year.
- *Interest Cost:* An interest cost is recorded to reflect the effective interest that accrues each year on the company's obligations to the pension and/or post-retirement plans. This cost is calculated by multiplying the Projected Post Retirement Benefit Obligation at the beginning of the year by the discount rate.
- *Actuarial Gains and Losses:* Each year the actuarial assumptions used to estimate the firm's commitments are reviewed and, if appropriate, changes are made. The effect of these changes is shown as Actuarial Gains and Losses.
- *Benefits Paid:* The plan commitments are reduced as the plan makes payments to retirees each year.

For example, in its financial statement footnotes, General Motors (GM) provided the following information on its projected obligation under its U.S. Other Benefits Plan (primarily representing future commitments for health benefits) for the years ended December 31, 2005 and 2004:

($ Millions)	2005	2004
U.S. Other Benefits Obligation		
Benefit obligation at beginning of year	$73,772	$64,547
Service cost	702	566
Interest cost	4,107	3,726
Plan participants' contributions	88	85
Actuarial losses	6,720	8,527
Benefits paid	(4,208)	(3,690)
Other	–	11
Benefit obligation at end of year	**$81,181**	**$73,772**

GM's obligation at the end of 2005 was $81.2 billion, a 10 percent increase over the prior year.

To meet their commitments under pension and other post-retirement plans, firms make contributions to the plans. These contributions are then invested in equities, debt, and other assets. Plan assets are therefore increased each year by new company contributions. They are also increased or decreased by the returns generated each year from plan investments. Finally, plan assets decline when the plan pays out benefits to retirees. For the years ended December 31, 2005 and 2004, GM reported the following assets for post-retirement plans:

($ Millions)	2005	2004
Plan Assets		
Fair value of plan assets at beginning of year	$16,016	$9,998
Actual return on plan assets	2,258	981
Employer contributions	2,008	5,037
Plan participants' contributions	–	–
Benefits paid	–	–
Fair value of plan assets at end of year	**$20,282**	**$16,016**

In 2005 GM's plan assets were $20.3 billion, an increase of over 25 percent from the previous year. The difference between GM's post-retirement plan obligations and the plan assets, $60.9 billion, represents the company's unfunded obligation to employees under the plan.

Of course, estimating pension and post-retirement obligations is highly subjective. It requires managers to forecast the future payouts under the plans, which in turn involves making projections of employees' service with the firm, retirement ages, and life expectancies, as well as future wage rates and health insurance costs. It also requires managers to select an interest rate to estimate the present value of the future benefits. For example, GM projected that health care costs would initially grow at 10 percent per year and then decline to a trend rate of 5 percent per year over the next 6 years. It also assumed that the appropriate discount rate was 5.0 percent. GM reports that a 1 percent increase in the health care cost trend rate would increase the post-retirement obligation by $9.3 billion. Given the management judgment involved in making these forecasts and assumptions, analysts should question whether reported obligations adequately reflect the firm's true commitments.

Since GM's unfunded post-retirement benefit obligation is $60.9 billion, it would seem reasonable to expect that the company will report a liability on its balance sheet for $60.9 billion. From December 31, 2006 onwards, SFAS 158 requires U.S. firms to recognize the full unfunded liability in the balance sheet. However, as discussed below, prior to this date, pension and post-retirement accounting was more complex. SFAS 87 required firms to smooth out shocks to plan obligations and assets. For example, under the former rules, if GM agrees to increase its post-retirement or pension benefits for current workers, the value of its obligation will increase, but it amortized this "prior period service obligation" over employees' average expected remaining years of service rather than right away. Also, if the value of plan assets increases or decreases unexpectedly in a given year, or there needs to be an adjustment in the actuarial assumptions made to estimate the obligation, the financial statement impact under SFAS 87 was reflected gradually rather than immediately. Thus, even though the actual gap between GM's post-retirement obligation and plan assets is $60.9 billion, this is not the value of the liability recorded on its 2005 balance sheet[24]. GM provides a separate disclosure that reconciles the actual and the reported obligation:

($ Millions)	2005	2004
Funded status	$(60,899)	$(57,756)
Unrecognized actuarial losses	30,592	27,345
Unrecognized prior service cost	(714)	(445)
Employer net contributions in the fourth quarter	(1,176)	4,000
Benefits paid in the fourth quarter	846	999
Net amount recognized	**$(31,351)**	**$(25,857)**

The unrecognized actuarial losses reported in these years arises because GM's earlier actuarial assumptions about parameters such as future health care costs, retirement rates, and assumed rates of return on plan assets have proven to be optimistic. These effects were recognized over time rather than right away. Similarly, prior service costs represent additional commitments from post-retirement plan changes that are recognized over time. Consequently, GM's 2005 reported post-retirement liability understated its real commitment by 29.5 billion ($60.9 billion less $31.4 billion).[25]

What does pension and post-retirement accounting imply for financial analysis? It is reasonable for the analyst to raise several questions about a firm's pension and post-retirement obligations, particularly for firms in labor-intensive industries.

1. Are the assumptions made by the firm to estimate its pension and post-retirement obligations realistic? These include assumptions about the discount rate, which is supposed to represent the current market interest rate on benefit obligations, as well as assumptions about increases in wage and benefit costs. If these assumptions are optimistic, the obligations recorded on the books understate the firm's real economic commitment. As discussed above, GM notes that a 1 percent increase in expected health care costs increases its obligation by $9.3 billion. The analyst can use this information to adjust for any optimism in management's assumptions. For example, if the analyst decided that GM's forecasts of future healthcare costs were too low and needed to increase by 1 percent, the post-retirement obligation would have to be increased by $9.3 billion, with offsetting declines to equity (for the after-tax effect) and to the deferred tax

liability. The adjustment to GM's 2005 balance sheet, assuming a 35 percent tax rate, would be as follows:

($ Millions)	Adjustment	
	Assets	Liabilities & Equity
Balance Sheet		
Benefit Obligations		+9,300
Deferred Tax Liability		−3,255
Common Shareholders' Equity		−6,045

2. For financial statements dated prior to December 31, 2006, the process of smoothing prior service costs and differences between actual and forecasted parameters for pension and other benefit plans affected the recognized obligation. For GM these factors have led to a substantial understatement of the reported liability. As noted above, GM reported a liability for unfunded post-retirement benefits that was $29.5 billion less than the actual obligations. The analyst can adjust for this distortion by increasing the firm's Benefit Obligations, and making offsetting adjustments to the Deferred Tax Liability (since the change would not affect the company's taxable income) and to Common Shareholders' Equity. Assuming a 35 percent tax rate, the adjustment to GM's 2005 balance sheet would be as follows:

($ Millions)	Adjustment	
	Assets	Liabilities & Equity
Balance Sheet		
Benefit Obligations		+29,548
Deferred Tax Liability		−10,342
Common Shareholders' Equity		−19,206

3. What effect do pension assumptions play in the income statement? The pension cost each year comprises (a) Service cost, plus (b) Interest cost, plus (c) Amortization of any prior period service costs, plus or minus (d) Amortization of actuarial gains and losses, minus (e) Expected return on plan assets (the expected long-term return multiplied by beginning assets under management). For example, GM shows that its post-retirement expenses for 2005 and 2004 are as follows:

($ Millions)	2005	2004
Service cost	$702	$566
Interest cost	4,107	3,726
Expected return on plan assets	(1,684)	(1,095)
Amortization of prior service cost	(70)	(87)
Recognized net actuarial loss/(gain)	2,250	1,138
Net expense	**$5,305**	**$4,248**

This expense reflects the effect of smoothing actual asset returns, prior period service costs, and revisions in actuarial assumptions discussed earlier. If these effects are reflected in the pension/benefit obligation in full (as discussed above), their amortization can be excluded from the current year expense. However, the revised expense will need to be adjusted to include the actual return on plan assets for the current year rather than the expected return. Let's see how this would affect the expense reported by GM. The benefit expense for 2005 would decline by $2.18 billion, representing the amortization of recognized net actuarial losses ($2.25 billion) and prior period service cost (−$0.07 billion). In addition, the actual return on post-retirement plan assets in 2005 was $0.574 billion higher than the expected return reflected in the expense. The net effect of these adjustments would be to reduce the benefit expense by $2.754 billion. Since this adjustment would not change the firm's tax books, it would increase the Tax Expense by $0.964 billion (.35 · $2.754 m). The full income statement adjustment would therefore be as follows:

($ Millions)	Adjustment
Income Statement	
SG&A Expense	(2,754)
Tax Expense	+964
Net Income	+1,790

4. Once the analyst is satisfied that the financial statements reflect realistic assumptions about pension/post-retirement costs and obligations, it is possible to assess the overall impact of these arrangements on a firm's cost structure relative to its competitors. For GM, this could lead the analyst to assess how GM is positioned relative to other U.S. manufacturers (such as Ford) and to non-U.S. competitors (such as Toyota, Honda, and Volkswagon).

EQUITY DISTORTIONS

Accounting treats stockholders' equity as a residual claim on the firm's assets after paying off the other claimholders. Consequently, equity distortions arise primarily from distortions in assets and liabilities. For example, distortions in assets or liabilities that affect earnings also lead to distortions in equity. However, equity distortions can also arise that are not captured in an asset and liability analysis. One such distortion is for hybrid securities.

Hybrid securities include convertible debt and debt with warrants attached. These securities are partially pure debt and partially equity. Current accounting rules do not separate these components, typically implying that the balance sheet overstates firm debt and understates its equity. Without adjusting for this distortion, it can be difficult to understand the real financial risks and returns for firms with different types of hybrids. New accounting rules proposed by the FASB are likely to address this issue by requiring securities such as convertible debt to be separated into two components on the balance sheet, a debt component and an equity component. Each would be valued at its fair value at the date of issue. This approach could be adopted by the analyst.

Examples of How to Correct for Equity Distortions

We illustrate the equity distortion arising from the issuance of hybrid securities and the corrections that the analyst can make to reduce bias in the financial statements.

Hybrid Securities

On February 3, 1999, Amazon.com completed an offering of $1.25 billion of 4.75 percent Convertible Subordinated Notes due in 2009. Several months earlier Amazon had issued senior notes with an annual interest rate of 10 percent. The conversion premium was therefore significant—if the notes had not included a conversion option, Amazon would probably have had to pay a coupon rate in excess of 10 percent. The value of the $1.25 billion convertible issue at a 10 percent discount rate is only $0.87 billion, implying that the convertibility premium was worth roughly $0.38 billion. One way to adjust for this effect is to record the debt component at $0.87 billion and to show the $0.38 billion conversion premium as part of Common Shareholders' Equity. Interest on the debt would then be based on the 10 percent coupon rate rather than the 4.75 percent (which reflects the conversion premium).

The effect of this adjustment on Amazon's financial statements at March 31, 2002, would be as follows:

($ billions)	Assets	Liabilities & Equity
Adjustment for March 31, 2002		
Balance Sheet		
Long-Term Debt		−0.38
Common Shareholders Equity		+0.38

SUMMARY

To implement accounting analysis, the analyst must first recast the financial statements into a common format so that financial statement terminology and formatting is comparable between firms and across time. A standard template for recasting the financials, presented in this chapter, is used throughout the remainder of the book.

Once the financial statements are standardized, the analyst can determine what accounting distortions exist in the firm's assets, liabilities, and equity. Common distortions that overstate assets include delays in recognizing asset impairments, underestimated reserves, aggressive revenue recognition leading to overstated receivables, and optimistic assumptions on long-term asset depreciation. Asset understatements can arise if managers overstate asset write-offs, use operating leases to keep assets off the balance sheet, or make conservative assumptions for asset depreciation. They can also arise because accounting rules require outlays for key assets (e.g., R&D and brands) to be immediately expensed. For liabilities, the primary concern for the analyst is whether the firm understates its real commitments. This can arise from off-balance liabilities (e.g., operating lease obligations), from questionable management judgment and limitations in accounting rules for estimating pension and benefit plan liabilities, and from aggressive revenue recognition that understates unearned revenue obligations. Equity distortions frequently arise when there are distortions in assets and liabilities. However, they can also arise if firms issue hybrid securities.

Adjustments for distortions can, therefore, arise because accounting standards, although applied appropriately, do not reflect a firm's economic reality. They can also arise if the analyst has a different point of view than management about the estimates and assumptions made in preparing the financial statements. Once distortions have been identified, the analyst can use footnote and cash flow statement information to make adjustments to the balance sheet at the beginning and/or end of the current year, as well as any needed adjustments to revenues and expenses in the latest income statement. This ensures that the most recent financial ratios used to evaluate a firm's performance and to forecast its future results are based on financial data that appropriately reflect its business economics.

Several points are worth remembering when doing accounting analysis. First, the bulk of the analyst's time and energy should be focused on evaluating and adjusting accounting policies and estimates that describe the firm's key strategic value drivers. Of course, this does not mean that management bias is not reflected in other accounting estimates and policies, and the analyst should certainly examine these. But given the importance of evaluating how the firm is managing its key success factors and risks, the bulk of the accounting analysis should be spent examining those policies that represent these key factors and risks.

It is also important to recognize that many accounting adjustments can only be approximations rather than precise calculations since much of the information necessary for making precise adjustments is not disclosed. The analyst should therefore try to avoid worrying about being overly precise in making accounting adjustments. By making even crude adjustments, it is usually possible to mitigate some of the limitations of accounting standards and problems of management bias in financial reporting.

DISCUSSION QUESTIONS

1. Use the templates shown in Tables 4-1, 4-2, and 4-3 to recast the following financial statements for Dell Inc.

Dell Inc. Consolidated Statements of Financial Position
(in millions)

	February 3, 2006	January 28, 2005
ASSETS		
Current assets:		
Cash and cash equivalents	$7,042	$4,747
Short-term investments	2,016	5,060
Accounts receivable, net	4,089	3,563
Financing receivables, net	1,363	985
Inventories	576	459
Other	2,620	2,083
Total current assets	17,706	16,897
Property, plant, and equipment, net	2,005	1,691
Investments	2,691	4,294
Long-term financing receivables, net	325	199
Other non-current assets	382	134
Total assets	$23,109	$23,215

(continued)

Dell Inc. Consolidated Statements of Financial Position
(in millions)

	February 3, 2006	January 28, 2005
LIABILITIES AND STOCKHOLDERS' DEFICIT		
Current liabilities:		
Accounts payable	$9,840	$8,895
Accrued and other	6,087	5,241
Total current liabilities	15,927	14,136
Long-term debt	504	505
Other non-current liabilities	2,549	2,089
Total Liabilities	18,980	16,730
Commitments and contingent liabilities	–	–
Stockholders' equity:		
Preferred stock and capital in excess of $.01 par value; shares issued and outstanding: none	–	–
Common stock and capital in excess of $.01 par value; shares authorized: 7,000; shares issued: 2,818 and 2,769, respectively	9,540	8,195
Treasury stock, at cost; 488 and 284 shares, respectively	(18,007)	(10,758)
Retained earnings	12,746	9,174
Other comprehensive loss	(103)	(82)
Other	(47)	(44)
Total stockholders' equity	4,129	6,485
Total liabilities and stockholders' equity	$23,109	$23,215

Dell Inc. Consolidated Statements of Income
(in millions)

	February 3, 2006	January 28, 2005	January 30, 2004
Net revenue	$55,908	$49,205	$41,444
Cost of revenue	45,958	40,190	33,892
Gross margin	9,950	9,015	7,552
Operating expenses:			
Selling, general, and administrative	5,140	4,298	3,544
Research, development, and engineering	463	463	464
Total operating expenses	5,603	4,761	4,008
Operating income	4,347	4,254	3,544
Investment and other income, net	227	191	180
Income before income taxes	4,574	4,445	3,724
Income tax provision	1,002	1,402	1,079
Net income	$3,572	$3,043	$2,645

Dell Inc. Consolidated Statements of Cash Flows (in millions)

	February 3, 2006	January 28, 2005	January 30, 2004
CASH FLOWS FROM OPERATING ACTIVITIES:			
Net income	$3,572	$3,043	$2,645
Adjustments to reconcile net income to net cash provided by operating activities:			
Depreciation and amortization	393	334	263
Tax benefits of employee stock plans	261	249	181
LIABILITIES denominated in foreign currencies	70	(602)	(677)
Other	188	78	113
Changes in:			
Operating working capital	(67)	1,755	872
Non-current assets and liabilities	422	453	273
Net cash provided by operating activities	4,839	5,310	3,670
CASH FLOWS FROM INVESTING ACTIVITIES:			
Investments:			
Purchases	(7,562)	(12,261)	(12,099)
Maturities and sales	12,168	10,469	10,078
Capital expenditures	(728)	(525)	(329)
Purchase of assets held in master lease facilities	–	–	(636)
Cash assumed in consolidation of Dell Financial Services L.P.	–	–	172
Net cash provided by (used in) investing activities	3,878	(2,317)	(2,814)
CASH FLOWS FROM FINANCING ACTIVITIES:			
Repurchase of common stock	(7,249)	(4,219)	(2,000)
Issuance of common stock under employee plans and other	1,023	1,091	617
Net cash used in financing activities	(6,226)	(3,128)	(1,383)
Effect of exchange-rate changes on cash and cashequivalents	(196)	565	612
Net increase in cash and cash equivalents	$2,295	$430	$85

2. Refer to the Creative Technology example on delaying write-downs of current assets. How much excess inventory do you estimate Creative Technology is holding in March 2005 if the firm's optimal days' inventory is 100 days? Calculate the inventory impairment charge for Creative Technology if 50 percent of this excess inventory is deemed worthless? Record the changes to Creative Technology's financial statements from adjusting for this impairment.

3. Acceptance Insurance Companies Inc. underwrites and sells specialty property and casualty insurance. The company is the third largest writer of crop insurance products

in the United States. In its 1998 10-K report to the SEC, it discloses the following information on the loss reserves created for claims originating in 1990:

Percentage of claim liability arising in 1990 paid as of:	
One year later	40.6%
Two years later	70.8
Three years later	88.5
Four years later	101.2
Five years later	107.5
Six years later	109.7
Seven years later	111.4
Eight years later	111.8
Net reserves for 1990 obligations re-estimated as of:	
One year later	100.3%
Two years later	102.3
Three years later	107.4
Four years later	110.7
Five years later	112.7
Six years later	112.0
Seven years later	112.5
Eight years later	113.4
Net cumulative deficiency	−13.4

Was the initial estimate for loss reserves originating in 1990 too low or too high? How has the firm updated its estimate of this obligation over time? What percentage of the original liability remains outstanding for 1990 claims at the end of 1998? As a financial analyst, what questions would you have for the CFO on its 1990 liability?

4. AMR, the parent of American Airlines, provides the following footnote information on its capital and operating leases:

> AMR's subsidiaries lease various types of equipment and property, primarily aircraft and airport facilities. The future minimum lease payments required under capital leases, together with the present value of such payments, and future minimum lease payments required under operating leases that have initial or remaining noncancelable lease terms in excess of one year as of December 31, 2005, were (in millions):

Year Ending December 31,	Capital Leases	Operating Leases
2006	$263	$1,065
2007	196	1,039
2008	236	973
2009	175	872
2010	140	815
2011 and thereafter	794	7,453
	$1,804	$12,217
Less amount representing interest	716	
Present value of net minimum lease payments	$1,088	

AMR further disclosed that "lease terms vary but are generally 10 to 25 years for air-craft and seven to 40 years for other leased property and equipment." Assuming that all leases are for aircraft with an average lease term of 15 years, what interest rate does AMR use to capitalize its capital leases? Use this rate to capitalize AMR's operating leases at December 31, 2005. Record the adjustment to AMR's balance sheet to reflect the capitalization of operating leases. How would this reporting change affect AMR's Income Statement in 2006?

5. What approaches would you use to estimate the value of brands? What assumptions underlie these approaches? As a financial analyst, what would you use to assess whether the brand value of £1.575 billion reported by Cadbury Schweppes in 1997 was a rea-sonable reflection of the future benefits from these brands? What questions would you raise with the firm's CFO about the firm's brand assets?

6. As the CFO of a company, what indicators would you look at to assess whether your firm's long-term assets were impaired? What approaches could be used, either by man-agement or an independent valuation firm, to assess the dollar value of any asset impairment? As a financial analyst, what indicators would you look at to assess whether a firm's long-term assets were impaired? What questions would you raise with the firm's CFO about any charges taken for asset impairment?

7. The cigarette industry is subject to litigation for health hazards posed by its products. The industry has been in an ongoing process of negotiating a settlement of these claims with state and federal governments. As the CFO for Altria Group, the parent company of Philip Morris, one of the larger firms in the industry, what information would you report to investors in the annual report on the firm's litigation risks? How would you assess whether the firm should record a liability for this risk, and if so, what approach would you use to assess the value of this liability? As a financial analyst following Altria, what questions would you raise with the CEO over the firm's litigation liability?

8. Refer to the General Motors example on post-retirement benefits. Show the adjust-ments that would be required to record the full amount of the unfunded post-retirement benefit on December 31, 2004. What factors account for the difference between the adjustments to Common Shareholders' Equity on December 31, 2004 and 2005?

9. Refer to the Lufthansa example on asset depreciation estimates. What adjustments would be required if Lufthansa's aircraft depreciation were computed using an average life of 25 years and salvage value of 5 percent (instead of the reported values of 12 years and 15 percent)? Show the adjustments to the 2004 and 2005 balance sheets, and to the 2005 income statement.

10. In early 2003 Bristol-Myers Squibb announced that it would have to restate its finan-cial statements as a result of stuffing as much as $3.35 billion worth of products into wholesalers' warehouses from 1999 through 2001. The company's sales and cost of sales during this period was as follows:

	2001	2000	1999
Net sales	$18,139	$17,695	$16,502
Cost of products sold	5,454	4,729	4,458

The company's marginal tax rate during the three years was 35 percent. What adjustments are required to correct Bristol-Myers Squibb's balance sheet for December 31, 2001? What assumptions underlie your adjustments? How would you expect the adjustments to affect Bristol-Myers Squibb's performance in the coming few years?

NOTES

1. If a firm's primary business income is from rentals, rental income will be classified as Sales, rather than Investment Income.

2. A notable exception in the U.S. is the requirement that software development costs be capitalized once the software reaches the stage of technological feasibility (see SFAS 86).

3. See P. Healy, S. Myers, and C. Howe, "R&D Accounting and the Tradeoff Between Relevance and Objectivity," *Journal of Accounting Research* 40 (June 2002): 677–711, for an analysis of the value of capitalizing R&D and then annually assessing impairment.

4. J. Elliott and D. Hanna find that the market anticipates large write-downs by about one quarter, consistent with managers' reluctance to take write-downs on a timely basis. See "Repeated Accounting Write-Offs and the Information Content of Earnings," *Journal of Accounting Research* 34, Supplement, 1996.

5. J. Francis, D. Hanna, and L. Vincent find that management is more likely to exercise judgment in its self-interest for goodwill write-offs and restructuring charges than for inventory or PP&E write-offs. See "Causes and Effects of Discretionary Asset Write-Offs," *Journal of Accounting Research* 34, Supplement, 1996.

6. P. Healy, K. Palepu, and R. Ruback find that acquisitions added value for only one third of the 50 largest acquisitions during the early 1980s, suggesting that acquirers frequently do not recover goodwill. See "Which Takeovers Are Profitable—Strategic or Financial?" *Sloan Management Review*, Summer 1997.

7. MicroStrategy 1998 10-K, Footnote 1—Organization and Summary of Significant Accounting Policies.

8. MicroStrategy 1999 10-K, Footnote 3—Restatement of Financial Statements.

9. Managers can avoid capitalizing leases by assuming long asset lives (that get around the 75% of asset life rule) and high discount rates (to avoid violating the 90% of present value rule). Research indicates that some firms responded to the adoption of SFAS 13, which changed the rules for lease capitalization, by grooming transactions to avoid having to capitalize leases. See E. Imhoff and J. Thomas, "Economic Consequences of Accounting Standards: The Lease Disclosure Rule Change," *Journal of Accounting & Economics* 10 (December 1988): 277–311, and S. El-Gazzar, S. Lilien, and V. Pastena, "Accounting for Leases by Lessees," *Journal of Accounting & Economics* 8 (October 1986): 217–238. FASB has responded by issuing ten standards on leases, five interpretations, ten technical bulletins, and 27 EITFs, many designed to reduce managers' ability to avoid capitalizing leases.

10. E. Imhoff, R. Lipe, and D. Wright show that adjustments to capitalize operating leases have a significant impact on leverage and other key financial ratios. See "Operating Leases: Impact of Constructive Capitalization," *Accounting Horizons* 5 (March 1991): 51–64.

11. Accounting rules in the U.S., the U.K., Canada, and Germany require expensing R&D outlays. Expensing is the norm in Japan and France, even though capitalization is permitted.

12. P. Healy, S. Myers, and C. Howe, "R&D Accounting and the Tradeoff Between Relevance and Objectivity," *Journal of Accounting Research* 40 (June 2002): 677–711, show that the magnitude of this bias is sizable.

13. See B. Bublitz and M. Ettredge, "The Information in Discretionary Outlays: Advertising, Research and Development," *The Accounting Review* 64 (1989): 108–124; S. Chan, J. Martin, and J. Kensinger, "Corporate Research and Development Expenditures and Share Value," *Journal of Financial Economics* 26 (1990): 255–276; R. Dukes, "An Investigation of the Effects of Expensing Research and Development Costs on Security Prices," in proceedings of the conference on topical research in accounting (New York University, 1976); J. Elliott, G. Richardson, T. Dyckman, and R. Dukes, "The Impact of SFAS No. 2 on Firm Expenditures on Research and Development: Replications and Extensions," *Journal of Accounting* 22 (1984): 85–102; M. Hirschey and J. Weygandt, "Amortization Policy for Advertising and Research and Development Expenditures," *Journal of Accounting Research* 23 (1985): 326–335; C. Wasley and T. Linsmeier, "A Further Examination of the Economic Consequences of SFAS No. 2," *Journal of Accounting Research* 30 (1992): 156–164; E. Eccher, "Discussion of the Value Relevance of Intangibles: The Case of Software Capitalization," *Journal of Accounting Research* 36 (1998): 193–198; B. Lev and T. Sougiannis, "The Capitalization, Amortization, and Value-Relevance of R&D," *Journal of Accounting and Economics* 21 (1996): 107–138; and D. Aboody and B. Lev, "The Value-Relevance of Intangibles: The Case of Software Capitalization" (working paper, University of California, 1998).

14. See Lufthansa, Annual Report 2005 (Cologne, Germany: Deutsche Lufthansa AG, 2006) and Air France-KLM 2005–06 Reference Document (Paris, France: Air France-KLM, 2006).

15. It is interesting to note that Lufthansa's depreciation expense for the year 2005 is significantly lower than expected given its 12-year life and 15 percent salvage estimates. The reported depreciation under these assumptions would have been €1,110 m ({13,048 + [(657 · .85)/2]}/12). The company provides no explanation for the difference.

16. See Japan Airlines, Annual Report 2006, Footnote 10.

17. JAL actually shows the present value of its lease commitments. However, most companies report the value of future lease payments for the next five years and then show a lump sum value for all payments beyond five years. To estimate the value of the lease liability, the analyst must decide how to allocate this lump sum over year six and beyond, and estimate a suitable interest rate on the lease debt. It is then possible to compute the present value of the lease payments.

18. When a firm records a capital lease, the Long-Term Tangible Asset equals the Long-Term Debt only at inception. Thereafter, the two numbers are unequal because the asset is reduced by depreciation expense while the debt is reduced by the lease payment net of interest expense. For most companies it is not possible to learn the book value of the asset, requiring the analyst to record the asset at the same value as the debt. However, JAL's annual report shows that, had it capitalized the leased assets, their net book value on March 31, 2005 would have been ¥388,896, while the liability would have been ¥396,006. Since this information is typically not available, we have chosen not to use it in our analysis.

19. M. Barth and M. McNichols discuss ways for investors to estimate the value of environmental liabilities. See "Estimation and Market Valuation of Environmental Liabilities Relating to Superfund Sites," *Journal of Accounting Research* 32, Supplement, 1994.

20. Defined contribution plans, where companies agree to contribute fixed amounts today to cover future benefits, require very little forecasting to estimate their annual cost since the firm's obligation is limited to its annual obligation to contribute to the employees' retirement funds.

21. E. Amir and E. Gordon show that firms with larger post-retirement benefit obligations and more leverage tend to make more aggressive estimates of post-retirement obligation parameters. See "A Firm's Choice of Estimation Parameters: Empirical Evidence from SFAS No. 106," *Journal of Accounting, Auditing & Finance* 11, no. 3, Summer 1996.

22. The interest expense is only a rough approximation of the amount that would be reported by CA since it does not adjust for the portion of the customer payments that were effectively interest for the bank given the premium rate charged.

23. In their footnotes, firms also report the Accumulated Benefit Obligation for the pension plan, which is the present value of plan commitments using current wage rates and salary scales.

24. In its 2006 financial statements, reported using SFAS 158, GM does record the full value of its U.S. post-retirement obligation as a Long-Term Liability. During 2006, GM amended its post-retirement plan to eliminate $15.1 billion of its obligation leaving its unfunded liability at $46.4 billion.

25. M. Barth finds that investors regard these footnote disclosures as more useful than the liability reported in the financial statements. See "Relative Measurement Errors Among Alternative Pension Asset and Liability Measures," *The Accounting Review* 66, no. 3, 1991.

APPENDIX: RECASTING FINANCIAL STATEMENTS INTO STANDARDIZED TEMPLATES

The following tables show the financial statements for Wal-Mart Stores, Inc., for the year ended January 2006, both as reported by the company and as standardized using the classifications discussed in this chapter. The first column in each reported financial statement presents the classifications that are used for each line item to standardize the statements. Note that the classifications are not applied to subtotal lines such as Total current assets or Net income. The recast financial statements for Wal-Mart are prepared by simply totaling the balances of line items with the same standard classifications. For example, on the balance sheet there are two line items classified as Other Current Liabilities – Accrued liabilities and Accrued income taxes.

Wal-Mart Reported Consolidated Balance Sheet
(in millions)

Fiscal Year Ended January 31		2006	2005	2004
	Assets			
	Current assets:			
Cash and Marketable Securities	Cash and cash equivalents	6,414	5,488	5,199
Accounts Receivable	Receivables	2,662	1,715	1,254
Inventory	Inventories	32,191	29,762	26,612
Other Current Assets	Prepaid expenses and other	2,557	1,889	1,356
	Total current assets	$43,824	$38,854	$34,421
	Property and equipment, at cost:			
Long-Term Tangible Assets	Land	16,643	14,472	12,699
Long-Term Tangible Assets	Buildings and improvements	56,163	46,574	40,192
Long-Term Tangible Assets	Fixtures and equipment	22,750	21,461	17,934
Long-Term Tangible Assets	Transportation equipment	1,746	1,530	1,269
	Property and equipment, at cost	$97,302	$84,037	$72,094
Long-Term Tangible Assets	Less accumulated depreciation	21,427	18,637	15,684
	Property and equipment, net	$75,875	$65,400	$56,410
	Property under capital lease:			
Other Long-Term Assets	Property under capital lease	5,578	4,556	4,286
Other Long-Term Assets	Less accumulated amortization	2,163	1,838	1,673
	Property under capital lease, net	$3,415	$2,718	$2,613
Long-Term Intangible Assets	Goodwill	12,188	10,803	9,882
Other Long-Term Assets	Other assets and deferred charges	2,885	2,379	2,079
	Total assets	$138,187	$120,154	$105,405

(continued)

Wal-Mart Reported Consolidated Balance Sheet
(in millions) (*continued*)

Fiscal Year Ended January 31		2006	2005	2004
	Liabilities and shareholders' equity			
	Current liabilities:			
Short-Term Debt	Commercial paper	3,754	3,812	3,267
Accounts Payable	Accounts payable	25,373	21,987	19,425
Other Current Liabilities	Accrued liabilities	13,465	12,120	10,671
Other Current Liabilities	Accrued income taxes	1,340	1,281	1,377
Short-Term Debt	Long-term debt due within one year	4,595	3,759	2,904
Short-Term Debt	Obligations under capital leases due within one year	299	223	196
	Total current liabilities	$48,826	$43,182	$37,840
Long-Term Debt	Long-term debt	26,429	20,087	17,102
Long-Term Debt	Long-term obligations under capital leases	3,742	3,171	2,997
Deferred Taxes– Long-Term Liability	Deferred income taxes and other	4,552	2,978	2,359
Minority Interest	Minority interest	1,467	1,340	1,484
	Shareholders' equity:			
Preferred Stock	Preferred stock ($0.10 par value; 100 shares authorized, none issued)	–	–	–
Common Shareholders' Equity	Common stock ($0.10 par value; 11,000 shares authorized, 4,165 and 4,234 issued and outstanding at January 31, 2006 and January 31, 2005, respectively)	417	423	431
Common Shareholders' Equity	Capital in excess of par value	2,596	2,425	2,135
Common Shareholders' Equity	Accumulated other comprehensive income	1,053	2,694	851
Common Shareholders' Equity	Retained earnings	49,105	43,854	40,206
	Total shareholders' equity	$53,171	$49,396	$43,623
	Total liabilities and shareholders' equity	138,187	120,154	105,405

Source: SEC 10-K filings.

Wal-Mart Reported Consolidated Statements of Income
(in millions except per share amounts)

Fiscal Year Ended January 31		2006	2005	2004
	Revenues:			
Sales	Net sales	312,427	285,222	256,329
Other Income	Other income, net	3,227	2,910	2,352
		$315,654	$288,132	$258,681
	Costs and expenses:			
Cost of Sales	Cost of sales	240,391	219,793	198,747
SG&A	Operating, selling, general and			
	administrative expenses	56,733	51,248	44,909
	Operating income	$18,530	$17,091	$15,025
	Interest:			
Interest Expense	Debt	1,171	934	729
Interest Expense	Capital leases	249	253	267
Interest Income	Interest income	(248)	(201)	(164)
	Interest, net	$1,172	$986	$832
	Income from continuing operations before income taxes and minority interest	17,358	16,105	14,193
	Provision for income taxes:			
Tax Expense	Current	5,932	5,326	4,941
Tax Expense	Deferred	(129)	263	177
		$5,803	$5,589	$5,118
	Income from continuing operations before minority interest	11,555	10,516	9,075
Minority Interest	Minority interest	(324)	(249)	(214)
	Income from continuing operations	$11,231	$10,267	$8,861
Unusual Items (after tax)	Income from discontinued operation, net of tax	–	–	193
	Net income	$11,231	$10,267	$9,054
	Basic net income per common share	2.68	2.41	2.08
	Diluted net income per common share	2.68	2.41	2.07
	Dividends per common share	0.60	0.52	0.36

Source: SEC 10-K filings.

Wal-Mart Reported Consolidated Statements of Cash Flows (in millions)

Fiscal Year Ended January 31		2006	2005	2004
	Cash flows from operating activities			
Net Income	Income from continuing operations	11,231	10,267	8,861
	Adjustments to reconcile net income to net cash provided by operating activities:			
Long-Term Operating Accruals	Depreciation and amortization	4,717	4,264	3,852
Long-Term Operating Accruals	Deferred income taxes	(129)	263	177
Long-Term Operating Accruals	Other operating activities	620	378	173
	Changes in certain assets and liabilities, net of effects of acquisitions:			
Net (Inv.) Liquidation of Op. WC	Decrease (increase) in accounts receivable	(456)	(304)	373
Net (Inv.) Liquidation of Op. WC	Increase in inventories	(1,733)	(2,494)	(1,973)
Net (Inv.) Liquidation of Op. WC	Increase in accounts payable	2,390	1,694	2,587
Net (Inv.) Liquidation of Op. WC	Increase in accrued liabilities	993	976	1,896
	Net cash provided by operating activities of continuing operations	$17,633	$15,044	$15,946
Net Income **	Net cash provided by operating activities of discontinued operation	–	–	50
	Net cash provided by operating activities	$17,633	$15,044	$15,996
	Cash flows from investing activities			
Net (Inv.) Liquidation of Op. L-T Assets	Payments for property and equipment	(14,563)	(12,893)	(10,308)
Net (Inv.) Liquidation of Op. L-T Assets	Investment in international operations, net of cash acquired	(601)	(315)	(38)
Net (Inv.) Liquidation of Op. L-T Assets	Proceeds from the disposal of fixed assets	1,049	953	481
Net (Inv.) Liquidation of Op. L-T Assets	Proceeds from the sale of McLane	–	–	1,500
Net (Inv.) Liquidation of Op. L-T Assets	Other investing activities	(68)	(96)	78
	Net cash used in investing activities of continuing operations	(14,183)	(12,351)	$(8,287)
Net (Inv.) Liquidation of Op. L-T Assets	Net cash used in investing activities of discontinued operation	–	–	(25)
	Net cash used in investing activities	$(14,183)	$(12,351)	$(8,312)

(continued)

Fiscal Year Ended January 31		**2006**	**2005**	**2004**
	Cash flows from financing activities			
Net Debt (Repayment) or Issuance	Increase (decrease) in commercial paper	(704)	544	688
Net Debt (Repayment) or Issuance	Proceeds from issuance of long-term debt	7,691	5,832	4,099
Net Stock (Repayment) or Issuance	Purchase of Company stock	(3,580)	(4,549)	(5,046)
Dividend (Payments)	Dividends paid	(2,511)	(2,214)	(1,569)
Net Debt (Repayment) or Issuance	Payment of long-term debt	(2,724)	(2,131)	(3,541)
Net Debt (Repayment) or Issuance	Payment of capital lease obligations	(245)	(204)	(305)
Net Stock (Repayment) or Issuance	Other financing activities	(349)	113	111
	Net cash used in financing activities	$(2,422)	$(2,609)	$(5,563)
Non-Operating Gains (Losses)	Effect of exchange rate changes on cash	(102)	205	320
	Net increase in cash and cash equivalents	$926	$289	$2,441
	Cash and cash equivalents at beginning of year	5,488	5,199	2,758
	Cash and cash equivalents at end of year	6,414	5,488	5,199

Source: SEC 10-K filings.

** *Wal-Mart separately reports cash from discontinued operations in its consolidated financial statements at a value of $50. We have included this as part of Net Income, rather than showing the full income effect of $193 million and including −$143 million of accruals for discontinued operations.*

The standardized financial statements for Wal-Mart are as follows:

Wal-Mart Standardized Consolidated Balance Sheet (in millions)

Fiscal Year Ended January 31	2006	2005	2004
ASSETS			
Cash and Marketable Securities	$6,414	$5,488	$5,199
Accounts Receivable	2,662	1,715	1,254
Inventory	32,191	29,762	26,612
Other Current Assets	2,557	1,889	1,356
Total Current Assets	43,824	38,854	34,421
Long-Term Tangible Assets	75,875	65,400	56,410
Long-Term Intangible Assets	12,188	10,803	9,882
Other Long-Term Assets	6,300	5,097	4,692
Total Long-Term Assets	94,363	81,300	70,984
Total Assets	$138,187	$120,154	$105,405
LIABILITIES			
Accounts Payable	$25,373	$21,987	$19,425
Short-Term Debt	8,648	7,794	6,367
Other Current Liabilities	14,805	13,401	12,048
Total Current Liabilities	48,826	43,182	37,840
Long-Term Debt	30,171	23,258	20,099
Deferred Taxes	4,552	2,978	2,359
Other Long-Term Liabilities (non-interest bearing)	–	–	–
Total Long-Term Liabilities	34,723	26,236	22,458
Total Liabilities	83,549	69,418	60,298
Minority Interest	1,467	1,340	1,484
SHAREHOLDERS' EQUITY			
Preferred Stock	–	–	–
Common Shareholders' Equity	53,171	49,396	43,623
Total Shareholders' Equity	53,171	49,396	43,623
Total Liabilities and Shareholders' Equity	$138,187	$120,154	$105,405

Wal-Mart Standardized Consolidated Statements of Income
(in millions except per share amounts)

Fiscal Year Ended January 31	2006	2005	2004
Sales	$ 312,427	$ 285,222	$ 256,329
Cost of Sales	240,391	219,793	198,747
Gross Profit	72,036	65,429	57,582
SG&A	56,733	51,248	44,909
Other Operating Expense	–	–	–
Operating Income	15,303	14,181	12,673
Investment Income	–	–	–
Other Income, net of Other Expense	3,227	2,910	2,352
Other Income	3,227	2,910	2,352
Other Expense	–	–	–
Net Interest Expense (Income)	1,172	986	832
Interest Income	248	201	164
Interest Expense	1,420	1,187	996
Minority Interest	(324)	(249)	(214)
Pre-Tax Income	17,034	15,856	13,979
Tax Expense	5,803	5,589	5,118
Unusual Gains, Net of Unusual Losses (after tax)	–	–	–
Net Income	$ 11,231	$ 10,267	$ 8,861
Preferred Dividends	–	–	–
Net Income to Common	$ 11,231	$ 10,267	$ 8,861

Wal-Mart Standardized Consolidated Statements of Cash Flows (in millions)

Fiscal Year Ended January 31	January 29, 2006	January 30, 2005	February 1, 2004
Net Income	$ 11,231	$ 10,267	$ 8,911
After-tax net interest expense (income)	773	638	527
Non-operating losses (gains)	102	(205)	(320)
Long-term operating accruals	5,208	4,905	4,202
Depreciation and amortization	4,717	4,264	3,852
Other	491	641	350
Operating cash flow before working capital investments	17,110	16,015	13,960
Net (investment in) or liquidation of operating working capital	1,194	(128)	2,883
Operating cash flow before investment in long-term assets	18,304	15,887	16,843
Net (investment in) or liquidation of operating long-term assets	(14,183)	(12,351)	(8,312)
Free cash flow available to debt and equity	4,121	3,536	8,531
After-tax net interest income (expense)	(773)	(638)	(527)
Net debt (repayment) or issuance	4,018	4,041	941
Free cash flow available to equity	7,366	6,939	8,945
Dividend (payments)	(2,511)	(2,214)	(1,569)
Net stock issuance (repurchase), and other equity changes	(3,929)	(4,436)	(4,935)
Net increase (decrease) in cash balance	$ 926	$ 289	$ 2,441

Chapter 5
Financial Analysis

The goal of financial analysis is to assess the performance of a firm in the context of its stated goals and strategy. There are two principal tools of financial analysis: ratio analysis and cash flow analysis. Ratio analysis involves an assessment of how various line items in a firm's financial statements relate to one another. Cash flow analysis allows the analyst to examine the firm's liquidity and to assess the management of operating, investment, and financing cash flows.

Financial analysis is used in a variety of contexts. Ratio analysis that compares a company's present performance to its past performance and/or to the performance of its peers provides the foundation for making forecasts of future performance. As we will discuss in later chapters, financial forecasting is useful in company valuation, credit evaluation, financial distress prediction, security analysis, and mergers and acquisitions analysis.

RATIO ANALYSIS

The value of a firm is determined by its profitability and growth. As shown in Figure 5-1, the firm's growth and profitability are influenced by its product market and financial market strategies. The product market strategy is implemented through the firm's competitive strategy, operating policies, and investment decisions. Financial market strategies are implemented through financing and dividend policies.

Thus, the four levers managers can use to achieve their growth and profit targets are (1) operating management, (2) investment management, (3) financing strategy, and (4) dividend policy. The objective of ratio analysis is to evaluate the effectiveness of the firm's policies in each of these areas. Effective ratio analysis involves relating the financial numbers to the underlying business factors in as much detail as possible. While ratio analysis may not give an analyst all the answers regarding the firm's performance, it will help the analyst frame questions for further probing.

In ratio analysis, the analyst can (1) compare ratios for a firm over several years (a time-series comparison), (2) compare ratios for the firm and other firms in the industry (cross-sectional comparison), and/or (3) compare ratios to some absolute benchmark. In a time-series comparison, the analyst can hold firm-specific factors constant and examine the effectiveness of a firm's strategy over time. Cross-sectional comparison facilitates examining the relative performance of a firm within its industry, holding industry-level factors constant. For most ratios there are no absolute benchmarks. The exceptions are measures of rates of return, which can be compared to the cost of the capital associated with the investment. For example, subject to distortions caused by accounting, the rate of return on equity (ROE) can be compared to the cost of equity capital.

In the discussion below, we will illustrate these approaches using the example of Wal-Mart Stores, Inc., the largest U.S. retailer. We will compare Wal-Mart's ratios for

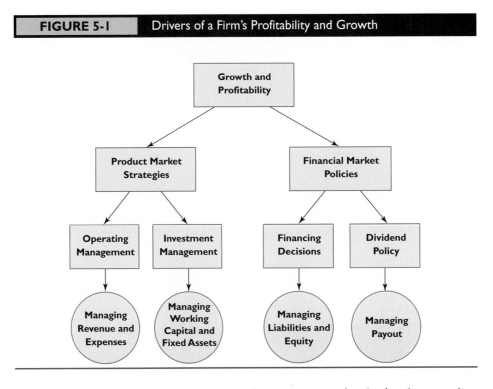

FIGURE 5-1   Drivers of a Firm's Profitability and Growth

the fiscal year ending January 31, 2006, with its own ratios for the fiscal year ending January 31, 2005, and with the ratios for Target Corporation, another U.S. retailer and one of Wal-Mart's principal competitors, for the fiscal year ending January 28, 2006.[1]

Wal-Mart has dominated, and continues to dominate, the retailing landscape in the U.S. As the second largest corporation in the U.S. when measured by revenue in 2005 (second only to Exxon Mobil), Wal-Mart has created a brand that is synonymous with low prices and value. Wal-Mart is known for effectively managing all aspects of its operating, investing, and financing activities, creating one of the pre-eminent global corporations. On the other hand, Target has, in many ways, reinvented itself over the past decade to successfully position itself as the discount retailer for the fashion conscious consumer. This has enabled Target to distinguish itself from Wal-Mart and carve out a market niche at the higher end of the discount retail market. We will examine whether this strategy has been successful for Target and how it compares to Wal-Mart across the various measures of financial performance that will be described in this chapter. We will also try to see which strategy is delivering better performance for shareholders.

In order to facilitate replication of the ratio calculations presented below, we present in the appendix to this chapter three versions of the financial statements of both these companies. The first version is the one reported by the two companies in their SEC filings. The second set of financial statements is presented in the standardized format described in Chapter 4. These "standardized financial statements" put both companies' financials in one standard format to facilitate direct comparison. The data is taken from Standard & Poor's Compustat database, which generally follows the format used by the companies in their own SEC filings, with minor modifications to make the data comparable across companies. A third format, labeled "Condensed Financial Statements," recasts the standardized financial statements to facilitate the calculation of several ratios discussed in the chapter. We will discuss later in the chapter how this recasting process works.

It is important to ensure that the financial statements of the company being analyzed do not include any data that will distort the analysis. Since the purpose of financial statement analysis is to better understand the performance of the firm as it relates to its strategy, care needs to be taken that any operations and events that are extraneous to that strategy do not change the picture that the analyst forms of the firm. The major categories of such distortions include one-time write-offs of assets and results from discontinued operations, including the gain or loss on the disposal of such operations. In such instances, it is useful to look at financial results of the core operations of the firm by adjusting the presented financial statements to exclude the impact of one-time effects. For example, in 2004 Target divested its interest in Marshall Field's and Mervyn's. Its 2004 results therefore reflected a partial year of revenues and earnings from those operations. In addition, its earnings were boosted by the gain on the sale of the discontinued operations. Without adjusting for these effects it is difficult to meaningfully use Target's 2004 results as a benchmark for performance in 2005 and beyond.

Background Information on Wal-Mart and Target

Wal-Mart Stores, Inc.

Wal-Mart is the number one retailer in the world, dwarfing its rivals in terms of both sales and earnings. Wal-Mart's success originates largely from its retailing philosophy, reflected in its slogan "every day low prices" (EDLP). EDLP entails offering a broad array of quality merchandise at low prices every day, giving customers the confidence that prices will not fluctuate as a result of promotional activity. This retailing proposition is delivered through more than 6,000 retail stores worldwide. While nearly two-thirds of its stores are located in the U.S., Wal-Mart has been expanding internationally and has grown to be the largest retailer in Canada, Mexico, and Puerto Rico. Wal-Mart reported a record $312.4 billion in net sales during the year ended January 31, 2006, and net income was a record $11.2 billion.

Wal-Mart offers its customers the full complement of products ranging from discount staples such as food and clothing to electronics, toys and entertainment, sporting goods, and prescription drugs. While generating impressive returns for its shareholders, Wal-Mart, through its breadth of affordable merchandise, has had a positive impact on the standard of living of its customers. According to a recently published study, Wal-Mart's lower prices and its impact on other retailers' prices saved consumers in the U.S. an estimated $263 billion in 2004, which translates into $2,329 per household.[a]

Wal-Mart's business is divided into three segments:

(1) Wal-Mart Stores, the primary U.S. retail business, accounts for 67 percent of the fiscal 2005[b] revenues from three retail store formats—supercenters, discount stores, and neighborhood markets. In addition, Wal-Mart operates an online retail store;

(2) SAM'S CLUB, which are membership warehouse clubs (and online retail) that account for 12.7 percent of fiscal 2005 sales. Members include both individuals and small and large businesses; and

(3) International operations, which account for 20.1 percent of fiscal 2005 sales through a variety of retail formats and restaurants including supercenters, discount stores, and SAM'S CLUB stores. As of January 31, 2006, Wal-Mart

had a presence in nine foreign countries and Puerto Rico. Subsequently, Wal-Mart increased its stake in CARHCO, a Central American retailer, giving it majority control over a retailer with a presence in five countries in the region.

While Wal-Mart has in many ways perfected the large discount retail model in the U.S., it is constantly improving on its strategy and operations and looking for innovative growth opportunities. Wal-Mart is currently opening stores in urban locations, which is a shift from its roots. It is also trying to replicate Target's success in catering to a higher-income customer with a selection of better designed and fashionable merchandise. In this attempt to appeal to a more affluent customer, Wal-Mart is remodeling a number of its stores, increasing the selection of designer apparel and organic foods, and is actively courting a class it terms "selective" shoppers. These customers come to the store for certain basic commodities but do not believe that Wal-Mart can cater to their quality and style requirements when it comes to apparel and home furnishings.

Wal-Mart has been looking increasingly to its international operations to drive profitable growth in the future. It has chosen a strategy of greenfield operations, joint ventures, and acquisitions to expand overseas, often leveraging a partner's local market knowledge while bringing its expertise in merchandising, supply chain management, and other facets of operations and finance. Two of Wal-Mart's earliest and most successful international operations were in neighboring Canada and Mexico. Wal-Mart was one of the early entrants into the Chinese market, establishing a presence there in 1996. Large acquisitions followed over the rest of the nineties in Germany, Brazil, and the UK, which were followed by acquisitions in Japan and Central America. Wal-Mart has also been lobbying to gain access to the high-growth Indian market. Wal-Mart has shown a willingness to rationalize international operations by disposing of underperforming assets as evidenced by recent exits from the highly competitive South Korean and German markets.

For all its successes, Wal-Mart attracts its fair share of criticism—from the media, its employees, politicians, and the community at large. Wal-Mart has long been vilified for what some have deemed unfair labor practices and poor benefits compensation, and it is the subject of numerous lawsuits alleging discrimination and violations of other wage-and-hour labor laws. Wal-Mart's attempts to address these claims, such as by improving health insurance for employees, will impact future profitability. Wal-Mart has also encountered resistance from community members and local governments as it has pursued expansion opportunities. For instance, some communities in California, a lucrative market for the retailer, have resisted planned Wal-Mart stores because of the perceived increase in traffic and a loss of open space in their neighborhoods. This opposition to Wal-Mart's expansion could limit its domestic growth prospects.

Wal-Mart clearly faces significant challenges and will rely on its seasoned executive team to continue to innovate and drive growth and profitability. In mid 2006, the sell side analyst community had mixed views about Wal-Mart's future success. Citigroup was positive on the stock and expected it to appreciate by 25 percent as a result of improved earnings per share growth from product mix enhancements.[c] On the other hand, JP Morgan's analysts gave the stock a "Neutral" rating, citing, among other reasons, an "augmented risk profile" due to factors such as "merchandise makeovers, international expansion, and field level management changes."[d]

Target Corporation

Target is the second largest discount chain in the U.S. behind Wal-Mart and operates close to 1,400 large-format, general merchandise discount stores. In the competitive world of retailing, Target seems to have identified a profitable market niche and created a sustainable position in the short and medium term. The company markets itself to discount store consumers who are more affluent, by appealing to their design sense and fashion consciousness. Target's brand promise, "Expect More. Pay Less," captures both its upscale appeal and its discount prices—the firm is widely recognized as having identified and successfully capitalized on a market for "cheap chic" goods. To augment this differentiated retailing strategy, Target has created a clever, trendy, and often non-traditional approach to its marketing campaigns. For the most recent fiscal year ended January 28, 2006, the company posted record core operating earnings ($2.4 billion) and record sales ($52.6 billion).

Target strives to create emotional ties with its customers, referred to as "guests," through superior design. Target's merchandising focuses on exclusive private-label collections from prominent designers while continuing to deliver the convenience and low prices that are central to its discount store heritage. Given Target's reliance on changing fashion trends, time to market is crucial. As a result, the company relies heavily on direct sourcing of merchandise and has invested in strengthening its supply chain. It has also invested in building Target.com, the online store which provides it with an integrated, multichannel approach to retailing.

Target's focus on design spills over to the stores themselves, as it experiments with different store design prototypes to refine its customers' shopping experience. In January 2006, Target operated 1,397 stores in the U.S. (compared to Wal-Mart's more than 3,200 domestic stores.) Target management expected to open more than 100 new stores in 2006 with a goal of 2,000 locations by 2010 and an ultimate vision of 3,000, implying an aggressive growth strategy. Management stressed that most of this expansion would come from within the U.S.—it was not yet looking to international growth.[e] Consistent with its focus on the core discount store business, in 2004 Target divested its stakes in Marshall Field's and Mervyn's department store chains.

Given Target's market niche, some analysts have expressed concern that its expansion could come at the expense of profitability. A February 2004 study by Morgan Stanley showed that Target already had a strong presence in California and the northeast corridor, two of the more affluent regions of the country where its value proposition had most traction. Expansion into less wealthy regions could mean a gradual reduction in both per store productivity and same store sales growth over time. This pressure could be offset by a general increase in living standards that would enable people to move up from being purely price-driven Wal-Mart shoppers to becoming style-driven Target shoppers.

Target National Bank, a wholly owned subsidiary of Target, has a credit card business which consists of both proprietary credit cards (usable either at Target stores or Target.com) and Target VISA cards. In fiscal 2005, credit cards contributed 2.6 percent of revenues. While there has been some concern that a credit card business could distract management from its core retailing operations, the customer information gathered from the card allows Target to better respond to its customer shopping needs and contributes to its ability to retain its margin on sales.

Although Target's strategy has paid off handsomely in recent years, it faces significant competitive threats. Wal-Mart is not likely to allow Target to solidify its market niche uncontested and is considering two competitive responses—to increase the appeal of its merchandise through better design and to widen the price gap with Target on commodity products to entice more shoppers to its stores. The other threat to Target is that customers begin splitting their shopping between two locations—for instance, shopping at Wal-Mart for consumables and commodities, which is essentially a price conscious decision, and then at another large retailer such as Kohl's for the purely fashion driven purchases.

Wall Street's view of Target was generally positive in mid 2006, with most analysts expecting price appreciation on Target's stock. Morgan Stanley, for instance, had a bullish outlook for the stock and expected its price to increase 25 percent.[f] Deutsche Bank, which expected a price rise of 20 percent, noted their confidence in Target management's "ability to execute against its long-term strategic plans, despite our expectations for a macro slowdown" and in the firm's ability to sustain 8–10 percent square foot growth for the next 12 years.[g]

a. Global Insight. *The Economic Impact of Wal-Mart,* November 2, 2005.
b. Wal-Mart refers to its fiscal year ended January 31, 2006, as fiscal 2006. However, for the sake of consistency, this book will refer to it as fiscal 2005.
c. Deborah Weinswig and Charmaine Tang, *Wal-Mart Stores, Inc.,* Citigroup, July 2, 2006, via Thomson Research/Investext (accessed July 2006).
d. Charles Grom, Matthew Boss, and Paul Trussel, *Wal-Mart Stores, Inc.,* JP Morgan, July 3, 2006, via Thomson Research/Investext (accessed July 2006).
e. Target Corporation, 2005 Annual Report (Minneapolis: Target Corporation, 2006), p. 8.
f. Gregory Melich, *Target Corp.,* Morgan Stanley, July 18, 2006, via Thomson Research/Investext (accessed July 2006).
g. William A. Dreher Jr., Vin Chao, and Shane Higgins, *Target,* Deutsche Bank, July 12, 2006, via Thomson Research/Investext (accessed July 2006).

Measuring Overall Profitability

The starting point for a systematic analysis of a firm's performance is its return on equity (ROE), defined as

$$\text{ROE} = \frac{\text{Net income}}{\text{Shareholder's equity}}$$

ROE is a comprehensive indicator of a firm's performance because it provides an indication of how well managers are employing the funds invested by the firm's shareholders to generate returns. On average over long periods, large publicly traded firms in the U.S. generate ROEs in the range of 11 to 13 percent.

In the long run, the value of the firm's equity is determined by the relationship between its ROE and its cost of equity capital.[2] That is, those firms that are expected over the long run to generate ROEs in excess of the cost of equity capital should have market values in excess of book value, and vice versa. (We will return to this point in more detail in the chapter on valuation.)

A comparison of ROE with the cost of capital is useful not only for analyzing the value of the firm but also in considering the path of future profitability. The generation of consistent supernormal profitability will, absent significant barriers to entry, attract competition. For that reason ROEs tend over time to be driven by competitive forces toward a "normal" level—the cost of equity capital. Thus, one can think of the cost of equity capital as establishing a benchmark for the ROE that would be observed in a long-run competitive equilibrium. Deviations from this level arise for two general reasons. One is the industry conditions and competitive strategy that cause a firm to generate supernormal (or subnormal) economic profits, at least over the short run. The second is distortions due to accounting.

Table 5-1 shows the ROE based on reported earnings for Wal-Mart and Target.

TABLE 5-1	Return on Equity for Wal-Mart and Target		
Ratio	**Wal-Mart FY2005**	**Wal-Mart FY2004**	**Target FY2005**
Return on equity	22.7%	23.5%	18.5%

Wal-Mart outperformed Target in 2005, despite the fact that Wal-Mart failed to sustain the level of profitability that it achieved in the prior year. Target's ROE of 18.5 percent trails the 22.7 percent earned by Wal-Mart in 2005. The performance of both companies over the past two years has exceeded both historical trends of ROE in the economy and reasonable estimates of the cost of equity capital for the firms.[3]

Wal-Mart's superior profitability performance relative to Target is reflected in the difference between the market value of equity to book value ratios for the two firms. As we will discuss in Chapter 7, ROE is a key determinant of a company's market to book ratio. As of early April 2006, when both companies had released their 2006 year-end results, Wal-Mart's market to book ratio was 3.6 and Target's ratio was 3.2. This differential in market valuation could be an indication that investors expected Wal-Mart to continue to outperform Target in the coming years and earn a superior return for its shareholders.

Decomposing Profitability: Traditional Approach

A company's ROE is affected by two factors: how profitably it employs its assets and how big the firm's asset base is relative to shareholders' investment. To understand the effect of these two factors, ROE can be decomposed into return on assets (ROA) and a measure of financial leverage, as follows:

$$\text{ROE} = \text{ROA} \times \text{Financial leverage}$$

$$= \frac{\text{Net income}}{\text{Assets}} \times \frac{\text{Assets}}{\text{Shareholders' equity}}$$

ROA tells us how much profit a company is able to generate for each dollar of assets invested. Financial leverage indicates how many dollars of assets the firm is able to deploy for each dollar invested by its shareholders.

The return on assets itself can be decomposed into a product of two factors:

$$\text{ROA} = \frac{\text{Net income}}{\text{Sales}} \times \frac{\text{Sales}}{\text{Assets}}$$

The ratio of net income to sales is called net profit margin or return on sales (ROS); the ratio of sales to assets is known as asset turnover. The profit margin ratio indicates how much the company is able to keep as profits for each dollar of sales it makes. Asset turnover indicates how many sales dollars the firm is able to generate for each dollar of its assets.

Table 5-2 displays the three drivers of ROE for our retail firms: net profit margins, asset turnover, and financial leverage. The small decline in Wal-Mart's ROE in 2005 was driven by a drop in asset utilization, from 2.73 to 2.61. Profit margins for Wal-Mart were steady and financial leverage increased modestly. Given its strategy, it is not surprising that Target had higher profit margins and lower asset turnover than Wal-Mart, However, the higher margins did not offset the lower turnover, resulting in a lower ROA for Target. Financial management of the two firms is similar. Consequently, Target's lower operating performance was also reflected in a lower ROE.

TABLE 5-2	Traditional Decomposition of ROE		
Ratio	**Wal-Mart FY2005**	**Wal-Mart FY2004**	**Target FY2005**
Net profit margin (ROS)	3.6%	3.6%	4.6%
× Asset turnover	2.61	2.73	1.63
= Return on assets (ROA)	9.3%	9.8%	7.5%
× Financial leverage	2.43	2.40	2.48
= Return on equity (ROE)	22.7%	23.5%	18.5%

Decomposing Profitability: Alternative Approach

Even though the above approach is popularly used to decompose a firm's ROE, it has several limitations. In the computation of ROA, the denominator includes the assets claimed by all providers of capital to the firm, but the numerator includes only the earnings available to equity holders. The assets themselves include both operating assets and financial assets such as cash and short-term investments. Further, net income includes income from operating activities as well as interest income and expense, which are consequences of financing decisions. Often it is useful to distinguish between these two drivers of performance. Finally, the financial leverage ratio used above does not recognize the fact that a firm's cash and short-term investments are in essence "negative debt" because they can be used to pay down the debt on the company's balance sheet.[4] These issues are addressed by an alternative approach to decomposing ROE.[5]

Before discussing this alternative ROE decomposition approach, we define in Table 5-3 some terminology used in this section as well as in the rest of this chapter.

TABLE 5-3	Definitions of Accounting Items Used in Ratio Analysis

Item	Definition
Net interest expense after tax	(Interest expense − Interest income) × (1 − Tax rate)[a]
Net operating profit after taxes (NOPAT)	Net income + Net interest expense after tax
Operating working capital	(Current assets − Cash and marketable securities) − (Current liabilities − Short-term debt and current portion of long-term debt)
Net long-term assets	Total long-term assets − Non-interest-bearing long-term liabilities
Net debt	Total interest bearing liabilities − Cash and marketable securities
Net assets	Operating working capital + Net long-term assets
Net capital	Net debt + Shareholders' equity

[a] *The calculation of net interest expense treats interest expense and interest income as absolute values, independent of how these figures are reported in the income statement.*

We use the terms defined above to recast the financial statements of Wal-Mart and Target. These recasted financial statements, which are shown in the appendix as condensed statements, are used to decompose ROE in the following manner:

$$\text{ROE} = \frac{\text{NOPAT}}{\text{Equity}} - \frac{(\text{Net interest expense after tax})}{\text{Equity}}$$

$$= \frac{\text{NOPAT}}{\text{Net assets}} \times \frac{\text{Net assets}}{\text{Equity}} - \frac{\text{Net interest expense after tax}}{\text{Net debt}} \times \frac{\text{Net debt}}{\text{Equity}}$$

$$= \frac{\text{NOPAT}}{\text{Net assets}} \times \left(1 + \frac{\text{Net debt}}{\text{Equity}}\right) - \frac{\text{Net interest expense after tax}}{\text{Net debt}} \times \frac{\text{Net debt}}{\text{Equity}}$$

$$= \text{Operating ROA} + (\text{Operating ROA} - \text{Effective interest rate after tax}) \times \text{Net financial leverage}$$

$$= \text{Operating ROA} + \text{Spread} \times \text{Net financial leverage}$$

Operating ROA is a measure of how profitably a company is able to deploy its operating assets to generate operating profits. This would be a company's ROE if it were financed entirely with equity. Spread is the incremental economic effect from introducing debt into the capital structure. This economic effect of borrowing is positive as long as the return on operating assets is greater than the cost of borrowing. Firms that do not earn adequate operating returns to pay for interest cost reduce their ROE by borrowing. Both the positive and negative effect is magnified by the extent to which a firm borrows relative to its equity base. The ratio of net debt to equity provides a measure of this net financial leverage. A firm's spread times its net financial leverage, therefore, provides a measure of the financial leverage gain to the shareholders.

Operating ROA can be further decomposed into NOPAT margin and operating asset turnover as follows:

$$\text{Operating ROA} = \frac{\text{NOPAT}}{\text{Sales}} \times \frac{\text{Sales}}{\text{Net assets}}$$

NOPAT margin is a measure of how profitable a company's sales are from an operating perspective. Operating asset turnover measures the extent to which a company is able to use its operating assets to generate sales.

Table 5-4 presents the alternative decomposition of ROE for Wal-Mart and Target. The ratios in this table show that Wal-Mart's operating ROA was nearly 75 percent higher than its traditional ROA. In 2005 for example, operating ROA (based on earnings before net interest expense) was 16.1 percent, whereas traditional ROA (based on earnings after net interest expense) was only 9.3 percent. Despite improved NOPAT margins in 2005, Wal-Mart's operating ROA declined during the year. This was attributable to declining net asset turnover, reflecting faster growth in net operating assets (stores) than in sales.

TABLE 5-4	Distinguishing Operating and Financing Components in ROE Decomposition		
Ratio	**Wal-Mart FY2005**	**Wal-Mart FY2004**	**Target FY2005**
Net operating profit margin	3.9%	3.8%	5.2%
× Net operating asset turnover	4.16	4.41	2.59
= Operating ROA	16.1%	16.9%	13.4%
Spread	12.7%	13.6%	9.1%
× Net financial leverage	0.53	0.49	0.56
= Financial leverage gain	6.7%	6.6%	5.1%
ROE = Operating ROA + Financial leverage gain	22.7%	23.5%	18.5%

The difference in ROA and operating ROA is equally pronounced for Target: its ROA in 2005 was 7.5 percent whereas the operating ROA was 13.3 percent. Like Wal-Mart, Target's NOPAT margin, which excludes the impact of its financing choices, was higher than its traditional return on sales ratio shown in Table 5-2. As Target is able to finance a portion of its net operating assets through non-interest-bearing long-term liabilities, its net operating asset turnover is significantly higher than its traditionally defined asset turnover shown in Table 5-2.

Both Wal-Mart and Target benefit from their financial management decisions as both show gains from financial leverage. However, the difference between the traditional ROA and its alternative operating ROA for both firms underscores the importance of distinguishing the operating performance of firms from the impact of its financial management to gain valuable insight into firm strategy and performance.

The key elements of operating ROA illustrate the different strategies pursued by the two firms. Wal-Mart dominates the low-end retail market, and its business model is dependent on high sales volumes of relatively low margin goods. Its

NOPAT margins of 3.9 percent combined with high asset turnover of over four demonstrates its ability to successfully execute that strategy, leading to a healthy operating ROA of over 16 percent in both 2004 and 2005. In contrast, Target has attempted to differentiate itself from its discount retail competitors by adding an element of design and fashion to its product offerings. This ensured that Target earned a higher NOPAT margin of 5.2 percent in 2005 versus 3.9 percent for Wal-Mart. Not surprisingly, however, it had a markedly lower operating asset turnover when compared to Wal-Mart. Overall, Wal-Mart's approach to discount retailing seems to be more successful than Target's, though it will be interesting to see how increased competition from Target will affect Wal-Mart's performance. One possibility is that Target's strategy to position itself at the higher end of the market is a defensible niche that is starting to pay off and Wal-Mart is beginning to lose ground to its design-centric rival. Another likely scenario is that Wal-Mart has not made its competitive response yet and that Target's margin performance is not sustainable in the face of a direct challenge by its larger rival.

Both firms are able to create shareholder value through their respective financing strategies. Given the financial strength of both firms—Wal-Mart is rated AA and Target has an A rating from S&P—both firms have a relatively low cost of debt. As a result, the spread between Wal-Mart's operating ROA and its after-tax interest cost was 12.7 percent in 2005. Wal-Mart's financing choices resulted in a net debt to equity ratio of around 50 percent. The combination of spread and leverage contributed to a net increment of 6.7 percent to Wal-Mart's ROE in 2005. Target's spread of 13.3 percent in 2005 is lower than Wal-Mart's, reflecting both its lower operating ROA and marginally higher cost of debt. Target's ROE in 2005 was enhanced by 5.2 percent as a result of its financing policies.

The appropriate benchmark for evaluating operating ROA is the weighted average cost of debt and equity capital, or WACC. In the long run, the value of a firm's assets is determined by how its operating ROA compares to this norm. Moreover, over the long run and absent some barrier to competitive forces, operating ROA will tend to be pushed toward the weighted average cost of capital. Since the WACC is typically lower than the cost of equity capital, operating ROA tends to be pushed to a level lower than that to which ROE tends.

The average operating ROA for large firms in the U.S. over long periods of time is in the range of 9 to 11 percent. In both 2004 and 2005, Wal-Mart comfortably exceeded these benchmarks. In addition, Target's performance in 2005 beat the long-run averages. This impressive operating performance of both firms would have been obscured by using the simple ROA measure.[6]

Assessing Operating Management: Decomposing Net Profit Margins

A firm's net profit margin or return on sales (ROS) shows the profitability of the company's operating activities. Further decomposition of a firm's ROS allows an analyst to assess the efficiency of the firm's operating management. A popular tool used in this analysis is the common-sized income statement in which all the line items are expressed as a percentage of sales revenues.

Common-sized income statements make it possible to compare trends in income statement relationships over time for the firm, and trends across different firms in the industry. To illustrate how the income statement analysis can be used, common-sized income statements for Wal-Mart and Target are shown in Table 5-5. The table also shows some commonly used profitability ratios. We will use the information in

TABLE 5-5	Common-Sized Income Statement and Profitability Ratios		
Ratio	**Wal-Mart FY2005**	**Wal-Mart FY2004**	**Target FY2005**
Line Items as a Percent of Sales			
Sales	100.0%	100.0%	100.0%
Cost of sales	75.2%	75.3%	66.4%
Selling, general & admin. expenses	18.1%	17.9%	22.8%
Other income/expense	0.6%	0.7%	2.7%
Net interest expense/income	0.4%	0.4%	1.0%
Income taxes	1.9%	2.0%	2.8%
Unusual gains/loss, net of taxes	0.0%	0.0%	0.0%
Net income	3.8%	3.8%	4.4%
Key Profitability Ratios			
Gross profit margin	24.8%	24.7%	33.6%
EBITDA margin	7.4%	7.5%	11.0%
NOPAT margin	3.9%	3.8%	5.2%
Recurring NOPAT margin	3.3%	3.4%	5.1%

Table 5-5 to investigate why Wal-Mart has had a steady net income margin (or return on sales) of 3.8 percent in both 2005 and 2004, while Target posted margins of 4.4 percent in 2005.

Gross Profit Margins

The difference between a firm's sales and cost of sales is gross profit. Gross profit margin is an indication of the extent to which revenues exceed direct costs associated with sales, and it is computed as

$$\text{Gross profit margin} = \frac{\text{Sales} - \text{Cost of sales}}{\text{Sales}}$$

Gross margin is influenced by two factors: (1) the price premium that a firm's products or services command in the marketplace and (2) the efficiency of the firm's procurement and production process. The price premium a firm's products or services can command is influenced by the degree of competition and the extent to which its products are unique. The firm's cost of sales can be low when it can purchase its inputs at a lower cost than competitors and/or run its production processes more efficiently. This is generally the case when a firm has a low-cost strategy.

Table 5-5 indicates that Wal-Mart's gross margin of 24.8 percent in 2005 was virtually unchanged from 2004, reflecting a relatively stable macroeconomic environment and no radical shift in the competitive environment or the firm's own strategy. As a consequence, Wal-Mart was able to maintain its prices and margins without having to resort to deep discounting to spur sales. Wal-Mart did not make any major changes to its strategy and product mix and continued to execute on its efficient sourcing systems.

Consistent with Target's premium product and price strategy relative to Wal-Mart, its gross margin in 2005 was significantly higher than Wal-Mart's gross margins in the same period. Target's impressive gross margin of 33.6 percent in 2005 reflects a combination of factors including an increased market acceptance for its premium, design-oriented discount strategy, better product mix and pricing, and strong sourcing and distribution capabilities.

Selling, General, and Administrative Expenses

A company's selling, general, and administrative (SG&A) expenses are influenced by the operating activities it has to undertake to implement its competitive strategy. As discussed in Chapter 2, firms with differentiation strategies have to undertake activities to achieve it. A company competing on the basis of quality and rapid introduction of new products is likely to have higher R&D costs relative to a company competing purely on a cost basis. Similarly, a company that attempts to build a brand image, distribute its products through full-service retailers, and provide significant customer service is likely to have higher selling and administration costs relative to a company that sells through warehouse retailers or direct mail and does not provide much customer support.

A company's SG&A expenses are also influenced by the efficiency with which it manages its overhead activities. The control of operating expenses is likely to be especially important for firms competing on the basis of low cost. However, even for differentiators, it is important to assess whether the cost of differentiation is commensurate with the price premium earned in the marketplace.

Several ratios in Table 5-5 allow us to evaluate the effectiveness with which Wal-Mart and Target managed their SG&A expenses. First, the ratio of SG&A expense to sales shows how much a company is spending to generate each sales dollar. Wal-Mart definitely had the edge in terms of a cost management strategy as demonstrated by its lower ratio of SG&A to sales. In 2005 Wal-Mart's SG&A expenses as a percent of sales was 18.1 percent compared to 22.8 percent for Target. It is interesting to note that Wal-Mart showed a small increases in its cost structure from 2004 to 2005.

Wal-Mart's lower gross margins and lower SG&A to sales are not surprising given its low cost strategy. In contrast, by catering to a slightly more affluent consumer, with higher prices, merchandising and service costs, Target had higher margins and also higher SG&A expenses. A key question is, when both these costs are netted out, which company performed better? Two ratios provide useful signals here: net operating profit margin (NOPAT margin) and EBITDA margin:

$$\text{NOPAT margin} = \frac{\text{NOPAT}}{\text{Sales}}$$

$$\text{EBITDA margin} = \frac{\text{Earnings before interest, taxes, depreciation, and amortization}}{\text{Sales}}$$

NOPAT margin provides a comprehensive indication of the operating performance of a company because it reflects all operating costs and eliminates the effects of debt policy. EBITDA margin provides similar information, except that it excludes depreciation and amortization expense, a significant non-cash operating expense. Some analysts prefer to use EBITDA margin because they believe that it focuses on "cash" operating items. While this is to some extent true, it can be potentially misleading for two reasons. EBITDA is not a strictly cash concept because sales, cost of sales, and SG&A expenses often include non-cash items. Also, depreciation is a real operating expense, and it reflects to some extent the consumption of resources. Therefore, ignoring it can be misleading.

Table 5-5 shows that Wal-Mart made a marginal improvement to its NOPAT margins from 2004 to 2005. Despite this improvement, Wal-Mart was able to earn only 3.9 cents in net operating profits out of every dollar of sales it generated, whereas Target earned 5.2 cents per sales dollar.

Recall that in Table 5-3 we define NOPAT as net income plus net interest expense. Therefore, NOPAT is influenced by any unusual or nonoperating income (expense) items included in net income. We can calculate a "recurring" NOPAT margin by eliminating these items. For both Wal-Mart and Target the major portion of their profits came from their core businesses. Wal-Mart's recurring NOPAT is lower than its NOPAT margin— 3.3 percent versus 3.9 percent in 2005—due to other income reported by the company, most likely a result of investment income. While Target divested itself of its Marshall Field's and Mervyn's subsidiaries in 2004, the impact of this change was not reflected in the 2005 results. As a result, its recurring NOPAT very closely approximated the regular NOPAT margin. In general, recurring NOPAT may be a better benchmark to use when extrapolating current performance into the future since it reflects margins from the core business activities of a firm, especially if in the particular years analyzed the firm generated income from non-core or discontinued operations.

Target also has a better EBITDA margin than Wal-Mart. Care needs to be taken when examining this ratio, especially in sectors such as retailing. Certain retailers choose to own both the land and the buildings for the stores that they operate, while others choose to enter into off-balance-sheet leases. As a result, the depreciation expenses can vary widely between firms choosing different strategies, and can lead to results that may be misleading. For Wal-Mart and Target, these differences appear to be modest: nearly 17 percent of Target's stores are either leased or built on leased land versus more than 21 percent for Wal-Mart's U.S. stores and 23 percent for SAM'S CLUB stores.

Tax Expense

Taxes are an important element of a firm's total expenses. Through a wide variety of tax planning techniques, firms can attempt to reduce their tax expenses.[7] There are two measures one can use to evaluate a firm's tax expense. One is the ratio of tax expense to sales, and the other is the ratio of tax expense to earnings before taxes (also known as the average tax rate). The firm's tax footnote provides a detailed account of why its average tax rate differs from the statutory tax rate.

Table 5-5 shows that Wal-Mart's income tax expenses as a percent of sales were lower than Target's. This was due in part to the fact that Target had higher pre-tax profits as a percent of sales. However, Wal-Mart's tax rate in 2005 was also lower than Target's— 33.4 percent versus 37.6 percent. This was a result of two factors: (1) Wal-Mart benefited from international operations, since its effective tax rate was lower on international operations than on domestic profits, and (2) Wal-Mart's mix of locations within the U.S. resulted in a lower state income tax liability. As Wal-Mart continues its domestic expansion, it will enter states with higher tax rates, leading to a gradual increase in its local tax liability. This is likely to be offset by the growing importance of the international operations and the lower tax rates on those earnings.

In summary, an examination of common-sized income statement ratios can illuminate strategic and operational differences among competitors. Wal-Mart's profitability is driven by a tight control over its expenses, which helps it compensate for lower gross margin when compared to Target.

Key Analysis Questions

A number of business questions will be useful to an analyst assessing the various elements of operating management:

- Are the company's margins consistent with its stated competitive strategy? For example, a differentiation strategy should usually lead to higher gross margins than a low-cost strategy.
- Are the company's margins changing? Why? What are the underlying business causes—changes in competition, changes in input costs, or poor overhead cost management?
- Is the company managing its overhead and administrative costs well? What are the business activities driving these costs? Are these activities necessary?
- Are the company's tax policies sustainable, or is the current tax rate influenced by one-time tax credits?
- Do the firm's tax planning strategies lead to other business costs? For example, if the operations are located in tax havens, how does this affect the company's profit margins and asset utilization? Are the benefits of tax planning strategies (reduced taxes) greater than the increased business costs?

Evaluating Investment Management: Decomposing Asset Turnover

Asset turnover is the second driver of a company's return on equity. Since firms invest considerable resources in their assets, using them productively is critical to overall profitability. A detailed analysis of asset turnover allows the analyst to evaluate the effectiveness of a firm's investment management. There are two primary areas of investment management: (1) working capital management and (2) management of long-term assets, both of which are discussed in further detail below.

Working Capital Management

Working capital is defined as the difference between a firm's current assets and current liabilities. However, this definition does not distinguish between operating components (such as accounts receivable, inventory, and accounts payable) and financing components (such as cash, marketable securities, and notes payable). An alternative measure that makes this distinction is operating working capital, defined in Table 5-3 as

$$\text{Operating working capital} = (\text{Current assets} - \text{cash and marketable securities}) \\ - (\text{Current liabilities} - \text{Short-term and current portion of long-term debt})$$

The components of operating working capital that analysts primarily focus on are accounts receivable, inventory, and accounts payable. A certain amount of investment in working capital is generally necessary for the firm to run its normal operations. For example, a firm's credit policies and distribution policies determine its optimal level of accounts receivable. The nature of the production process and the need for buffer stocks determine the optimal level of inventory. Finally, accounts payable is a routine source of financing for the firm's working capital, and payment practices in an industry determine the normal level of accounts payable.

The following ratios are useful in analyzing a firm's working capital management: operating working capital as a percent of sales, operating working capital turnover, accounts receivable turnover, inventory turnover, and accounts payable turnover. The turnover ratios can also be expressed in number of days of activity that the operating working capital (and its components) can support. These ratios are defined below:

$$\text{Operating working capital to sales ratio} = \frac{\text{Operating working capital}}{\text{Sales}}$$

$$\text{Operating working capital turnover} = \frac{\text{Sales}}{\text{Operating working capital}}$$

$$\text{Accounts receivable turnover} = \frac{\text{Sales}}{\text{Accounts receivable}}$$

$$\text{Inventory turnover} = \frac{\text{Cost of goods sold}^8}{\text{Inventory}}$$

$$\text{Accounts payable turnover} = \frac{\text{Purchases}}{\text{Accounts payable}} \quad or \quad \frac{\text{Cost of goods sold}}{\text{Accounts payable}}$$

$$\text{Days' receivables} = \frac{\text{Accounts receivable}}{\text{Average sales per day}}$$

$$\text{Days' inventory} = \frac{\text{Inventory}}{\text{Average cost of goods sold per day}}$$

$$\text{Days' payables} = \frac{\text{Accounts payable}}{\text{Average purchases (or cost of goods sold) per day}}$$

Operating working capital turnover indicates how many dollars of sales a firm is able to generate for each dollar invested in operating working capital. Accounts receivable turnover, inventory turnover, and accounts payable turnover allow the analyst to examine how productively the three principal components of working capital are being used. Days' receivables, days' inventory, and days' payables are another way to evaluate the efficiency of a firm's working capital management.[9]

Long-Term Assets Management

Another area of investment management concerns the utilization of a firm's long-term assets. It is useful to define again a firm's investment in long-term assets:

$$\text{Net long-term assets} = (\text{Total long-term assets} - \text{Non-interest-bearing long-term liabilities})$$

Long-term assets generally consist of net property, plant, and equipment (PP&E), intangible assets such as goodwill, and other assets. Non-interest-bearing long-term liabilities include items such as deferred taxes. We define net long-term assets and net working capital in such a way that their sum, net operating assets, is equal to the sum of net debt and equity, or net capital. This is consistent with the way we defined operating ROA earlier in the chapter.

The efficiency with which a firm uses its net long-term assets is measured by the following two ratios: net long-term assets as a percent of sales and net long-term asset turnover, defined as

$$\text{Net long-term asset turnover} = \frac{\text{Sales}}{\text{Net long-term assets}}$$

Property plant and equipment (PP&E) is the most important long-term asset in a firm's balance sheet. The efficiency with which a firm's PP&E is used is measured either by the ratio of PP&E to sales or by the PP&E turnover ratio:

$$\text{PP\&E turnover} = \frac{\text{Sales}}{\text{Net property, plant, and equipment}}$$

Key Analysis Questions

The ratios discussed in the two preceding sections allow the analyst to explore a number of business questions:

- How well does the company manage its inventory? Does the company use modern manufacturing techniques? Does it have good vendor and logistics management systems? If inventory ratios are changing, what is the underlying business reason? Are new products being planned? Is there a mismatch between the demand forecasts and actual sales?
- How well does the company manage its credit policies? Are these policies consistent with its marketing strategy? Is the company artificially increasing sales by loading the distribution channels?
- Is the company taking advantage of trade credit? Is it relying too much on trade credit? If so, what are the implicit costs?
- Is the company's investment in plant and equipment consistent with its competitive strategy? Does the company have a sound policy of acquisitions and divestitures?

Table 5-6 shows the asset turnover ratios for Wal-Mart and Target. Wal-Mart is extremely efficient at managing its working capital needs. Its negative operating working capital turnover ratio indicates that it finances its accounts receivable, inventory, and other operating current assets through accounts payable and other accrued liabilities. This is due to a combination of its efficient supply chain management, the fact that it does not have credit card operations that lead to large receivables, and its negotiating power based on its size, which results in favorable trade credit terms from its vendors. Wal-Mart's working capital management has been relatively stable for 2004 and 2005, though its long-term asset utilization deteriorated slightly, as both net long-term asset turnover and PP&E turnover declined.

Target's working capital management trails that of Wal-Mart by a significant margin. Target still has a large portion of its asset base tied up in operating working capital. Target's strategy of financing its customers through its in-house credit card operations leads to large accounts receivables and lengthy days' accounts receivable—38 days in 2005 compared to two days for Wal-Mart. In addition, its customer focus and higher margins lead to slower-turning inventory and long-term assets.

TABLE 5-6	Asset Management Ratios		
Ratio	**Wal-Mart FY2005**	**Wal-Mart FY2004**	**Target FY2005**
Operating working capital/Sales	−0.7%	−0.6%	7.5%
Net long-term assets/Sales	24.7%	23.3%	31.1%
PP&E/Sales	21.9%	20.5%	32.0%
Operating working capital turnover	−148.9	−156.4	13.3
Net long-term assets turnover	4.0	4.3	3.2
PP&E turnover	4.6	4.9	3.1
Accounts receivable turnover	182.7	228.2	9.6
Inventory turnover	8.0	8.1	6.5
Accounts payable turnover	10.9	11.1	6.0
Days' accounts receivable	2.0	1.6	38.1
Days' inventory	45.6	45.1	56.3
Days' account payable	33.6	32.7	60.4

Evaluating Financial Management: Analyzing Financial Leverage

Financial leverage enables a firm to have an asset base larger than its equity. The firm can augment its equity through borrowing and the creation of other liabilities such as accounts payable, accrued liabilities, and deferred taxes. Financial leverage increases a firm's ROE as long as the cost of the liabilities is less than the return from investing these funds. In this respect, it is important to distinguish between interest-bearing liabilities such as notes payable, other forms of short-term and long-term debt that carry an explicit interest charge, and other liabilities. Some of these other forms of liability, such as accounts payable or deferred taxes, do not carry any interest charge at all. Others, such as capital lease obligations and pension obligations, carry an implicit interest charge. Finally, some firms carry large cash balances or investments in marketable securities. These balances reduce a firm's net debt because conceptually the firm can pay down its debt using its cash and short-term investments.

While financial leverage can potentially benefit a firm's shareholders, it can also increase their risk. Unlike equity, liabilities have predefined payment terms, and the firm faces risk of financial distress if it fails to meet these commitments. There are a number of ratios to evaluate the degree of risk arising from a firm's financial leverage.

Current Liabilities and Short-Term Liquidity

The following ratios are useful in evaluating the risk related to a firm's current liabilities:

$$\text{Current ratio} = \frac{\text{Current assets}}{\text{Current liabilities}}$$

$$\text{Quick ratio} = \frac{\text{Cash} + \text{Short-term investments} + \text{Accounts receivable}}{\text{Current liabilities}}$$

$$\text{Cash ratio} = \frac{\text{Cash} + \text{Marketable securities}}{\text{Current liabilities}}$$

$$\text{Operating cash flow ratio} = \frac{\text{Cash flow from operations}}{\text{Current liabilities}}$$

All the above ratios attempt to measure the firm's ability to repay its current liabilities. The first three compare a firm's current liabilities with its short-term assets that can be used to repay those liabilities. The fourth ratio focuses on the ability of the firm's operations to generate the resources needed to repay its current liabilities.

Since both current assets and current liabilities have comparable duration, the current ratio is a key index of a firm's short-term liquidity. Analysts view a current ratio of more than one to be an indication that the firm can cover its current liabilities from the cash realized from its current assets. However, the firm can face a short-term liquidity problem even with a current ratio exceeding one when some of its current assets are not easy to liquidate. Quick ratio and cash ratio capture the firm's ability to cover its current liabilities from liquid assets. Quick ratio assumes that the firm's accounts receivable are liquid. This is true in industries where the credit-worthiness of the customers is beyond dispute, or when receivables are collected in a very short period. When these conditions do not prevail, cash ratio, which considers only cash and marketable securities, is a better indication of a firm's ability to cover its current liabilities in an emergency. Operating cash flow is another measure of the firm's ability to cover its current liabilities from cash generated from operations of the firm.

The liquidity ratios for Wal-Mart and Target are shown in Table 5-7. On all dimensions of liquidity, Target has a greater cushion than Wal-Mart. None of Wal-Mart's liquidity ratios were higher than one in either 2004 or 2005. Wal-Mart's lower level of liquidity reflects its tight working capital management. Given its financial strength and stability, Wal-Mart's short-term creditors are probably not very concerned about its ability to fulfill its obligations in a timely manner. Target's creditors are also likely to be very comfortable with the firm's liquidity situation.

TABLE 5-7 Liquidity Ratios			
Ratio	**Wal-Mart FY2005**	**Wal-Mart FY2004**	**Target FY2005**
Current ratio	0.90	0.92	1.69
Quick ratio	0.17	0.17	0.94
Cash ratio	0.13	0.14	0.27
Operating cash flow ratio	0.43	0.42	0.58

Debt and Long-Term Solvency

A company's financial leverage is also influenced by its debt financing policy. There are several potential benefits from debt financing. First, debt is typically cheaper than equity because the firm promises predefined payment terms to debt holders. Second, in most countries interest on debt financing is tax deductible whereas dividends to shareholders are not tax deductible. Third, debt financing can impose discipline on the firm's management and motivate it to reduce wasteful expenditures. Fourth, for non-public debt, it is likely to be easier for management to communicate their proprietary information on the firm's strategies and prospects to private lenders than to public capital markets. Such communication can potentially reduce a firm's cost of capital. For all these reasons, it is advantageous for firms to use at least some debt in their capital structure. Too much reliance on debt financing, however, is potentially costly to the firm's shareholders. The firm will face financial distress if it defaults on the interest and principal payments. Debt holders also impose covenants on the firm, restricting the firm's operating, investment, and financing decisions.

The optimal capital structure for a firm is determined primarily by its business risk. A firm's cash flows are highly predictable when there is little competition or there is little threat of technological changes. Such firms have low business risk and hence they can rely heavily on debt financing. In contrast, if a firm's operating cash flows are highly volatile and its capital expenditure needs are unpredictable, it may have to rely primarily on equity financing. Managers' attitude towards risk and financial flexibility also often determine a firm's debt policies.

There are a number of ratios which help the analyst in this area. To evaluate the mix of debt and equity in a firm's capital structure, the following ratios are useful:

$$\text{Liabilities-to-equity ratio} = \frac{\text{Total liabilities}}{\text{Shareholders' equity}}$$

$$\text{Debt-to-equity ratio} = \frac{\text{Short-term debt} + \text{Long-term debt}}{\text{Shareholders' equity}}$$

Net-debt-to-equity ratio

$$= \frac{\text{Short-term debt} + \text{Long-term debt} - \text{Cash and marketable securities}}{\text{Shareholders' equity}}$$

Debt-to-capital ratio =

$$\frac{\text{Short-term debt} + \text{Long-term debt}}{\text{Short-term debt} + \text{Long-term debt} + \text{Shareholders' equity}}$$

Net-debt-to-net-capital ratio =

$$\frac{\text{Interest bearing liabilities} - \text{Cash and marketable securities}}{\text{Interest bearing liabilities} - \text{Cash and marketable securities} + \text{Shareholders' equity}}$$

The first ratio reformulates one of the three primary ratios underlying ROE, the assets-to-equity ratio (it is the assets-to-equity ratio minus one). The second ratio provides an indication of how many dollars of debt financing the firm is using for each dollar invested by its shareholders. The third ratio uses net debt, which is total debt minus cash and marketable securities, as the measure of a firm's borrowings. The fourth and fifth ratios measure debt as a proportion of total capital. In calculating all the above ratios, it is important to include all interest-bearing obligations, whether the interest charge is explicit or implicit. Recall that examples of line items which carry an implicit interest charge include capital lease obligations and pension obligations.

Analysts sometimes include any potential off-balance-sheet obligations that a firm may have, such as non-cancellable operating leases, in the definition of a firm's debt.

The ease with which a firm can meet its interest payments is an indication of the degree of risk associated with its debt policy. The interest coverage ratio provides a measure of this construct:

$$\text{Interest coverage (earnings basis)} = \frac{\text{Net income} + \text{Interest expense} + \text{Tax expense}}{\text{Interest expense}}$$

Interest coverage (cash flow basis)

$$= \frac{\text{Cash flow from operations} + \text{Interest expense} + \text{Taxes paid}}{\text{Interest expense}}$$

One can also calculate coverage ratios that measure a firm's ability to measure all fixed financial obligations, such as interest payment, lease payments, and debt repayments, by appropriately redefining the numerator and denominator in the above ratios. In doing so it is important to remember that some fixed charge payments, such as interest and lease rentals, are paid with pretax dollars while others, such as debt repayments, are made with after-tax dollars.

The earnings-based coverage ratio indicates the dollars of earnings available for each dollar of required interest payment; the cash-flow-based coverage ratio indicates the dollars of cash generated by operations for each dollar of required interest payment. In both these ratios, the denominator is the interest expense. In the numerator we add taxes back because taxes are computed only after interest expense is deducted. A coverage ratio of one implies that the firm is barely covering its interest expense through its operating activities, which is a very risky situation. The larger the coverage ratio, the greater the cushion the firm has to meet interest obligations.

Key Analysis Questions

Some of the business questions to ask when the analyst is examining a firm's debt policies follow:

- Does the company have enough debt? Is it exploiting the potential benefits of debt—interest tax shields, management discipline, and easier communication?
- Does the company have too much debt given its business risk? What type of debt covenant restrictions does the firm face? Is it bearing the costs of too much debt, risking potential financial distress and reduced business flexibility?
- What is the company doing with the borrowed funds? Investing in working capital? Investing in fixed assets? Are these investments profitable?
- Is the company borrowing money to pay dividends? If so, what is the justification?

We show debt and coverage ratios for Wal-Mart and Target in Table 5-8.

Wal-Mart's net debt to equity ratios in 2004 and 2005 were close to 50 percent, implying it financed its net assets conservatively with an equal mix of debt and equity. Target's leverage ratios in 2005 were very similar to those of Wal-Mart.

TABLE 5-8	Debt and Coverage Ratios		
Ratio	Wal-Mart FY2005	Wal-Mart FY2004	Target FY2005
Liabilities to equity	1.41	1.37	1.48
Debt to equity	0.64	0.61	0.73
Net debt to equity	0.53	0.49	0.56
Debt to capital	0.39	0.38	0.42
Net debt to net capital	0.34	0.33	0.36
Net debt to equity, including operating lease obligations[a]	0.61	0.58	0.65
Interest coverage (earnings based)	11.80	13.13	8.26
Interest coverage (cash flow based)	15.86	16.79	12.10
Fixed charges coverage, including lease payments (earnings based)	6.92	7.32	6.63
Fixed charges coverage, including lease payments (cash flow based)	9.15	9.23	9.60

[a] Present value of leases estimated using the cost of debt and an approximation of average life

Given that both companies rely on operating leases for about one-fifth of their stores, it is important to estimate the impact of the operating lease obligations on the firms' leverage and interest coverage. Using the respective costs of debt and an estimate of average life of the operating leases, it is possible to form an estimate of the implicit leverage on the balance sheet of both firms. As Table 5-8 shows, the net debt to equity ratio goes from 0.53 to 0.61 for Wal-Mart if the impact of operating leases is included. The ratio for Target increases from 0.56 to 0.65 for the year 2005.

In general, both companies are in an extremely comfortable situation relative to their fixed obligations, even after factoring in operating leases commitments. Wal-Mart's coverage ratios are consistently superior to those of Target, primarily as a result of its higher profitability.

Ratios of Disaggregated Data

So far we have discussed how to compute ratios using information in the financial statements. Analysts often probe the above ratios further by using disaggregated financial and physical data. For example, for a multibusiness company, one could analyze the information by individual business segments. Such an analysis can reveal potential differences in the performance of each business unit, allowing the analyst to pinpoint areas where a company's strategy is working and where it is not. It is also possible to probe financial ratios further by computing ratios of physical data pertaining to a company's operations. The appropriate physical data to look at varies from industry to industry. As an example in retailing, one could compute productivity statistics such as sales per store, sales per square foot, customer transactions per store, and average amount of sale per customer transaction. In the hotel industry, room occupancy rates provide important information; in the cellular telephone industry, acquisition cost per new subscriber and subscriber retention rate are important. These disaggregated ratios are particularly useful for young firms and young industries such as Internet firms, where accounting data may not fully capture the business economics due to conservative accounting rules.

Putting It All Together: Assessing Sustainable Growth Rate

Analysts often use the concept of sustainable growth as a way to evaluate a firm's ratios in a comprehensive manner. A firm's sustainable growth rate is defined as

$$\text{Sustainable growth rate} = \text{ROE} \times (1 - \text{Dividend payout ratio})$$

We already discussed the analysis of ROE in the previous four sections. The dividend payout ratio is defined as

$$\text{Divided payout ratio} = \frac{\text{Cash dividends paid}}{\text{Net income}}$$

A firm's dividend payout ratio is a measure of its dividend policy. Firms pay dividends for several reasons. They provide a way to return to shareholders any cash generated in excess of the firm's operating and investment needs. When there are information asymmetries between a firm's managers and its shareholders, dividend payments can serve as a signal to shareholders about managers' expectation of the firm's future prospects. Firms may also pay dividends to attract a certain type of shareholder base.

Sustainable growth rate is the rate at which a firm can grow while keeping its profitability and financial policies unchanged. A firm's return on equity and its dividend payout policy determine the pool of funds available for growth. Of course the firm can grow at a rate different from its sustainable growth rate if its profitability, payout policy, or financial leverage changes. Therefore, the sustainable growth rate provides a benchmark against which a firm's growth plans can be evaluated. Figure 5-2 shows how a firm's sustainable growth rate can be linked to all the ratios discussed in this chapter. These linkages allow an analyst to examine the drivers of a firm's current sustainable growth rate. If the firm intends to grow at a higher rate than its sustainable growth rate, one could assess which of the ratios are likely to change in the process.

Key Analysis Questions

Analysis of sustainable growth can lead to asking the following types of business questions:
- How quickly can the firm grow its business by keeping its profitability and financial policies unchanged?
- If it intends growing faster, where is the growth going to come from? Is management expecting profitability to increase? Or asset productivity to improve? Are these expectations realistic? Is the firm planning for these changes?
- If the firm is planning to increase its financial leverage or cut dividends, what is the likely impact of these financial policy changes?

| FIGURE 5-2 | Sustainable Growth Rate Framework for Financial Ratio Analysis |

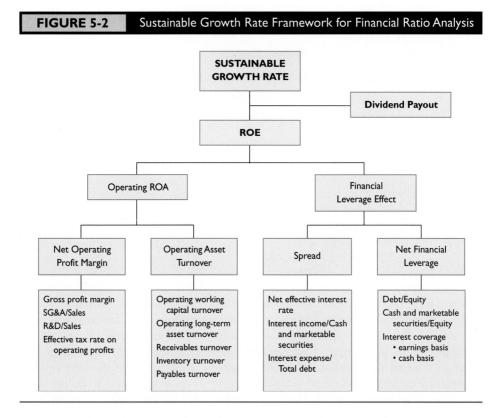

Table 5-9 shows the sustainable growth rate and its components for Wal-Mart and Target. Recall that Wal-Mart was considerably more profitable than Target in 2005. Despite its higher return on equity, Wal-Mart's higher dividend payout ratio narrows the sustainable growth rate gap between Target and itself. Wal-Mart's actual sales and asset growth rates in 2005 were lower than implied by its 2004 sustainable growth rate due to a number of factors including a drop in operating asset turnover and a share repurchase program. Wal-Mart grew sales by only 9.5 percent and its operating ROA declined while its leverage increased marginally.

| TABLE 5-9 | Sustainable Growth Rate |

Ratio	Wal-Mart FY2005	Wal-Mart FY2004	Target FY2005
Return on equity	22.7%	23.5%	18.5%
Dividend payout ratio	22.4%	21.6%	13.2%
Sustainable growth rate	17.7%	18.5%	16.0%

In 2005 it appears that Wal-Mart's and Target's sustainable growth rates are converging. This implies that growth rates for the two firms are about the same if they choose to maintain their current operating and financing policies.

Historical Patterns of Ratios for U.S. Firms

To provide a benchmark for analysis, Table 5-10 reports historical values of the key ratios discussed in this chapter. These ratios are calculated using financial statement data for all publicly listed U.S. companies. The table shows the values of ROE, its key components, and the sustainable growth rate for each of the years 1988 to 2005, and the average for this period. The data show that the average ROE over this time frame has been 10.5 percent, average operating ROA has been 8.5 percent, and the average spread between operating ROA and net borrowing costs after tax has been 2.1 percent. The average sustainable growth rate for U.S. companies during this period has been 4.9 percent. Of course, an individual company's ratios might depart from these economy-wide averages for a number of reasons, such as industry effects, company strategies, and management effectiveness. Nonetheless, the average values in the table serve as useful benchmarks in financial analysis.

TABLE 5-10	Historical Values of Key Financial Ratios

Year	ROE	NOPAT Margin	Operating Asset Turnover	Operating ROA	Spread	Net Financial Leverage	Sustainable Growth Rate
1988	13.1%	7.7%	1.73	12.0%	2.7%	0.88	6.3%
1989	11.5%	7.8%	1.65	10.8%	2.6%	1.11	5.1%
1990	9.7%	6.9%	1.64	10.1%	1.5%	1.21	3.5%
1991	6.8%	6.3%	1.56	7.4%	0.0%	1.22	0.7%
1992	4.4%	4.3%	1.60	6.1%	−0.6%	1.17	−1.6%
1993	9.1%	5.0%	1.67	6.6%	0.9%	1.19	2.9%
1994	13.9%	7.2%	1.76	10.8%	3.8%	1.19	7.9%
1995	13.8%	6.1%	1.82	8.3%	6.8%	1.15	7.4%
1996	14.7%	6.7%	1.82	9.3%	7.5%	1.18	8.7%
1997	13.9%	7.6%	1.82	10.4%	3.7%	1.16	8.3%
1998	13.1%	8.1%	1.76	9.7%	2.3%	1.28	7.4%
1999	13.6%	8.0%	1.69	9.9%	3.8%	1.29	8.5%
2000	10.1%	7.3%	1.71	8.0%	1.8%	1.35	5.4%
2001	1.3%	3.9%	1.47	2.8%	−3.3%	1.29	−2.7%
2002	−0.3%	2.4%	1.35	−1.1%	−6.4%	1.35	−4.4%
2003	13.2%	8.2%	1.58	9.4%	3.3%	1.46	8.6%
2004	13.2%	8.0%	1.70	10.0%	3.2%	1.36	8.3%
2005	13.9%	9.1%	1.78	12.1%	3.5%	1.12	8.3%
Average	**10.5%**	**6.7%**	**1.67**	**8.5%**	**2.1%**	**1.22**	**4.9%**

Ratios are based on beginning balance sheet data.

Source: Financial statement data for all publicly traded U.S. companies between 1987 and 2005, listed in Standard & Poor's Compustat database.

CASH FLOW ANALYSIS

The ratio analysis discussion focused on analyzing a firm's income statement (net profit margin analysis) or its balance sheet (asset turnover and financial leverage). The analyst can get further insights into the firm's operating, investing, and financing policies by examining its cash flows. Cash flow analysis also provides an indication of the quality of the information in the firm's income statement and balance sheet. As before, we will illustrate the concepts discussed in this section using Wal-Mart's and Target's cash flows.

Cash Flow and Funds Flow Statements

All U.S. companies are required to include a statement of cash flows in their financial statements under Statement of Financial Accounts Standard No. 95 (SFAS 95). In the cash flow statement, firms report their cash flows in three categories: cash flow from operations, cash flow related to investments, and cash flow related to financing activities. Cash flow from operations is the cash generated by the firm from the sale of goods and services after paying for the cost of inputs and operations. Cash flow related to investment activities shows the cash paid for capital expenditures, intercorporate investments, acquisitions, and cash received from the sales of long-term assets. Cash flow related to financing activities shows the cash raised from (or paid to) the firm's stockholders and debt holders.

Firms use two cash flow statement formats: the direct format and the indirect format. The key difference between the two formats is the way they report cash flow from operating activities. In the direct cash flow format, which is used by only a small number of firms, operating cash receipts and disbursements are reported directly. In the indirect format, firms derive their operating cash flows by making adjustments to net income. Because the indirect format links the cash flow statement with the firm's income statement and balance sheet, many analysts and managers find this format more useful. As a result, the FASB required firms using the direct format to report operating cash flows in the indirect format as well.

Recall from Chapter 3 that net income differs from operating cash flows because revenues and expenses are measured on an accrual basis. There are two types of accruals embedded in net income. First, there are current accruals like credit sales and unpaid expenses. Current accruals result in changes in a firm's current assets (such as accounts receivable, inventory, prepaid expenses) and current liabilities (such as accounts payable and accrued liabilities). The second type of accruals included in the income statement is noncurrent accruals such as depreciation, deferred taxes, and equity income from unconsolidated subsidiaries. To derive cash flow from operations from net income, adjustments have to be made for both these types of accruals. In addition, adjustments have to be made for nonoperating gains included in net income such as profits from asset sales.

Some firms outside the U.S. report a funds flow statement rather than a cash flow statement of the type described above. Prior to SFAS 95, U.S. firms also reported a similar statement. Funds flow statements show working capital flows, not cash flows. It is useful for analysts to know how to convert a funds flow statement into a cash flow statement.

Funds flow statements typically provide information on a firm's working capital from operations, defined as net income adjusted for noncurrent accruals, and gains from the sale of long-term assets. As discussed above, cash flow from operations essentially involves a third adjustment, the adjustment for current accruals. Thus it is relatively straightforward to convert working capital from operations to cash flow from operations by making the relevant adjustments for current accruals related to operations.

Information on current accruals can be obtained by examining changes in a firm's current assets and current liabilities. Typically, operating accruals represent changes in all the current asset accounts other than cash and cash equivalents, and changes in all the current liabilities other than notes payable and the current portion of long-term debt.[10] Cash from operations can be calculated as follows:

Working capital from operations
− Increase (or + decrease) in accounts receivable
− Increase (or + decrease) in inventory
− Increase (or + decrease) in other current assets excluding cash and cash equivalents
+ Increase (or − decrease) in accounts payable
+ Increase (or − decrease) in other current liabilities excluding debt.

Funds flow statements also often do not classify investment and financing flows. In such a case, the analyst has to classify the line items in the funds flow statement into these two categories by evaluating the nature of the business transactions that give rise to the flow represented by the line items.

Analyzing Cash Flow Information

Cash flow analysis can be used to address a variety of questions regarding a firm's cash flow dynamics:

- How strong is the firm's internal cash flow generation? Is the cash flow from operations positive or negative? If it is negative, why? Is it because the company is growing? Is it because its operations are unprofitable? Or is it having difficulty managing its working capital properly?
- Does the company have the ability to meet its short-term financial obligations, such as interest payments, from its operating cash flow? Can it continue to meet these obligations without reducing its operating flexibility?
- How much cash did the company invest in growth? Are these investments consistent with its business strategy? Did the company use internal cash flow to finance growth, or did it rely on external financing?
- Did the company pay dividends from internal free cash flow, or did it have to rely on external financing? If the company had to fund its dividends from external sources, is the company's dividend policy sustainable?
- What type of external financing does the company rely on? Equity, short-term debt, or long-term debt? Is the financing consistent with the company's overall business risk?
- Does the company have excess cash flow after making capital investments? Is it a long-term trend? What plans does management have to deploy the free cash flow?

While the information in reported cash flow statements can be used to answer the above questions directly in the case of some firms, it may not be easy to always do so for a number of reasons. First, even though SFAS 95 provides broad guidelines on the format of a cash flow statement, there is still significant variation across firms in how cash flow data are disclosed. Therefore, to facilitate a systematic analysis and comparison across firms, analysts often recast the information in the cash flow statement using their own cash flow model. Second, firms include interest expense and interest income in computing their cash flow from operating activities. However, these two items are not strictly related to a firm's operations. Interest expense is a function of financial leverage, and interest income is derived from financial assets rather than operating assets. Therefore it is useful to restate the cash flow statement to take this into account.

Analysts use a number of different approaches to restate the cash flow data. One such model is shown in Table 5-11. This presents cash flow from operations in two stages. The first step computes cash flow from operations before operating working capital investments. In computing this cash flow, the model excludes interest expense and interest income. To compute this number starting with a firm's net income, an analyst adds back three types of items: (1) after-tax net interest expense because this is a financing item that will be considered later; (2) nonoperating gains or losses typically arising out of asset disposals or asset write-offs because these items are investment related and will be considered later; and (3) long-term operating accruals such as depreciation and deferred taxes because these are non-cash operating charges.

TABLE 5-11	Cash Flow Analysis		
Ratio	**Wal-Mart FY2005**	**Wal-Mart FY2004**	**Target FY2005**
Net Income	**11,231.0**	**10,267.0**	**2,408.0**
After-tax net interest expense (income)	876.2	716.2	315.0
Non-operating losses (gains)	0.0	0.0	70.0
Long-term operating accruals	5,208.0	5,046.0	1,813.0
Operating cash flow before working capital investments	**17,315.2**	**16,029.2**	**4,606.0**
Net (investments in) or liquidation of operating working capital	1,194.0	(269.0)	160.0
Operating cash flow before investment in long-term assets	**18,509.2**	**15,760.2**	**4,766.0**
Net (investment in) or liquidation of operating long-term assets	**(14,183.0)**	**(12,351.0)**	**(4,149.0)**
Free cash flow available to debt and equity	4,326.2	3,409.2	617.0
After-tax net interest income (expense)	(876.2)	(716.2)	(315.0)
Net debt (repayment) or issuance	4,018.0	4,041.0	386.0
Free cash flow available to equity	**7,468.0**	**6,734.0**	**688.0**
Dividend (payments)	(2,511.0)	(2,214.0)	(318.0)
Net stock issuance (repurchase), and other equity changes	(4,031.0)	(4,231.0)	(1,026.0)
Net increase (decrease) in cash balance	**926.0**	**289.0**	**(656.0)**
Cash flow from Discontinued Operations	0.0	0.0	0.0
Net increase (decrease) in cash balance – As reported	**926.0**	**289.0**	**(656.0)**

Several factors affect a firm's ability to generate positive cash flow from operations. Healthy firms that are in a steady state should generate more cash from their customers than they spend on operating expenses. In contrast, growing firms—especially those with heavy outlays for research and development, advertising and marketing, or building an organization to sustain future growth—may experience negative operating cash flow. Firms' working capital management also affects whether they generate positive cash flow from operations. Firms in the growing stage typically use cash flow for operating working capital items such as funding customers (accounts receivable) and purchasing inventories (net of accounts payable financing from suppliers). Net investments in working capital are a function of firms' credit policies (accounts receivable), payment policies (payables, prepaid expenses, and accrued liabilities), and expected growth in sales (inventories). Thus, in interpreting firms' cash flow from operations after working capital, it is important to keep in mind their growth strategy, industry characteristics, and credit policies.

The cash flow analysis model next focuses on cash flows related to long-term investments. These investments take the form of capital expenditures, intercorporate investments, and mergers and acquisitions. Any positive operating cash flow after making operating working capital investments allows the firm to pursue long-term growth opportunities. If the firm's operating cash flows after working capital investments are not sufficient to finance its long-term investments, it has to rely on external financing to fund its growth. Such firms have less flexibility to pursue long-term investments than those that can fund their growth internally. There are both costs and benefits from being able to fund growth internally. The cost is that managers can use the internally generated free cash flow to fund unprofitable investments. Such wasteful capital expenditures are less likely if managers are forced to rely on external capital suppliers. However, reliance on external capital markets may make it difficult for managers to undertake long-term risky investments if it is not easy to communicate to the capital markets the benefits from such investments.

Any excess cash flow after these long-term investments is free cash flow that is available for both debt holders and equity holders. Debt cash transactions include interest payments and principal payments as well as new borrowing. Cash flow after payments to debt holders is free cash flow available to equity holders. Cash transactions involving shareholders include dividend payments and stock repurchases, as well as issues of new equity.

Firms with negative free cash flow to both debt and equity have to borrow additional funds to meet their interest and debt repayment obligations, cut dividend payments, or issue additional equity. Managers of firms in this situation are often reluctant to cut dividends for fear that it will be viewed negatively by investors. While this may be feasible in the short term, it is not prudent for a firm to continue to pay dividends to equity holders unless it has a positive free cash flow on a sustained basis. In contrast, firms with large positive free cash flow to debt and equity run the risk of making unproductive investments to pursue growth for its own sake. An analyst, therefore, should carefully examine the investment plans of such firms.

The model in Table 5-11 suggests that the analyst should focus on a number of cash flow measures: (1) cash flow from operations before investment in working capital and interest payments, to examine whether or not the firm is able to generate a cash surplus from operations; (2) cash flow from operations after investment in working capital, to assess how the firm's working capital is being managed and whether or not it has the flexibility to invest in long-term assets for future growth; (3) free cash flow available to debt and equity holders, to assess a firm's ability to meet its interest and principal payments; and (4) free cash flow available to equity holders, to assess the firm's financial ability to sustain its dividend policy and to identify potential agency problems from excess free cash flow. These measures have to be evaluated in the context of the company's business, its growth strategy, and its financial policies. Further, changes in these measures from year to year provide valuable information on the stability of the cash flow dynamics of the firm.

Key Analysis Questions

The cash flow model in Table 5-11 can be also used to assess a firm's earnings quality. The reconciliation of a firm's net income with its cash flow from operations facilitates this exercise. Following are some of the questions an analyst can probe in this respect:

- Are there significant differences between a firm's net income and its operating cash flow? Is it possible to clearly identify the sources of this difference? Which accounting policies contribute to this difference? Are there any one-time events contributing to this difference?
- Is the relationship between cash flow and net income changing over time? Why? Is it because of changes in business conditions or because of changes in the firm's accounting policies and estimates?
- What is the time lag between the recognition of revenues and expenses and the receipt and disbursement of cash flows? What type of uncertainties need to be resolved in between?
- Are the changes in receivables, inventories, and payables normal? If not, is there adequate explanation for the changes?

Finally, as we will discuss in Chapter 7, free cash flow available to debt and equity and free cash flow available to equity are critical inputs into the cash-flow-based valuation of firms' assets and equity, respectively.

Analysis of Wal-Mart's and Target's Cash Flow

Both Wal-Mart and Target reported their cash flows using the indirect cash flow statement. Table 5-11 recasts these statements using the approach discussed above so that we can analyze the two companies' cash flow dynamics.

The cash flow analysis presented in Table 5-11 shows that Wal-Mart had an operating cash flow before working capital investments of $17.3 billion in 2005. The difference between its earnings and this cash flow is attributable primarily to depreciation and amortization charges, which is a non-cash expense that is included in the company's income statement.

In 2005 Wal-Mart was able to generate a further $1.2 billion from the liquidation of operating working capital, due in large part to an increase in its accounts payable. As mentioned before, Wal-Mart's size and the volume of its purchases make it an attractive client to most suppliers, enabling it to manage its relations with suppliers to generate additional cash flow. As a result of this improved working capital management, Wal-Mart had an operating cash flow before investment in long-term assets of $18.5 billion. In 2004 Wal-Mart also generated significant cash flows from its operations despite making a small net investment in operating working capital.

In both years Wal-Mart was able to finance substantial investments in long-term assets from cash flow from operations. The firm invested $12.4 billion and $14.2 billion in long-term assets in 2004 and 2005, respectively, still leaving positive cash flow for its debt and equity holders. Since Wal-Mart was a net borrower during this period, free cash flow available to its equity holders exceeded that available to debt and equity. The company utilized this free cash flow to pay regular dividends, to buy back company shares, and to build up its cash balance.

Like Wal-Mart, Target's non-cash operating charges had a significant impact on the firm's net income. Operating cash flow before working capital investments was 70 percent higher than net income in 2005. Despite increases in accounts receivables and inventory, Target was able to reduce its working capital investments in 2005 by increasing use of supplier credit through accounts payable and other accrued liabilities.

In 2005 Target used $4.1 billion of its operating cash flow to invest in long-term assets, primarily to open new stores and refurbish existing ones, leaving $617.0 million available to debt and equity holders. The company was also a net borrower, with a modest increase in outstanding debt. As a result, $688 million was available for stockholders. Dividends and stock buybacks were $1,344 million, leading to a decline in the cash balance in 2005.

SUMMARY

This chapter presents two key tools of financial analysis: ratio analysis and cash flow analysis. Both these tools allow the analyst to examine a firm's performance and its financial condition given its strategy and goals. Ratio analysis involves assessing the firm's income statement and balance sheet data. Cash flow analysis relies on the firm's cash flow statement.

The starting point for ratio analysis is the company's ROE. The next step is to evaluate the three drivers of ROE, which are net profit margin, asset turnover, and financial leverage. Net profit margin reflects a firm's operating management, asset turnover reflects its investment management, and financial leverage reflects its financing policies. Each of these areas can be further probed by examining a number of ratios. For example, common-sized income statement analysis allows a detailed examination of a firm's net margins. Similarly, turnover of key working capital accounts such as accounts receivable, inventory, and accounts payable, and turnover of the firm's fixed assets allow further examination of a firm's asset utilization. Finally, short-term liquidity ratios, debt policy ratios, and coverage ratios provide a means of examining a firm's financial leverage.

A firm's sustainable growth rate—the rate at which it can grow without altering its operating, investment, and financing policies—is determined by its ROE and its dividend policy. The concept of sustainable growth provides a way to integrate the different elements of ratio analysis and to evaluate whether or not a firm's growth strategy is sustainable. If a firm's plans call for growing at a rate above its current sustainable rate, then one can analyze which of the firm's ratios is likely to change in the future.

Cash flow analysis supplements ratio analysis in examining a firm's operating activities, investment management, and financial risks. Firms in the U.S. are currently required to report a cash flow statement summarizing their operating, investment, and financing cash flows. Firms in other countries typically report working capital flows, but it is possible to use this information to create a cash flow statement.

Since there are wide variations across firms in the way cash flow data are reported, analysts often use a standard format to recast cash flow data. We discussed one such cash flow model in this chapter. This model allows the analyst to assess whether a firm's operations generate cash flow before investments in operating working capital, and how much cash is being invested in the firm's working capital. It also enables the analyst to calculate the firm's free cash flow after making long-term investments, which is an indication of the firm's ability to meet its debt and dividend payments. Finally, the cash flow analysis shows how the firm is financing itself, and whether its financing patterns are too risky.

The insights gained from analyzing a firm's financial ratios and its cash flows are valuable in forecasts of the firm's future prospects.

DISCUSSION QUESTIONS

1. Which of the following types of firms do you expect to have particularly high or low asset turnover? Explain why.
   - a supermarket
   - a pharmaceutical company
   - a jewelry retailer
   - a steel company

2. Which of the following types of firms do you expect to have high or low sales margins? Why?
   - a supermarket
   - a pharmaceutical company
   - a jewelry retailer
   - a software company

3. James Broker, an analyst with an established brokerage firm, comments: "The critical number I look at for any company is operating cash flow. If cash flows are less than earnings, I consider a company to be a poor performer and a poor investment prospect." Do you agree with this assessment? Why or why not?

4. In 2005 IBM had a return on equity of 26.7 percent, whereas Hewlett-Packard's return was only 6.4 percent. Use the decomposed ROE framework to provide possible reasons for this difference based on the data below:

	IBM	HP
NOPAT/Sales	9.0%	2.7%
Sales/Net Assets	2.16	2.73
Effective After Tax Interest Rate	2.4%	1.1%
Net Financial Leverage	0.42	−0.16

5. Joe Investor asserts, "A company cannot grow faster than its sustainable growth rate." True or false? Explain why.

6. What are the reasons for a firm having lower cash from operations than working capital from operations? What are the possible interpretations of these reasons?

7. ABC Company recognizes revenue at the point of shipment. Management decides to increase sales for the current quarter by filling all customer orders. Explain what impact this decision will have on
   • Days' receivable for the current quarter
   • Days' receivable for the next quarter
   • Sales growth for the current quarter
   • Sales growth for the next quarter
   • Return on sales for the current quarter
   • Return on sales for the next quarter

8. What ratios would you use to evaluate operating leverage for a firm?

9. What are the potential benchmarks that you could use to compare a company's financial ratios? What are the pros and cons of these alternatives?

10. In a period of rising prices, how would the following ratios be affected by the accounting decision to select LIFO, rather than FIFO, for inventory valuation?
   • Gross margin
   • Current ratio
   • Asset turnover
   • Debt-to-equity ratio
   • Average tax rate

NOTES

1. We will call the fiscal year ending January 31, 2006, as the year 2005, and the fiscal year ending January 31, 2005, as the year 2004.

2. In computing ROE, one can either use the beginning equity, ending equity, or an average of the two. Conceptually, the average equity is appropriate, particularly for rapidly growing companies. However, for most companies, this computational choice makes little difference as long as the analyst is consistent. Therefore, in practice most analysts use ending balances for simplicity. This comment applies to all ratios discussed in this chapter where one of the items in the ratio is a flow variable (items in the income statement or cash flow statement) and the other item is a stock variable (items in the balance sheet). Throughout this chapter we use the beginning balances of the stock variables.

3. We discuss in greater detail in Chapter 8 how to estimate a company's cost of equity capital. The cost of equity for Wal-Mart and Target is in the 10 to 12 percent range.

4. Strictly speaking, part of a cash balance is needed to run the firm's operations, so only the excess cash balance should be viewed as negative debt. However, firms do not provide

information on excess cash, so we subtract all cash balances in our definitions and computations. An alternative possibility is to subtract only short-term investments and ignore the cash balance completely.

5. See D. Nissim and S. Penman, "Ratio Analysis and Valuation: From Research to Practice," *Review of Accounting Studies* 6 (2001): 109–154, for a more detailed description of this approach.

6. Both Wal-Mart and Target have a solid credit rating and a relatively low cost of debt. Given the level of leverage, the weighted average cost of capital will be lower than the cost of equity. We will discuss in Chapter 8 how to estimate a company's weighted average cost of capital.

7. See *Taxes and Business Strategy* by Myron Scholes and Mark Wolfson (Englewood Cliffs, NJ: Prentice-Hall, 1992).

8. If firms that are analyzed use different inventory methods, the analyst can adjust to a common method for computing inventory turnover and days inventory. This can be accomplished by adjusting LIFO inventory and LIFO cost of sales to FIFO values using disclosures on the effect of LIFO inventory valuation in the inventory footnote disclosure.

9. There are a number of issues related to the calculation of these ratios in practice. First, in calculating all the turnover ratios, the assets used in the calculations can either be beginning of the year values, year-end values, or an average of the beginning and ending balances in a year. We use the beginning of the year values in our calculations. Second, strictly speaking, one should use credit sales to calculate accounts receivable turnover and days' receivables. But since it is usually difficult to obtain data on credit sales, total sales are used instead. Similarly, in calculating accounts payable turnover or days' payables, cost of goods sold is substituted for purchases for data availability reasons.

10. Changes in cash and marketable securities are excluded because this is the amount being explained by the cash flow statement. Changes in short-term debt and the current portion of long-term debt are excluded because these accounts represent financing flows, not operating flows.

APPENDIX
PART A: WAL-MART STORES, INC. FINANCIAL STATEMENTS

Wal-Mart's financial statements as reported by the firm are shown in the appendix to Chapter 4.

Note: The standardized statements shown below are generated by the BAV software tool and based on data reported by the Standard & Poor's Compustat database, which makes minor modifications to the data as reported by the firm. As a consequence, the standardized statements shown below will not be an exact match to the standardized statements shown in the appendix to Chapter 4.

Wal-Mart Stores, Inc.
Standardized Statements of Income ($ millions)

Fiscal Year Ended January 31	2006	2005	2004
Sales	**313,335**	**286,103**	**257,157**
Cost of Sales	235,691	215,493	195,247
Gross Profit	**77,644**	**70,610**	**61,910**
SG&A	56,733	51,105	44,909
Other Operating Expense	4,700	4,300	3,500
Operating Income	**16,211**	**15,205**	**13,501**
Investment Income	–	–	–
Other Income, net of Other Expense	2,476	2,006	1,668
Other Income	2,476	2,006	1,668
Other Expense	–	–	–
Net Interest Expense (Income)	1,329	1,106	976
Interest Income	248	201	164
Interest Expense	1,577	1,307	1,140
Minority Interest	324	249	214
Pre-Tax Income	**17,034**	**15,856**	**13,979**
Tax Expense	5,803	5,589	5,118
Unusual Gains, Net of Unusual Losses (after tax)	–	–	193
Net Income	**11,231**	**10,267**	**9,054**
Preferred Dividends	–	–	–
Net Income to Common	**11,231**	**10,267**	**9,054**

Source: Standard & Poor's Compustat database and BAV Model v4.3.

Wal-Mart Stores, Inc.
Standardized Balance Sheet ($ millions)

Year Beginning February 1	2006	2005	2004
Assets			
Cash and Marketable Securities	6,414	5,488	5,199
Accounts Receivable	2,662	1,715	1,254
Inventory	32,191	29,447	26,612
Other Current Assets	2,557	1,841	1,356
Total Current Assets	**43,824**	**38,491**	**34,421**
Long-Term Tangible Assets	79,290	68,567	58,530
Long-Term Intangible Assets	12,188	10,803	9,882
Other Long-Term Assets	2,885	2,362	2,079
Total Long-Term Assets	**94,363**	**81,732**	**70,491**
Total Assets	**138,187**	**120,223**	**104,912**
Liabilities			
Accounts Payable	25,373	21,671	19,332
Short-Term Debt	8,648	7,781	6,367
Other Current Liabilities	14,805	13,436	11,719
Total Current Liabilities	**48,826**	**42,888**	**37,418**
Long-Term Debt	30,171	23,669	20,099
Deferred Taxes	–	–	–
Other Long-Term Liabilities (non-interest bearing)	4,552	2,947	2,288
Total Long-Term Liabilities	**34,723**	**26,616**	**22,387**
Total Liabilities	**83,549**	**69,504**	**59,805**
Minority Interest	1,467	1,323	1,484
Shareholders' Equity			
Preferred Stock	–	–	–
Common Shareholders' Equity	53,171	49,396	43,623
Total Shareholders' Equity	**53,171**	**49,396**	**43,623**
Total Liabilities and Shareholders' Equity	**138,187**	**120,223**	**104,912**

Source: Standard & Poor's Compustat database and BAV Model v4.3.

Wal-Mart Stores, Inc.
Standardized Statements of Cash Flows ($ millions)

Year Ended January 31	2006	2005	2004
Net Income	11,231	10,267	9,054
After-tax net interest expense (income)	876	716	619
Non-operating losses (gains)	–	–	–
Long-term operating accruals	5,208	5,046	4,084
Depreciation and amortization	4,717	4,405	3,852
Other	491	641	232
Operating cash flow before working capital investments	**17,315**	**16,029**	**13,757**
Net (investments in) or liquidation of operating working capital	1,194	(269)	2,858
Operating cash flow before investment in long-term assets	**18,509**	**15,760**	**16,615**
Net (investment in) or liquidation of operating long-term assets	(14,183)	(12,351)	(8,312)
Free cash flow available to debt and equity	**4,326**	**3,409**	**8,303**
After-tax net interest income (expense)	(876)	(716)	(619)
Net debt (repayment) or issuance	4,018	4,041	941
Free cash flow available to equity	**7,468**	**6,734**	**8,625**
Dividend (payments)	(2,511)	(2,214)	(1,569)
Net stock issuance (repurchase), and other equity changes	(4,031)	(4,231)	(4,615)
Net increase (decrease) in cash balance	**926**	**289**	**2,441**

Source: Standard & Poor's Compustat database and BAV Model v4.3.

Wal-Mart Stores, Inc.
Condensed Statements of Income ($ millions)

Year Ended January 31	2006	2005	2004
Sales	**313,335**	**286,103**	**257,157**
Net Operating Profit after Tax	12,107	10,983	9,673
Net Income	11,231	10,267	9,054
+ Net Interest Expense after Tax	876	716	619
= **Net Operating Profit after Tax**	**12,107**	**10,983**	**9,673**
− Net Interest Expense after Tax	876	716	619
Interest Expense	1,577	1,307	1,140
− Interest Income	248	201	164
= Net Interest Expense (Income)	1,329	1,106	976
× (1 − Tax Expense/Pre-Tax Income)	0.659	0.648	0.634
= **Net Interest Expense after Tax**	**876**	**716**	**619**
= **Net Income**	**11,231**	**10,267**	**9,054**
− Preferred Stock Dividends	–	–	–
= **Net Income to Common**	**11,231**	**10,267**	**9,054**

Source: BAV Model v4.3.

Wal-Mart Stores, Inc.
Condensed Balance Sheet ($ millions)

Year Beginning February 1	2006	2005	2004
Beginning Net Working Capital	**(2,768)**	**(2,104)**	**(1,829)**
Accounts Receivable	2,662	1,715	1,254
+ Inventory	32,191	29,447	26,612
+ Other Current Assets	2,557	1,841	1,356
− Accounts Payable	25,373	21,671	19,332
− Other Current Liabilities	14,805	13,436	11,719
= **Beginning Net Working Capital**	**(2,768)**	**(2,104)**	**(1,829)**
+ **Beginning Net Long-Term Assets**	**88,344**	**77,462**	**66,719**
Long-Term Tangible Assets	79,290	68,567	58,530
+ Long-Term Intangible Assets	12,188	10,803	9,882
+ Other Long-Term Assets	2,885	2,362	2,079
− Minority Interest	1,467	1,323	1,484
− Deferred Taxes	–	–	–
− Other Long-Term Liabilities (non-interest bearing)	4,552	2,947	2,288
= **Beginning Net Long-Term Assets**	**88,344**	**77,462**	**66,719**
= **Total Assets**	**85,576**	**75,358**	**64,890**
Beginning Net Debt	**32,405**	**25,962**	**21,267**
Short-Term Debt	8,648	7,781	6,367
+ Long-Term Debt	30,171	23,669	20,099
− Cash	6,414	5,488	5,199
= **Beginning Net Debt**	**32,405**	**25,962**	**21,267**
+ **Beginning Preferred Stock**	–	–	–
+ **Beginning Shareholders' Equity**	53,171	49,396	43,623
= **Total Net Capital**	**85,576**	**75,358**	**64,890**

Source: BAV Model v4.3.

APPENDIX
PART B: TARGET CORPORATION FINANCIAL STATEMENTS

Note: The standardized statements shown below are generated by the BAV software tool and based on data reported by the Standard & Poor's Compustat database, which makes minor modifications to the data as reported by the firm. As a consequence, the standardized statements shown below will not be an exact match to the standardized statements that would result from the preceding manual standardization exercise.

Target Corporation
Standardized Statements of Income ($ millions)

Fiscal Year Ended January	2006	2005	2004
Sales	52,620	46,839	48,163
Cost of Sales	34,927	31,445	31,790
Gross Profit	17,693	15,394	16,373
SG&A	11,988	10,534	11,534
Other Operating Expense	1,409	1,259	1,320
Operating Income	4,296	3,601	3,519
Investment Income	–	–	–
Other Income, net of Other Expense	69	(89)	–
Other Income	69	(89)	–
Other Expense	–	–	–
Net Interest Expense (Income)	505	481	559
Interest Income	27	–	–
Interest Expense	532	481	559
Minority Interest	–	–	–
Pre-Tax Income	3,860	3,031	2,960
Tax Expense	1,452	1,146	1,119
Unusual Gains, Net of Unusual Losses (after tax)	–	1,313	–
Net Income	2,408	3,198	1,841
Preferred Dividends	–	–	–
Net Income to Common	2,408	3,198	1,841

Source: Standard & Poor's Compustat database and BAV Model v4.3.

Target Corporation
Standardized Balance Sheet ($ millions)

Year Beginning February	2006	2005	2004
Assets			
Cash and Marketable Securities	1,648	2,245	716
Accounts Receivable	6,226	5,497	5,776
Inventory	5,838	5,384	5,343
Other Current Assets	693	796	1,093
Total Current Assets	**14,405**	**13,922**	**12,928**
Long-Term Tangible Assets	19,038	16,860	16,969
Long-Term Intangible Assets	183	206	364
Other Long-Term Assets	1,369	1,305	1,131
Total Long-Term Assets	**20,590**	**18,371**	**18,464**
Total Assets	**34,995**	**32,293**	**31,392**
Liabilities			
Accounts Payable	6,268	5,779	5,448
Short-Term Debt	753	504	866
Other Current Liabilities	2,567	1,937	2,000
Total Current Liabilities	**9,588**	**8,220**	**8,314**
Long-Term Debt	9,119	9,034	10,217
Deferred Taxes	851	973	–
Other Long-Term Liabilities (non-interest bearing)	1,232	1,037	1,796
Total Long-Term Liabilities	**11,202**	**11,044**	**12,013**
Total Liabilities	**20,790**	**19,264**	**20,327**
Minority Interest	–	–	–
Shareholders' Equity			
Preferred Stock	–	–	–
Common Shareholders' Equity	14,205	13,029	11,065
Total Shareholders' Equity	**14,205**	**13,029**	**11,065**
Total Liabilities and Shareholders' Equity	**34,995**	**32,293**	**31,392**

Source: Standard & Poor's Compustat database and BAV Model v4.3.

Target Corporation
Standardized Statements of Cash Flows ($ millions)

Year Ended January	2006	2005	2004
Net Income	2,408	3,198	1,841
After-tax net interest expense (income)	315	299	348
Non-operating losses (gains)	70	59	54
Long-term operating accruals	1,813	120	2,131
Depreciation and amortization	1,409	1,259	1,320
Other	404	(1,139)	811
Operating cash flow before working capital investments	4,606	3,676	4,374
Net (investments in) or liquidation of operating working capital	160	(182)	(866)
Operating cash flow before investment in long-term assets	4,766	3,494	3,508
Net (investment in) or liquidation of operating long-term assets	(4,149)	1,179	(2,919)
Free cash flow available to debt and equity	617	4,673	589
After-tax net interest income (expense)	(315)	(299)	(348)
Net debt (repayment) or issuance	386	(1,477)	(72)
Free cash flow available to equity	688	2,897	169
Dividend (payments)	(318)	(272)	(237)
Net stock issuance (repurchase), and other equity changes	(1,026)	(1,088)	26
Net increase (decrease) in cash balance	**(656)**	**1,537**	**(42)**

Source: Standard & Poor's Compustat database and BAV Model v4.3.

Target Corporation
Condensed Statements of Income ($ millions)

Year Ended January	2006	2005	2004
Sales	52,620	46,839	48,163
Net Operating Profit after Tax	2,723	3,497	2,189
Net Income	2,408	3,198	1,841
+ Net Interest Expense after Tax	315	299	348
= Net Operating Profit after Tax	2,723	3,497	2,189
− Net Interest Expense after Tax	315	299	348
Interest Expense	532	481	559
− Interest Income	27	–	–
= Net Interest Expense (Income)	505	481	559
× (1 − Tax Expense/Pre-Tax Income)	0.624	0.622	0.622
= Net Interest Expense after Tax	315	299	348
= Net Income	2,408	3,198	1,841
− Preferred Stock Dividends	–	–	–
= Net Income to Common	2,408	3,198	1,841

Source: BAV Model v4.3.

Target Corporation
Condensed Balance Sheet ($ millions)

Year Beginning February	2006	2005	2004
Beginning Net Working Capital	3,922	3,961	4,764
Accounts Receivable	6,226	5,497	5,776
+ Inventory	5,838	5,384	5,343
+ Other Current Assets	693		1,093
− Accounts Payable	6,268	5,779	5,448
− Other Current Liabilities	2,567	1,937	2,000
= **Beginning Net Working Capital**	3,922	3,961	4,764
+ **Beginning Net Long-Term Assets**	18,507	16,361	16,668
Long-Term Tangible Assets	19,038	16,860	16,969
+ Long-Term Intangible Assets	183	206	364
+ Other Long-Term Assets	1,369	1,305	1,131
− Minority Interest	–	–	–
− Deferred Taxes	851	973	–
− Other Long-Term Liabilities (non-interest bearing)	1,232	1,037	1,796
= **Beginning Net Long-Term Assets**	18,507	16,361	16,668
= **Total Assets**	22,429	20,322	21,432
Beginning Net Debt	8,224	7,293	10,367
Short-Term Debt	753	504	866
+ Long-Term Debt	9,119	9,034	10,217
− Cash	1,648	2,245	716
= **Beginning Net Debt**	8,224	7,293	10,367
+ **Beginning Preferred Stock**	–	–	–
+ **Beginning Shareholders' Equity**	14,205	13,029	11,065
= **Total Net Capital**	22,429	20,322	21,432

Source: BAV Model v4.3.

Chapter 6

Prospective Analysis: Forecasting

M**ost** financial statement analysis tasks are undertaken with a forward-looking decision in mind—and much of the time it is useful to summarize the view developed in the analysis with an explicit forecast. Managers need forecasts to formulate business plans and provide performance targets; analysts need forecasts to help communicate their views of the firm's prospects to investors; and bankers and debt market participants need forecasts to assess the likelihood of loan repayment. Moreover, there are a variety of contexts (including but not limited to security analysis) where the forecast is usefully summarized in the form of an estimate of the firm's value. This estimate can be viewed as an attempt to best reflect in a single summary statistic the manager's or analyst's view of the firm's prospects.

Prospective analysis includes two tasks—forecasting and valuation—that together represent approaches to explicitly summarizing the analyst's forward-looking views. In this chapter we focus on forecasting; valuation is the topic of the next two chapters. Forecasting is not so much a separate analysis as it is a way of summarizing what has been learned through business strategy analysis, accounting analysis, and financial analysis. However, there are certain techniques and knowledge that can help a manager or analyst to structure the best possible forecast, conditional on what has been learned in the previous steps. Below we summarize an approach to structuring the forecast, offer information useful in getting started, explore the relationship between the other analytical steps and forecasting, and give detailed steps to forecast earnings, balance sheet data, and cash flows. The key concepts discussed in this chapter are illustrated using a forecast for Wal-Mart, the discount retailer examined in Chapter 5.

THE OVERALL STRUCTURE OF THE FORECAST

The best way to forecast future performance is to do it comprehensively—producing not only an earnings forecast, but also a forecast of cash flows and the balance sheet. A comprehensive approach is useful, even in cases where one might be interested primarily in a single facet of performance, because it guards against unrealistic implicit assumptions. For example, if an analyst forecasts growth in sales and earnings for several years without explicitly considering the required increases in working capital and plant assets and the associated financing, the forecast might possibly imbed unreasonable assumptions about asset turnover, leverage, or equity capital infusions.

A comprehensive approach involves many forecasts, but in most cases they are all linked to the behavior of a few key "drivers." The drivers vary according to the type of business, but for businesses outside the financial services sector, the sales forecast is nearly always one of the key drivers; profit margin is another. When asset turnover is expected to remain stable—often a realistic assumption—working capital accounts and investment in plant should track the growth in sales closely. Most major expenses also track sales, subject to expected shifts in profit margins. By linking forecasts of such amounts to the sales forecast, one can avoid internal inconsistencies and unrealistic implicit assumptions.

In some contexts the manager or analyst is interested ultimately in a forecast of cash flows, not earnings per se. Nevertheless, in practice even forecasts of cash flows tend to be grounded on forecasts of accounting numbers, including sales, earnings, assets, and liabilities. Of course it would be possible in principle to move directly to forecasts of cash flows—inflows from customers, outflows to suppliers and laborers, and so forth—and in some businesses this is a convenient way to proceed. In most cases, however, the growth prospects, profitability, and investment and financing needs of the firm are more readily framed in terms of accrual-based sales, operating earnings, assets, and liabilities. These amounts can then be converted to cash flow measures by adjusting for the effects of non-cash expenses and expenditures for working capital and plant, property, and equipment.

A Practical Framework for Forecasting

The most practical approach to forecasting a company's financial statements is to focus on projecting "condensed" financial statements, as used in the ratio analysis in Chapter 5, rather than attempting to project detailed financial statements at the level that the company reports. There are several reasons for this recommendation. Forecasting condensed financial statements involves a relatively small set of assumptions about the future of the firm, so the analyst will have more ability to think about each of the assumptions carefully. A detailed line-item forecast is likely to be very tedious, and an analyst may not have a good basis to make all the assumptions necessary for such forecasts. Further, for most purposes, condensed financial statements are all that are needed for analysis and decision making. We therefore approach the task of financial forecasting with this framework.

Recall that the condensed income statement that we used in Chapter 5 consists of the following elements: sales, net operating profits after tax (NOPAT), net interest expense after tax, taxes, and net income. The condensed balance sheet consists of net operating working capital, net long-term assets, net debt, and equity. Also recall that we start with a balance sheet at the beginning of the forecasting period. Assumptions about how we use the beginning balance sheet and run the firm's operations will lead to the income statement for the forecasting period; assumptions about investment in working capital and long-term assets, and how we finance these assets, results in a balance sheet at the end of the forecasting period.

To forecast the condensed income statement, one needs to begin with an assumption about next period's sales. Beyond that, assumptions about NOPAT margin, interest rate on beginning debt, and tax rate are all that are needed to prepare the condensed income statement for the period.

To forecast the condensed balance sheet for the end of the period (or the equivalent, the beginning of the next period), we need to make the following additional assumptions: (1) the ratio of net operating working capital to sales, to estimate the level of working capital needed to support those sales; (2) the ratio of net operating long-term assets to the following year's sales, to calculate the expected level of net operating long-term assets; and (3) the ratio of net debt to capital to estimate the levels of debt and equity needed to finance the estimated amount of assets on the balance sheet.

Once we have the condensed income statement and balance sheet, it is relatively straightforward to compute the condensed cash flow statement, including cash flow from operations before working capital investments, cash flow from operations after working capital investments, free cash flow available to debt and equity, and free cash flow available to equity.

We discuss how best to make the necessary assumptions to forecast the condensed income statement, balance sheet, and cash flow statements below.

PERFORMANCE BEHAVIOR: A STARTING POINT

Every forecast has, at least implicitly, an initial benchmark—some notion of how a particular amount, such as sales or earnings, would be expected to behave in the absence of detailed information. For example, in beginning to contemplate fiscal 2006 profitability for Wal-Mart, 2005 performance might be a starting point. Another potential starting point might be 2005 performance adjusted for recent trends. A third possibility that might seem reasonable—but one that generally turns out not to be very useful—is the average performance over several prior years.

By the time one has completed a business strategy analysis, an accounting analysis, and a detailed financial analysis, the resulting forecast might differ significantly from the original point of departure. Nevertheless, for purposes of having a starting point that can help anchor the detailed analysis, it is also useful to know how certain financial statistics behave "on average" for all firms.

In the case of some key statistics, such as earnings, a point of departure based only on prior behavior of the number is more powerful than one might expect. Research demonstrates that some such benchmarks for earnings are almost as accurate as the forecasts of professional security analysts, who have access to a rich information set (we return to this point in more detail below). Thus, the benchmark is often not only a good starting point but also close to the amount forecast after detailed analysis. Large departures from the benchmark could be justified only in cases where the firm's situation is demonstrably unusual.

Reasonable points of departure for forecasts of key accounting numbers can be based on the evidence summarized below. Such evidence may also be useful for checking the reasonableness of a completed forecast.

Sales Growth Behavior

Sales growth rates tend to be "mean-reverting": firms with above-average or below-average rates of sales growth tend to revert over time to a "normal" level (historically in the range of 7 to 9 percent for U.S. firms) within three to ten years. Figure 6-1 documents this effect for 1988 through 2005 for all the publicly traded, nonfinancial services U.S. firms covered by the Compustat database. All firms are ranked in terms of their sales growth in 1988 (year 1) and formed into five portfolios based on the relative ranking of their sales growth in that year. Firms in portfolio 1 are in the top 20 percent of rankings in terms of their sales growth in 1988, those in portfolio 2 fall into the next 20 percent, while those in portfolio 5 are in the bottom 20 percent when ranked by sales growth. The sales growth rates of firms in each of these five portfolios are traced from 1988 through the subsequent nine years (years 2 to 10). The same experiment is repeated with 1992 and then 1996 as the base year (year 1). The results are averaged over the three experiments and the resulting sales growth rates of each of the five portfolios for years 1 through 10 are plotted in Figure 6-1.

| FIGURE 6-1 | Behavior of Sales Growth for U.S. Firms over Time, 1988–2005 |

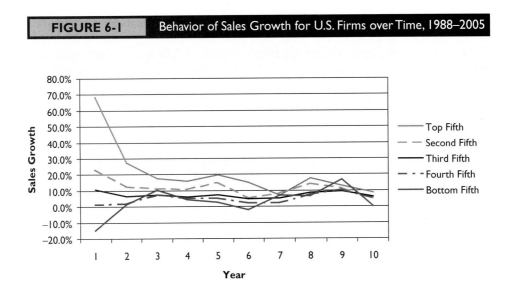

The figure shows that the group of firms with the highest growth initially—sales growth rates of close to 70 percent—experience a decline to about an 18 percent growth rate within two years and are never above 20 percent in the next seven years. Those with the lowest initial sales growth rates, negative 15 percent, improve immediately to a marginally positive sales growth in year 2. Over years 6 to 10 these firms average 7.5 percent growth annually. One explanation for the pattern of sales growth seen in Figure 6-1 is that as industries and companies mature, their growth rate slows down due to demand saturation and intra-industry competition. Therefore, even when a firm is growing rapidly at present, it is generally unrealistic to assume that the current high growth will persist indefinitely. Of course, how quickly a firm's growth rate reverts to the average depends on the characteristics of its industry and its own competitive position within an industry.

Earnings Behavior

Earnings have been shown on average to follow a process that can be approximated by a "random walk" or "random walk with drift." This implies that the prior year's earnings is a good starting point in considering future earnings potential. Even a simple random walk forecast—one that predicts next year's earnings will be equal to last year's earnings—is surprisingly useful. One study documents that professional analysts' year-ahead forecasts are only 22 percent more accurate, on average, than a simple random walk forecast.[1] Thus a final earnings forecast will usually not differ dramatically from a random walk benchmark. In addition, it is reasonable to adjust this simple benchmark for the earnings changes of the most recent quarter, i.e., changes relative to the comparable quarter of the prior year after controlling for the long-run trend in the series.

Although the average level of earnings over several prior years is not useful, long-term trends in earnings tend to be sustained on average, and so they are also worthy of consideration. If quarterly data are also included, then some consideration should usually be given to any departures from the long-run trend that occurred in the most recent quarter. For most firms, these most recent changes tend to be partially repeated in subsequent quarters.[2]

Return on Equity Behavior

Given that prior earnings serve as a useful benchmark for future earnings, one might expect the same to be true of measures of return on investment such as ROE. That, however, is not the case for two reasons. First, even though the average firm tends to sustain the current earnings level, this is not true of firms with unusual levels of ROE. Firms with abnormally high (low) ROE tend to experience earnings declines (increases).[3]

Second, firms with higher ROEs tend to expand their investment bases more quickly than others, which causes the denominator of the ROE to increase. Of course, if firms could earn returns on the new investments that match the returns on the old ones, then the level of ROE would be maintained. However, firms have difficulty continuing to generate those impressive ROEs. Firms with higher ROEs tend to find that, as time goes by, their earnings growth does not keep pace with growth in their investment base, and ROE ultimately falls.

The resulting behavior of ROE and other measures of return on investment is characterized as mean-reverting, a pattern similar to that observed for sales growth rates earlier. Firms with above-average or below-average rates of return tend to revert over time to a "normal" level (historically in the range of 10 to 15 percent for U.S. firms) within no more than ten years.[4] Figure 6-2 documents this effect for U.S. firms from 1988 through 2005. All firms are ranked in terms of their ROE in 1988 (year 1) and formed into five portfolios in a similar fashion to the sales growth analysis above. Firms in portfolio 1 have the top 20 percent ROE rankings in 1988, those in portfolio 2 fall into the next 20 percent, and those in portfolio 5 have the bottom 20 percent. The average ROE of firms in each of these five portfolios is then traced through nine subsequent years (years 2 to 10). The same experiment is repeated with 1992 and 1996 as the base year (year 1). Figure 6-2 plots the average ROE of each of the five portfolios in years 1 to 10 averaged across these three experiments.

Though the five portfolios start out in year 1 with a wide range of ROEs (−65 percent to +32 percent), by year 10 the pattern of mean-reversion is clear. The most profitable group of firms initially—with average ROEs of 32 percent—experience a decline to 23 percent within three years. By year 10 this group of firms has an ROE of 15 percent. Those with the lowest initial ROEs (−65 percent) experience a

| **FIGURE 6-2** | Behavior of ROE for U.S. Firms over Time, 1988–2005 |

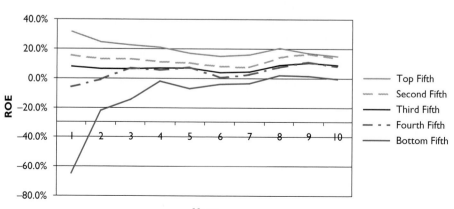

dramatic increase in ROE in the first four years and are marginally profitable or breakeven by the final three years.

The pattern in Figure 6-2 is not a coincidence—it is exactly what the economics of competition would predict. The tendency of high ROEs to fall is a reflection of high profitability attracting competition; the tendency of low ROEs to rise reflects the mobility of capital away from unproductive ventures toward more profitable ones.

Despite the general tendencies documented in Figure 6-2, there are some firms whose ROEs may remain above or below normal levels for long periods of time. In some cases the phenomenon reflects the strength of a sustainable competitive advantage (e.g., Wal-Mart), but in other cases it is purely an artifact of conservative accounting methods. A good example of the latter phenomenon in the U.S. is pharmaceutical firms, whose major economic asset, the intangible value of research and development, is not recorded on the balance sheet and is therefore excluded from the denominator of ROE. For these firms, one could reasonably expect high ROEs—in excess of 20 percent—over the long run, even in the face of strong competitive forces.

The Behavior of Components of ROE

The behavior of rates of return on equity can be analyzed further by looking at the behavior of its key components. Recall from Chapter 5 that ROEs and profit margins are linked as follows:

$$ROE = \text{Operating ROA} + (\text{Operating ROA} - \text{Net interest rate after tax}) \times \text{Net financial leverage}$$

$$= \text{NOPAT margin} \times \text{Operating asset turnover} + \text{Spread} \times \text{Net financial leverage}$$

The time-series behavior of the primary components of ROE for U.S. companies for 1988 through 2005 are shown in a series of figures in the appendix to this chapter. Some major conclusions can be drawn from these figures:

(1) Operating asset turnover tends to be rather stable, in part because it is largely a function of the technology of the industry. The only exception to this is the set of firms with very high asset turnover, which tends to decline somewhat over time before stabilizing;

(2) Net financial leverage also tends to be stable, simply because management policies on capital structure aren't often changed; and

(3) NOPAT margin stands out as the most variable component of ROE. If the forces of competition drive abnormal ROEs toward more normal levels, the change is most likely to arrive in the form of changes in profit margins. The change in NOPAT margin will drive changes in the spread, since the cost of borrowing is likely to remain stable because leverage tends to be stable.

To summarize, profit margins and ROEs tend to be driven by competition to normal levels over time. What constitutes normal varies widely according to the technology employed within an industry and the corporate strategy pursued by the firm, both of which influence turnover and leverage.[5] In a fully competitive equilibrium, profit margins should remain high for firms that must operate with a low turnover, and vice versa.

The above discussion of rates of return and margins implies that a reasonable starting point for forecasting such statistics should consider more than just the most recent observation. One should also consider whether that rate or margin is above or below a normal level. If so, then absent detailed information to the contrary, one would expect some movement over time toward that norm. Of course this central tendency might be overcome in some cases—for example, where the firm has erected barriers to competition that can protect margins, even for extended periods. The lesson from the evidence, however, is that such cases are unusual.

In contrast to rates of return and margins, it is reasonable to assume that asset turnover, financial leverage, and net interest rate remain relatively constant over time. Unless there is an explicit change in technology or financial policy being contemplated for future periods, a reasonable starting point for assumptions for these variables is the current period level. The only exceptions to this appear to be firms with either very high asset turns that experience some decline in this ratio before stabilizing, or those firms with very low (usually negative) net debt to capital that appear to increase leverage before stabilizing. In addition, firms with very high levels of leverage tend to survive at a lower rate than more conservatively financed firms, driving down averages over time.

As we proceed with the steps involved in producing a detailed forecast, the reader will note that we draw on knowledge of the behavior of accounting numbers to some extent. However, it is important to keep in mind that a knowledge of average behavior will not fit all firms well. The art of financial statements analysis requires not only knowing what the "normal" patterns are but also having expertise in identifying those firms that will not follow the norm.

RELATIONSHIP OF FORECASTING TO THE OTHER ANALYSES

In general, the mean-reverting behavior of sales growth and return on equity that is demonstrated by the broader market should hold true. The starting point for any forecast should therefore be the time-series behavior of the various measures of firm performance, as discussed. However, the three levels of analysis that precede prospective analysis—strategy, accounting, and financial performance—can also lead to informed decisions by an analyst about expected performance, especially in the short and medium term.

We use the example of Wal-Mart, the discount retailer discussed in Chapter 5, to illustrate the strategic analysis that informs the forecast as well as the mechanics of forecasting. A projection of the future performance of Wal-Mart for year 2006[6] must be grounded in an understanding of questions such as these:

- From business strategy analysis: Has Wal-Mart been able to create a retailing infrastructure that will allow it to continue to dominate the U.S. market? Will Wal-Mart be able to replicate this market dominance internationally? At what rate will the company be able to grow its sales, both in the short term and the long term, without sacrificing its margins? Will competitors such as Target be able to replicate Wal-Mart's efficiency while competing with a differentiated product offering?
- From accounting analysis: Are there any aspects of Wal-Mart's accounting that suggest past earnings and assets are misstated, or expenses or liabilities are misstated? If so, what are the implications for future accounting statements?
- From financial analysis: What are the sources of Wal-Mart's superior performance? Is this performance sustainable? Is there any discernible pattern in Wal-Mart's past performance? If so, are there any reasons why this trend is likely to continue or to change?

The key challenge in building a forecast, therefore, is to predict whether Wal-Mart will be able to maintain its competitive advantage and current performance levels or whether competition will force Wal-Mart to follow the general mean-reverting trends discussed above.

Macroeconomic Factors

In the first half of 2006, the U.S. economy was in a period of relative stability. The economy had recovered from the low points in 2001 and 2002, and consumer spending had shown modest growth. Wal-Mart's proposition of a wide variety of dependable products at low prices continued to appeal to the millions of low-income shoppers that patronized the store.

However, several factors are worrying from the perspective of Wal-Mart's growth prospects and could lead to short-term profit concerns. High gas prices tend to temper consumer enthusiasm for driving to suburban stores in search of discounts, which could lead to a drop in Wal-Mart's sales outside of its limited urban presence. The spectacular increase in real estate values over the past decade, which fueled increases in consumer spending, was viewed by many market experts as susceptible to a market correction. Falling real estate prices, rising interest rates, and increased bank foreclosures could put pressure on discretionary spending, leading to a potential drop in Wal-Mart's sales. However, a loss in sales from traditional Wal-Mart shoppers could be counterbalanced by a widening of Wal-Mart's customer base, as higher income consumers turn to Wal-Mart stores in an effort to save money. Finally, Wal-Mart's business model, which is based on domestic sales of internationally sourced products, is susceptible to changes in the relative value of the U.S. dollar. If the dollar weakens relative to the Chinese yuan, for instance, the cost of Wal-Mart's imports from China could rise sharply, negatively impacting margins.

The impact of changing macro-economic conditions on Wal-Mart's performance in the short, medium, and long term cannot be forecast with a high degree of certainty. Consequently, it is advisable to focus on the firm's particular strategy and competitive position and assume that the impact of changes in the business cycle will even out in the long run.

Sales Growth

Despite the intense competition in retailing, the seasoned executive team at Wal-Mart has built an impressive track record of meeting and exceeding investor expectations, and it is reasonable to expect that they will continue to deliver the same strong growth that they have in the past. Wal-Mart has essentially two growth drivers—domestic sales in the U.S., which show signs of stagnating as a result of the intensity of competition and market saturation; and international sales, where the growth opportunities, especially in large emerging markets such as China, India, and Brazil seem extremely attractive.

Wal-Mart currently operates over 3,200 stores in the U.S. among its various Wal-Mart store formats. Sales for Wal-Mart Stores grew 9.4 percent in the year ending January 2006, compared to 10.1 and 10.9 percent in each of the previous two years. Comparable store sales grew by only 3 percent, a relatively low level that is likely to persist as Wal-Mart continues its new store expansion program. Given that Wal-Mart has a fairly comprehensive retail network, new store openings tend to cannibalize sales from existing stores in the same area, reducing growth in comparable store sales. New store openings are also likely to slow as unique attractive locations become increasingly scarce. At the same time, Wal-Mart is actively courting more affluent customers and working to make its product offerings more stylish and appealing. However, it is unclear whether this initiative will be successful in offsetting the slowdown in same store sales. Wal-Mart also faces a discount retail paradigm-shifting threat from Target that could erode its market leadership. Thus, it is reasonable to expect that Wal-Mart Stores' overall sales growth will trend downward, though probably at a slower pace than would be implied by the mean-reverting tendency of sales growth for the overall market.

SAM'S CLUB sales grew 7.2 percent during the year ended January 2006, and it has exhibited a slowing trend in sales growth over the last three years similar to that of Wal-Mart Stores. In fiscal year 2005, comparable club sales grew 5.0 percent and square footage grew 3.8 percent. SAM'S CLUB faces formidable competition from other wholesale club operators, primarily Costco and BJ's Wholesale Club. Though it is reasonable to expect that sales growth at SAM'S CLUB will slow, the slowdown is likely to be more gradual than at Wal-Mart Stores as its current comparable store sales growth remains robust and it has a smaller base of stores (fewer than 600 stores), giving it more expansion opportunities.

Wal-Mart's International operations present an interesting forecasting challenge. The subtleties of local tastes and bureaucratic complexities in local real estate markets have made it extremely challenging for nondomestic retailing companies to establish market leadership outside their home markets. Although Wal-Mart has achieved dominant positions in the Canadian and Mexican markets through a mixture of acquisitions and joint ventures, its ability to replicate this success in what are widely acknowledged to be the major growth markets—the emerging consumer economies in China, India, Brazil, and Russia—remains to be seen. Wal-Mart's value-oriented philosophy, which was extremely successful in the underserved and fragmented markets of suburban and rural America, may well be replicable in many of the key developing economies with similar market characteristics, implying that international sales are likely to outpace U.S. sales over the forecast horizon. Thus, the projections suggest that in ten years nearly 30 percent of Wal-Mart's sales will be generated by its overseas operations, compared to the current 20 percent. A key question is whether this growth will add value for Wal-Mart if the international expansion comes from acquisitions, which for many companies are zero net present value undertakings.

Overall, the projections in Table 6-1 show a gradual improvement in sales growth over the next couple of years, followed by a slow decline in growth. While this pattern is based on a mixture of business intelligence and a knowledge of long-term trends in the market, it is important to note that an analyst could capture much of the dynamics of the projections merely by assuming that Wal-Mart will not be immune to the long-run forces of competition and mean reversion.

TABLE 6-1	Forecasted Sales Growth for Wal-Mart									
Forecast year	2006	2007	2008	2009	2010	2011	2012	2013	2014	2015
Wal-Mart Stores	9.0%	9.0%	8.8%	8.5%	8.3%	8.0%	7.8%	7.5%	7.3%	7.0%
SAM'S CLUB	7.0%	7.0%	6.9%	6.8%	6.7%	6.5%	6.3%	6.1%	6.0%	6.0%
International	12.0%	13.0%	14.0%	14.0%	14.0%	13.0%	12.0%	11.0%	10.0%	10.0%
Overall Sales Growth	9.3%	9.6%	9.6%	9.5%	9.4%	9.0%	8.6%	8.2%	7.8%	7.7%

NOPAT Margins

In the highly competitive U.S. market, Wal-Mart Stores is likely to have to resort to deeper discounting to offset the threat of competition from other discount retailers such as Target. At the same time, Wal-Mart is trying to beat Target at its own game by increasing the design component of its product offerings and appealing to more affluent discount shopping consumers. This improved merchandising could lead to a narrowing of the margin gap seen in the comparison of Wal-Mart and Target in Chapter 5, at least on selective merchandise. However, Wal-Mart's shift in strategy away from its now synonymous "every day low prices" strategy could also lead to some short-term execution missteps, such as overstocked inventory and mispricing. Thus, there could be unexpected short-term disruptions to Wal-Mart's margin growth as a result of its strategy of pursuing higher-income consumers. Overall, it is likely that the competitive pressures will have a greater impact than the modifications to product strategy and sourcing that Wal-Mart expects to implement, leading to a gradual but steady decline in NOPAT margins.

International operations of Wal-Mart are expected to show higher growth but have relatively low margins, which will have an impact on overall margins for the firm. Several offsetting forces are likely to affect International margins in the medium-term. As transportation and general infrastructure improves in many of Wal-Mart's developing economy markets, and as Wal-Mart is able to impose its efficiency in supply chain management on its international operations, it is possible that International margins will show some improvement in the medium term. More direct sourcing and improved in-country distribution will also help improve margins. At the same time, as large economies such as China develop, competition is likely to heat up, leading to margin declines that mimic mean-reverting trends seen in the U.S. We predict that international margins are likely to improve in the medium term due to improvements in developing country infrastructure, but in the longer term there is likely to be mean reversion. As shown in Table 6-2, Wal-Mart's average NOPAT margins are expected to decline due to the increased importance of the faster growing, but lower margin, International business.

TABLE 6-2	Forecasted NOPAT Margins for Wal-Mart									
Forecast year	2006	2007	2008	2009	2010	2011	2012	2013	2014	2015
Wal-Mart Stores	4.4%	4.3%	4.2%	4.1%	4.0%	3.9%	3.8%	3.6%	3.4%	3.2%
SAM'S CLUB	2.1%	2.1%	2.1%	2.0%	2.0%	1.9%	1.9%	1.8%	1.8%	1.8%
International	3.2%	3.2%	3.3%	3.4%	3.4%	3.4%	3.4%	3.3%	3.3%	3.2%
Overall Margins	**3.9%**	**3.8%**	**3.8%**	**3.7%**	**3.7%**	**3.6%**	**3.5%**	**3.4%**	**3.2%**	**3.1%**

Working Capital to Sales

Wal-Mart's working capital management has consistently beaten that of its peers, and this dominance is likely to continue. Wal-Mart currently has a negative net operating working capital to sales ratio. This implies that Wal-Mart is able to fund its working capital needs—primarily for accounts receivable and inventory—through trade and other short-term creditors and accruals.

Wal-Mart continues to invest heavily in its logistics and distribution network, keeping inventory levels at a minimum. As the firm increases its reliance on direct sourcing, its working capital advantage is likely to increase further. Working capital needs are also likely to decline as it improves operations in its International business and takes advantage of its growing international presence to negotiate more favorable terms with its suppliers. Therefore, it is reasonable to expect that its net operating working capital to sales ratio will remain at or near zero as the firm's market power grows and it continues to invest in its supply chain.

Long-Term Assets to Sales

As the pace of Wal-Mart's new store openings in the U.S. slows, comparable store sales growth should improve as fewer new stores will open up near existing stores, reducing the risk of customer cannibalization. This should have a beneficial impact on the firm's long-term asset use in both Wal-Mart and SAM'S CLUB divisions. Counteracting this improvement is the fact that new store openings are likely to be more capital intensive than in the past for two reasons. First, real estate prices in the U.S. have risen sharply over the past decade. Additionally, Wal-Mart is moving away from its rural base into regions where average real estate prices are higher. This change in the cost structure of Wal-Mart's domestic long-term asset base could lead to a reduction in asset turns.

The International business is currently extremely asset intensive when compared to the firm's U.S. businesses. However, as Wal-Mart gains traction in many of its developing markets, same store sales growth is likely to improve. Additionally, as the firm's market power grows, its relationships with host countries could strengthen, giving it access to cheaper real estate and better locations. A combination of these factors should enhance asset utilization in International operations, though it will still trail the performance of U.S. stores.

Overall, as International sales growth outpaces that of the U.S. businesses, Wal-Mart's ratio of long-term assets to sales is likely to gradually deteriorate over the forecast horizon.

Capital Structure

Wal-Mart's Board of Directors authorized a $10.0 billion share repurchase program in September 2004. At the end of January 2006, approximately $6.1 billion of shares had yet to be purchased under this buyback authorization. There is no time limit within which the program needs to be completed, and decisions are made in light of the firm's overall leverage, among other factors. Thus, it is unlikely that the share repurchase will lead to any fundamental, long-term change in Wal-Mart's capital structure, and leverage should remain relatively stable. Given the financial strength of the firm, any short-term fluctuations in leverage should not have any impact on the cost of debt.

MAKING FORECASTS

The analysis of Wal-Mart's performance in Chapter 5, and the preceding discussions about general market behavior and Wal-Mart's strategic positioning, leads to the conclusion that while Wal-Mart consistently generated above-market returns for its shareholders, in the long run it is likely that a portion of the firm's abnormal profits will be competed away. The performance of the firm will revert towards the mean, as has been the general trend that we have seen earlier in the chapter.

Table 6-3 shows the forecasting assumptions for years 2006 to 2015. Table 6-4 shows the forecasted income statements for these same fiscal years, and beginning of the year balance sheets for years 2007 to 2016. Recall that the balance sheet at the beginning of fiscal 2006 is the same as the balance sheet reported by the company for the year ending January 31, 2006. We have chosen a ten-year forecasting period because we believe that the firm should reach a relatively steady state of performance by then (discussed in further detail in Chapter 8). We discuss below the forecasting assumptions, which are based on the foregoing discussion of the various elements that comprise the forecast.

The Overall One Year Ahead Forecast

As mentioned above, we have the actual balance sheet for the beginning of 2006, so there is no need to forecast this. Making a short-term income statement forecast, such as a one year ahead forecast, is usually a straightforward extrapolation of recent performance. This is a particularly valid approach for an established company such as Wal-Mart for several reasons. First, the company is unlikely to effect major changes to its operating and financing policies in the short term unless it is in the middle of a restructuring program. Second, the beginning of the year balance sheet for any given year will put constraints on operating activities during that fiscal year. For example, inventories at the beginning of the year will determine to some extent the sales activities during the year; stores in operation at the beginning of the year also determine to some extent the level of sales achievable during the year. To put it another way, since our discussion above shows that asset turns for a company do not usually change significantly in a short time, sales in any period are to some extent constrained by the beginning of the period assets in place in the company's balance sheet. Of course Wal-Mart is likely to achieve some flexibility in this regard as it has explicit plans to expand assets during the year through new store openings. Changes in the asset utilization could also be driven by increases in same store sales and changes to its product mix.

As shown below in Table 6-3, we assume that sales will grow at 9.3 percent. This is marginally lower than the 9.5 percent sales growth that the company achieved in

TABLE 6-3	Forecasting Assumptions for Wal-Mart									
Forecast year	2006	2007	2008	2009	2010	2011	2012	2013	2014	2015
Sales growth rate	9.3%	9.6%	9.6%	9.5%	9.4%	9.0%	8.6%	8.2%	7.8%	7.7%
NOPAT margin	3.9%	3.8%	3.8%	3.7%	3.7%	3.6%	3.5%	3.4%	3.2%	3.1%
Beginning net operating working capital/sales	−0.8%	0.0%	0.0%	0.0%	0.0%	0.0%	0.0%	0.0%	0.0%	0.0%
Beginning net operating long-term assets/sales	25.8%	25.2%	25.4%	25.6%	25.9%	26.0%	26.0%	26.3%	26.5%	26.8%
Beginning net debt to capital ratio	37.9%	37.9%	37.9%	37.9%	37.9%	37.9%	37.9%	37.9%	37.9%	37.9%
After tax cost of debt	3.3%	3.3%	3.3%	3.3%	3.3%	3.3%	3.3%	3.3%	3.3%	3.3%

2005. While the consensus among analysts that follow the stock is for higher growth, our strategic analysis led to an expectation of slowing growth in the U.S. market that offsets possible increases in international sales, leading to an overall slowdown. This growth rate leads to an expected sales level in 2006 of $342.6 billion, up from $313.3 billion in 2005 as Table 6-4 shows.

The next key assumption to be made about Wal-Mart's performance in 2006 is its NOPAT margin. We expect Wal-Mart to be able to maintain its margin of 3.9 percent from the previous year. Wal-Mart's market leadership in the U.S. should allow the firm to protect its margins in the domestic business. Furthermore, improvements in the International business should maintain Wal-Mart's overall margins in the short-term.

The next two forecast items—net operating working capital to sales and net operating long-term assets to sales—have already been determined by the balance sheet position at January 31, 2006. Therefore, we are starting with a given level of assets to work with. So we can either make an assumption about sales growth rate and check the implied ratio of beginning net assets to sales for reasonableness, or make an assumption of the beginning net assets to sales ratio for the year and check for the reasonableness of the implied sales growth rate. In other words, we are free to make only one of the two assumptions—either sales growth or net asset turns. In subsequent years in the forecast horizon, we relax this constraint because we can build up both a desired beginning balance sheet and income statement for the following years.

The third assumption we make to forecast Wal-Mart's income statement for 2006 relates to the after-tax cost of debt. The company's beginning level of debt and its beginning debt to capital ratio for 2006 are determined by its actual balance sheet at the start of the fiscal year. Although the firm is in the middle of completing a share repurchase program, the effect on leverage is not likely to affect its cost of debt (adjusting for any changes in overall market interest rates). As a result, it is reasonable to assume that the firm's relative cost of debt will be similar to its cost of borrowing in prior years as reflected in the yield on its intermediate term bonds. Given stable interest rates, the cost of borrowing is expected to remain stable at 5.15 percent, or 3.35 percent on an after-tax basis.

These assumptions together lead to a projected $12.2 billion net income in fiscal year compared with a reported net income of $11.2 billion in 2005.

Overall Forecasts for Years Two to Ten

In making longer-term forecasts, in this instance for years two to ten, we have relied on our analysis of the firm and its prospects as well as the time-series behavior of various performance ratios discussed earlier. Given our assumptions of increased growth in international markets, we assume that Wal-Mart will be able to increase its sales growth rate to 9.6 percent in years two and three. Thereafter, sales growth will gradually decline as the firm finds fewer locations in the U.S. in which to profitably expand, and comparable store domestic sales growth flatten out. While the International business is expected to maintain its high growth rate over the medium term, the relatively smaller scale of those operations leads to a gradual overall decline in sales growth.

The pattern of margins in Wal-Mart's domestic and foreign businesses is likely to diverge, as International operations initially show improvements in margins. For the firm overall, we assume a pattern of steady and then declining NOPAT margins over time. These assumptions are again consistent with the time-series trend we documented earlier in the chapter for firms with initially high NOPAT and with our

TABLE 6-4 Forecasted Financial Statements for Wal-Mart

Forecast year	2006	2007	2008	2009	2010	2011	2012	2013	2014	2015
Beginning Balance Sheet										
Beg. Net Working Capital	–2,768	0	0	0	0	0	0	0	0	0
+ Beg. Net Long-Term Assets	88,344	94,546	104,527	115,477	127,486	139,917	151,937	166,343	181,019	196,873
= **Net Operating Assets**	**85,576**	**94,546**	**104,527**	**115,477**	**127,486**	**139,917**	**151,937**	**166,343**	**181,019**	**196,873**
Net Debt	32,405	35,802	39,581	43,728	48,275	52,982	57,534	62,989	68,546	74,550
+ Preferred Stock	0	0	0	0	0	0	0	0	0	0
+ Shareholders' Equity	53,171	58,744	64,946	71,749	79,211	86,935	94,403	103,354	112,473	122,323
= **Net Capital**	**85,576**	**94,546**	**104,527**	**115,477**	**127,486**	**139,917**	**151,937**	**166,343**	**181,019**	**196,873**
Income Statement										
Sales	342,629	375,435	411,628	450,786	493,126	537,648	584,130	632,291	681,861	734,359
Net operating profits after tax	13,284	14,360	15,531	16,755	18,034	19,288	20,483	21,264	21,958	22,644
– Net interest expense after tax	1,085	1,198	1,325	1,464	1,616	1,774	1,926	2,109	2,295	2,496
= Net income	12,199	13,162	14,206	15,291	16,418	17,515	18,557	19,155	19,664	20,149
– Preferred dividends	0	0	0	0	0	0	0	0	0	0
= **Net income to common**	**12,199**	**13,162**	**14,206**	**15,291**	**16,418**	**17,515**	**18,557**	**19,155**	**19,664**	**20,149**
Operating Return on Assets	15.5%	15.2%	14.9%	14.5%	14.1%	13.8%	13.5%	12.8%	12.1%	11.5%
Return on Common Equity	22.9%	22.4%	21.9%	21.3%	20.7%	20.1%	19.7%	18.5%	17.5%	16.5%
Book Value of Assets Growth Rate	13.6%	10.5%	10.6%	10.5%	10.4%	9.8%	8.6%	9.5%	8.8%	8.8%
Book Value of Common Equity										
Growth Rate	7.6%	10.5%	10.6%	10.5%	10.4%	9.8%	8.6%	9.5%	8.8%	8.8%
Net Operating Asset Turnover	4.0	4.0	3.9	3.9	3.9	3.8	3.8	3.8	3.8	3.7
Net income	12,199	13,162	14,206	15,291	16,418	17,515	18,557	19,155	19,664	20,149
– Change in net working capital	(2,768)	-	-	-	-	-	-	-	-	-
– Change in net long-term assets	(6,202)	(9,981)	(10,950)	(12,009)	(12,431)	(12,020)	(14,406)	(14,676)	(15,854)	(15,089)
+ Change in net debt	3,397	3,779	4,147	4,547	4,707	4,552	5,455	5,557	6,004	4,349
= Free cash flow to equity	6,626	6,960	7,403	7,829	8,694	10,047	9,606	10,036	9,814	9,409
Net operating profit after tax	13,284	14,360	15,531	16,755	18,034	19,288	20,483	21,264	21,958	22,644
– Change in net working capital	(2,768)	-	-	-	-	-	-	-	-	-
– Change in net long-term assets	(6,202)	(9,981)	(10,950)	(12,009)	(12,431)	(12,020)	(14,406)	(14,676)	(15,854)	(15,089)
= Free cash flow to capital	4,314	4,379	4,581	4,746	5,603	7,268	6,077	6,588	6,104	5,359

assessment of the competitive response of the other players in Wal-Mart's industry. While Wal-Mart clearly has a significant competitive advantage over its rivals, it is prudent to assume, given the history of U.S. firms, that this advantage will decline over time. Wal-Mart Stores faces the greatest competitive threats, so we assume that its NOPAT margins decline steadily at the rate of 0.1 percent per year. SAM'S CLUB stores are assumed to maintain their margins for a period of three years, after which they decline gradually from 2.1 percent in year three to 1.8 percent by year 10. Wal-Mart International is able to increase its margins from years two through four and then hold them steady for a further period of three years. Eventually, even margins in the International business decline as competition heats up. Overall, we assume that the company's NOPAT margin is steady to declining and by year 10, Wal-Mart's NOPAT margins are expected to have dropped to 3.1 percent compared to the current margin of 3.9 percent.

Wal-Mart currently has a negative net working capital to sales ratio of −0.7 percent. Based on the sales growth assumption for year one, this is projected to be −0.8 percent at the beginning of year two. The forecast assumes that the situation deteriorates marginally until net working capital is zero at the beginning of year three, and this is maintained throughout the forecast horizon.

As discussed, Wal-Mart's International business is highly asset intensive when compared to domestic operations. As International sales growth outpaces domestic growth, asset turns firm-wide should deteriorate. Consequently, the ratio of net long-term assets to sales is expected to increase from 25.2 percent in year two to 26.8 by year 10.

The company's capital structure should remain relatively unchanged. Although the firm is in the midst of executing an authorized share repurchase, we do not expect leverage to be materially different from the past. As a result, the ratio of net debt to book value of net capital of 37.9 percent is maintained for the duration of the forecast horizon. This assumption of a constant capital structure policy is consistent with the general pattern observed in the historical data discussed earlier in the chapter. Consequently, the forecast assumes that Wal-Mart's cost of debt remains at 5.15 percent, or an after-tax cost of 3.35 percent. The cost of debt is expected to be equal to the yield on an intermediate-term bond issued by Wal-Mart.

Having made this set of key assumptions, it is a straightforward task to derive the forecasted income statements and beginning balance sheets for years 2006 through 2015 as shown in Table 6-4. Under these forecasts, Wal-Mart's sales will grow to $734.4 billion, more than double the level in 2005. By 2015, the firm will have a net operating asset base of $196.9 billion and shareholders' equity of $122.3 billion. Consistent with market-wide patterns of mean-reversion in returns, Wal-Mart's return on equity will decline steadily from the 22.7 percent reported in 2005 to 16.5 percent by 2015, and operating return on assets will show a similar pattern.

Cash Flow Forecasts

Once we have forecasted income statements and balance sheets, we can derive cash flows for the years 2006 through 2015. Note that we need to forecast the beginning balance sheet for 2016 to compute the cash flows for 2015. This balance sheet is not shown in Table 6-4. For the purpose of illustration, we assume that all the sales growth and the balance sheet ratios remain the same in 2016 as in 2015. Based on this, we project a beginning balance sheet for 2016 and compute the cash flows for 2015. Cash flow to capital is equal to NOPAT minus increases in net working capital and net long-term assets. Cash flow to equity is cash flow to capital minus net interest after tax plus increase in net debt. These two sets of forecasted cash flows are presented in Table 6-4. As the table shows, the free cash flow to all providers of capital increases from $4.3 billion to a high of $7.3 billion in 2011 before declining to $5.4 billion by 2015. In addition, the firm is expected to increase the free cash flow it generates to its equity holders from $6.6 billion in 2006 to $9.4 billion by 2015.

SENSITIVITY ANALYSIS

The projections discussed thus far represent nothing more than an estimation of a most likely scenario for Wal-Mart. Managers and analysts are typically interested in a broader range of possibilities. For example, an analyst estimating the value of Wal-Mart might consider the sensitivity of projections to the key assumptions about sales growth, profit margins, and asset utilization. What if Wal-Mart is able to retain more of its competitive advantage in the U.S. than assumed in the above forecasts? Alternatively, what if it is unable to improve its levels of asset utilization as assumed or to maintain its high growth rates in the International business division? It is wise to also generate projections based on a variety of assumptions to determine the sensitivity of the forecasts to these assumptions.

There is no limit to the number of possible scenarios that can be considered. One systematic approach to sensitivity analysis is to start with the key assumptions underlying a set of forecasts, and then examine the sensitivity to the assumptions with greatest uncertainty in a given situation. For example, if a company has experienced a variable pattern of gross margins in the past, it is important to make projections using a range of margins. Alternatively, if a company has announced a significant change in its expansion strategy, asset utilization assumptions might be more uncertain. In determining where to invest one's time in performing sensitivity analysis, it is therefore important to consider historical patterns of performance, changes in industry conditions, and changes in a company's competitive strategy.

In the case of Wal-Mart, two likely alternatives to the forecast can be readily envisioned. The forecast presented above expects that Wal-Mart's dominance of the U.S. market gradually wanes, while the International division contributes stellar growth and improvement in performance. An upside case for Wal-Mart would have the firm continuing to dominate the U.S. retail industry and resisting the mean-reverting trends that characterize the market in general, in addition to the increased contribution from international operations. On the downside, the projected boost from the International business could fail to materialize, hastening the decline in Wal-Mart's overall performance towards the market averages.

Seasonality and Interim Forecasts

Thus far, we have concerned ourselves with annual forecasts. However, especially for security analysts in the U.S., forecasting is very much a quarterly exercise. Forecasting quarter-by-quarter raises a new set of questions. How important is seasonality? What is a useful starting point—the most recent quarter's performance? The comparable quarter of the prior year? Some combination of the two? How should quarterly data be used in producing an annual forecast? Does the item-by-item approach to forecasting used for annual data apply equally well to quarterly data?

Full consideration of these questions lies outside the scope of this chapter, but we can begin to answer some of them.

Seasonality is a more important phenomenon in sales and earning behavior than one might guess. It is present for more than just the retail sector firms that benefit from holiday sales. Seasonality also results from weather-related phenomena (e.g., for electric and gas utilities, construction firms, and motorcycle manufacturers), new product introduction patterns (e.g., for the automobile industry), and other factors. Analysis of the time series behavior of earnings for U.S. firms suggests that at least some seasonality is present in nearly every major industry.

The implication for forecasting is that one cannot focus only on performance of the most recent quarter as a starting point. In fact, the evidence suggests that, in forecasting earnings, if one had to choose only one quarter's performance as a basis for forecasting, it would be the comparable quarter of the prior year, not the most recent quarter. Note how this finding is consistent with the reports of analysts or the financial press; when they discuss a quarterly earnings announcement, it is nearly always evaluated relative to the performance of the comparable quarter of the prior year, not the most recent quarter.

Research has produced models that forecast sales, earnings, or EPS based solely on prior quarters' observations. These models are not used by many analysts since they have access to much more information than such simple models contain. However, the models are useful for helping those unfamiliar with the behavior of earnings data to understand how it tends to evolve over time. Such an understanding can provide useful general background, a point of departure in forecasting that can be adjusted to reflect details not revealed in the history of earnings, or a "reasonableness" check on a detailed forecast.

One model of the earnings process that fits well across a variety of industries is the so-called Foster model.[7] Using Q_t to denote earnings (or EPS) for quarter t, and $E(Q_t)$ as its expected value, the Foster model predicts that

$$E(Q_t) = Q_{t-4} + \delta + \phi(Q_{t-1} - Q_{t-5})$$

Foster shows that a model of the same form also works well with quarterly sales data.

The form of the Foster model confirms the importance of seasonality because it shows that the starting point for a forecast for quarter t is the earnings four quarters ago, Q_{t-4}. It states that, when constrained to using only prior earnings data, a reasonable forecast of earnings for quarter t includes the following elements:

- the earnings of the comparable quarter of the prior year (Q_{t-4});
- a long-run trend in year-to-year quarterly earnings increases (δ); and
- a fraction (ϕ) of the year-to-year increase in quarterly earnings experienced most recently ($Q_{t-1} - Q_{t-5}$).

The parameters δ and ϕ can easily be estimated for a given firm with a simple linear regression model available in most spreadsheet software.[8] For most firms the parameter ϕ tends to be in the range of .25 to .50, indicating that 25 to 50 percent of an increase in quarterly earnings tends to persist in the form of another increase in the subsequent quarter. The parameter δ reflects in part the average year-to-year change in quarterly earnings over past years, and it varies considerably from firm to firm.

Research indicates that the Foster model produces one quarter ahead forecasts that vary from actual results by $.30 to $.35 per share, on average. Such a degree of accuracy stacks up surprisingly well with that of security analysts, who obviously have access to much information ignored in the model. As one would expect, most of the evidence supports analysts' being more accurate, but the models are good enough to be a reasonable approximation in most circumstances. While it would certainly be unwise to rely completely on such a mechanistic model, an understanding of the typical earnings behavior reflected by the model is useful.

SUMMARY

Forecasting represents the first step of prospective analysis and serves to summarize the forward-looking view that emanates from business strategy analysis, accounting analysis, and financial analysis. Although not every financial statement analysis is accompanied by such an explicit summarization of a view of the future, forecasting is still a key tool for managers, consultants, security analysts, investment bankers, commercial bankers and other credit analysts, among others.

The best approach to forecasting future performance is to do it comprehensively—producing not only an earnings forecast but also a forecast of cash flows and the balance sheet as well. Such a comprehensive approach provides a guard against internal inconsistencies and unrealistic implicit assumptions. The approach described here involves a condensed, line-by-line analysis, so as to recognize that different items on the income statement and balance sheet are influenced by different drivers. Nevertheless, it remains the case that a few key projections—such as sales growth and profit margin—usually drive most of the projected numbers.

The forecasting process should be embedded in an understanding of how various financial statistics tend to behave on average, and what might cause a firm to deviate from that average. Absent detailed information to the contrary, one would expect sales and earnings numbers to persist at their current levels, adjusted for overall trends of recent years. However, rates of return on investment (ROEs) tend, over several years, to move from abnormal to normal levels—close to the cost of equity capital—as the forces of competition come into play. Profit margins also tend to shift to normal levels, but for this statistic "normal" varies widely across firms and industries, depending on the levels of asset turnover and leverage. Some firms are capable of creating barriers to entry that enable them to fight these tendencies toward normal returns, even for many years, but such firms are the unusual cases.

Forecasting should be preceded by a comprehensive business strategy, accounting, and financial analysis. It is important to understand the dynamics of the industry in which the firm operates and its competitive positioning within that industry. Therefore, while general market trends provide a useful benchmark, it is critical that the analyst incorporate the views developed about the firm's prospects to guide the forecasting process.

For some purposes, including short-term planning and security analysis, forecasts for quarterly periods are desirable. One important feature of quarterly data is seasonality; at least some seasonality exists in the sales and earnings data of nearly every industry. An understanding of a firm's intra-year peaks and valleys is a necessary ingredient of a good forecast of performance on a quarterly basis.

Forecasts provide the input for estimating a firm's value, which can be viewed as the best attempt to reflect in a single summary statistic the manager's or analyst's view of the firm's prospects. The process of converting a forecast into a value estimate is labeled valuation and is discussed next.

DISCUSSION QUESTIONS

1. Merck is one of the largest pharmaceutical firms in the world, and over an extended period of time in the recent past, it consistently earned higher ROEs than the pharmaceutical industry as a whole. As a pharmaceutical analyst, what factors would you consider to be important in making projections of future ROEs for Merck? In particular, what factors would lead you to expect Merck to continue to be a superior performer in its industry, and what factors would lead you to expect Merck's future performance to revert to that of the industry as a whole?

2. John Right, an analyst with Stock Pickers Inc., claims, "It is not worth my time to develop detailed forecasts of sales growth, profit margins, etcetera, to make earnings projections. I can be almost as accurate, at virtually no cost, using the random walk model to forecast earnings." What is the random walk model? Do you agree or disagree with John Right's forecast strategy? Why or why not?

3. Which of the following types of businesses do you expect to show a high degree of seasonality in quarterly earnings? Explain why.
   • a supermarket
   • a pharmaceutical company
   • a software company
   • an auto manufacturer
   • a clothing retailer

4. What factors are likely to drive a firm's outlays for new capital (such as plant, property, and equipment) and for working capital (such as receivables and inventory)? What ratios would you use to help generate forecasts of these outlays?

5. How would the following events (reported this year) affect your forecasts of a firm's future net income?
   • an asset write-down
   • a merger or acquisition
   • the sale of a major division
   • the initiation of dividend payments

6. Consider the following two earnings forecasting models:

$$E(EPS_{t+1}) = EPS_t$$

Model 1:

$$E(EPS_{t+1}) = \frac{1}{5}\sum_{t=1}^{5} EPS_t$$

$E(EPS_{t+1})$ is the expected forecast of earnings per share for year $t + 1$, given information available at t. Model 1 is usually called a random walk model for earnings, whereas Model 2 is called a mean-reverting model. The earnings per share for Wal-Mart Stores for the fiscal years ending January 2001 (FY2000) through January 2005 (FY2004) are as follows:

Fiscal Year	2000	2001	2002	2003	2004
EPS	$1.41	$1.48	$1.80	$2.08	$2.41

a. What would the forecast for earnings per share in FY2005 be for each model?

b. Actual earnings per share for Wal-Mart in FY2005 were $2.68. Given this information, what would be the FY2006 forecast for earnings per share for each model? Why do the two models generate quite different forecasts? Which do you think would better describe earnings per share patterns? Why?

7. Joe Fatcat, an investment banker, states, "It is not worth my while to worry about detailed long-term forecasts. Instead, I use the following approach when forecasting cash flows beyond three years: I assume that sales grow at the rate of inflation, capital expenditures are equal to depreciation, and that net profit margins and working capital to sales ratios stay constant." What pattern of return on equity is implied by these assumptions? Is this reasonable?

NOTES

1. See P. O'Brien, "Analysts' Forecasts as Earnings Expectations," *Journal of Accounting and Economics* (January 1988): 53–83.

2. See G. Foster, "Quarterly Accounting Data: Time Series Properties and Predictive Ability Results," *The Accounting Review* (January 1977): 1–21.

3. See R. Freeman, J. Ohlson, and S. Penman, "Book Rate-of-Return and Prediction of Earnings Changes: An Empirical Investigation," *Journal of Accounting Research* (Autumn 1982): 639–53.

4. See S. Penman, "An Evaluation of Accounting Rate-of-Return," *Journal of Accounting, Auditing, and Finance* (Spring 1991): 233–56; E. Fama and K. French, "Size and Book-to-Market Factors in Earnings and Returns," *Journal of Finance* (March 1995): 131–56; and V. Bernard, "Accounting-Based Valuation Methods: Evidence on the Market-to-Book Anomaly and Implications for Financial Statements Analysis," (working paper, University of Michigan, 1994). Ignoring the effects of accounting artifacts, ROEs should be driven in a competitive equilibrium to a level approximating the cost of equity capital.

5. A "normal" profit margin is that which, when multiplied by the turnover achievable within an industry and with a viable corporate strategy, yields a return on investment that just covers the cost of capital. However, as mentioned above, accounting artifacts can cause returns on investment to deviate from the cost of capital for long periods, even in a competitive equilibrium.

6. Wal-Mart's fiscal year ends on January 31. Throughout the chapter we refer to the forecast for the year ended January 31, 2007 as the 2006 year, since eleven of the twelve months of operations occur in 2006.

7. See Foster, op. cit. A somewhat more accurate model is furnished by Brown and Rozeff, but it requires interactive statistical techniques for estimation. See L. Brown and M. Rozeff, "Univariate Time Series Models of Quarterly Accounting Earnings per Share," *Journal of Accounting Research* (Spring 1979): 179–89.

8. To estimate the model, we write in terms of realized earnings (as opposed to expected earnings) and move Q_{t-4} to the left-hand side:

$$Q_t - Q_{t-4} = \delta + \phi(Q_{t-1} - Q_{t-5}) + e_t$$

We now have a regression where $(Q_t - Q_{t-4})$ is the dependent variable, and its lagged value—$(Q_{t-1} - Q_{t-5})$—is the independent variable. Thus, to estimate the equation, prior earnings data must first be expressed in terms of year-to-year changes; the change for one quarter is then regressed against the change for the most recent quarter. The intercept provides an estimate of δ, and the slope is an estimate of ϕ. The equation is typically estimated using 24 to 40 quarters of prior earnings data.

9. See O'Brien, op. cit.

APPENDIX: THE BEHAVIOR OF COMPONENTS OF ROE

In Figure 6-2 we show that ROEs tend to be mean-reverting. In this appendix we show the behavior of the key components of ROE—operating ROA, operating margin, operating asset turnover, and net financial leverage. These ratios are computed using the same portfolio approach described in the chapter, based on the data for all publicly listed U.S. firms for the time period 1988 through 2005.

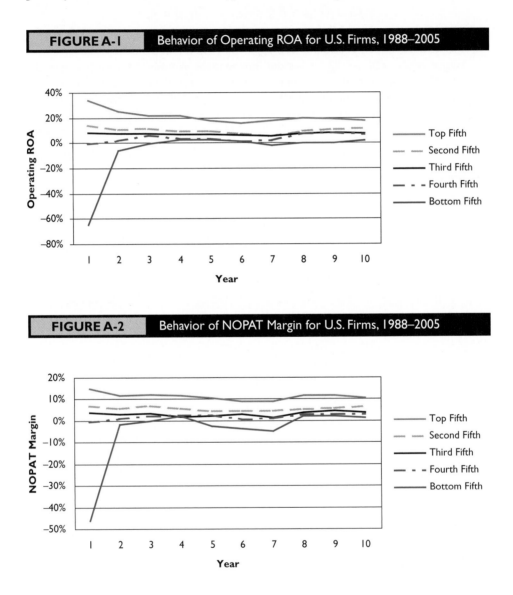

FIGURE A-1   Behavior of Operating ROA for U.S. Firms, 1988–2005

FIGURE A-2   Behavior of NOPAT Margin for U.S. Firms, 1988–2005

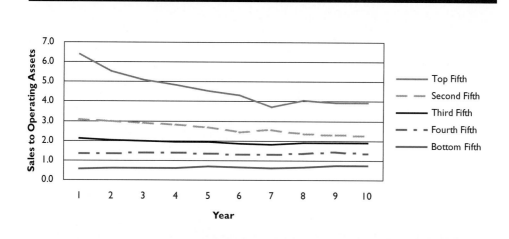

FIGURE A-3   Behavior of Operating Asset Turnover for U.S. Firms, 1988–2005

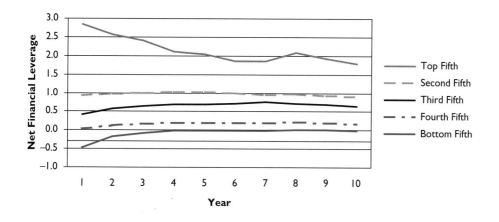

FIGURE A-4   Behavior of Net Financial Leverage for U.S. Firms, 1988–2005

Chapter 7

Prospective Analysis: Valuation Theory and Concepts

The previous chapter introduced forecasting, the first stage of prospective analysis. In this and the following chapter we describe valuation, the second and final stage of prospective analysis. This chapter focuses on valuation theory and concepts, and the following chapter discusses implementation issues.

Valuation is the process of converting forecasts into an estimate of the value of the firm's assets or equity. At some level, nearly every business decision involves valuation, at least implicitly. Within the firm, capital budgeting involves considering how a particular project will affect firm value. Strategic planning focuses on how value is influenced by larger sets of actions. Outside the firm, security analysts conduct valuation to support their buy/sell decisions, and potential acquirers (often with the assistance of investment bankers) estimate the value of target firms and the synergies they might offer. Even credit analysts, who typically do not explicitly estimate firm value, must at least implicitly consider the value of the firm's equity "cushion" if they are to maintain a complete view of the risk associated with lending activity.

In practice a wide variety of valuation approaches are employed. For example, in evaluating the fairness of a takeover bid, investment bankers commonly use five to ten different methods of valuation. Among the available methods are the following:

- *Discounted dividends.* This approach expresses the value of the firm's equity as the present value of forecasted future dividends.
- *Discounted abnormal earnings.* Under this approach, the value of the firm's equity is expressed as the sum of its current book value and the present value of forecasted abnormal earnings.
- *Valuation based on price multiples.* Under this approach, a current measure of performance or single forecast of performance is converted into value by applying an appropriate price multiple derived from the value of comparable firms. For example, firm value can be estimated by applying a price-to-earnings ratio to a forecast of the firm's earnings for the coming year. Other commonly used multiples include price-to-book ratios and price-to-sales ratios.
- *Discounted cash flow (DCF) analysis.* This approach involves the production of detailed, multiple-year forecasts of cash flows. The forecasts are then discounted at the firm's estimated cost of capital to arrive at an estimated value.

These methods are developed throughout the chapter, and their pros and cons discussed. All of the approaches can be structured in two ways. The first is to directly value the equity of the firm, since this is usually the variable the analyst is interested in estimating. The second is to value the assets of the firm, that is, the claims of equity and net debt, and then to deduct the value of net debt to arrive at the final equity estimate. Theoretically, both approaches should generate the same values. However, as we will see in the next chapter, there are implementation issues in reconciling the approaches. In this chapter we illustrate valuation using an all-equity firm to simplify the discussion. A brief discussion of the theoretical issues in valuing a firm's assets is included in Appendix A.

THE DISCOUNTED DIVIDENDS VALUATION METHOD

How should shareholders think about the value of their equity claims on a firm? Finance theory holds that the value of any financial claim is simply the present value of the cash payoffs that its claimholders receive. Since shareholders receive cash payoffs from a company in the form of dividends, the value of their equity is the present value of future dividends (including any liquidating dividend).

$$\text{Equity value} = \text{PV of expected future dividends}$$

If we denote the expected future dividend for a given year as DIV and r_e as the cost of equity capital (the relevant discount rate), the stock value is as follows:

$$\text{Equity value} = \frac{DIV_1}{(1 + r_e)} + \frac{DIV_2}{(1 + r_e)^2} + \frac{DIV_3}{(1 + r_e)^3} + \dots$$

Notice that the valuation formula views a firm as having an indefinite life. But in reality firms can go bankrupt or get taken over. In these situations shareholders effectively receive a terminating dividend on their stock.

If a firm had a constant dividend growth rate (g_d) indefinitely, its value would simplify to the following formula, which represents the present value of a growing perpetuity:

$$\text{Equity value} = \frac{DIV_1}{r_e - g_d}$$

To better understand how the discounted dividend approach works, consider the following example. At the beginning of year 1, Down Under Company raises $60 million of equity and uses the proceeds to buy a fixed asset. Operating profits before depreciation (all received in cash) are expected to be $40 million in year 1, $50 million in year 2, and $60 million in year 3. The firm pays out all operating profits as dividends and pays no taxes. At the end of year 3, the company terminates and has no residual value. If the cost of equity capital for this firm is 10 percent, the value of the firm's equity is computed as follows:

Year	Dividend	PV Factor	PV of Dividend
1	$40 m	0.909	$36.4 m
2	50 m	0.826	41.3 m
3	60 m	0.751	45.1 m
Equity value			$122.8 m

The above valuation method is called the dividend discount model. It forms the basis for most of the popular theoretical approaches to stock valuation. The remainder of the chapter discusses how this model can be recast to generate the discounted abnormal earnings, price multiple, and discounted cash flow models of value.

THE DISCOUNTED ABNORMAL EARNINGS VALUATION METHOD

There is a direct link between dividends and earnings. If all equity effects (other than capital transactions) flow through the income statement,[1] the expected book value of equity for existing shareholders at the end of year 1 (BVE_1) is simply the book value at the beginning of the year (BVE_0) plus expected net income (NI_1) less expected dividends (DIV_1).[2] This relation can be rewritten as follows:

$$DIV_1 = NI_1 + BVE_0 - BVE_1$$

By substituting this identity for dividends into the dividend discount formula and rearranging the terms, stock value can be rewritten as follows (Appendix B provides a simple proof of this formula):

Equity value = Book value of equity + PV of expected future abnormal earnings

Abnormal earnings are net income adjusted for a capital charge, which is computed as the discount rate multiplied by the beginning book value of equity. Abnormal earnings incorporate an adjustment to reflect the fact that accountants do not recognize any opportunity cost for equity funds used. Thus, the discounted abnormal earnings valuation formula is:

Equity value

$$= BVE_0 + \frac{NI_1 - r_e \cdot BVE_0}{(1 + r_e)} + \frac{NI_2 - r_e \cdot BVE_1}{(1 + r_e)^2} + \frac{NI_3 - r_e \cdot BVE_2}{(1 + r_e)^3} + \cdots$$

The earnings-based formulation has intuitive appeal. If a firm can earn only the required rate of return on its book value, then investors should be willing to pay no more than book value for the stock. Investors should pay more or less than book value if earnings are above or below this normal level. Thus, the deviation of a firm's market value from book value depends on its ability to generate "abnormal earnings." The formulation also implies that a firm's stock value reflects the cost of its existing net assets (i.e., its book equity) plus the present value of future growth options (represented by cumulative abnormal earnings).

To illustrate the earnings-based valuation approach, let's return to the Down Under Company example. Assuming the company depreciates its fixed assets using the straight-line method, its accounting-based earnings will be $20 million lower than dividends in each of the three years. The firm's beginning book equity, earnings, capital charges, abnormal earnings, and valuation will be as follows:

Year	Beginning Book Value	Earnings	Capital Charge	Abnormal Earnings	PV Factor	PV of Abnormal Earnings
1	$60 m	$20 m	$6 m	$14 m	0.909	$12.7 m
2	40 m	30 m	4 m	26 m	0.826	21.5 m
3	20 m	40 m	2 m	38 m	0.751	28.6 m
Cumulative PV of abnormal earnings						62.8 m
+ Beginning book value						60.0 m
= Equity value						$122.8 m

This stock valuation of $122.8 million is identical to the value estimated when the expected future dividends are discounted directly.

Key Analysis Questions

Valuation of equity under the discounted abnormal earnings method requires the analyst to answer the following questions:

- What are expected future net income and book values of equity (and therefore abnormal earnings) over a finite forecast horizon (usually five to ten years) given the firm's industry competitiveness and the firm's positioning?
- What is expected future abnormal net income beyond the final year of the forecast horizon (called the "terminal year") based on some simplifying assumptions? If abnormal returns are expected to persist, what are the barriers to entry that deter competition?
- What is the firm's cost of equity used to compute the present value of abnormal earnings?

Accounting Methods and Discounted Abnormal Earnings

One question that arises when valuation is based directly on earnings and book values is how the estimate is affected by managers' choice of accounting methods and accrual estimates. Would estimates of value differ for two otherwise identical firms if one used more conservative accounting methods than the other? We will see that, provided analysts recognize the impact of differences in accounting methods on future earnings (and hence their earnings forecasts), the accounting effects per se should have no influence on their value estimates. There are two reasons for this. First, accounting choices that affect a firm's current earnings also affect its book value, and therefore they affect the capital charges used to estimate future abnormal earnings. For example, conservative accounting not only lowers a firm's current earnings and book equity but also reduces future capital charges and inflates its future abnormal earnings. Second, double-entry bookkeeping is by nature self-correcting. Inflated earnings for one period have to ultimately be reversed in subsequent periods.

To understand how these two effects undo the effect of differences in accounting methods or accrual estimates, let's return to Down Under Company and see what happens if its managers choose to be conservative and expense some unusual costs that could have been capitalized as inventory in year 1. This accounting decision causes earnings and ending book value to be lower by $10 million. The inventory is then sold in year 2. For the time being, let's say the accounting choice has no influence on the analyst's view of the firm's real performance.

Management's choice reduces abnormal earnings in year 1 and book value at the beginning of year 2 by $10 million. However, future earnings will be higher, for two reasons. First, future earnings will be higher (by $10 million) when the inventory is sold in year 2. Second, the capital charge for normal earnings will be based on a book value of equity that is lower by $10 million. The $10 million decline in abnormal earnings in year 1 is perfectly offset (on a present value basis) by the $11 million higher abnormal earnings in year 2. As a result, the value of Down Under Company under conservative reporting is identical to the value under the earlier accounting method ($122.8 million).

Year	Beginning Book Value	Earnings	Abnormal Earnings	PV Factor	PV of Abnormal Earnings
1	$60 m	$10 m	$4 m	0.909	$3.6 m
2	30 m	40 m	37 m	0.826	30.6 m
3	20 m	40 m	38 m	0.751	28.6 m
Cumulative PV of abnormal earnings					62.8 m
+ Beginning book value					60.0 m
= Equity value					$122.8 m

Provided the analyst is aware of biases in accounting data that arise from managers' using aggressive or conservative accounting choices, abnormal earnings-based valuations are unaffected by variation in accounting decisions. This shows that strategic and accounting analyses are critical precursors to abnormal earnings valuation. The strategic and accounting analysis tools help the analyst to identify whether abnormal earnings arise from sustainable competitive advantage or from unsustainable accounting manipulations. For example, consider the implications of failing to understand the reasons for a decline in earnings from a change in inventory policy for Down Under Company. If an analyst mistakenly interpreted the decline as indicating that the firm was having difficulty moving its inventory, rather than that it had used conservative accounting, the analyst might reduce expectations of future earnings. The estimated value of the firm *would* then be lower than that reported in our example.

VALUATION USING PRICE MULTIPLES

Valuations based on price multiples are widely used by analysts. The primary reason for the popularity of this method is its simplicity. Unlike the discounted dividend, discounted abnormal earnings, and discounted cash flow methods, multiples-based valuations do not require detailed multiyear forecasts of a number of parameters such as growth, profitability, and cost of capital.

Valuation using multiples involves the following steps:

Step 1: Select a measure of performance or value (e.g., earnings, sales, cash flows, book equity, book assets) as the basis for multiple calculations. The two most commonly used metrics are based on earnings and book equity.

Step 2: Calculate price multiples for comparable firms, i.e., the ratio of the market value to the selected measure of performance or value.

Step 3: Apply the comparable firm multiple to the performance or value measure of the firm being analyzed.

Under this approach, the analyst relies on the market to undertake the difficult task of considering the short- and long-term prospects for growth and profitability and their implications for the values of the comparable firms. Then the analyst assumes that the pricing of the comparable firms is applicable to the firm at hand.

Main Issues with Multiples-Based Valuation

On the surface, using multiples seems straightforward. Unfortunately, in practice it is not as simple as it would appear. Identification of comparable firms is often quite difficult. There are also some choices to be made concerning how multiples will be calculated. Finally, understanding why multiples vary across firms, and how applicable another firm's multiple is to the one at hand, requires a sound knowledge of the determinants of each multiple.

Selecting Comparable Firms

Ideally, price multiples used in a comparable firm analysis are those for firms with similar operating and financial characteristics. Firms within the same industry are the most obvious candidates. But even within narrowly defined industries, it is often difficult to identify comparable firms. Many firms are in multiple industries, making it difficult to identify representative benchmarks. In addition, firms within the same industry frequently have different strategies, growth opportunities, and profitability, creating selection problems.

One way of dealing with these issues is to average across *all* firms in the industry. The analyst implicitly assumes that the various sources of noncomparability cancel each other out, so that the firm being valued is comparable to a "typical" industry member. Another approach is to focus on only those firms within the industry that are most similar.

For example, consider using multiples to value Wal-Mart. Business databases such as OneSource and Hoover's classify Wal-Mart as a discount and variety retailer in the nonapparel sector. Its closest competitors include Big Lots, BJ's Wholesale Club, Costco, Dollar General, Dollar Tree, Family Dollar, Sears, and Target. The average price–earnings ratio for these competitors was 22.19 and the average price-to-book ratio was 2.54. However, it is unclear whether these multiples are useful benchmarks for valuing Wal-Mart. Wal-Mart has a wider product offering than most of these competitors and operates on a significantly larger scale, both in terms of revenue and geographic reach. In addition, it competes in a variety of sectors against specialized retailers such as grocery stores and home improvement stores.

Multiples for Firms with Poor Performance

Price multiples can be affected when the denominator variable is temporarily performing poorly. This is especially common when the denominator is a flow measure, such as earnings or cash flows. For example, Big Lots, one of Wal-Mart's competitors, was unprofitable in the fiscal year ended January 2006 and marginally profitable in the twelve months ended July 2006. As a result, Big Lots had a price–earnings ratio of 51.54, well above the industry average.

Analysts have numerous options for handling the problems for multiples created by transitory shocks to the denominator. One option is to simply exclude firms with large transitory effects from the set of comparable firms. If Big Lots were excluded from Wal-Mart's peer group, the average price–earnings ratio for the industry declines from 22.19 to 17.53, which is much closer to the overall median ratio of 17.20. The magnitude of this effect illustrates how sensitive price–earnings multiples can be to transitory shocks. If poor performance is due to a one-time write-down or special item, analysts can simply exclude that effect from their computation of the comparable multiple. Finally, analysts can reduce the effect on multiples of temporary problems in past performance by using a denominator that is a forecast of future performance rather than the past measure itself. Multiples based on forecasts are termed *leading* multiples, whereas those based on historical data are called *trailing* multiples. Leading multiples are less likely to include one-time gains and losses in the denominator, simply because such items are difficult to anticipate.

Adjusting Multiples for Leverage

Price multiples should be calculated in a way that preserves consistency between the numerator and denominator. Consistency is an issue for those ratios where the denominator reflects performance *before* servicing debt. Examples include the price-to-sales multiple and any multiple of operating earnings or operating cash flows. When calculating these multiples, the numerator should include not just the market value of equity but the value of debt as well.

Determinants of Value-to-Book and Value–Earnings Multiples

Even across relatively closely related firms, price multiples can vary considerably. The abnormal earnings valuation method provides insight into factors that lead to differences in value-to-book and value–earnings multiples across firms.

If the abnormal earnings formula is scaled by book value, the left-hand side becomes the equity value-to-book ratio as opposed to the equity value itself. The right-hand side variables now reflect three multiple drivers: (1) earnings deflated by book value, or our old friend return on equity (ROE), discussed in Chapter 5, (2) the growth in equity book value over time, and (3) the firm's cost of equity. The actual valuation formula is as follows:

$$\text{Equity value-to-book ratio} = 1 + \frac{ROE_1 - r_e}{(1 + r_e)} + \frac{(ROE_2 - r_e)(1 + gbve_1)}{(1 + r_e)^2}$$
$$+ \frac{(ROE_3 - r_e)(1 + gbve_1)(1 + gbve_2)}{(1 + r_e)^3} + \dots$$

where $gbve_t$ = growth in book value (BVE) from year $t - 1$ to year t or

$$\frac{BVE_t - BVE_{t-1}}{BVE_{t-1}}$$

A firm's value-to-book ratio is largely driven by the magnitude of its future abnormal ROEs, defined as ROE less the cost of equity capital ($ROE - r_e$). Firms with positive abnormal ROEs are able to invest their net assets that create value for shareholders and will have price-to-book ratios greater than one. In contrast, firms with negative abnormal ROEs are unable to invest shareholder funds at a rate greater than their cost of capital and have ratios below one.

The magnitude of a firm's value-to-book multiple also depends on the amount of growth in book value. Firms can grow their equity base by issuing new equity or by reinvesting profits. If this new equity is invested in positive valued projects for shareholders, that is, projects with ROEs that exceed the cost of capital, the firm will boost its equity value-to-book multiple. Conversely, for firms with ROEs that are less than the cost of capital, equity growth further lowers the multiple.

The valuation task can now be framed in terms of the following essential questions about the firm's value drivers:

- Will the firm be able to generate ROEs that exceed its cost of equity capital? If so, for how long?
- How quickly will the firm's investment base (book value) grow?

If desired, the equation can be rewritten so that future ROEs are expressed as the product of their components: profit margins, sales turnover, and leverage. Thus the approach permits us to build directly on projections of the same accounting numbers utilized in financial analysis (see Chapter 5) without the need to convert projections of those numbers into cash flows. Yet in the end, the estimate of value should be the same as that from the dividend discount model.[3]

Returning to the Down Under Company example, the implied equity value-to-book multiple can be estimated as follows:

	Year 1	Year 2	Year 3
Beginning book value	$60 m	$40 m	$20 m
Earnings	$20 m	$30 m	$40 m
ROE	0.33	0.75	2.00
− Cost of capital	0.10	0.10	0.10
= Abnormal ROE	0.23	0.65	1.90
× (1 + compound book value growth)	1.00	0.67	0.33
= Abnormal ROE scaled by book value growth	0.23	0.43	0.63
× PV factor	0.909	0.826	0.751
= PV of abnormal ROE scaled by book value growth	0.212	0.358	0.476
Cumulative PV of abnormal ROE scaled by book value growth	1.046		
+ 1.00	1.000		
= Equity value-to-book multiple	2.046		

The equity value-to-book multiple for Down Under is therefore 2.046, and the implied stock value is $122.8 ($60 times 2.046), once again identical to the dividend discount model value.

The equity value-to-book formulation can also be used to construct the equity value–earnings multiple as follows:

$$\text{Equity value-to-earnings multiple} = \text{Equity value-to-book multiple} \times \frac{\text{Book value of equity}}{\text{Earnings}}$$

$$= \frac{\text{Equity value-to-book multiple}}{\text{ROE}}$$

In other words, the same factors that drive a firm's equity value-to-book multiple also explain its equity value–earnings multiple. The key difference between the two multiples is that the value–earnings multiple is affected by the firm's current level of ROE performance, whereas the value-to-book multiple is not. Firms with low current ROEs therefore have very high value–earnings multiples and vice versa. If a firm has a zero or negative ROE, its PE multiple is not defined. Value–earnings multiples are therefore more volatile than value-to-book multiples.

The following data for a subset of comparable firms in the discount and variety retail industry illustrate the relation between ROE, equity growth, the price-to-book ratio, and the price–earnings ratio:

Company	ROE	Book Value Growth	Price-to-Book Ratio	Price–Earnings Ratio
Wal-Mart	22.3%	18.1%	3.36	16.33
Sears	10.3%	2.7%	1.96	19.49
Target	18.2%	6.3%	2.92	16.96
Big Lots	4.0%	−9.3%	2.02	51.54

The price-to-book multiples indicate that investors expect that Wal-Mart will have the highest future abnormal ROEs, highest net asset growth, and/or lowest cost of capital combination of the four firms, followed by Target. Expectations for Sears and Big Lots are similar, but somewhat lower than for Wal-Mart or Target. In contrast, the price-to-earnings multiples are highest for Big Lots and Sears. Given their relatively low price-to-book multiples, the explanation for their price–earnings multiples rests in their low current ROEs. The price–earnings multiples imply that the market believes that Big Lots' current 4% ROE will improve substantially in the future, whereas Sears is expected to show modest improvement in its ROE.

Key Analysis Questions

To value a firm using multiples, an analyst must assess the quality of the variable used as the multiple basis and determine the appropriate peer firms to include in the benchmark multiple. Analysts are therefore likely to be interested in answering the following questions:

- How well does the denominator used in the multiple reflect the firm's performance? For example, if earnings or book equity are used as the denominator, has the firm made conservative or aggressive accounting choices that affect these variables and that are likely to unwind in the coming years? Is the firm likely to show strong growth in earnings or book equity? If earnings are the denominator, does the firm have temporarily poor or strong performance?
- What is the sustainability of the firm's growth and ROE based on the competitive dynamics of its industry and product market and its own competitive position?
- Which are the most suitable peer companies to include in the benchmark multiple computation? Have these firms had growth (earnings or book values), profitability, and quality of earnings comparable to the firm being analyzed? Do they have the same risk characteristics?

SHORTCUT FORMS OF EARNINGS-BASED VALUATION

The discounted abnormal earnings valuation formula can be simplified by making assumptions about the relation between a firm's current and future abnormal earnings. Similarly, the equity value-to-book formula can be simplified by making assumptions about long-term ROEs and growth.

Abnormal Earnings Simplification

Several assumptions about the relation between current and future net income are popular for simplifying the abnormal earnings model. First, abnormal earnings can be assumed to follow a random walk. The random walk model for abnormal earnings implies that an analyst's best guess about future expected abnormal earnings are current abnormal earnings. The model assumes that past shocks to abnormal earnings persist forever, but that future shocks are random or unpredictable. The random walk model can be written as follows:

$$\text{Forecasted } AE_1 = AE_0$$

Forecasted AE_1 is the forecast of next year's abnormal earnings and AE_0 is current period abnormal earnings. Under the model, forecasted abnormal earnings for two years ahead are simply abnormal earnings in year one, or once again current abnormal earnings. In other words, the best guess of abnormal earnings in any future year is just current abnormal earnings. It is also possible to include a drift term in the model, allowing earnings to grow by a constant amount, or at a constant rate in each period.

How does the above assumption about future abnormal earnings simplify the discounted abnormal earnings valuation model? If abnormal earnings follow a random walk, all future forecasts of abnormal earnings are simply current abnormal earnings. Consequently, the present value of future abnormal earnings can be calculated by valuing the current level of abnormal earnings as a perpetuity. It is then possible to rewrite value as follows:

$$\text{Stock value} = BVE_0 + \frac{AE_0}{r_e}$$

The stock value is the book value of equity at the end of the year plus current abnormal earnings divided by the cost of capital. The perpetuity formula can be adjusted to incorporate expectations of constant growth in future abnormal earnings.

In reality, shocks to abnormal earnings are unlikely to persist forever. Firms that have positive shocks are likely to attract competitors that will reduce opportunities for future abnormal performance. Firms with negative abnormal earnings shocks are likely to fail or to be acquired by other firms that can manage their resources more effectively. The persistence of abnormal performance will therefore depend on strategic factors such as barriers to entry and switching costs, discussed in Chapter 2. To reflect this, analysts frequently assume that current shocks to abnormal earnings decay over time. Under this assumption, abnormal earnings are said to follow an autoregressive model. Forecasted abnormal earnings are then

$$\text{Forecasted } AE_1 = \beta AE_0$$

β is a parameter that captures the speed with which abnormal earnings decay over time. If there is no decay, β is 1 and abnormal earnings follow a random walk. If β is 0, abnormal earnings decay completely within one year. Estimates of β using actual company data indicate that for a typical U.S. firm, β is approximately 0.6. However, it varies by industry and is smaller for firms with large accruals and one-time accounting charges.[4]

The autoregressive model implies that stock values can again be written as a function of current abnormal earnings and book values[5]:

$$\text{Stock value} = \text{BVE}_0 + \frac{\beta AE_0}{r_e + (1 - \beta)}$$

This formulation implies that stock values are simply the sum of current book value plus current abnormal earnings weighted by the cost of equity capital and persistence in abnormal earnings.

ROE and Growth Simplifications

It is also possible to make simplifications about long-term ROEs and equity growth to reduce forecast horizons for estimating the equity value-to-book multiple. Firms' long-term ROEs are affected by such factors as barriers to entry in their industries, change in production or delivery technologies, and quality of management. As discussed in Chapter 6, these factors tend to force abnormal ROEs to decay over time. One way to model this decay is to assume that ROEs revert to the mean. Forecasted ROE after one period then takes the following form:

$$\text{Forecasted } ROE_1 = ROE_0 + \beta(ROE_0 - \overline{ROE})$$

$\overline{ROE}$ is the steady state ROE (either the firm's cost of capital or the long-term industry ROE) and β is a "speed of adjustment factor" that reflects how quickly it takes the ROE to revert to its steady state.[6]

Growth rates in the book value of equity are driven by several factors. First, the size of the firm is important. Small firms can sustain very high growth rates for an extended period, whereas large firms find it more difficult to do so. Second, firms with high rates of growth are likely to attract competitors, which reduces their growth rates. As a result, steady-state rates of growth in book equity are likely to be similar to rates of growth in the overall economy, which in the U.S. have averaged 3–4 percent per year.

The long-term patterns in ROE and book equity growth rates imply that for most companies there is limited value in making forecasts for valuation beyond a relatively short horizon, generally five to ten years. Powerful economic forces tend to lead firms with superior or inferior performance early in the forecast horizon to revert to a level that is comparable to that of other firms in the industry or the economy. For a firm in steady state, that is, expected to have a stable ROE and book equity growth rate ($gbve$), the value-to-book multiple formula simplifies to the following:

$$\text{Equity value-to-book multiple} = 1 + \frac{ROE_0 - r_e}{r_e - gbve}$$

Consistent with this simplified model, there is a strong relation between price-to-book ratios and current ROEs. Figure 7-1 shows the relation between these variables for firms in the variety and discount retail industry we discussed earlier. The correlation between the two variables is 0.69.

| FIGURE 7-1 | Relationship Between ROE and Price-to-Book Multiples |

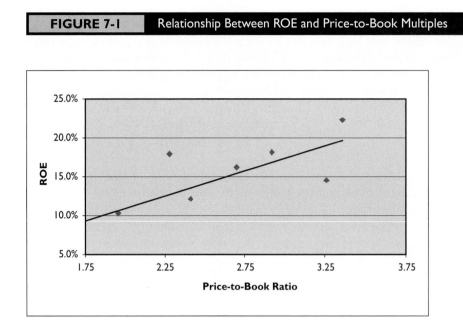

Of course, analysts can make a variety of simplifying assumptions about a firm's ROE and growth. For example, they can assume that they decay slowly or rapidly to the cost of capital and the growth rate for the economy. They can assume that the rates decay to the industry or economy average ROEs and book value growth rates. The valuation formula can easily be modified to accommodate these assumptions

THE DISCOUNTED CASH FLOW MODEL

The final valuation method discussed here is the discounted cash flow approach, the valuation method taught in most finance classes. Like the abnormal earnings approach, it is derived from the dividend discount model. It is based on the insight that dividends can be recast as free cash flows,[7] as follows:

$$\text{Dividends} = \text{Operating cash flow} - \text{Capital outlays} + \text{Net cash flows from debt owners}$$

As discussed in Chapter 5, operating cash flows to equity holders are simply net income plus depreciation less changes in working capital accruals. Capital outlays are capital expenditures less asset sales. Finally, net cash flows from debt owners are issues of new debt less retirements less the after-tax cost of interest. By rearranging these terms, the free cash flows to equity can be written as

$$\text{Dividends} = \text{Free cash flows to equity} = NI - \Delta BVA + \Delta BVND$$

where NI is net income, ΔBVA is the change in book value of net operating assets (including changes in working capital plus capital expenditures less depreciation expense), and $\Delta BVND$ is the change in book value of net debt (interest-bearing debt less excess cash).

The dividend discount model can therefore be written as the present value of free cash flows to equity. Under this formulation, value to shareholders is estimated as follows:

Equity value = PV of free cash flows to equity claim holders

$$= \frac{NI_1 - \Delta BVA_1 + \Delta BVND_1}{(1 + r_e)} + \frac{NI - \Delta BVA_2 + \Delta BVND_2}{(1 + r_e)^2} + \dots$$

Valuation under the discounted cash flow method therefore involves the following steps:

Step 1: Forecast free cash flows available to equity holders over a finite forecast horizon (usually five to ten years).

Step 2: Forecast free cash flows beyond the terminal year based on some simplifying assumption.

Step 3: Discount free cash flows to equity holders at the cost of equity. The discounted amount represents the estimated value of free cash flows available to equity.

Returning to the Down Under Company example, there is no debt, so the free cash flows to owners are simply the operating profits before depreciation. Since the company's cost of equity is assumed to be 10 percent, the present value of the free cash flows is calculated as follows:

Year	Free Cash Flows	PV Factor	PV of Free Cash Flows
1	$40 m	0.909	$36.4 m
2	50 m	0.826	41.3 m
3	60 m	0.751	45.1 m
Equity value			$122.8 m

Notice that the value of Down Under's equity is exactly the same as that estimated using the discounted abnormal earnings method. This should not be surprising. Both methods are derived from the dividend discount model. And in estimating value under the two approaches, we have used the same underlying assumptions to forecast earnings and cash flows.

COMPARING VALUATION METHODS

We have discussed three methods of valuation derived from the dividend discount model: discounted dividends, discounted abnormal earnings (or abnormal ROEs), and discounted cash flows. Since the methods are all derived from the same underlying model, no one version can be considered superior to the others. As long as analysts make the same assumptions about firm fundamentals, value estimates under all three methods will be identical. However, we discuss below important differences between the models.

Differences in Focus

The methods frame the valuation task differently and can in practice focus the analyst's attention on different issues. The earnings-based approaches frame the issues in terms of accounting data such as earnings and book values rather than cash flows. Analysts spend considerable time analyzing historical income statements and balance sheets, and their primary forecasts are typically for these accounting variables.

Defining values in terms of ROEs has the advantage that it focuses analysts' attention on ROE, the same key measure of performance that is decomposed in a standard financial analysis. Furthermore, because ROEs control for firm scale, it is likely to be easier for analysts to evaluate the reasonableness of their forecasts by benchmarking them with ROEs of other firms in the industry and in the broader economy. This type of benchmarking is more challenging for free cash flows and abnormal earnings.

Differences in Required Structure

The methods differ in the amount of analysis and structure required for valuation. The discounted abnormal earnings and ROE methods require analysts to construct both pro forma income statements and balance sheets to forecast future earnings and book values. In contrast, the discounted cash flow method requires analysts to forecast income statements and changes in working capital and long-term assets to generate free cash flows. Finally, the discounted dividend method requires analysts to forecast dividends.

The discounted abnormal earnings, ROE, and free cash flow models all require more structure for analysis than the discounted dividend approach. They therefore help analysts avoid structural inconsistencies in their forecasts of future dividends by specifically requiring a prediction of firms' future performance and investment opportunities. Similarly, the discounted abnormal earnings/ROE method requires more structure and work than the discounted cash flow method to build full pro forma balance sheets. This allows analysts to avoid inconsistencies in the firm's financial structure.

Differences in Terminal Value Implications

A third difference between the methods is in the effort required for estimating terminal values. Terminal value estimates for the abnormal earnings and ROE methods tend to represent a much smaller fraction of total value than under the discounted cash flow or dividend methods. On the surface, this would appear to mitigate concerns about the aspect of valuation that leaves the analyst most uncomfortable. Is this apparent advantage real? As explained below, the answer turns on how well value is already reflected in the accountant's book value.

The abnormal earnings valuation does not eliminate the discounted cash flow terminal value problem, but it does reframe it. Discounted cash flow terminal values include the present value of *all* expected cash flows beyond the forecast horizon. Under abnormal earnings valuation, that value is broken into two parts: the present values of *normal* earnings and *abnormal* earnings beyond the terminal year. The terminal value in the abnormal earnings technique includes only the *abnormal* earnings. The present value of *normal* earnings is already reflected in the original book value.

The abnormal earnings approach, then, recognizes that current book value and earnings over the forecast horizon already reflect many of the cash flows expected to arrive after the forecast horizon. The approach builds directly on accrual accounting. For example, under accrual accounting book equity can be thought of as the minimum recoverable future benefits attributable to the firm's net assets. In addition, revenues are typically realized when earned, not when cash is received. The discounted cash flow approach, on the other hand, "unravels" all of the accruals, spreads the resulting cash flows over longer horizons, and then reconstructs its own "accruals" in the form of discounted expectations of future cash flows. The essential difference between the two approaches is that abnormal earnings valuation recognizes that the accrual process may already have performed a portion of the valuation task, whereas the discounted cash flow approach ultimately moves back to the primitive cash flows underlying the accruals.

The usefulness of the accounting-based perspective thus hinges on how well the accrual process reflects future cash flows. The approach is most convenient when the accrual process is "unbiased," so that earnings can be abnormal only as the result of economic rents and not as a product of accounting itself.[8] The forecast horizon then extends to the point where the firm is expected to approach a competitive equilibrium and earn only normal earnings on its projects. Subsequent abnormal earnings would be zero, and the terminal value at that point would be zero. In this case, *all* of the firm's value is reflected in the book value and earnings projected over the forecast horizon.

Of course, accounting rarely works so well. For example, in most countries research and development costs are expensed, and book values fail to reflect any research and development assets. As a result, firms that spend heavily on research and development—such as pharmaceutical companies—tend, on average, to generate abnormally high earnings even in the face of stiff competition. Purely as an artifact of research and development accounting, abnormal earnings would be expected to remain positive indefinitely for such firms, and the terminal value could represent a substantial fraction of total value.

If desired, the analyst can alter the accounting approach used by the firm in his or her own projections. "Better" accounting would be viewed as that which reflects a larger fraction of the firm's value in book values and earnings over the forecast horizon.[9] This same view underlies analysts' attempts to "normalize" earnings; the adjusted numbers are intended to provide better indications of value, even though they reflect performance only over a short horizon.

Recent research has focused on the performance of earnings-based valuation relative to discounted cash flow and discounted dividend methods. The findings indicate that over relatively short forecast horizons, ten years or less, valuation estimates using the abnormal earnings approach generate more precise estimates of value than either the discounted dividend or discounted cash flow models. This advantage for the earnings-based approach persists for firms with conservative or aggressive accounting, indicating that accrual accounting in the U.S. does a reasonably good job of reflecting future cash flows.[10]

Research also indicates that abnormal earnings estimates of value outperform traditional multiples, such as price–earnings ratios, price-to-book ratios, and dividend yields, for predicting future stock movements.[11] Firms that have high abnormal earnings model estimates of value relative to their current price show positive abnormal future stock returns, whereas firms with low estimated value-to-price ratios have negative abnormal stock performance.

Key Analysis Questions

The above discussion on the trade-offs between different methods of valuing a company raises several questions for analysts about comparing methods and considering which is likely to be most reliable for their analysis:

- What are the key performance parameters that the analyst forecasts? Is more attention given to forecasting accounting variables, such as earnings and book values, or to forecasting cash flow variables?

- Has the analyst linked forecasted income statements and balance sheets? If not, is there any inconsistency between the two statements, or in the implications of the assumptions for future performance? If so, what is the source of this inconsistency and does it affect discounted earnings-based and discounted cash flow methods similarly?
- How well does the firm's accounting capture its underlying assets and obligations? Does it do a good enough job that we can rely on book values as the basis for long-term forecasts? Alternatively, does the firm rely heavily on off-balance-sheet assets, such as R&D, which make book values a poor lower bound on long-term performance?
- Has the analyst made very different assumptions about long-term performance in the terminal value computations under the different valuation methods? If so, which set of assumptions is more plausible given the firm's industry and its competitive positioning?

SUMMARY

Valuation is the process by which forecasts of performance are converted into estimates of price. A variety of valuation techniques are employed in practice, and there is no single method that clearly dominates others. In fact, since each technique involves different advantages and disadvantages, there are gains to considering several approaches simultaneously.

For shareholders, a stock's value is the present value of future dividends. This chapter described three valuation techniques directly based on this dividend discount definition of value: discounted dividends, discounted abnormal earnings/ROEs, and discounted free cash flows. The discounted dividend method attempts to forecast dividends directly. The abnormal earnings approach expresses the value of a firm's equity as book value plus discounted expectations of future abnormal earnings. Finally, the discounted cash flow method represents a firm's stock value through expected future free cash flows discounted at the cost of capital.

Although these three methods were derived from the same dividend discount model, they frame the valuation task differently. In practice they focus the analyst's attention on different issues and require different levels of structure in developing forecasts of the underlying primitive, future dividends.

Price-multiple valuation methods were also discussed. Under these approaches, analysts calculate ratios of current price to historical or forecasted measures of performance for comparable firms. The benchmarks are then used to value the performance of the firm being analyzed. Multiples have traditionally been popular, primarily because they do not require analysts to make multiyear forecasts of performance. However, it can be difficult to identify comparable firms to use as benchmarks. Even across highly related firms, there are differences in performance that are likely to affect their multiples.

The chapter discussed the relation between two popular multiples, value-to-book and value–earnings ratios, and the discounted abnormal earnings valuation. The resulting formulations indicate that value-to-book multiples are a function of future abnormal ROEs, book value growth, and the firm's cost of equity. The value–earnings multiple is a function of the same factors and the current ROE.

DISCUSSION QUESTIONS

1. Joe Watts, an analyst at EMH Securities, states: "I don't know why anyone would ever try to value earnings. Obviously, the market knows that earnings can be manipulated and only values cash flows." Discuss.

2. Explain why terminal values in accounting-based valuation are significantly lower than those for DCF valuation.

3. Manufactured Earnings is a "darling" of Wall Street analysts. Its current market price is $15 per share, and its book value is $5 per share. Analysts forecast that the firm's book value will grow by 10 percent per year indefinitely, and the cost of equity is 15 percent. Given these facts, what is the market's expectation of the firm's long-term average ROE?

4. Given the information in question 3, what will be Manufactured Earnings' stock price if the market revises its expectations of long-term average ROE to 20 percent?

5. Analysts reassess Manufactured Earnings' future performance as follows: growth in book value increases to 12 percent per year, but the ROE of the incremental book value is only 15 percent. What is the impact on the market-to-book ratio?

6. How can a company with a high ROE have a low PE ratio?

7. What types of companies have
    a. a high PE and a low market-to-book ratio?
    b. a high PE ratio and a high market-to-book ratio?
    c. a low PE and a high market-to-book ratio?
    d. a low PE and a low market-to-book ratio?

8. Free cash flows (FCF) used in DCF valuations discussed in the chapter are defined as follows:

    FCF to debt and equity = Earnings before interest and taxes $\times$ (1 − tax rate) + Depreciation and deferred taxes − Capital expenditures −/+ Increase/decrease in working capital

    FCF to equity = Net income + Depreciation and deferred taxes − Capital expenditures −/+ Increase/decrease in working capital +/− Increase/decrease in debt

    Which of the following items affect free cash flows to debt and equity holders? Which affect free cash flows to equity alone? Explain why and how.
    * An increase in accounts receivable
    * A decrease in gross margins
    * An increase in property, plant, and equipment
    * An increase in inventory
    * Interest expense
    * An increase in prepaid expenses
    * An increase in notes payable to the bank.

9. Starite Company is valued at $20 per share. Analysts expect that it will generate free cash flows to equity of $4 per share for the foreseeable future. What is the firm's implied cost of equity capital?

10. Janet Stringer argues that "the DCF valuation method has increased managers' focus on short-term rather than long-term performance, since the discounting process places much heavier weight on short-term cash flows than long-term ones." Comment.

NOTES

1. The incorporation of all noncapital equity transactions into income is called clean surplus accounting. It is analogous to comprehensive income, the concept defined in FAS 130.

2. Changes in book value also include new capital contributions. However, the dividend discount model assumes that new capital is issued at fair value. As a result, any incremental book value from capital issues is exactly offset by the discounted value of future dividends to new shareholders. Capital transactions, therefore, do not affect firm valuation.

3. It may seem surprising that one can estimate value with no explicit attention to two of the cash flow streams considered in DCF analysis, investments in working capital and capital expenditures. The accounting-based technique recognizes that these investments cannot possibly contribute to value without impacting abnormal earnings and, therefore, only their earnings impacts need be considered. For example, the benefit of an increase in inventory turnover surfaces in terms of its impact on ROE (and thus, abnormal earnings) without the need to consider explicitly the cash flow impacts involved.

4. See P. M. Dechow, A. P. Hutton, and R. G. Sloan, "An empirical assessment of the residual income valuation model," *Journal of Accounting and Economics* 23, January 1999.

5. This formulation is a variant of a model proposed by J. Ohlson, "Earnings, book values, and dividends in security valuation," *Contemporary Accounting Research* 11, Spring 1995. Ohlson includes in his forecasts of future abnormal earnings a variable that reflects relevant information other than current abnormal earnings. This variable then also appears in the stock valuation formula. Empirical research by Dechow, Hutton, and Sloan, "An empirical assessment of the residual income valuation model," *Journal of Accounting and Economics* 23, January 1999, indicates that financial analysts' forecasts of abnormal earnings do reflect considerable information other than current abnormal earnings, and that this information is useful for valuation.

6. This specification is similar to the model for dividends developed by J. Lintner, "Distribution of incomes of corporations among dividends, retained earnings, and taxes," *American Economic Review* 46 (May 1956): 97–113.

7. In practice, firms do not have to pay out all of their free cash flows as dividends; they can retain surplus cash in the business. The conditions under which a firm's dividend decision affects its value are discussed by M. H. Miller and F. Modigliani in "Dividend Policy, Growth and the Valuation of Shares," *Journal of Business* 34 (October 1961): 411–33.

8. Unbiased accounting is that which, in a competitive equilibrium, produces an expected ROE equal to the cost of capital. The actual ROE thus reveals the presence of economic rents. Market-value accounting is a special case of unbiased accounting that produces an expected ROE equal to the cost of capital, even when the firm is not in a competitive equilibrium. That is, market-value accounting reflects the present value of future economic rents in book value, driving the expected ROEs to a normal level. For a discussion of unbiased and biased accounting, see G. Feltham and J. Ohlson, "Valuation and Clean Surplus Accounting for Operating and Financial Activities," *Contemporary Accounting Research* 11, No. 2 (Spring 1995): 689–731.

9. In Bennett Stewart's book on EVA valuation, *The Quest for Value* (New York: HarperBusiness, 1999), he recommends a number of accounting adjustments including the capitalization of research and development.

10. S. Penman and T. Sougiannis, "A Comparison of Dividend, Cash Flow, and Earnings Approaches to Equity Valuation," *Contemporary Accounting Research* (Fall 1998): 343–83, compares the valuation methods using actual realizations of earnings, cash flows, and dividends to estimate prices. J. Francis, P. Olsson, and D. Oswald, "Comparing Accuracy and Explainability of Dividend, Free Cash Flow and Abnormal Earnings Equity Valuation Models," *Journal of Accounting Research* 38 (Spring 2000): 45–70, estimates values using *Value Line* forecasts.

11. See C. Lee, J. Myers, and B. Swaminathan, "What is the Intrinsic Value of the Dow?" *Journal of Finance* (October 1999): 1693–1741.

APPENDIX A: ASSET VALUATION METHODOLOGIES

All of the valuation approaches discussed in this chapter can also be structured to estimate the value of a firm's assets (or the combined debt and equity) rather than its equity. Switching from equity valuation to asset valuation is often as simple as substituting financial measures related to equity for financial measures related to the entire firm. For example, in the earnings-based valuation model, net income (the earnings flow to equity) is replaced by NOPAT (the earnings available for debt and equity), and book values of assets replace the book value of equity. Value multiples are based on ROEs for the equity formulation and on ROAs for valuing asset multiples. And the discount rate for equity models is the cost of equity compared to the weighted average cost of capital (or WACC) for asset valuation models.

The formulas used for asset valuation under the various approaches are presented below.

Abnormal Earnings Valuation

Under the earnings-based approach, the value of the assets is

Assets value

$$= BVA_0 + \frac{NOPAT_1 - WACC \cdot BVA_0}{(1 + WACC)} + \frac{NOPAT_2 - WACC \cdot BVA_1}{(1 + WACC)^2} + \ldots$$

BVA is the book value of the firm's assets, NOPAT is net operating profit (before interest) after tax, and WACC is the firm's weighted-average cost of debt and equity. From this asset value, the analyst can deduct the market value of net debt to generate an estimate of the value of equity.

Valuation Using Price Multiples

The multiple valuation can be structured as the debt plus equity value-to-book assets ratio by scaling the abnormal NOPAT formula by book value of net operating assets. The valuation formula then becomes

Debt plus equity value-to-book ratio

$$= 1 + \frac{ROA_1 - WACC}{(1 + WACC)} + \frac{(ROA_2 - WACC)(1 + gbva_1)}{(1 + WACC)^2}$$

$$+ \frac{(ROA_3 - WACC)(1 + gbva_1)(1 + gbva_2)}{(1 + WACC)^3} + \ldots$$

where ROA = operating return on asset = NOPAT/(Operating working capital + Net long-term assets)

WACC = weighted average cost of debt and equity

$gbva_t$ = growth in book value of assets (BVA) from year $t - 1$ to year t or

$$\frac{BVA_t - BVA_{t-1}}{BVA_{t-1}}$$

The value of a firm's debt and equity to net operating assets multiple therefore depends on its ability to generate asset returns that exceed its WACC, and on its ability to grow its asset base. The value of equity under this approach is then the estimated multiple times the current book value of assets less the market value of debt.

Discounted Cash Flow Model

The free cash flow formulation can be structured by estimating the value of claims to net debt and equity and then deducting the market value of net debt. This approach is more widely used in practice because it does not require explicit forecasts of changes in debt balances. The value of debt plus equity is computed as follows:

Debt plus equity value = PV of free cash flows to net debt and equity claim holders

$$= \frac{NOPAT_1 - \Delta BVA_1}{(1 + WACC)} + \frac{NOPAT_2 - \Delta BVA_2}{(1 + WACC)^2} + \dots$$

The firm's asset valuation therefore depends on the expected free cash flows to debt and equity holders during the forecast horizon, the forecasted terminal value of free cash flows, and the weighted average cost of capital.

APPENDIX B: RECONCILING THE DISCOUNTED DIVIDENDS AND DISCOUNTED ABNORMAL EARNINGS MODELS

To derive the earnings-based valuation from the dividend discount model consider the following two-period valuation:

$$\text{Equity value} = \frac{DIV_1}{(1 + r_e)} + \frac{DIV_2}{(1 + r_e)^2}$$

With clean surplus accounting, dividends (DIV) can be expressed as a function of net income (NI) and the book value of equity (BVE):

$$DIV_t = NI_t + BVE_{t-1} - BVE_t$$

Substituting this expression into the dividend discount model yields the following:

$$\text{Equity value} = \frac{NI_1 + BVE_0 - BVE_1}{(1 + r_e)} + \frac{NI_2 + BVE_1 - BVE_2}{(1 + r_e)^2}$$

This can be rewritten as follows:

$$\text{Equity value} = \frac{NI_1 - r_e BVE_0 + BVE_0(1 + r_e) - BVE_1}{(1 + r_e)}$$
$$+ \frac{NI_2 - r_e BVE_1 + BVE_1(1 + r_e) - BVE_2}{(1 + r_e)^2}$$
$$= BVE_0 + \frac{NI_1 - r_e BVE_0}{(1 + r_e)} + \frac{NI_2 - r_e BVE_1}{(1 + r_e)^2} - \frac{BVE_2}{(1 + r_e)^2}$$

As the forecast horizon expands, the final term (the present value of liquidating book value) becomes inconsequential. The value of equity is therefore the current book value plus the present value of future abnormal earnings.

Chapter 8

Prospective Analysis: Valuation Implementation

To move from the valuation theory discussed in the previous chapter to the actual task of valuing a company, we have to deal with two key issues. First, we have to estimate the cost of capital to discount our forecasts. And second, we have to make forecasts of financial performance stated in terms of abnormal earnings and book values, or free cash flows, over the life of the firm. The forecasting task itself is divided into two subcomponents: (1) detailed forecasts over a finite number of years and (2) a forecast of terminal value, which represents a summary of performance beyond the detailed forecast horizon.

This chapter builds on the forecast developed in Chapter 6 and provides guidance on calculating cost of capital, computing a terminal value, and synthesizing the different pieces of the analytical process to estimate firm or equity value.

COMPUTING A DISCOUNT RATE

To value a company's assets, the analyst discounts abnormal NOPAT, abnormal operating ROA, or cash flows available to both debt and equity holders. The proper discount rate to use is, therefore, the weighted average cost of capital (WACC). The WACC is calculated by weighting the costs of debt and equity capital according to their respective market values:

$$\text{WACC} = \text{Percent debt financing} \times \text{Cost of debt (after tax)} + \text{Percent}$$
$$\text{equity financing} \times \text{Cost of equity capital}$$

Weighting the Costs of Debt and Equity

The weights assigned to debt and equity represent their respective fractions of total capital provided, measured in terms of economic values. Computing an economic value for debt should not be difficult. It is reasonable to use book values if interest rates have not changed significantly since the time the debt was issued. Otherwise, the value of the debt can be estimated by discounting the future payouts at current market rates of interest applicable to the firm.

What is included in debt? Should short-term as well as long-term debt be included? Should payables and accruals be included? The answer is revealed by recalling that abnormal NOPAT and free cash flows to debt and equity are the earnings and cash flows *before* servicing short-term and long-term debt—indicating that both short-term and long-term debt should be considered a part of capital when computing the WACC. Servicing of other liabilities, such as accounts payable or accruals, should already have been considered as we computed abnormal NOPAT or free cash flows. Thus internal consistency requires that operating liabilities not be considered a part of capital when computing the WACC.

The tricky problem we face is assigning an economic value to equity. That is the very amount we are trying to estimate in the first place! How can the analyst possibly assign an economic value to equity at this intermediate stage, given that the estimate will not be known until all steps in the DCF analysis are completed?

One common approach to the problem is to insert at this point "target" ratios of debt to capital and equity to capital. For example, one might expect that a firm will, over the long run, maintain a capital structure that is 40 percent debt and 60 percent equity. The long-run focus is reasonable because we are discounting cash flows over a long horizon.

Another way around the problem is to start with book value of equity as a weight for purposes of calculating an initial estimate of the WACC, which in turn can be used in the discounting process to generate an initial estimate of the value of equity. That initial estimate can then be used in place of the book value to arrive at a new WACC, and a second estimate of the value of equity can be produced. This process can be repeated until the value used to calculate the WACC and the final estimated value converge. However, the analyst needs to be cautious in using this approach if the firm's economic leverage is likely to change over time.

Estimating the Cost of Debt

The cost of debt is the interest rate on the debt. If the assumed capital structure in future periods is the same as the historical structure, then the current interest rate on debt will be a good proxy for this. However, if the analyst assumes a change in capital structure, then it is important to estimate the expected interest rate given the new level of debt. One approach to this would be to estimate the expected credit rating of the company at the new level of debt and use the appropriate interest rates for that credit category.

It is also worth noting that the cost of debt will change over time if market interest rates are expected to change. This can arise if investors expect inflation to increase or decrease over the forecast horizon. Since we typically discount nominal earnings or cash flows, the cost of debt is a nominal rate, and will change over time to reflect changes in inflation. This can be handled by scaling the cost of debt up or down over time to reflect expected changes in interest rates each year. If interest rates are projected to rise by 3 percent as a result of expected inflation, the cost of debt for the firm we are analyzing should also increase by 3 percent. The yield curve, which shows how investors expect interest rates to change over time can be used to assess whether time-varying interest rates are likely to be important to include in the analysis.

Finally, the cost of debt should be expressed on a net-of-tax basis because it is after-tax cash flows that are being discounted. In most settings the market rate of interest can be converted to a net-of-tax basis by multiplying it by one minus the marginal corporate tax rate.

Estimating the Cost of Equity

Estimating the cost of equity can be difficult, and a full discussion of the topic lies beyond the scope of this chapter. At any rate, even an extended discussion would not supply answers to all the questions that might be raised in this area because the field of finance is in a state of flux over what constitutes an appropriate measure of the cost of equity.

One common approach is to use the capital asset pricing model (CAPM), which expresses the cost of equity as the sum of a required return on riskless assets plus a premium for beta or systematic risk:

Cost of equity = Riskless rate of return + Beta risk × Market risk premium

To estimate the required return on riskless assets, analysts often use the rate on intermediate-term treasury bonds, based on the observation that it is cash flows beyond the short term that are being discounted.[1]

The systematic or beta risk of a stock reflects the sensitivity of its cash flows and earnings (and hence stock price) to economy-wide market movements.[2] A firm whose performance increases or decreases at the same rate as changes in the economy as a whole will have a beta of one. Firms whose performance is highly sensitive to economy-wide changes, such as luxury goods producers, capital goods manufacturers, and construction firms, will have beta risks that exceed one. And firms whose earnings and cash flows are less sensitive to economic changes, such as regulated utilities or supermarkets, will have betas that are lower than one. Financial services firms, such as Standard & Poor's and Value Line, provide estimates of beta for publicly-listed companies that are based on the historical relation between the firm's stock returns and the returns on the market index. These estimates provide a useful way to assess publicly-traded firms' beta risks. For firms that are not publicly-traded, analysts can use betas for publicly-traded firms in the same industries, adjusting for any differences in financial leverage, as an indicator of their likely beta risks.

Finally, the market risk premium is the amount that investors demand as additional return for bearing beta risk. It is the excess of the expected return on the market index over the riskless rate. Over the 1926–2005 period, returns to the Standard and Poor's 500 index have exceeded the rate on intermediate-term treasury bonds by 6.8 percent.[3] As a result, many analysts assume that the market risk premium is around 7 percent. However, others argue that a variety of changes in the U.S. economy make the historical risk premium an invalid basis for forecasting expected risk premium going forward. Recent academic research suggests that the expected risk premium in the market in recent years has declined substantially to between 3 and 4 percent, leading some analysts to use these lower rates in their valuations.[4]

Although the above CAPM is often used to estimate the cost of capital, the evidence indicates that the model is incomplete. Assuming stocks are priced competitively, stock returns should be expected to compensate investors for just the cost of their capital. Thus, long-run average returns should be close to the cost of capital and should (according to the CAPM) vary across stocks according to their systematic risk. However, factors beyond just systematic risk seem to play some role in explaining variation in long-run average returns. The most important such factor is labeled the "size effect": smaller firms (as measured by market capitalization) tend to generate higher returns in subsequent periods. The reason for this size effect is unclear. It could mean either that smaller firms are riskier than indicated by the CAPM or that they are underpriced at the point their market capitalization is measured, or some combination of the two. Average stock returns for U.S. firms (including NYSE, AMEX, and NASDAQ firms) varied across size deciles from 1926 to 2005 as shown in Table 8-1.

The table shows that, historically, investors in firms in the top two deciles of the size distribution have realized returns of only 11.3 and 13.2 percent. In contrast, firms in the smallest two size deciles have realized significantly higher returns, ranging from 17.5 to 21.6 percent. Not surprisingly, however, the volatility of large stocks has been

| TABLE 8-1 | Stock Returns, Volatility, and Firm Size | | | | |

Size Decile	Market value of largest company in decile in 2005 ($ millions)	Fraction of total market value represented by decile in 2005 (%)	Average annual stock return, 1926–2005 (%)	Beta, 1926–2005	Size Premium (return in excess of CAPM – %)
1–smallest	265.0	0.8	21.6	1.41	6.4
2	586.4	1.0	17.5	1.34	2.7
3	872.1	1.3	16.6	1.28	2.3
4	1,281.0	1.7	15.6	1.23	1.7
5	1,728.9	2.4	15.3	1.18	1.7
6	2,519.3	3.2	14.9	1.16	1.5
7	3,961.4	4.7	14.3	1.13	1.1
8	7,187.2	7.6	13.8	1.10	0.9
9	16,016.5	14.0	13.2	1.04	0.7
10–largest	367,495.1	63.3	11.3	0.91	−0.4

Source: Ibbotson and Associates, *Stocks, Bonds, Bills, and Inflation* (2006).

significantly lower than that of smaller stocks. Stocks in the largest decile have a beta of less than one compared to 1.41 for the smallest decile. Note, however, that if we use returns based on firm size as an indicator of the cost of capital, we are implicitly assuming that large size is indicative of lower risk. Firms in the smallest decile have earned an average of 6.4 percent above the theoretical CAPM return over time. Yet finance theorists have not developed a well accepted explanation for why that should be the case.

One method for estimating the cost of capital combines the CAPM and the "size effect." The approach calls for adjusting the CAPM-based cost of capital for the difference between the average return on the market index used in the CAPM (the Standard and Poor's 500) and the average return on firms of size comparable to the firm being evaluated. The resulting cost of capital is

$$\text{Cost of equity} = \text{Riskless rate of return} + \text{Beta risk} \times \text{Market risk premium} + \text{Size premium}$$

In light of the continuing debate on how to measure the cost of capital, it is not surprising that managers and analysts often consider a range of estimates. In addition to the question about whether or not the historical risk premium of approximately 7 percent is valid today, there is debate over whether beta is a relevant measure of risk, and whether other metrics such as size should be reflected in cost of capital estimates. Since these debates are still unresolved, it is prudent for analysts to use a range of risk premium estimates in computing a firm's cost of capital.

Adjusting Cost of Equity for Changes in Leverage

The cost of both debt and equity change as a function of a firm's economic leverage. As leverage increases, debt and equity become more risky and therefore more costly. If an analyst is contemplating changing capital structure during the forecasting time period, either relative to the historical capital structure of the firm or over time, it is important to re-estimate the cost of debt and equity to take these changes into account. We describe below a simple approach to this task.

We begin with the observation that the beta of a firm's assets is equal to the weighted average of its debt and equity betas, weighted by the economic values of debt and equity to total economic capital. As noted above, financial services firms report estimates of betas for publicly-traded firms based on the historical relation between their stock returns and returns on the market index. Debt betas can be inferred from the capital asset pricing model if we have information on the current interest rate and risk-free rate. The economic value of debt is typically estimated using the book value of debt whereas the economic value of equity is usually estimated using the firm's market equity capitalization. From these estimated equity and debt betas and the estimated economic capital structure, we can infer the firm's asset beta.

When the firm's economic capital structure changes, its equity and debt betas will change but its asset beta remains the same. We can take advantage of this fact to estimate the expected equity beta for the new capital structure. We first have to get an estimate of the interest rate on debt at the new capital structure level. Once we have this information, we can estimate the implied debt beta using the capital asset pricing model and the risk-free rate. Now we can estimate the equity beta for the new capital structure using the identity that the new equity beta and the new debt beta, weighted by the new economic capital structure weights, have to add up to the asset beta estimated earlier.

Estimating Wal-Mart's Cost of Capital

To estimate the cost of capital for Wal-Mart, we start with the assumption that its pre-tax cost of debt is 5.15 percent, based on the yield on its intermediate-term bonds at the beginning of fiscal 2006 (with an assumed tax rate of 35 percent, this translates into a after-tax cost of debt of 3.3 percent). The company's equity beta was calculated in February 2006 to be 0.90. The ten-year Treasury bond rate at that time was yielding 4.5 percent. Using the historical risk premium for equities of 6.8 percent, we can calculate its cost of equity to be 10.6 percent. Clearly this estimate is only a starting point, and the analyst can change the estimate by changing the assumed market risk premium or by adjusting for the size effect.

Wal-Mart's equity market value in February 2006, after the financial performance of the preceding fiscal year had been announced, was approximately $191 billion and its net book debt was $32.4 billion. Using these numbers we can calculate the "economic value" weights of debt and equity in the company's capital structure as 15 percent and 85 percent, respectively. Based on these weights and the above estimates of costs of equity and debt, our estimate of Wal-Mart's weighted average cost of capital (WACC) in February 2006 is 9.5 percent, as shown in Table 8-2. We keep Wal-Mart's book leverage constant throughout the forecasting period. But this does not necessarily ensure that economic leverage will be constant. Economic leverage will change if book debt grows at a different rate than the economic value of equity. Growth in future book debt is driven by the forecasted growth in Wal-Mart's sales and profitability. These factors are capitalized in Wal-Mart's current economic equity valuation. As a result, estimated future economic equity values for the firm are driven by its cost of capital and dividend

TABLE 8-2	Wal-Mart's Weighted Average Cost of Capital		
	Cost of Funds ×	**Economic Weighting** =	**Weighted Cost**
Debt	3.3%	15.0%	0.5%
Equity	10.6%	85.0%	9.0%
Capital			9.5%

policy. As we will see later in this chapter, if the economic capital structure is not stable, using the current weights to estimate WACC will result in economic asset valuations that do not reconcile with those for debt and equity.

These calculations imply that, as a starting point, we will use a 10.6 percent cost of equity to discount forecasts of abnormal earnings and cash flows available to Wal-Mart's equity holders, and the 9.5 percent WACC to discount forecasts of abnormal NOPAT and cash flows generated for all of its capital contributors (debt and equity).

DETAILED FORECASTS OF PERFORMANCE

The horizon over which detailed forecasts are made is itself a choice variable. We will discuss later in this chapter how the analyst might make this choice. Once it is made, the next step is to consider the set of assumptions regarding a firm's performance that are needed to arrive at the forecasts. We described in Chapter 6 the general framework of financial forecasting and illustrated the approach using Wal-Mart.

The key to sound forecasts is that the underlying assumptions are grounded in a company's business reality. Strategy analysis provides a critical understanding of a company's value proposition, and whether current performance is likely to be sustainable in future. Accounting analysis and ratio analysis provide a deep understanding of a company's current performance, and whether the ratios themselves are reliable indicators of performance. It is, therefore, important to see the valuation forecasts as a continuation of the earlier steps in business analysis rather than as a discrete exercise not connected to the rest of the analysis.

Since valuation involves forecasting over a long time horizon, it is not practical to forecast all the line items in a company's financial statements. Instead, the analyst has to focus on the important elements of a firm's performance. Specifically, we forecasted Wal-Mart's condensed income statement, beginning balance sheet, and free cash flows for a period of ten years starting in fiscal year 2006 (year beginning in February 2006). We will use these same forecasting assumptions and financial forecasts, which are repeated here in Tables 8-3 and 8-4, as a starting point to value Wal-Mart as of February 1, 2006.

TABLE 8-3	Forecasting Assumptions for Wal-Mart									
For fiscal year	2006	2007	2008	2009	2010	2011	2012	2013	2014	2015
Sales growth rate	9.3%	9.6%	9.6%	9.5%	9.4%	9.0%	8.6%	8.2%	7.8%	7.7%
NOPAT margin	3.9%	3.8%	3.8%	3.7%	3.7%	3.6%	3.5%	3.4%	3.2%	3.1%
Beginning net operating working capital/sales	−0.8%	0.0%	0.0%	0.0%	0.0%	0.0%	0.0%	0.0%	0.0%	0.0%
Beginning net operating long-term assets/sales	25.8%	25.2%	25.4%	25.6%	25.9%	26.0%	26.0%	26.3%	26.5%	26.8%
Beginning net debt to capital ratio	37.9%	37.9%	37.9%	37.9%	37.9%	37.9%	37.9%	37.9%	37.9%	37.9%
After-tax cost of debt	3.3%	3.3%	3.3%	3.3%	3.3%	3.3%	3.3%	3.3%	3.3%	3.3%

TABLE 8-4 Forecasted Financial Statements for Wal-Mart

For fiscal year	2006	2007	2008	2009	2010	2011	2012	2013	2014	2015
Beginning Balance Sheet										
Beg. net working capital	−2,768	0	0	0	0	0	0	0	0	0
+ Beg. net long-term assets	88,344	94,546	104,527	115,477	127,486	139,917	151,937	166,343	181,019	196,873
= **Net operating assets**	**85,576**	**94,546**	**104,527**	**115,477**	**127,486**	**139,917**	**151,937**	**166,343**	**181,019**	**196,873**
Net debt	32,405	35,802	39,581	43,728	48,275	52,982	57,534	62,989	68,546	74,550
+ Preferred stock	0	0	0	0	0	0	0	0	0	0
+ Shareholders' equity	53,171	58,744	64,946	71,749	79,211	86,935	94,403	103,354	112,473	122,323
= **Net capital**	**85,576**	**94,546**	**104,527**	**115,477**	**127,486**	**139,917**	**151,937**	**166,343**	**181,019**	**196,873**
Income Statement										
Sales	342,629	375,435	411,628	450,786	493,126	537,648	584,130	632,291	681,861	734,359
Net operating profits after tax	13,284	14,360	15,531	16,755	18,034	19,288	20,483	21,264	21,958	22,644
− Net interest expense after tax	1,085	1,198	1,325	1,464	1,616	1,774	1,926	2,109	2,295	2,496
= Net income	12,199	13,162	14,206	15,291	16,418	17,515	18,557	19,155	19,664	20,149
− Preferred dividends	0	0	0	0	0	0	0	0	0	0
= **Net income to common**	**12,199**	**13,162**	**14,206**	**15,291**	**16,418**	**17,515**	**18,557**	**19,155**	**19,664**	**20,149**
Operating return on assets	15.5%	15.2%	14.9%	14.5%	14.1%	13.8%	13.5%	12.8%	12.1%	11.5%
Return on equity	22.9%	22.4%	21.9%	21.3%	20.7%	20.1%	19.7%	18.5%	17.5%	16.5%
Book value of assets growth rate	13.6%	10.5%	10.6%	10.5%	10.4%	9.8%	8.6%	9.5%	8.8%	8.8%
Book value of equity growth rate	7.6%	10.5%	10.6%	10.5%	10.4%	9.8%	8.6%	9.5%	8.8%	8.8%
Net operating asset turnover	4.0	4.0	3.9	3.9	3.9	3.8	3.8	3.8	3.8	3.7
Net income	12,199	13,162	14,206	15,291	16,418	17,515	18,557	19,155	19,664	20,149
− Change in net working capital	(2,768)	-	-	-	-	-	-	-	-	-
− Change in net long-term assets	(6,202)	(9,981)	(10,950)	(12,009)	(12,431)	(12,020)	(14,406)	(14,676)	(15,854)	(15,089)
+ Change in net debt	3,397	3,779	4,147	4,547	4,707	4,552	5,455	5,557	6,004	4,349
= Free cash flow to equity	6,626	6,960	7,403	7,829	8,694	10,047	9,606	10,036	9,814	9,409
Net operating profit after tax	13,284	14,360	15,531	16,755	18,034	19,288	20,483	21,264	21,958	22,644
− Change in net working capital	(2,768)	-	-	-	-	-	-	-	-	-
− Change in net long-term assets	(6,202)	(9,981)	(10,950)	(12,009)	(12,431)	(12,020)	(14,406)	(14,676)	(15,854)	(15,089)
= Free cash flow to capital	4,314	4,379	4,581	4,746	5,603	7,268	6,077	6,588	6,104	5,359

Making Performance Forecasts for Valuing Wal-Mart

As discussed in Chapter 7, the forecasts required to convert the financial forecasts shown above into estimates of value differ depending on whether we wish to value a firm's equity or its assets. To value equity, the essential inputs are

- Abnormal earnings: net income less shareholders' equity at the beginning of the year times cost of equity;
- Abnormal ROE: the difference between ROE and cost of equity; or
- Free cash flows to equity: net income less the increase in operating working capital less the increase in net long-term assets plus the increase in net debt.

Alternatively, to value a company's assets, the significant performance forecasts would be

- Abnormal NOPAT: NOPAT less total net capital at the beginning of the year times the weighted average cost of capital;
- Abnormal operating ROA: the difference between operating ROA and the weighted average cost of capital; or
- Free cash flows to capital: NOPAT less the increase in operating working capital less the increase in net long-term assets.

Table 8-5 shows Wal-Mart's performance forecasts for all six of these financial statement variables for the ten-year period 2006 to 2015.

TABLE 8-5	Performance Forecasts for Wal-Mart									
For fiscal year	2006	2007	2008	2009	2010	2011	2012	2013	2014	2015
Equity Valuation										
Abonormal earnings	6,552	6,923	7,308	7,671	8,006	8,282	8,532	8,179	7,719	7,158
Abnormal ROE	12.3%	11.8%	11.3%	10.7%	10.1%	9.5%	9.0%	7.9%	6.9%	5.9%
Free cash flow to equity	6,626	6,960	7,402	7,830	8,694	10,046	9,606	10,037	9,813	9,409
Asset Valuation										
Abnormal NOPAT	5,122	5,343	5,561	5,741	5,875	5,944	5,992	5,399	4,693	3,868
Abnormal Operating ROA	6.0%	5.7%	5.3%	5.0%	4.6%	4.2%	3.9%	3.2%	2.6%	2.0%
Free cash flow to capital	4,314	4,379	4,580	4,746	5,603	7,269	6,077	6,588	6,105	5,359
Discount factors:										
Equity	0.904	0.817	0.739	0.668	0.604	0.546	0.493	0.446	0.403	0.364
Assets	0.913	0.833	0.761	0.695	0.634	0.579	0.529	0.482	0.440	0.402
Growth factors*:										
Equity	1.00	1.10	1.22	1.35	1.49	1.64	1.78	1.94	2.12	2.30
Assets	1.00	1.10	1.22	1.35	1.49	1.64	1.78	1.94	2.12	2.30

The growth factor is relevant only for calculating the present value for abnormal ROE and ROA.

As discussed earlier, to derive cash flows in 2015, we need to make assumptions about sales growth rate and balance sheet ratios in 2016. The cash flow forecasts shown in Table 8-5 are based on the simple assumption that the sales growth and beginning balance sheet ratios in 2016 remain the same as in 2015. We discuss the sensitivity of this assumption and the terminal value assumption later in the chapter.

Wal-Mart's projected abnormal ROE declines steadily over the forecast horizon, from 12.3 percent in 2006 to 5.9 percent in 2015. Abnormal Operating ROA also shows a similar trend, in keeping with the expected gradual attrition due to the forces of competition. A somewhat different pattern is shown for abnormal earnings and abnormal NOPAT, which both trend upward for the first six to seven years before declining. This pattern arises because Wal-Mart is able to increase the investment base on which it earns it abnormal profits for a period of time, leading to increasing abnormal earnings and NOPAT. However, after 2012 declining profitability drives even the absolute level of abnormal profits down.

TERMINAL VALUES

Explicit forecasts of the various elements of a firm's performance generally extend for a period of five to ten years. The final year of this forecast period is labeled the *terminal year* (selection of an appropriate terminal year is discussed later in this section). Terminal value is then the present value of either abnormal earnings or free cash flows occurring beyond the terminal year. Since this involves forecasting performance over the remainder of the firm's life, the analyst must adopt some assumption that simplifies the process of forecasting. A key question is whether it is reasonable to assume a continuation of the terminal year performance or whether some other pattern is expected.

Clearly, the continuation of a sales growth that is significantly greater than the average growth rate of the economy is unrealistic over a very long horizon. That rate would likely outstrip inflation in the dollar and the real growth rate of the world economy. Over many years, it would imply that the firm would grow to a size greater than that of all other firms in the world combined. But what would be a suitable alternative assumption? Should we expect the firm's sales growth rate to ultimately settle down to the rate of inflation? Or to a higher rate, such as the nominal GDP growth rate? And perhaps equally important, will a firm that earns abnormal profits continue to do so by maintaining its profit margins on a growing, or even existing, base of sales?

To answer these questions, we must consider how much longer the rate of growth in industry sales can outstrip overall economic growth, and how long a firm's competitive advantages can be sustained. Clearly, looking eleven or more years into the future, any forecast is likely to be subject to considerable error. Below we discuss a variety of alternative approaches to the task of calculating a terminal value.

Terminal Values with the Competitive Equilibrium Assumption

Fortunately, in many if not most situations, how we deal with the seemingly imponderable questions about long-range growth in sales simply *does not matter very much!* In fact, under plausible economic assumptions, there is no practical need to consider sales growth beyond the terminal year. Such growth may be *irrelevant* so far as the firm's current value is concerned.

How can long-range growth in sales *not* matter? The reasoning revolves around the forces of competition. One impact of competition is that it tends to constrain a firm's ability to identify, on a consistent basis, growth opportunities that generate supernormal profits. The other dimension that competition tends to impact is a firm's margins. Ultimately, we would expect high profits to attract enough competition to drive down a firm's margins, and therefore its returns, to a normal level. At this point, the firm will earn its cost of capital, with no abnormal returns or terminal value. (Recall the evidence in Chapter 6 concerning the reversion of ROEs to normal levels over a horizon of five to ten years.)

Certainly a firm may at a point in time maintain a competitive advantage that permits it to achieve returns in excess of the cost of capital. When that advantage is protected with patents or a strong brand name, the firm may even be able to maintain it for many years, perhaps indefinitely. With hindsight, we know that some such firms—Coca-Cola and Wal-Mart, for instance—were able not only to maintain their competitive edge but also to expand it across a dramatically increasing investment base. However, with a few exceptions, it is reasonable to assume that the terminal value of the firm will be zero under the competitive equilibrium assumption, obviating the need to make assumptions about long-term growth rates.

Competitive Equilibrium Assumption Only on Incremental Sales

An alternative version of the competitive equilibrium assumption is to assume that a firm will continue to earn abnormal earnings forever on the sales it had in the terminal year, but there will be no abnormal earnings on any incremental sales beyond that level. If we invoke the competitive equilibrium assumption on incremental sales beyond the terminal year, then it does not matter what sales growth rate we use beyond that year, and we may as well simplify our arithmetic by treating sales *as if* they will be constant at the terminal year level. Then operating ROA, ROE, NOPAT, net income, free cash flow to capital, and free cash flow to equity will all remain constant at the terminal year level.

For example, by treating Wal-Mart as if its competitive advantage can be maintained only on the *nominal* sales level achieved in the year 2015, we will be assuming that in *real* terms its competitive advantage will shrink. Under this scenario, it is simple to estimate the terminal value by dividing the 2015 level of each of the variables by the appropriate discount rate. As one would expect, terminal values in this scenario will be higher than those with no abnormal returns on all sales in years 2016 and beyond. This is entirely due to the fact that we are now assuming that Wal-Mart can retain indefinitely its superior performance on its existing base of sales.

Terminal Value with Persistent Abnormal Performance and Growth

Each of the approaches described above appeals in some way to the competitive equilibrium assumption. However, there are circumstances where the analyst is willing to assume that the firm may defy competitive forces and earn abnormal rates of return on new projects for many years. If the analyst believes supernormal profitability can be extended to larger markets for many years, it can be accommodated within the context of a valuation analysis.

One possibility is to project earnings and cash flows over a longer horizon, i.e., until the competitive equilibrium assumption can reasonably be invoked. In the case of

Wal-Mart, for example, we could assume that the supernormal profitability will continue for five years beyond 2015 (for a total forecasting horizon of 15 years from the beginning of the forecasting period), but after that period the firm's ROE and Operating ROA will be equal to its cost of equity and its weighted average cost of capital, respectively.

Another possibility is to project growth in abnormal earnings or cash flows at some constant rate. For instance, one could expect Wal-Mart to maintain its advantage on a sales base that remains constant in *real* terms, implying that sales grow beyond the year 2015 at the expected long-run U.S. inflation rate of 3.5 percent. Beyond our terminal year, 2015, as the sales growth rate remains constant at 3.5 percent, abnormal earnings, free cash flows, and book values of assets and equity also grow at a constant rate of 3.5 percent. This is simply because we held all other performance ratios constant in this period. As a result, abnormal operating ROA and abnormal ROE remain constant at the same level as in the terminal year.

This approach is more aggressive than the preceding assumptions about terminal value, but it may be more realistic. After all, there is no obvious reason why the *real* size of the investment base on which Wal-Mart earns abnormal returns should depend on inflation rates. The approach, however, still relies to some extent on the competitive equilibrium assumption. The assumption is now invoked to suggest that supernormal profitability can be extended only to an investment base that remains constant in real terms. In rare situations, if the company has established a market dominance that the analyst believes is immune to the threat of competition, the terminal value can be based on both positive real sales growth and abnormal profits. As mentioned earlier, Wal-Mart might be just such a company.

When we assume that the abnormal performance persists at the same level as in the terminal year, projecting abnormal earnings and free cash flows is a simple matter of growing them at the assumed sales growth rate. Since the rate of growth in abnormal earnings and cash flows is constant starting in the year after the terminal year, it is also straightforward to discount those flows. The present value of the flow stream is the flow at the end of the first year divided by the difference between the discount rate and steady-state growth rate, provided that the discount rate exceeds the growth rate. There is nothing about this valuation method that requires reliance on the competitive equilibrium assumption, so it could be used with *any* rate of growth in sales. The question is not whether the arithmetic is available to handle such an approach but rather how realistic it is.

Terminal Value Based on a Price Multiple

A popular approach to terminal value calculation is to apply a multiple to abnormal earnings, cash flows, or book values of the terminal period. The approach is not as ad hoc as it might first appear. Note that under the assumption of no sales growth, abnormal earnings or cash flows beyond the terminal year remain constant. Capitalizing these flows in perpetuity by dividing by the cost of capital is equivalent to multiplying them by the inverse of the cost of capital. For example, in the case of Wal-Mart, capitalizing free cash flows to equity at its cost of equity of 10.6 percent is equivalent to assuming a terminal cash flow multiple of 9.4. Thus, applying a multiple in this range to Wal-Mart is similar to discounting all free cash flows beyond 2015 while invoking the competitive equilibrium assumption on incremental sales.

The mistake to avoid here is to capitalize the future abnormal earnings or cash flows using a multiple that is too high. The earnings or cash flow multiples might be high currently because the market anticipates abnormally profitable growth. However, once that growth is realized, the price–earnings multiple should fall to a normal level. It is that normal price–earnings ratio, applicable to a stable firm or one that can grow only through zero net present value projects, that should be used in the terminal value calculation. Thus, multiples in the range of 7 to 10—close to the reciprocal of cost of equity and WACC—should be used here. Higher multiples are justifiable only when the terminal year is closer and there are still abnormally profitable growth opportunities beyond that point. A similar logic applies to the estimation of terminal values using book value multiples.

Selecting the Terminal Year

A critical question posed by the above discussion is how long to make the detailed forecast horizon. When the competitive equilibrium assumption is used, the answer is whatever time is required for the firm's returns on incremental investment projects to reach that equilibrium—an issue that turns on the sustainability of the firm's competitive advantage. As indicated in Chapter 6, historical evidence indicates that most firms in the U.S. should expect ROEs to revert to normal levels within five to ten years. But for the typical firm, we can justify ending the forecast horizon even earlier as the return on *incremental* investment can be normal even while the return on *total* investment (and therefore ROE) remains abnormal. Thus a five- to ten-year forecast horizon should be more than sufficient for most firms. Exceptions would include firms so well insulated from competition (perhaps due to the power of a brand name) that they can extend their investment base to new markets for many years and still expect to generate supernormal returns.

Estimates of Wal-Mart's Terminal Value

Choosing Terminal Year

In the case of Wal-Mart, the terminal year used is ten years beyond the current one. Table 8-4 shows that the ROE (and operating ROA) is forecasted to decline only gradually over these ten years, from 22.9 percent in 2006 to 16.5 percent by 2015. At this level the company will earn an abnormal return on equity of approximately 5.9 percent, since its cost of equity is estimated to be 10.6 percent.

Based on the foregoing strategic assessment of Wal-Mart, we believe that the firm has created a competitive advantage that should be sustainable in the long term. Consequently, we assume that the firm will have reached a steady state of performance in 2015 and extending the forecast horizon will not lead to further insights into how market dynamics will impact Wal-Mart's performance. The overall projection, therefore, expects that while Wal-Mart's current level of market dominance is not sustainable and that growth will slow and margins will get squeezed, the firm has created a market position that will allow it to make some level of abnormal earnings in the long term that drives its terminal value. Based on this logic, we will fix 2015 as the terminal year for Wal-Mart and attempt to estimate its terminal value at that time.

Terminal Value Under Varying Assumptions

Table 8-6 shows Wal-Mart's terminal value under the various theoretical approaches we discussed above. Scenario 1 of this table shows the terminal value if we assume that Wal-Mart will continue to grow its sales at 7.7 percent beyond fiscal year 2015, and that it will continue to earn the same level of abnormal returns as in 2015 (that is, we assume that all the other forecasting assumptions will be the same as in 2015). This scenario essentially summarizes Wal-Mart performance in perpetuity under the assumption that the firm will continue to make persistent abnormal returns and leads

TABLE 8-6	Terminal Values for Wal-Mart Under Various Assumptions (Using Abnormal Earnings Methodology)				
Scenario Number	Approach	Scenario	Terminal Sales Growth	Terminal NOPAT Margins	Value Beyond Forecast Horizon (Terminal Value)
1	Persistent Abnormal Performance	Sales growth and margins based on detailed analysis and forecast	7.7%	3.0%	87,108
2	Abnormal Returns on Constant Sales (Real Terms)	Sales grow at the rate of inflation, margins maintained	3.5%	3.0%	34,113
3	Abnormal Returns on Constant Sales (Nominal Terms)	Essentially zero sales growth, margins maintained	0.0%	3.0%	22,097
4	Competitive Equilibrium	Margins reduced so no abnormal earnings	7.7%	2.1%	0

to a terminal value of $87.1 billion. Scenario 2 assumes that Wal-Mart is able to maintain its abnormal returns only on a base of sales that is constant in real terms. Scenario 2 calculates the terminal value assuming that Wal-Mart will maintain its margins only on sales that grow at the long-run expected rate of inflation, assumed to be 3.5 percent, dropping the terminal value down to $34.1 billion. Scenario 3 shows the terminal value if we assume that the company's competitive advantage can be maintained only on the nominal sales level achieved in 2015. As a result, sales growth beyond the terminal year is assumed to be zero, which is equivalent to assuming that incremental sales do not produce any abnormal returns. The terminal value under this scenario drops to $22.1 billion. The final scenario invokes the competitive equilibrium assumption, i.e., margins will be eroded such that the firm will have no abnormal returns irrespective of the rate of sales growth, leading to no terminal value. For the sake of illustration, the expected sales growth of 7.7 percent is maintained. To portray the competitive equilibrium, margins are lowered to eliminate any competitive advantage that Wal-Mart will have.

COMPUTING ASSET AND EQUITY VALUES

Table 8-7 shows the estimated value of Wal-Mart's assets and equity, each using the three different methods discussed in Chapter 7. The value of assets is estimated using abnormal operating ROA, abnormal NOPAT, and free cash flows to debt and equity. The value of equity is estimated using operating ROE, abnormal NOPAT, and free cash flow to equity. These values are computed using the financial forecasts in Table 8-5 and the terminal value forecast using the persistent abnormal performance scenario.

In Table 8-7, present values of abnormal NOPAT and free cash flow to capital are computed using a WACC of 9.5 percent, and present values of abnormal earnings and free cash flow to equity are computed using a cost of equity of 10.6 percent. To calculate the present values of abnormal operating ROA and abnormal ROE, the

TABLE 8-7	Valuation Summary for Wal-Mart Using Various Methodologies				
	Beginning Book Value	Value from Forecast Period 2006 to 2015	Value Beyond Forecast Horizon (Terminal Value)	Total Value	Value Per Share ($)
Equity Value					
Abnormal earnings	53,171	45,035	87,108	185,314	44.49
Abnormal ROE	53,171	45,035	87,108	185,314	44.49
Free cash flows to equity	N/A	49,708	135,606	185,314	44.49
Asset Value					
Abnormal NOPAT	85,576	33,910	74,179	193,665	N/A
Abnormal ROA	85,576	33,910	74,179	193,665	N/A
Free cash flow to capital	N/A	33,365	160,299	193,665	N/A

values for each year are first multiplied by the corresponding growth factor, as shown in the formulae in Chapter 7, and then they are discounted using the WACC and cost of equity, respectively. Under the assumptions and forecast we have made, Wal-Mart's estimated value per share is $44.49 and the total firm value is $193.7 billion.

Value estimates show that the abnormal returns method, abnormal earnings method, and the free cash flow method result in the same value, as claimed in Chapter 7. Note also that Wal-Mart's terminal value represents a significantly larger fraction of the total value of assets and equity under the free cash flow method relative to the other methods. As discussed, this is due to the fact that the abnormal returns and earnings methods rely on a company's book value of assets and equity, so the terminal value estimates are estimates of incremental values over book values. In contrast, the free cash flow approach ignores the book values, so the terminal value forecasts are estimates of total value during this period.

The primary calculations in the above estimates treat all flows as if they arrive at the end of the year. Of course, they are likely to arrive throughout the year. If we assume for the sake of simplicity that cash flows will arrive mid-year, then we should adjust adjust our value estimates upward by the amount $\left[1 + \left(\frac{r}{2}\right)\right]$, where r is the discount rate.

Finally, it is worth noting that the asset valuation ($193,665) and the equity valuation ($185,314) imply that the value of debt should be $8,315, which differs from the actual value of $32,405. This arises because Wal-Mart's economic leverage increases over the forecast horizon. The estimated WACC used to compute asset valuations is based on the beginning economic leverage and therefore does not correctly capture these changes. Given the difficulties of forecasting these subtle changes in economic leverage, we recommend valuing equity directly using abnormal earnings, abnormal ROEs, or equity free cash flows.

Value Estimates Versus Market Values

As the discussion above shows, valuation involves a substantial number of assumptions by analysts. Therefore, the estimates of value will vary from one analyst to the other. The only way to ensure that one's estimates are reliable is to make sure that the assumptions are grounded in the economics of the business being valued. It is also useful to check the assumptions against the time-series trends for performance ratios discussed in Chapter 6. While it is legitimate to make assumptions that differ markedly from these trends in any given case, it is important for the analyst to be able to articulate the business and strategy reasons for making such assumptions.

When a company being valued is publicly traded, it is possible to compare one's own estimated value with the market value of a company. When an estimated value differs substantially from a company's market value, it is useful for the analyst to understand why such differences arise. A way to do this is to redo the valuation exercise and figure out what valuation assumptions are needed to arrive at the observed stock price. One can then examine whether the market's assumptions are more or less valid relative to one's own assumptions. As we discuss in the next chapter, such an analysis can be invaluable in using valuation to make buy or sell decisions in the security analysis context.

In the case of Wal-Mart, our estimated value of the firm's equity is almost identical to the observed value at the end of February 2006, when the market had assimilated the announced results for the quarter and fiscal year ended January 31, 2006.

Sensitivity Analysis

Recall that in Chapter 6, we developed what we believed to be a reasonable assessment of Wal-Mart's expected future performance. The resulting valuation seems to be in line with the market's expectations, as the imputed value per share closely approximated the traded value per share at the time. However, we acknowledged that the company's future could play out in multiple ways and proposed two alternative scenarios. As shown in Table 8-8, if Wal-Mart is able to maintain higher growth rates and better NOPAT margins in its domestic business, its value per share would be $55.80. If, on the other hand, its international business fails to deliver the expected returns in conjunction with increased domestic competition, its stock would be worth only $38.10 per share. The changes in stock value in these scenarios are driven primarily by changes in sales growth and margins, performance measures that are most strongly affected by the forces of competition.

TABLE 8-8	Equity Valuation Under Various Scenarios Using Abnormal Earnings				
Scenario	**Beginning Book Value**	**Value from Forecast Period 2006 to 2015**	**Value Beyond Forecast Horizon (Terminal Value)**	**Total Value**	**Value Per Share ($)**
U.S. Market Slowdown Balanced by International Growth	53,171	45,035	87,108	185,314	44.49
Maintain U.S. Market Growth, Supplement with International Growth	53,171	47,408	131,809	232,389	55.80
Strong Competition on Both Domestic and International Fronts	53,171	43,748	61,788	158,707	38.10

SOME PRACTICAL ISSUES IN VALUATION

The above discussion provides a blueprint for doing valuation. In practice, the analyst has to deal with a number of other issues that have an important effect on the valuation task. We discuss below three frequently encountered complications—accounting distortions, negative book values, and excess cash.

Dealing with Accounting Distortions

We know from the discussion in Chapter 7 that accounting methods per se should have no influence on firm value, despite the fact that abnormal returns and earnings valuation approaches used here are based on numbers that vary with accounting method choices.

Since accounting choices must affect both earnings *and* book value, and because of the self-correcting nature of double-entry bookkeeping (all "distortions" of accounting must ultimately reverse), estimated values will not be affected by accounting choices *as long as the analyst recognizes the accounting distortions.*[5]

If accounting reliability is a concern, the analyst has to expend resources on accounting adjustments. When a company uses "biased" accounting—either conservative or aggressive—the analyst needs to recognize the bias to ensure that value estimates are not biased. If a thorough analysis is not performed, a firm's accounting choices can influence analysts' perceptions of the real performance of the firm and hence the forecasts of future performance. Accounting choice would affect expectations of future earnings and cash flows, and distort the valuation, regardless of whether the valuation is based on DCF or discounted abnormal earnings. For example, if a firm overstates current revenue growth through aggressive revenue recognition, failure to appreciate the effect is likely to lead the analyst to overstate future revenues, affecting both earnings and cash flow forecasts.

An analyst who encounters biased accounting has two choices—either to adjust current earnings and book values to eliminate managers' accounting biases, or to recognize these biases and adjust future forecasts accordingly. Whereas both approaches lead to the same estimated firm value, the choice will have an important impact on what fraction of the firm's value is captured within the forecast horizon, and what remains in the terminal value. Holding forecasting horizon and future growth opportunities constant, higher accounting quality allows a higher fraction of a firm's value to be captured by the current book value and the abnormal earnings within the forecasting horizon.

Dealing with Negative Book Values

A number of firms have negative earnings and/or negative values of book equity. Firms in the start-up phase have negative equity. These firms incur large investments whose payoff is uncertain. Accountants write off these investments as a matter of conservatism, leading to negative book equity. Examples of firms in this situation include biotechnology firms, Internet firms, telecommunication firms, and other high technology firms. A second category of firms with negative book equity are those that are performing poorly, resulting in cumulative losses exceeding the original investment by the shareholders.

Negative book equity makes it difficult to use the accounting-based approach to value a firm's equity. There are several possible ways to get around this problem. The first approach is to value the firm's assets (using, for example, abnormal operating ROA or abnormal NOPAT) rather than equity. Then, based on an estimate of the value of the firm's debt, one can estimate the equity value. Another alternative is to "undo" accountants' conservatism by capitalizing the investment expenditures written off. This is possible if the analyst is able to establish that these expenditures are value creating. A third alternative, feasible for publicly-traded firms, is to start from the observed stock price and work backwards. Using reasonable estimates of cost of equity and steady-state growth rate, the analyst can calculate the average long-term level of abnormal earnings needed to justify the observed stock price. Then the analytical task can be framed in terms of examining the feasibility of achieving this abnormal earnings "target."

It is important to note that the value of firms with negative book equity often consists of a significant option value. For example, the value of high-tech firms is driven not only by the expected earnings from their current technologies but also the payoff from technology options embedded in their research and development efforts. Similarly, the value of troubled companies is driven to some extent by the "abandonment option"—shareholders with limited liability can put the firm to debt holders and creditors. One can use the options theory framework to estimate the value of these "real options."

Dealing with Excess Cash and Excess Cash Flows

Firms with excess cash balances, or large free cash flows, also pose a valuation challenge. In our projections in Table 8-4, we implicitly assumed that cash beyond the level required to finance a company's operations will be paid out to the firm's shareholders. Excess cash flows are assumed to be paid out to shareholders either in the form of dividends or stock repurchases. Notice that these cash flows are already incorporated into the valuation process when they are earned, so there is no need to take them into account when they are paid out.

It is important to recognize that both the accounting-based valuation and the discounted cash flow valuation assume a dividend payout that can potentially vary from period to period. This dividend policy assumption is required as long as one wishes to assume a constant level of financial leverage, a constant cost of equity, and a constant level of weighted average cost of capital used in the valuation calculations. Firms rarely have such a variable dividend policy in practice. However, this in itself does not make the valuation approaches invalid, as long as a firm's dividend policy does not affect its value. That is, the valuation approaches assume that the well known Modigliani-Miller theorem regarding the irrelevance of dividends holds.

A firm's dividend policy can affect its value if managers do not invest free cash flows optimally. For example, if a firm's managers are likely to use excess cash to undertake value-destroying acquisitions, then our approach overestimates the firm's value. If the analyst has these types of concerns about a firm, one approach is to first estimate the firm according to the approach described earlier and then adjust the estimated value for whatever agency costs the firm's managers may impose on its investors. One way to evaluate whether or not a firm suffers from severe agency costs is to examine the effectiveness of its corporate governance processes.

SUMMARY

We illustrate in this chapter how to apply the valuation theory discussed in Chapter 7. The chapter explains the set of business and financial assumptions needed to complete the valuation exercise. We first discuss how to compute cost of equity and the weighted average cost of capital. We then build on the detailed forecasts developed in Chapter 6 and illustrate the mechanics of estimating terminal values of earnings, free cash flows, and accounting rates of return. Using a detailed example, we show how a firm's equity values and asset values can be computed using earnings, cash flows, and rates of return. The sensitivity of equity and firm value to the assumptions, both during the forecast horizon and for the terminal value, are highlighted. Finally, we offer ways to deal with some commonly encountered practical issues, including accounting distortions, negative book values, and excess cash balances.

DISCUSSION QUESTIONS

1. How would the forecasts in Table 8-4 change if Wal-Mart were to maintain a sales growth rate of 10 percent per year from 2006 to 2016 (and all the other assumptions are kept unchanged)?

2. Recalculate the forecasts in Table 8-4 assuming that the NOPAT profit margin is held steady for the first five years of the forecast and then declines by 0.1 percentage points per year thereafter (keeping all the other assumptions unchanged).

3. Recalculate the forecasts in Tables 8-4 and 8-5 assuming that the ratio of net operating working capital to sales is 3 percent, and the ratio of net long-term assets to sales is 30 percent for all the years from fiscal 2006 to fiscal 2015. Keep all the other assumptions unchanged.

4. Calculate Wal-Mart's cash payouts to its shareholders in the years 2006–2015 that are implicitly assumed in the projections in Table 8-4.

5. How would the abnormal earnings calculations in Table 8-5 change if the cost of equity assumption is changed to 12 percent?

6. How would the terminal values in Table 8-6 change if the sales growth in years 2016 and beyond is 10 percent, and the company keeps forever its abnormal returns at the same level as in fiscal 2015 (keeping all the other assumptions in the table unchanged)?

7. Calculate the proportion of terminal values to total estimated values of equity under the abnormal earnings method and the discounted cash flow method for the results shown in Table 8-7. Why are these proportions different?

8. What will Wal-Mart's cost of equity be if the equity market risk premium is 5 percent?

9. Assume that Wal-Mart changes its capital structure so that its market value weight of debt to capital increases to 20 percent, and its after-tax interest rate on debt at this new leverage level is 4 percent. Assume that the equity market risk premium is 7 percent. What will be the cost of equity at the new debt level? What will be the weighted average cost of capital?

10. Nancy Smith says she is uncomfortable making the assumption that Wal-Mart's dividend payout will vary from year to year. If she makes a constant dividend payout assumption, what changes does she have to make in her other valuation assumptions to make them internally consistent with each other?

NOTES

1. See T. Copeland, T. Koller, and J. Murrin, *Valuation: Measuring and Managing the Value of Companies,* 2nd edition (New York: John Wiley & Sons, 1994). Theory calls for the use of a short-term rate, but if that rate is used here, a difficult practical question rises: How does one reflect the premium required for expected inflation over long horizons? While the premium could, in principle, be treated as a portion of the term $[E(r_m) - r_f]$, it is probably easier to use an intermediate- or long-term riskless rate that presumably reflects expected inflation.

2. One way to estimate systematic risk is to regress the firm's stock returns over some recent time period against the returns on the market index. The slope coefficient represents an estimate of β. More fundamentally, systematic risk depends on how sensitive the firm's operating profits are to shifts in economy-wide activity and the firm's degree of leverage. Financial analysis that assesses these operating and financial risks should be useful in arriving at reasonable estimates of β. See W. Beaver, P. Kettler, and M. Scholes, "The Association Between Market Determined and Accounting Determined Risk Measures," *The Accounting Review,* Vol. XLV, No. 4 (1970), who develop a model for estimating beta using financial statement data.

3. The average return reported here is the arithmetic mean as opposed to the geometric mean. Ibbotson and Associates explain why this estimate is appropriate in this context (see *Stocks, Bonds, Bills, and Inflation,* 2006 Yearbook, Chicago).

4. See W. Gebhardt, C. Lee, and B. Swaminathan, "Toward an Implied Cost of Capital," *Journal of Accounting Research* 39, no. 1 (2001): 135–176, and J. Claus and J. Thomas, "The Equity Premium Is Much Lower Than You Think It Is: Empirical Estimates from a New Approach," *Journal of Finance* 56 (2001): 1629–1666.

5. Valuation based on discounted abnormal earnings does require one property of the forecasts: that they be consistent with "clean surplus accounting." Such accounting requires the following relation:

$$\text{End-of-period book value} = \text{Beginning book value} \cdot \text{earnings} - \text{dividends} \pm \text{capital contributions/withdrawals}$$

Clean surplus accounting rules out situations where some gain or loss is excluded from earnings but is still used to adjust the book value of equity. For example, under U.S. GAAP, gains and losses on foreign currency translations are handled this way. In applying the valuation technique described here, the analyst would need to deviate from GAAP in producing forecasts and treat such gains/losses as a part of earnings. However, the technique does *not* require that clean surplus accounting has been applied *in the past*—so the existing book value, based on U.S. GAAP or any other set of principles, can still serve as the starting point. All the analyst needs to do is apply clean surplus accounting in his/her forecasts. That is not only easy but also usually the natural thing to do anyway.

PART THREE

BUSINESS ANALYSIS
AND VALUATION
APPLICATIONS

CHAPTER 9
Equity Security Analysis

CHAPTER 10
Credit Analysis and Distress
Prediction

CHAPTER 11
Mergers and Acquisitions

CHAPTER 12
Communication and
Governance

Chapter 9
Equity Security Analysis

Equity security analysis is the evaluation of a firm and its prospects from the perspective of a current or potential investor in the firm's stock. Security analysis is, however, just one step in a larger investment process that involves (1) establishing the objectives of the investor, (2) forming expectations about the future returns and risks of individual securities, and then (3) combining individual securities into portfolios to maximize progress toward the investment objectives.

Security analysis is the foundation for the second step of projecting future returns and assessing risk. Security analysis is typically conducted with an eye toward identifying mispriced securities in the hopes of generating returns that more than compensate the investor for risk. However, that need not be the case. For analysts who do not have a comparative advantage in identifying mispriced securities, the focus should be on gaining an appreciation for how a security would affect the risk of a given portfolio, and whether it fits the profile that the portfolio is designed to maintain.

Security analysis is undertaken by individual investors, by analysts at brokerage houses and investment banks (sell-side analysts), and by analysts that work at the direction of fund managers for various institutions (buy-side analysts). The institutions employing buy-side analysts include mutual funds, hedge funds, insurance companies, universities, and others.

A variety of questions are dealt with in security analysis:

- A sell-side analyst asks: Is the industry I am covering attractive, and if so why? How do different firms within the industry position themselves? What are the implications for my earnings forecasts? Given my expectations for a firm, does its stock appear to be mispriced? Should I recommend this stock as a buy, a sell, or a hold?
- A buy-side analyst for a "value stock fund" asks: Does this stock possess the characteristics we seek in our fund, that is, does it have a relatively low ratio of price–earnings, low price-to-book value, and other fundamental indicators? Do its prospects for earnings improvement suggest good potential for high future returns on the stock?
- An individual investor asks: Does this stock present the risk profile that suits my investment objectives? Does it enhance my ability to diversify the risk of my portfolio? Is the firm's dividend payout rate low enough to minimize my tax liability while I continue to hold the stock?

As the above questions underscore, there is more to security analysis than estimating the value of stocks. Nevertheless, for most sell-side and buy-side analysts, the key goal remains the identification of mispriced stocks.

INVESTOR OBJECTIVES AND INVESTMENT VEHICLES

The investment objectives of individual savers in the economy are highly idiosyncratic. For any given saver they depend on factors such as income, age, wealth, tolerance for risk, and tax status. For example, savers with many years until retirement are likely to prefer to have a relatively large share of their portfolio invested in equities, which offer a higher expected return than fixed income (or debt) securities and higher short-term variability. Investors in high tax brackets are likely to prefer to have a large share of their portfolio in stocks that generate tax-deferred capital gains rather than stocks that pay dividends or interest-bearing securities.

Mutual funds (or unit trusts as they are termed in some countries) have become popular investment vehicles for savers to achieve their investment objectives. Mutual funds sell shares in professionally managed portfolios that invest in specific types of stocks and/or fixed income securities. They therefore provide a low-cost way for savers to invest in a portfolio of securities that reflects their particular appetite for risk.

The major classes of mutual fund include (1) money market funds that invest in CDs and treasury bills, (2) bond funds that invest in debt instruments, (3) equity funds that invest in equity securities, (4) balanced funds that hold money market, bond, and equity securities, and (5) real estate funds that invest in commercial real estate. Within the bond and equities classes of funds, however, there are wide ranges of fund types. For example, bond funds include

- *Corporate bond funds* that invest in investment-grade rated corporate debt instruments,
- *High yield funds* that invest in non-investment-grade rated corporate debt,
- *Mortgage funds* that invest in mortgage-backed securities, and
- *Municipal funds* that invest in municipal debt instruments, which generate income that can be exempt from federal and often state and local taxes.

Equity funds include

- *Income funds* that invest in stocks that are expected to generate dividend income,
- *Growth funds* that invest in stocks expected to generate long-term capital gains,
- *Income and growth funds* that invest in stocks that provide a balance of dividend income and capital gains,
- *Value funds* that invest in equities that are considered to be undervalued,
- *Short funds* that sell short equity securities that are considered to be overvalued,
- *Index funds* that invest in stocks that track a particular market index, such as the S&P 500,
- *Size-based funds* that invest based on the market capitalization of the company, such as large-cap and small-cap funds,
- *Sector funds* that invest in stocks in a particular industry segment, such as the technology or health sciences sectors, and
- *Regional funds* that invest in equities from a particular country or geographic region, such as Japan, Europe, or the Asia-Pacific region.

Since the 1990s, hedge funds have gained increased prominence and the assets controlled by these funds have grown significantly. While generally open only to institutional investors and certain qualified wealthy individuals, hedge funds are becoming an increasingly important force in the market. Hedge funds employ a variety of investment strategies including

- *Market neutral funds* that typically invest equal amounts of money in purchasing undervalued securities and shorting overvalued ones to neutralize market risk,
- *Short-selling funds,* which short sell the securities of companies that they believe are overvalued, and

- *Special situations funds* that invest in undervalued securities in anticipation of an increase in value resulting from a favorable turn of events.

These fund types employ very different strategies. But for many, fundamental analysis of companies is the critical task. This chapter focuses on applying the tools we have developed in Part 2 of the book to analyze equity securities.

EQUITY SECURITY ANALYSIS AND MARKET EFFICIENCY

How a security analyst should invest his or her time depends on how quickly and efficiently information flows through markets and becomes reflected in security prices. In the extreme, information would be reflected in security prices fully and immediately upon its release. This is essentially the condition posited by the *efficient markets hypothesis*. This hypothesis states that security prices reflect all available information, as if such information could be costlessly digested and translated immediately into demands for buys or sells without regard to frictions imposed by transactions costs. Under such conditions, it would be impossible to identify mispriced securities on the basis of public information.

In a world of efficient markets, the expected return on any equity security is just enough to compensate investors for the unavoidable risk the security involves. Unavoidable risk is that which cannot be "diversified away" simply by holding a portfolio of many securities. Given efficient markets, the investor's strategy shifts away from the search for mispriced securities and focuses instead on maintaining a well diversified portfolio. Aside from this, the investor must arrive at the desired balance between risky securities and risk-free short-term government bonds. The desired balance depends on how much risk the investor is willing to bear for a given increase in expected returns.

The above discussion implies that investors who accept that stock prices already reflect available information have no need for analysis involving a search for mispriced securities. If all investors adopted this attitude, of course no such analysis would be conducted, mispricing would go uncorrected, and markets would no longer be efficient![1] This is why the efficient markets hypothesis cannot represent an equilibrium in a strict sense. In equilibrium there must be just enough mispricing to provide incentives for the investment of resources in security analysis.

The existence of some mispricing, even in equilibrium, does not imply that it is sensible for just anyone to engage in security analysis. Instead, it suggests that securities analysis is subject to the same laws of supply and demand faced in all other competitive industries: It will be rewarding only for those with the strongest comparative advantage. How many analysts are in that category depends on a number of factors, including the liquidity of a firm's stock and investor interest in the company.[2] For the smallest publicly traded firms in the U.S., there is typically no formal following by analysts, and would-be investors and their advisors are left to form their own opinions on a stock. Recent research shows a trend of reduced sell-side analyst coverage following new regulations for investment banks following the scandals of the late 1990s.[3] Coverage of IBM, for example, has declined from about 40 sell-side professional analysts in March 2003 to 25 analysts in September 2006. This decline has been at least partially offset by an increase in the number of analysts employed on the buy-side.

Market Efficiency and the Role of Financial Statement Analysis

The degree of market efficiency that arises from competition among analysts and other market agents is an empirical issue addressed by a large body of research spanning the last three decades. Such research has important implications for the role of financial statements in security analysis. Consider for example the implications of an extremely efficient market, where information is fully impounded in prices within minutes of its revelation. In such a market, agents could profit from digesting financial statement information in two ways. First, the information would be useful to the select few who receive newly announced financial data, interpret it quickly, and trade on it within minutes. Second, and probably more important, the information would be useful for gaining an understanding of the firm, so as to place the analyst in a better position to interpret future news (from financial statements as well as other sources) as it arrives.

On the other hand, if securities prices fail to reflect financial statement data fully, even days or months after its public revelation, market agents could profit from such data by creating trading strategies designed to exploit any systematic ways in which the publicly available data are ignored or discounted in the price-setting process.

Market Efficiency and Managers' Financial Reporting Strategies

The degree to which markets are efficient also has implications for managers' approaches to communicating with their investment communities. The issue becomes most important when the firm pursues an unusual strategy, or when the usual interpretation of financial statements would be misleading in the firm's context. In such a case, the communication avenues managers can successfully pursue depend not only on management's credibility but also on the degree of understanding present in the investment community. We will return to the issue of management communications in more detail in Chapter 12.

Evidence of Market Efficiency

There is an abundance of evidence consistent with a high degree of efficiency in the primary U.S. securities markets.[4] In fact, during the 1960s and 1970s, the evidence was so one-sided that the efficient markets hypothesis gained widespread acceptance within the academic community and had a major impact on the practicing community as well.

Evidence pointing to very efficient securities markets comes in several forms:

- When information is announced publicly, the markets react *very* quickly.
- It is difficult to identify specific funds or analysts who have consistently generated abnormally high returns.
- A number of studies suggest that stock prices reflect a rather sophisticated level of fundamental analysis.

While a large body of evidence consistent with efficiency exists, recent years have witnessed a re-examination of the once widely accepted thinking. A sampling of the research includes the following:

- On the issue of the speed of stock price response to news, a number of studies suggest that even though prices react quickly, the initial reaction tends to be incomplete.[5]
- A number of studies point to trading strategies that could have been used to outperform market averages.[6]
- Related evidence—still subject to ongoing debate about its proper interpretation—suggests that even though market prices reflect some relatively sophisticated analysis, prices still do not fully reflect all the information that could be garnered from publicly available financial statements.[7]

The controversy over the efficiency of securities markets is unlikely to be resolved soon. However, there are some lessons that are accepted by most researchers. First, securities markets not only reflect publicly available information, but they also anticipate much of it before it is released. The open question is what fraction of the response remains to be impounded in price once the day of the public release comes to a close. Second, even in most studies that suggest inefficiency, the degree of mispricing is relatively small for large stocks.

Finally, even if some of the evidence is currently difficult to align with the efficient markets hypothesis, it remains a useful benchmark (at a minimum) for thinking about the behavior of security prices. The hypothesis will continue to play that role unless it can be replaced by a more complete theory. Some researchers are developing theories that encompass the existence of market agents who are forced to trade for unpredictable "liquidity" reasons, and prices that differ from so-called "fundamental values," even in equilibrium.[8] Also, behavioral finance models recognize that cognitive biases can affect investor behavior.[9]

APPROACHES TO FUND MANAGEMENT AND SECURITIES ANALYSIS

Approaches used in practice to analyze securities and manage funds are quite varied. One dimension of variation is the extent to which the investments are actively or passively managed. Another is whether a quantitative or a traditional fundamental approach is used. Security analysts also vary considerably in terms of whether they produce formal or informal valuations of the firm.

Active Versus Passive Management

Active portfolio management relies heavily on security analysis to identify mispriced securities. The passive portfolio manager serves as a price taker, avoiding the costs of security analysis and turnover while typically seeking to hold a portfolio designed to match some overall market index or sector performance. Combined approaches are also possible. For example, one may actively manage 20 percent of a fund balance while passively managing the remainder. The widespread growth of passively managed funds in the U.S. over the past 20 years serves as testimony to the growing belief that it is difficult to consistently earn returns that are superior to broad market indices such as the S&P 500 Index.

Quantitative Versus Traditional Fundamental Analysis

Actively managed funds must depend on some form of security analysis. Some funds employ *technical analysis,* which attempts to predict stock price movements on the basis of market indicators (prior stock price movements, volume of shares traded, etc.). In contrast, *fundamental analysis,* the primary approach for security analysis, attempts to evaluate the current market price relative to projections of the firm's future earnings and cash-flow generating potential. Fundamental analysis involves all the steps described in the previous chapters of this book: business strategy analysis, accounting analysis, financial analysis, and prospective analysis (forecasting and valuation). In recent years, some analysts have supplemented traditional fundamental analysis, which involves a substantial amount of subjective judgment, with more quantitative approaches.

The quantitative approaches themselves are quite varied. Some involve simply "screening" stocks on the basis of some set of factors, such as trends in analysts' earnings revisions, price–earnings ratios, price-to-book ratios, and so on. Whether such approaches are useful depends on the degree of market efficiency relative to the screens. Quantitative approaches can also involve implementation of some formal model to predict future stock returns. Longstanding statistical techniques such as regression analysis and probit analysis can be used, as can more recently developed, computer-intensive techniques such as neural network analysis. Again, the success of these approaches depends on the degree of market efficiency and whether the analysis can exploit information in ways not otherwise available to market agents as a group.

Quantitative approaches play a more important role in security analysis today than they did a decade or two ago. However, by and large, analysts still rely primarily on fundamental analysis involving complex human judgments.

Formal Versus Informal Valuation

Full-scale, formal valuations based on the methods described in Chapter 7 have become more common in recent years. However, less formal approaches are also popular. For example, an analyst can compare his or her long-term earnings projection with the consensus forecast to generate a buy or sell recommendation. Another possible approach, that might be labeled "marginalist," involves no attempt to value the firm. The analyst simply assumes that if he or she has unearthed favorable (or unfavorable) information believed not to be recognized by others, the stock should be bought (or sold).

Unlike many security analysts, investment bankers produce formal valuations as a matter of course. Investment bankers, who estimate values for the purpose of bringing a private firm to the public market, for evaluating a merger or buyout proposal, for issuing a fairness opinion or for making a periodic managerial review, must document their valuation in a way that can readily be communicated to management and, if necessary, to the courts.

THE PROCESS OF COMPREHENSIVE SECURITY ANALYSIS

Given the variety of approaches practiced in security analysis, it is impossible to summarize all of them here. Instead, we briefly outline steps to be included in a comprehensive security analysis. The amount of attention focused on any given step varies among analysts.

Selection of Candidates for Analysis

No analyst can effectively investigate more than a small fraction of the securities on a major exchange, and thus some approach to narrowing the focus must be employed. Sell-side analysts are often organized within an investment house by industry or sector. Thus they tend to be constrained in their choices of firms to follow. However, from the perspective of a fund manager or an investment firm as a whole, there is usually the freedom to focus on any firm or sector.

As noted earlier, funds typically specialize in investing in stocks with certain risk profiles or characteristics (e.g., growth stocks, "value" stocks, technology stocks, and cyclical stocks). Managers of these types of funds seek to focus the energies of their analysts on identifying stocks that fit their fund objective. In addition, individual investors who seek to maintain a well diversified portfolio without holding many stocks also need information about the nature of a firm's risks and how they fit with the risk profile of their overall portfolio.

An alternative approach to stock selection is to screen firms on the basis of some potential mispricing followed by a detailed analysis of only those stocks that meet the specified criteria. For example, one fund managed by a large U.S. insurance company screens stocks on the basis of recent "earnings momentum" as reflected in revisions in the earnings projections of sell-side and buy-side analysts. Upward revisions trigger investigations for possible purchase. The fund operates on the belief that earnings momentum is a positive signal of future price movements. Another fund complements the earnings momentum screen with one based on recent short-term stock price movements, in the hopes of identifying earnings revisions not yet reflected in stock prices.

Key Analysis Questions

Depending on whether fund managers follow a strategy of targeting stocks with specific types of characteristics, or of screening stocks that appear to be mispriced, the following types of questions are likely to be useful:

- What is the risk profile of a firm? How volatile is its earnings stream and stock price? What are the most likely bad outcomes in the future? What is the upside potential? How closely linked are the firm's risks to the health of the overall economy? Are the risks largely diversifiable, or are they systematic?
- Does the firm possess the characteristics of a growth stock? What is the expected pattern of sales and earnings growth for the coming years? Is the firm reinvesting most or all of its earnings?
- Does the firm match the characteristics desired by "income funds"? Is it a mature or maturing company, prepared to "harvest" profits and distribute them in the form of high dividends?
- Is the firm a candidate for a "value fund"? Does it offer measures of earnings, cash flow, and book value that are high relative to the price? What specific screening rules can be implemented to identify misvalued stocks?

Inferring Market Expectations

If the security analysis is conducted with an eye toward the identification of mispricing, it must ultimately involve a comparison of the analyst's expectations with those of "the market." One possibility is to view the observed stock price as the reflection of market expectations and to compare the analyst's own estimate of value with that price. However, a stock price is only a "summary statistic." It is useful to have a more detailed idea of the market's expectations about a firm's future performance, expressed in terms of sales, earnings, and other measures. For example, assume that an analyst has developed new insights about a firm's near-term sales. Whether those insights represent new information for the stock market, and whether they indicate that a "buy" recommendation is appropriate, can be easily determined if the analyst knows the market consensus sales forecast.

Around the world a number of agencies summarize analysts' forecasts of sales and earnings. Forecasts for the next year or two are commonly available, and for many firms, a "long-run" earnings growth projection is also available—typically for three to five years. Some financial information providers in the U.S provide continuous on-line updates to such data, so if an analyst revises a forecast, that can be made known to fund managers and other analysts within seconds.

As useful as analysts' forecasts of sales and earnings are, they do not represent a complete description of expectations about future performance, and there is no guarantee that consensus analyst forecasts are the same as those reflected in market prices. Further, financial analysts typically forecast performance for only a few years, so it is helpful to understand what types of long-term forecasts are reflected in stock prices. Armed with the model in Chapters 7 and 8 that expresses price as a function of future cash flows or earnings, an analyst can draw some educated inferences about the expectations embedded in stock prices.

For example, consider the valuation of Electronic Arts Inc. (EA), a developer of interactive software video games. On November 15, 2006, EA's stock price closed at $58.84, giving it a market capitalization of $18.1 billion. Through September 30, 2006, the company suffered eight consecutive quarters of year-over-year profit declines and reported a 53 percent decline in earnings for the fiscal year ended March 31, 2006. Earnings per share (EPS) declined from $1.87 in fiscal year 2004 to $0.75 in fiscal year 2006. The stock was trading at over 100 times trailing twelve months earnings, clearly indicating that the market was expecting earnings to rebound. Performance in the quarter ended September 30, 2006, showed early evidence of this rebound as the firm returned to profitability after two consecutive quarters of losses.

The decline in profitability was driven by a variety of reasons. The major video game hardware manufacturers such as Sony and Nintendo, for which EA published game software, were in the midst of releasing new and more powerful game consoles following the release of Microsoft's new game player. EA had been aggressively investing in the development of new video game titles for these new consoles. The company was also investing in games for the online market as well as handheld devices and cell phones. In addition to incurring these additional research and development costs, the company experienced declining sales in anticipation of the transition to the new hardware, lower margins as a result of price cuts to stimulate sales, and higher marketing and sales costs.

The market expected EA's financial downturn to continue through the fiscal year ending March 2007. Analysts expected EA to generate EPS of only $0.11 in 2007, an 85 percent decrease from the prior year. However, EPS were expected to rebound to $0.95 (an increase of 764 percent) and $2.03 (an increase of 114 percent) in the following two years. Most analysts projected earnings only over a three-year period.[10]

How do these forecasts by analysts reconcile with the actual market valuation of EA? What were the market's implicit assumptions about the short-term and long-term earnings growth for the company? By altering the amounts for key value drivers and arriving at combinations that generate an estimated value equal to the observed market price, the analyst can infer what the market might have been expecting for EA in November 2006.

A reasonable estimate of EA's cost of equity capital is in the range of 10 percent to 12 percent. As a result of strong revenue growth, the company's book value has grown at an average of 20 percent over the past five years, and it is likely that this growth will persist over the next five years. Focusing on earnings as the value driver, critical questions for judging the market valuation of EA are (1) how quickly the company's earnings will rebound to the levels of two years ago, (2) what the firm's near-term earnings growth prospects are, and (3) whether the company will continue to outperform the earnings growth rates of the average firms in the economy, which has historically been around 4 percent? The analysis in Table 9-1 shows different scenarios for EA's future performance that would justify its current stock price, assuming a cost of equity capital of 10 percent.

Table 9-1 shows the implications for EA's earnings growth using the three-year estimates of the various sell-side analysts covering the stock as well as scenarios if the expected short-term turnaround does not materialize as expected. The table also shows the implied EPS and ROEs that the various turnaround scenarios would imply. Even using the market's estimates for the first three years, EA would need to maintain an impressive rate of earnings growth through 2011. If the turnaround is faster than the market consensus, EA's earnings could show only a modest decline in 2007 and grow by 150 percent the following year as the firm's investments pay off. However, the company still needs to achieve impressively high average growth through 2011 to justify the $58 stock price. If, on the other hand, the turnaround in the current year's performance is slower than anticipated, the pressure on EA to produce superior earnings growth in the short term is intensified, with required growth rates of 100 percent even four years in the future. Critically, all three scenarios require strong earnings growth beyond the forecast horizon. For instance, in the scenario of a slow turnaround, EA would need to maintain an earnings growth rate of 7 percent in perpetuity, a rate that few companies have managed to maintain. In addition, any missteps could lead the stock to become more risky and volatile, implying a higher cost of capital. In this case, even higher rates of earnings growth would be needed to justify the current market price.

This type of scenario analysis provides the analyst with insights about investors' expectations for EA, and is useful for judging whether the stock is correctly valued. Security analysis need not involve such a detailed attempt to infer market

TABLE 9-1	Alternative Assumptions About Value Drivers for Electronic Arts Consistent with Observed Market Price of $58.84 (Assuming 10 Percent Cost of Equity Capital)

Analysts' Mean Earnings Forecast Through 2009	2007	2008	2009	2010	2011	Post 2011
Earnings Growth	−85%	764%	114%	75%	50%	6.0%
Earnings Per Share	0.11	0.95	2.03	3.56	5.34	
Return on Equity	1%	7%	13%	19%	24%	

Turnaround Faster Than Predicted	2007	2008	2009	2010	2011	Post 2011
Earnings Growth	−25%	150%	100%	60%	30%	5.0%
Earnings Per Share	0.56	1.41	2.82	4.51	5.86	
Return on Equity	5%	11%	18%	24%	26%	

Turnaround Slower Than Predicted	2007	2008	2009	2010	2011	Post 2011
Earnings Growth	−85%	350%	200%	100%	57%	7.0%
Earnings Per Share	0.11	0.50	1.49	2.98	4.67	
Return on Equity	1%	4%	10%	16%	21%	

expectations. However, whether or not an explicit analysis is made, a good analyst understands what economic scenarios could plausibly be reflected in the observed price.

Key Analysis Questions

By using the discounted abnormal earnings/ROE valuation model, analysts can infer the market's expectations for a firm's future performance. This permits analysts to ask whether the market is over- or undervaluing a company. Typical questions that analysts might ask from this analysis include the following:

- What are the market's assumptions about long-term ROE and growth? For example, is the market forecasting that the company can grow its earnings without a corresponding level of expansion in its asset base (and hence equity)? If so, how long can this persist?
- How do changes in the cost of capital affect the market's assessment of the firm's future performance? If the market's expectations seem to be unexpectedly high or low, has the market reassessed the company's risk? If so, is this change plausible?

Developing the Analyst's Expectations

Ultimately, a security analyst must compare his or her own view of a stock with the view embedded in the market price. The analyst's view is generated using the same analytical tools discussed in Chapters 2 through 8. The final product of this work is, of course, a forecast of the firm's future earnings and cash flows and an estimate of the firm's value. However, that final product is less important than the understanding of the business and its industry that the analysis provides. It is such understanding that enables the analyst to interpret new information as it arrives and to infer its implications.

Key Analysis Questions

In developing expectations about a firm's future performance using the financial analysis tools discussed throughout this book, the analyst is likely to ask the following types of questions:

- How profitable is the firm? In light of industry conditions, the firm's corporate strategy, and its barriers to competition, how sustainable is that rate of profitability?
- What are the opportunities for growth for this firm?
- How risky is this firm? How vulnerable are operations to general economic downturns? How highly levered is the firm? What does the riskiness of the firm imply about its cost of capital?
- How do answers to the above questions compare to the expectations embedded in the observed stock price?

The Final Product of Security Analysis

For financial analysts, the final product of security analysis is a recommendation to buy, sell, or hold the stock (or some more refined ranking). The recommendation is supported by a set of forecasts and a report summarizing the foundation for the recommendation. Analysts' reports often delve into significant detail and include an assessment of a firm's business as well as a line-by-line income statement, balance sheet, and cash flow forecasts for one or more years.

In making a recommendation to buy or sell a stock, the analyst has to consider the investment time horizon required to capitalize on the recommendation. Are anticipated improvements in performance likely to be confirmed in the near term, allowing investors to capitalize quickly on the recommendation? Or do expected performance improvements reflect long-term fundamentals that will take several years to play out? Longer investment horizons impose greater risk to investors that the company's performance will be affected by changes in economic conditions that cannot be anticipated by the analyst, reducing the value of the recommendation. Consequently, thorough analysis requires the ability not only to recognize whether a stock is misvalued, but also to anticipate when a price correction is likely to take place.

Because there are additional investment risks from following recommendations that require long-term commitments, security analysts tend to focus on making recommendations that are likely to pay off in the short term. This might explain why so few analysts recommended selling dot-com and technology stocks during the late 1990s when their prices would be difficult to justify on the basis of long-term fundamentals. It also explains why analysts recommended Enron's stock at its peak, even though the kind of analysis performed in this chapter would have shown that the future growth and ROE performance implied by this price would be extremely difficult to achieve. It also implies that to take advantage of long-term fundamental analysis can often require access to patient, long-term capital.

PERFORMANCE OF SECURITY ANALYSTS AND FUND MANAGERS

There has been extensive research on the performance of sell-side security analysts and fund managers during the last three decades. A few of the key findings are summarized below.

Performance of Sell-Side Analysts

Despite the recent failure of sell-side analysts to foresee the dramatic price declines for dot-com and telecommunications stocks, and to detect the financial shenanigans and overvaluation of companies such as Enron and WorldCom, research shows that analysts generally add value in the capital market. Analyst earnings forecasts are more accurate than those produced by time series models that use past earnings to predict future earnings.[11] Of course, this should not be too surprising since analysts can update their earnings forecasts between quarters to incorporate new firm and economy information, whereas time-series models cannot. In addition, stock prices tend to respond positively to upward revisions in analysts' earnings forecasts and recommendations, and negatively to downward revisions.[12] Further, recent research indicates that sell-side analysts' buy recommendations outperform the market index and risk benchmarks by 6.5 percent and 7.5 percent per year, respectively.[13] Finally, recent research finds that analysts play a valuable role in improving market efficiency.

For example, stock prices for firms with higher analyst following incorporate more rapidly information on accruals and cash flows than prices of less followed firms.[14]

Several factors seem to be important in explaining analysts' earnings forecast accuracy. Not surprisingly, forecasts of near-term earnings are much more accurate than those of long-term performance.[15] This probably explains why analysts typically make detailed forecasts for only one or two years ahead. Studies of differences in earnings forecast accuracy among analysts find that the more accurate ones tend to specialize by industry and work for large, well funded firms that employ other analysts who follow the same industry.[16]

Although analysts perform a valuable function in the capital market, research shows that their forecasts and recommendations tend to be biased. Early evidence on bias indicated that analyst earnings forecasts tended to be optimistic and that their recommendations were almost exclusively for buys.[17] Several factors potentially explain this finding. First, security analysts at brokerage houses are typically compensated on the basis of the trading volume that their reports generate. Given the costs of short selling and the restrictions on short selling by many institutions, brokerage analysts have incentives to issue optimistic reports that encourage investors to buy stocks rather than to issue negative reports that create selling pressure.[18] Second, until 2003 analysts that worked for investment banks were rewarded for promoting public issues by current clients and for attracting new banking clients, creating incentives for optimistic forecasts and recommendations. Studies show that analysts who work for lead underwriters make more optimistic long-term earnings forecasts and recommendations for firms raising equity capital than unaffiliated analysts.[19]

Evidence indicates that during the late 1990s there was a marked decline in analyst optimism in forecasts of near-term earnings.[20] One explanation offered for this change is that during this time analysts relied heavily on private discussions with top management to make their earnings forecasts. Management allegedly used these personal connections to manage analysts' short-term expectations downward so that the firm could subsequently report earnings that beat analysts' expectations. In response to concerns about this practice, in October 2000 the SEC approved Regulation Fair Disclosure, which prohibits management from making selective disclosures of nonpublic information. Studies show that this regulatory intervention has led to greater independence from management by analysts and an increased effort in independent information discovery.[21]

There has also been a general decline in sell-side analysts' optimistic recommendations during the past few years. Many large investment banks now require analysts to use a forced curve to rate stocks, leading to a greater number of the lowest ratings. Factors that underlie this change include a sharp rise in trading by hedge funds, which actively seek stocks to short-sell. In contrast, traditional money management firms are typically restricted from short-selling, and are more interested in analysts' buy recommendations than their sells. Second, regulatory changes in the U.S. under the Global Settlement require tight separation between investment banking and equity research at investment banks.

Performance of Fund Managers

Measuring whether mutual and pension fund managers earn superior returns is a difficult task for several reasons. First, there is no agreement about how to estimate benchmark performance for a fund. Studies have used a number of approaches—some have used the Capital Asset Pricing Model (CAPM) as a benchmark while others have used multifactor pricing models. For studies using the CAPM, there are questions about what type of market index to use. For example, should it be an equal- or value-weighted index, a NYSE index or a broader market index? Second, many of the traditional measures of fund performance abstract from market-wide performance, which understates fund abnormal performance if fund managers can time the market by reducing portfolio risk prior to market declines and increasing risks before a market run-up. Third, the overall volatility of stock returns stretches the limits of statistical power needed to measure fund performance. Finally, tests of fund performance are likely to be highly sensitive to the time period examined. Value or momentum investing could therefore appear to be profitable depending on when the tests are conducted.

Perhaps because of these challenges, there is no consistent evidence that actively managed mutual funds generate superior returns for investors. While some studies find evidence of positive abnormal returns for the industry, others conclude that returns are generally negative.[22] Of course even if mutual fund managers on average can only generate "normal" returns for investors, it is still possible for the best managers to show consistently strong performance. Some studies do in fact document that funds earning positive abnormal returns in one period continue to outperform in subsequent periods. However, more recent evidence suggests that these findings are caused by general momentum in stock returns or are offset by high fund expenses from management fees and/or trading costs.[23] Researchers have also examined which, if any, investment strategies are most successful. However, no clear consensus appears—several studies have found that momentum and high turnover strategies generate superior returns, whereas others conclude that value strategies are better.[24]

Finally, recent research has examined whether fund managers tend to buy and sell many of the same stocks at the same time. There is evidence of "herding" behavior, particularly by momentum fund managers.[25] This could arise because managers have access to common information, because they are affected by similar cognitive biases, or because they have incentives to follow the crowd.[26] For example, consider the rationale of a fund manager who holds a stock but who, through long-term fundamental analysis, estimates that it is misvalued. If the manager changes the fund's holdings accordingly and the stock price returns to its intrinsic value in the next quarter, the fund will show superior relative portfolio performance and will attract new capital. However, if the stock continues to be misvalued for several quarters, the informed fund manager will underperform the benchmark and capital will flow to other funds. In contrast, a risk-averse manager who simply follows the crowd will not be rewarded for detecting the misvaluation, but neither will this manager be blamed for a poor investment decision when the stock price ultimately corrects, since other funds made the same mistake.

There has been considerably less research on the performance of pension fund managers. Overall, the findings show little consistent evidence that pension fund managers either over- or under-perform traditional benchmarks.[27]

SUMMARY

Equity security analysis is the evaluation of a firm and its prospects from the perspective of a current or potential investor in the firm's stock. Security analysis is one component of a larger investment process that involves (1) establishing the objectives of the investor or fund, (2) forming expectations about the future returns and risks of individual securities, and then (3) combining individual securities into portfolios to maximize progress toward the investment objectives.

Some security analysis is devoted primarily to assuring that a stock possesses the proper risk profile and other desired characteristics prior to inclusion in an investor's portfolio. However, especially for many professional buy-side and sell-side security analysts, the analysis is also directed toward the identification of mispriced securities. In equilibrium, such activity will be rewarding for those with the strongest comparative advantage. They will be the ones able to identify any mispricing at the lowest cost and exert pressure on the price to correct the mispricing. What kinds of efforts are productive in this domain depends on the degree of market efficiency. A large body of evidence exists that is supportive of a high degree of efficiency in the U.S. market, but recent studies have reopened the debate on this issue.

In practice, a wide variety of approaches to fund management and security analysis are employed. However, at the core of the analyses are the same steps outlined in Chapters 2 through 8 of this book: business strategy analysis, accounting analysis, financial analysis, and prospective analysis (forecasting and valuation). For the professional analyst, the final product of the work is, of course, a forecast of the firm's future earnings and cash flows, and an estimate of the firm's value. But that final product is less important than the understanding of the business and its industry, which the analysis provides. It is such understanding that positions the analyst to interpret new information as it arrives and infer its implications.

Finally, the chapter summarizes some key findings of the research on the performance of both sell-side and buy-side security analysts.

DISCUSSION QUESTIONS

1. Despite many years of research, the evidence on market efficiency described in this chapter appears to be inconclusive. Some argue that this is because researchers have been unable to link company fundamentals to stock prices precisely. Comment.

2. Geoffrey Henley, a professor of finance, states, "The capital market is efficient. I don't know why anyone would bother devoting time to following individual stocks and doing fundamental analysis. The best approach is to buy and hold a well diversified portfolio of stocks." Do you agree? Why or why not?

3. What is the difference between fundamental and technical analysis? Can you think of any trading strategies that use technical analysis? What are the underlying assumptions made by these strategies?

4. Investment funds follow many different types of investment strategies. Income funds focus on stocks with high dividend yields, growth funds invest in stocks that are expected to have high capital appreciation, value funds follow stocks that are considered to be undervalued, and short funds bet against stocks they consider to be overvalued. What types of investors are likely to be attracted to each of these types of funds? Why?

5. Intergalactic Software Company went public three months ago. You are a sophisticated investor who devotes time to fundamental analysis as a way of identifying mispriced stocks. Which of the following characteristics would you focus on in deciding whether to follow this stock?
   • The market capitalization
   • The average number of shares traded per day
   • The bid–ask spread for the stock

- Whether the underwriter that brought the firm public is a Top Five investment banking firm
- Whether the firm's audit company is a Big Four firm
- Whether there are analysts from major brokerage firms following the company
- Whether the stock is held mostly by retail or by institutional investors

6. Intergalactic Software Company's stock has a market price of $20 per share and a book value of $12 per share. If its cost of equity capital is 15 percent and its book value is expected to grow at 5 percent per year indefinitely, what is the market's assessment of its steady state return on equity? If the stock price increases to $35 and the market does not expect the firm's growth rate to change, what is the revised steady state ROE? If instead the price increase was due to an increase in the market's assessments about long-term book value growth rather than long-term ROE, what would the price revision imply for the steady state growth rate?

7. There are two major types of financial analysts: buy-side and sell-side. Buy-side analysts work for investment firms and make stock recommendations that are available only to the management of funds within that firm. Sell-side analysts work for brokerage firms and make recommendations that are used to sell stock to the brokerage firms' clients, which include individual investors and managers of investment funds. What would be the differences in tasks and motivations of these two types of analysts?

8. Many market participants believe that sell-side analysts are too optimistic in their recommendations to buy stocks and too slow to recommend sells. What factors might explain this bias?

9. Joe Klein is an analyst for an investment banking firm that offers both underwriting and brokerage services. Joe sends you a highly favorable report on a stock that his firm recently helped go public and for which it currently makes the market. What are the potential advantages and disadvantages in relying on Joe's report in deciding whether to buy the stock?

10. Joe states, "I can see how ratio analysis and valuation help me do fundamental analysis, but I don't see the value of doing strategy analysis." Can you explain to him how strategy analysis could be potentially useful?

NOTES

1. P. Healy and K. Palepu, "The Fall of Enron," *Journal of Economic Perspectives* 17, no. 2 (Spring 2003): 3–26, discuss how weak money manager incentives and a lack of proper long-term analysis contributed to the stock price run-up and subsequent collapse of Enron. A similar discussion on factors affecting the rise and fall of dot-com stocks is provided in "The Role of Capital Market Intermediaries in the Dot-Com Crash of 2000," Harvard Business School Case 9-101–110, 2001.

2. See R. Bhushan, "Firm characteristics and analyst following," *Journal of Accounting and Economics* 11 (2/5), July 1989: 255–75, and P. O'Brien and R. Bhushan, "Analyst following and institutional ownership," *Journal of Accounting Research* 28, Supplement (1990): 55–76.

3. P. Mohanram and S. Sunder, "How Has Regulation FD Affected the Operations of Financial Analysts?" *Contemporary Accounting Research 23*, no. 2 (2006): 491–525.

4. Reviews of evidence on market efficiency are provided by E. Fama, "Efficient Capital Markets: II," *Journal of Finance* 46 (December 1991): 1575–1617; S. Kothari, "Capital Markets Research in Accounting," *Journal of Accounting and Economics* 31 (September 2001):105–231; and C. Lee, "Market Efficiency in Accounting Research," *Journal of Accounting and Economics* 31 (September 2001): 233–53.

5. For example, see V. Bernard and J. Thomas, "Evidence That Stock Prices Do Not Fully Reflect the Implications of Current Earnings for Future Earnings," *Journal of Accounting and Economics* 13 (December 1990): 305–41.

6. For example, the superior returns earned by pursuing a "value stock" strategy were examined by J. Lakonishok, A. Shleifer, and R. Vishny, "Contrarian Investment, Extrapolation, and Risk," *Journal of Finance* 49 (December 1994): 1541–78, and R. Frankel and C. Lee, "Accounting Valuation, Market Expectation, and Cross-Sectional Stock Returns," *Journal of Accounting and Economics* 25 (June 1998): 283–319.

7. For example, see J. Ou and S. Penman, "Financial Statement Analysis and the Prediction of Stock Returns," *Journal of Accounting and Economics* 11 (November 1989): 295–330; R. Holthausen and D. Larcker, "The Prediction of Stock Returns Using Financial Statement Information," *Journal of Accounting and Economics* 15 (June/September 1992): 373–412; and R. Sloan, "Do Stock Prices Fully Reflect Information in Accruals and Cash Flows about Future Earnings?" *The Accounting Review* 71 (July 1996): 298–325.

8. A. Shleifer, "Do Demand Curves for Stocks Slope Down," *Journal of Finance and Quantitative Analysis* 34 (March 1986): 579–90, argues that stocks show a positive abnormal returns immediately after entering the S&P 500 Index as a result of increased demand from index funds. While extensive research exists on the idea that trading as a result of investor preference creates short-term price pressure in spin-off transactions, J. Abarbanell, B. Bushee, and J. Raedy, "Institutional Investor Preferences and Price Pressure: The Case of Corporate Spin-Offs," *Journal of Business* 76 (2003): 233–61, finds that this trading is not associated with abnormal price movements for parents or subsidiaries around the spin-off.

9. For an overview of research in behavioral finance, see R. Thaler, *Advances in Behavioral Finance* (New York: Russell Sage Foundation, 1993), and A. Shleifer, *Inefficient Markets: An Introduction to Behavioral Finance* (Oxford: Oxford University Press, 2000). Numerous studies have documented the bias introduced by various elements of irrational behavior such as overconfidence, herding, regret, and loss aversion.

10. These forecasts were taken from Thomson One Analytics.

11. See L. Brown and M. Rozeff, "The Superiority of Analyst Forecasts as Measures of Expectations: Evidence from Earnings," *Journal of Finance* 33 (1978): 1–16; L. Brown, P. Griffin, R. Hagerman, and M. Zmijewski, "Security Analyst Superiority Relative to Univariate Time-Series Models in Forecasting Quarterly Earnings," *Journal of Accounting and Economics* 9 (1987): 61–87; and D. Givoly, "Financial Analysts' Forecasts of

Earnings: A Better Surrogate for Market Expectations," *Journal of Accounting and Economics* 4, no. 2 (1982): 85–108.

12. See D. Givoly and J. Lakonishok, "The Information Content of Financial Analysts' Forecasts of Earnings: Some Evidence on Semi-Strong Efficiency," *Journal of Accounting and Economics* 2 (1979): 165–86; T. Lys and S. Sohn, "The Association Between Revisions of Financial Analysts' Earnings Forecasts and Security Price Changes," *Journal of Accounting and Economics* 13 (1990): 341–64; and J. Francis and L. Soffer, "The Relative Informativeness of Analysts' Stock Recommendations and Earnings Forecast Revisions," *Journal of Accounting Research* 35, no. 2 (1997): 193–212.

13. See B. Groysberg, P. Healy, C. Chapman, and Y. Gui, "Do Buy-Side Analysts Out-Perform the Sell-Side?" (working paper, Harvard Business School, June 2006). The study also finds that buy-side analysts at a large money management firm make more optimistic earnings forecasts and less profitable buy recommendations than sell-side analysts.

14. See M. Brennan, N. Jegadeesh, and B. Swaminathan, "Investment Analysis and the Adjustment of Stock Prices to Common Information," *Review of Financial Studies* 6, no. 4 (1993): 799–824, and B. Ayers and R. Freeman, "Evidence That Analyst Following and Institutional Ownership Accelerate the Pricing of Future Earnings," *Review of Accounting Studies* 8, no. 1 (2003): 47–67.

15. See P. O'Brien, "Forecasts Accuracy of Individual Analysts in Nine Industries." *Journal of Accounting Research* 28 (1990): 286–304.

16. See M. Clement, "Analyst Forecast Accuracy: Do Ability, Resources, and Portfolio Complexity Matter?" *Journal of Accounting and Economics* 27 (1999): 285–304; J. Jacob, T. Lys, and M. Neale, "Experience in Forecasting Performance of Security Analysts." *Journal of Accounting and Economics* 28 (1999): 51–82; and S. Gilson, P. Healy, C. Noe, and K. Palepu, "Analyst Specialization and Conglomerate Stock Breakups," *Journal of Accounting Research* 39 (December 2001): 565–73.

17. See L. Brown, G. Foster, and E. Noreen, "Security Analyst Multi-Year Earnings Forecasts and the Capital Market," *Studies in Accounting Research*, no. 23, American Accounting Association (Sarasota, FL), 1985. In addition, M. McNichols and P. O'Brien, in "Self-Selection and Analyst Coverage," *Journal of Accounting Research*, Supplement (1997): 167–208, find that analyst bias arises primarily because analysts issue recommendations on firms for which they have favorable information and withhold recommending firms with unfavorable information.

18. See A. Cowen, B. Groysberg, and P. Healy, "Which Types of Analyst Firms Are More Optimistic?" *Journal of Accounting and Economics* 41 (2006): 119–146.

19. See H. Lin and M. McNichols, "Underwriting Relationships, Analysts' Earnings Forecasts and Investment Recommendations," *Journal of Accounting and Economics* 25, no. 1 (1998): 101–28; R. Michaely and K. Womack, "Conflict of Interest and the Credibility of Underwriter Analyst Recommendations," *Review of Financial Studies* 12, no. 4 (1999): 653–86; and P. Dechow, A. Hutton, and R. Sloan, "The Relation Between Analysts' Forecasts of Long-Term Earnings Growth and Stock Price Performance Following Equity Offerings," *Contemporary Accounting Research* 17, no. 1 (2000): 1–32.

20. See L. Brown, "Analyst Forecasting Errors: Additional Evidence," *Financial Analysts' Journal* (November/December 1997): 81–88, and D. Matsumoto, "Management's Incentives to Avoid Negative Earnings Surprises," *The Accounting Review* 77 (July 2002): 483–515.

21. See P. Mohanram and S. Sunder, "How Has Regulation FD Affected the Functioning of Financial Analysts?" *Contemporary Accounting Research* 23, no. 2 (2006): 491–525.

22. For example, evidence of superior fund performance is reported by M. Grinblatt and S. Titman, "Mutual Fund Performance: An Analysis of Quarterly Holdings, *Journal of Business* 62 (1994), and by D. Hendricks, J. Patel, and R. Zeckhauser, "Hot Hands in Mutual Funds: Short-Run Persistence of Relative Performance," *The Journal of Finance* 48 (1993): 93–130. In contrast, negative fund performance is shown by M. Jensen, "The Performance of Mutual Funds in the Period 1945–64," *The Journal of Finance* 23 (May 1968): 389–416, and B. Malkiel, "Returns from Investing in Equity Mutual Funds from 1971 to 1991," *Journal of Finance* 50 (June 1995): 549–73.

23. M. Grinblatt and S. Titman, "The Persistence of Mutual Fund Performance," *Journal of Finance* 47 (December 1992): 1977–86, and D. Hendricks, J. Patel, and R. Zeckhauser, "Hot Hands in Mutual Funds: Short-Run Persistence of Relative Performance," *Journal of Finance* 48 (March 1993): 93–130, find evidence of persistence in mutual fund returns. However, M. Carhart, "On Persistence in Mutual Fund Performance," *The Journal of Finance* 52 (March 1997): 57–83, shows that much of this is attributable to momentum in stock returns and to fund expenses; B. Malkiel, "Returns from Investing in Equity Mutual Funds from 1971 to 1991," *The Journal of Finance* 50 (June 1995): 549–73, shows that survivorship bias is also an important consideration.

24. See M. Grinblatt, S. Titman, and R. Wermers, "Momentum Investment Strategies, Portfolio Performance, and Herding: A Study of Mutual Fund Behavior," *The American Economic Review* 85 (December 1995): 1088–105.

25. For example, J. Lakonishok, A. Shleifer, and R. Vishny, "Contrarian Investment, Extrapolation, and Risk," *Journal of Finance* 49 (December 1994): 1541–79, find that value funds show superior performance, whereas M. Grinblatt, S. Titman, and R. Wermers, "Momentum Investment Strategies, Portfolio Performance, and Herding: A Study of Mutual Fund Behavior," *The American Economic Review* 85 (December 1995): 1088–105, find that momentum investing is profitable.

26. See D. Scharfstein and J. Stein, "Herd Behavior and Investment," *The American Economic Review* 80 (June 1990): 465–80, and P. Healy and K. Palepu, "The Fall of Enron," *Journal of Economic Perspectives* 17, no. 2 (Spring 2003): 3–26.

27. For evidence on performance by pension fund managers, see J. Lakonishok, A. Shleifer, and R. Vishny, "The Structure and Performance of the Money Management Industry," *Brookings Papers on Economic Activity*, Washington, DC (1992): 339–92; T. Coggin, F. Fabozzi, and S. Rahman, "The Investment Performance of U.S. Equity Pension Fund Managers: An Empirical Investigation," *The Journal of Finance* 48 (July 1993): 1039–56; and W. Ferson and K. Khang, "Conditional Performance Measurement Using Portfolio Weights: Evidence for Pension Funds," *Journal of Financial Economics* 65 (August 2002): 249–282.

Chapter 10

Credit Analysis and Distress Prediction

redit analysis is the evaluation of a firm from the perspective of a holder or potential holder of its debt, which includes trade payables, loans, and public debt securities. A key element of credit analysis is the prediction of the likelihood a firm will face financial distress. Credit analysis is involved in a wide variety of decision contexts:

- A commercial banker asks: Should we extend a loan to this firm? If so, how should it be structured? How should it be priced?
- If the loan is granted, the banker must later ask: Are we still providing the services, including credit, that this firm needs? Is the firm still in compliance with the loan terms? If not, is there a need to restructure the loan, and if so, how? Is the situation serious enough to call for accelerating the repayment of the loan?
- A potential investor asks: Are these debt securities a sound investment? What is the probability that the firm will face distress and default on the debt? Does the yield provide adequate compensation for the default risk involved?
- An investor contemplating purchase of debt securities in default asks: How likely is it that this firm can be turned around? In light of the high yield on this debt relative to its current price, can I accept the risk that the debt will not be repaid in full?
- A potential supplier asks: Should I sell products or services to this firm? The associated credit will be extended only for a short period, but the amount is large and I should have some assurance that collection risks are manageable.

Finally, there are third parties—those other than borrowers and lenders—who are interested in the general issue of how likely it is that a firm will avoid financial distress:

- An auditor asks: How likely is it that this firm will survive beyond the short run? In evaluating the firm's financials, should I consider it a going concern?
- An actual or potential employee asks: How confident can I be that this firm will be able to offer employment over the long term?
- A potential customer asks: What assurance is there that this firm will survive to provide warranty services, replacement parts, product updates, and other services?
- A competitor asks: Will this firm survive the current industry shakeout? What are the implications of potential financial distress at this firm for my pricing and market share?

This chapter develops a framework to evaluate a firm's creditworthiness and assess the likelihood of financial distress.

WHY DO FIRMS USE DEBT FINANCING?

Before discussing the credit market and credit analysis, it is worth understanding why firms use debt financing. Debt financing is attractive to firms for two key reasons:

- *Corporate interest tax shields.* In many countries including the U.S., tax laws provide for the corporate tax deductibility of interest paid on debt. No such corporate tax shield is available for dividend payments or retained earnings. Therefore, corporate tax benefits should encourage firms with high effective tax rates and few forms of tax shields other than interest to favor debt financing.
- *Management incentives for value creation.* Firms with relatively high leverage face pressures to generate cash flows to meet payments of interest and principal, reducing resources available to fund unjustifiable expenses and investments that do not maximize shareholder value. Debt financing, therefore, focuses management on value creation, reducing conflicts of interest between managers and shareholders.

However, there are also costs of debt financing. As a firm increases its use of debt financing, it increases the likelihood of financial distress, where it is unable to meet interest or principal repayment obligations to creditors. This forces the firm to restructure its financial claims, either under formal bankruptcy proceedings or out of bankruptcy. Financial distress has multiple negative consequences for the firm:

- *Legal costs of financial distress.* Restructurings are likely to be costly, since the parties involved have to hire lawyers, bankers, and accountants to represent their interests, and to pay court costs if there are formal legal proceedings. These are often called the direct costs of financial distress.
- *Costs of foregone investment opportunities.* Distressed firms face significant challenges in raising capital as potential new investors and creditors will be wary of becoming embroiled in the firm's legal disputes. Thus, firms in distress are often unable to finance new investments even though they may be profitable for its owners.
- *Costs of conflicts between creditors and stockholders.* When faced with financial distress, creditors focus on the firm's ability to service its debt while shareholders worry that their equity will revert to the creditors if the firm defaults. Thus, managers face increased pressure to make decisions that typically serve the interests of the stockholders, and creditors react by increasing the costs of borrowing for the firm's stockholders.

Firms are more likely to fall into financial distress if they have high business risks and their assets are easily destroyed in financial distress. For example, firms with human capital and brand intangibles are particularly sensitive to financial distress since dissatisfied employees and customers can leave or seek alternative suppliers. In contrast, firms with tangible assets can sell their assets if they get into financial distress, providing additional security for lenders and lowering the costs of financial distress. Firms with intangible assets are therefore less likely to be highly leveraged than firms whose assets are mostly tangible.

The above discussion implies that a firm's long-term decisions on the use of debt financing reflects a trade-off between the corporate interest tax shield and incentive benefits of debt against the costs of financial distress. As the firm becomes more highly leveraged, the costs of leverage presumably begin to outweigh the tax and monitoring benefits of debt.

Table 10-1 shows median leverage ratios for all publicly-traded stocks in selected industries for the year ended December 31, 2005. Median debt-to-book equity ratios are highest for the water supply and electric services industries, which are typically not highly sensitive to economy risk and whose core assets are primarily physical equipment and property that are readily transferable to debt holders in the event

TABLE 10-1	Median Leverage in Selected Industries – Year-end 2005	

Industry	Net Interest-Bearing Debt-to-Book Equity	
	All Listed Firms	**NYSE Firms**
Prepackaged Computer Software	−54.5%	−41.6%
Pharmaceuticals	−60.9%	−11.8%
Petroleum Refining	−2.2%	−2.2%
Hotels & Motels	40.0%	45.9%
Water Supply	78.0%	78.0%
Electric Services	92.4%	95.1%

of financial distress. In contrast, the software and pharmaceutical industries' core assets are their research staffs. Ownership of these types of assets cannot be easily transferred to debt holders if the firm is in financial distress and researchers are sensitive to budget cuts. As a result, firms in these industries have relatively conservative capital structures. Petroleum refining and hotel firms have leverage in between these extremes, reflecting the need to balance the impact of having extensive physical assets and being subject to more volatile revenue streams.

It is also interesting to note that NYSE firms in general tend to have higher debt financing than non-NYSE firms in the same industries, with the difference most pronounced in pharmaceuticals. This probably reflects the fact that larger NYSE firms tend to have more product offerings and to be more diversified geographically, reducing their vulnerability to negative events for a single product or market, and enabling them to take on more debt.

THE MARKET FOR CREDIT

An understanding of credit analysis requires an appreciation for the various players in the market for credit. We briefly describe below the major suppliers of debt financing:

Commercial Banks

Commercial banks are important players in the market for credit. Since banks tend to provide a range of services to a client, and have intimate knowledge of the client and its operations, they have a comparative advantage in extending credit in settings where (1) knowledge gained through close contact with management reduces the perceived riskiness of the credit and (2) credit risk can be contained through careful monitoring of the firm.

Bank lending operations are constrained by a low tolerance for risk to ensure that the overall loan portfolio will be of acceptably high quality to bank regulators. Because of the importance of maintaining public confidence in the banking sector and the desire to shield government deposit insurance from risk, governments have incentives to constrain banks' exposure to credit risk. Banks also tend to shield themselves from the risk of shifts in interest rates by avoiding fixed-rate loans with long maturities. Since banks' capital comes mostly from short-term deposits, such long-term loans leave them exposed to increases in interest rates, unless the risk can be hedged with derivatives. Thus banks are less likely to play a role when a firm requires a very long-term commitment to financing. However, in some cases banks place the debt with investors looking for longer-term credit exposure.

Non-Bank Financial Institutions

Banks face competition in the commercial lending market from a variety of sources. In the U.S., there is competition from savings and loans institutions, though these firms tend to focus on financing mortgages. Finance companies compete with banks in the market for asset-based lending (i.e., the secured financing of specific assets such as receivables, inventory, or equipment). Insurance companies are also involved in a variety of lending activities. Since life insurance companies face obligations of a long-term nature, they often seek investments of long duration (e.g., long-term bonds or loans to support large, long-term commercial real estate and development projects). Investment bankers are prepared to place debt securities with private investors or in the public markets (discussed below). Various government agencies are also a source of credit.

Public Debt Markets

Some firms have the size, strength, and credibility necessary to bypass the banking sector and seek financing directly from investors, either through sales of commercial paper or through the issuance of bonds. Such debt issues are facilitated by the assignment of a debt rating, which measures the underlying credit strength of the firm and determines the yield that must be offered to investors.

Banks often provide financing in tandem with a public debt issue or other source of financing. In highly levered transactions, such as leveraged buyouts, banks commonly provide financing along with public debt that has a lower priority in case of bankruptcy. The bank's "senior financing" would typically be scheduled for earlier retirement than the public debt, and it would carry a lower yield. For smaller or start-up firms, banks often provide credit in conjunction with equity financing from venture capitalists. Note that in the case of both the leveraged buyout and the start-up company, the bank helps provide the cash needed to make the deal happen, but it does so in a way that shields it from risks that would be unacceptably high for the banking sector.

Sellers Who Provide Financing

Another sector of the market for credit is manufacturers and other suppliers of goods and services. As a matter of course, such firms tend to finance their customers' purchases on an unsecured basis for periods of 30 to 60 days. Suppliers will, on occasion, also agree to provide more extended financing, usually with the support of a secured note. A supplier may be willing to grant such a loan in the expectation that the creditor will survive a cash shortage and remain an important customer in the future. However, the customer would typically seek such an arrangement only if bank financing is unavailable because it could constrain flexibility in selecting among and/or negotiating with suppliers.

THE CREDIT ANALYSIS PROCESS IN PRIVATE DEBT MARKETS

Credit analysis is more than just establishing the creditworthiness of a firm, that is, its ability to pay its debts at the scheduled times. The decision to extend credit is not a binary one—the firm's exact value, its upside potential, and its distance from the threshold of creditworthiness are all equally important. There are ranges of credit-worthiness, and it is important for purposes of pricing and structuring a loan to understand where a firm lies within that range. While downside risk must be the primary consideration in credit analysis, a firm with growth potential offers opportunities for future income-generating financial services from a continued relationship.

This broader view of credit analysis involves most of the issues already discussed in the prior chapters on business strategy analysis, accounting analysis, financial analysis, and prospective analysis. Perhaps the greatest difference is that credit analysis rarely involves any explicit attempt to estimate the value of the firm's equity. However, the determinants of that value are relevant in credit analysis because a larger equity cushion translates into lower risk for the creditor.

Below we describe a representative but comprehensive series of steps that is used by commercial lenders in credit analysis. However, not all credit providers follow these guidelines. For example, when compared to a banker, manufacturers conduct a less extensive analysis on their customers since the credit is very short-term and the manufacturer is willing to bear some credit risk in the interest of generating a profit on the sale.

We present the steps in a particular order, but they are in fact all interdependent. Thus analysis at one step may need to be rethought depending on the analysis at some later step.

Step 1: Consider the Nature and Purpose of the Loan

Understanding the purpose of a loan is important not only for deciding whether it should be granted but also for structuring the loan based on duration, purpose, and size. Loans might be required for only a few months, for several years, or even as a permanent part of a firm's capital structure. Loans might be used for replacement of other financing, to support working capital needs, or to finance the acquisition of long-term assets or another firm.

The required amount of the loan must also be established. In the case of small and medium-sized companies, bankers typically prefer to be the sole financier of the business. This preference is not only to gain an advantage in providing a menu of financial services to the firm but also to maintain a superior interest in case of bankruptcy. If other creditors are willing to subordinate their positions to the bank, that would of course be acceptable as far as the bank is concerned.

Often the commercial lender deals with firms that may have parent-subsidiary relations, posing the question of the appropriate counterparty. In general, the entity that owns the assets that will serve as collateral (or that could serve as such if needed in the future) acts as the borrower. If this entity is the subsidiary and the parent presents some financial strength independent of the subsidiary, a guarantee of the parent could be considered.

Step 2: Consider the Type of Loan and Available Security

The type of loan is a function of not only its purpose but also the financial strength of the borrower. Thus, to some extent, the loan type will be dictated by the financial analysis described in Step 3. Some of the possible loan types are as follows:

- *Open line of credit.* An open line of credit permits the borrower to receive cash up to some specified maximum on an as-needed basis for a specified term, such as one year. To maintain this option, the borrower pays a fee (e.g., 3/8 of 1 percent) on the unused balance in addition to a market rate of interest on any used amount. An open line of credit is useful in cases where the borrower's cash needs are difficult to anticipate.

- *Revolving line of credit.* When it is clear that a firm will need credit beyond the short run, financing may be provided in the form of a "revolver." The terms of a revolver, which is sometimes used to support working capital needs, requires the borrower to make payments as the operating cycle proceeds and inventory and receivables are converted to cash. However, it is also expected that cash will continue to be advanced as long as the borrower remains in good standing. In addition to interest on amounts outstanding, a fee is charged on the unused line.
- *Working capital loan.* Such a loan is used to finance inventory and receivables, and it is usually secured. The maximum loan balance may be tied to the balance of the working capital accounts. For example, the loan may be allowed to rise to no more than 80 percent of receivables less than 60 days old.
- *Term loan.* Term loans are used for long-term needs and are often secured with long-term assets such as plant or equipment. Typically, the loan will be amortized, requiring periodic payments to reduce the loan balance.
- *Trade credit.* Trade credit generally takes two forms—an interim loan to an exporter to be repaid when the exports are paid for by the foreign importer, or credit extended by an exporter to an importer, allowing them to pay at some time after they take delivery.
- *Mortgage loan.* Mortgages support the financing of real estate, have long terms, and generally require periodic amortization of the loan balance.
- *Lease financing.* Lease financing can be used to facilitate the acquisition of any asset but is most commonly used for equipment, including vehicles, and buildings. Leases may be structured over periods of 1 to 15 years, depending on the life of the underlying asset.

Much bank lending is done on a secured basis, especially with smaller and more highly levered companies. Security will be required unless the loan is short-term and the borrower exposes the bank to only minimal default risk. When security is required, an important consideration is whether the amount of available security is sufficient to support the loan. The amount that a bank will lend based on given security involves business judgment and depends on a variety of factors that affect the liquidity of the security should the firm face financial distress. The following are some rules of thumb often applied in commercial lending to various categories of security:

- *Receivables.* Accounts receivable are usually considered the most desirable form of security because they are the most liquid. One large regional bank allows loans of 50 to 80 percent of the balance of nondelinquent accounts. The percentage applied is lower when (1) there are many small accounts that would be costly to collect in case the firm is distressed; (2) there are a few very large accounts, such that problems with a single customer could be serious; and/or (3) the customer's financial health is closely related to that of the borrower, so that collectibility is endangered just when the borrower is in default. On the latter score, banks often refuse to accept receivables from affiliates as effective security.
- *Inventory.* The desirability of inventory as security varies widely. The best-case scenario is inventory consisting of a common commodity that can easily be sold to other parties if the borrower defaults. More specialized inventory, with appeal to only a limited set of buyers or that is costly to store or transport, is less desirable. The large regional bank mentioned above lends up to 60 percent on raw materials, 50 percent on finished goods, and 20 percent on work in process.
- *Machinery and equipment.* Machinery and equipment is less desirable as collateral. It is likely to be used, and it must be stored, insured, and marketed. Keeping the costs of these activities in mind, banks typically will lend only up to 50 percent of the estimated value of such assets in a forced sale such as an auction.

- *Real estate.* The value of real estate as collateral varies considerably. Banks will often lend up to 80 percent of the appraised value of readily salable real estate. On the other hand, a factory designed for a unique purpose would be much less desirable.

Even when a loan is not secured initially, a bank can require a "negative pledge" on the firm's assets—a pledge that the firm will not use the assets as security for any other creditor. In that case, if the borrower begins to experience difficulty and defaults on the loan, and if there are no other creditors in the picture, the bank can demand the loan become secured if it is to remain outstanding.

Step 3: Conduct a Financial Analysis of the Potential Borrower

This portion of the analysis involves all the steps discussed in our chapters on business strategy analysis, accounting analysis, and financial analysis. The emphasis, however, is on the firm's ability to service the debt at the scheduled rate. All the factors that could impact that ability, such as the presence of off-balance-sheet lease obligations and the sustainability of the firm's operating profit stream, need to be carefully examined. The focus of the analysis depends on the type of financing under consideration. For example, if a short-term loan is needed to support seasonal fluctuations in inventory, the emphasis would be on the ability of the firm to convert the inventory into cash on a timely basis. In contrast, a term loan to support plant and equipment must be made with confidence in the long-run earnings prospects of the firm. This step incorporates both an assessment of the potential borrower's financial status using ratio analysis and a forecast to determine future payment prospects.

Ratio Analysis

Ultimately, since the key issue in the financial analysis is the likelihood that cash flows will be sufficient to repay the loan, lenders focus much attention on solvency ratios: the magnitude of various measures of profits and cash flows relative to debt service and other requirements. Therefore, ratio analysis from the perspective of a creditor differs somewhat from that of an owner. There is greater emphasis on cash flows and earnings available to *all* claimants (not just owners) *before* taxes (since interest is tax-deductible and paid out of pretax dollars). The *funds flow coverage ratio* illustrates the creditor's perspective:

$$\text{Funds flow coverage} = \frac{\text{EBIT} + \text{Depreciation}}{\text{Interest} + \dfrac{\text{Debt repayment}}{(1 - \text{tax rate})} + \dfrac{\text{Preferred dividends}}{(1 - \text{tax rate})}}$$

Earnings before both interest and taxes in the numerator is compared directly to the interest expense in the denominator, because interest expense is paid out of pre-tax dollars. In contrast, any payment of principal scheduled for a given year is non-deductible and must be made out of after-tax profits. In essence, with a 50 percent tax rate, one dollar of principal payment is "twice as expensive" as a one-dollar interest payment. Scaling the payment of principal by (1 − tax rate) accounts for this. The same idea applies to preferred dividends, which are not tax deductible.

The funds flow coverage ratio provides an indication of how comfortably the funds flow can cover unavoidable expenditures. The ratio excludes payments such as common dividends and capital expenditures on the premise that they could be reduced to zero to make debt payments if necessary.[1] Clearly, however, if the firm is to survive in the long run, funds flow must be sufficient to not only service debt but also maintain plant assets. Thus long-run survival requires a funds flow coverage ratio well in excess of 1.[2]

To the extent the ratio exceeds 1, it indicates the "margin of safety" the lender faces. When such a ratio is combined with an assessment of the variance in its numerator, it provides an indication of the probability of nonpayment. However, it would be overly simplistic to establish any particular threshold above which a ratio indicates a loan is justified. A creditor clearly wants to be in a position to be repaid on schedule, even when the borrower faces a reasonably foreseeable difficulty. That argues for lending only when the funds flow coverage is expected to exceed 1, even in a recession scenario—and higher if some allowance for capital expenditures is prudent.

The financial analysis should produce more than an assessment of the risk of nonpayment. It should also identify the nature of the significant risks. At many commercial banks it is standard operating procedure to summarize the analysis of the firm by listing the key risks that could lead to default and factors that could be used to control those risks if the loan were made. That information can be used in structuring the detailed terms of the loan so as to trigger default when problems arise, at a stage early enough to permit corrective action.

Forecasting

Implicit in the discussion of the ratio analysis is a forward-looking view of the firm's ability to service the loan. Good credit analysis should also be supported by explicit forecasts. The basis for such forecasts is usually management, though lenders perform their own tests as well. An essential element of this step is a sensitivity analysis to examine the ability of the borrower to service the debt under a variety of scenarios such as changes in the economy or in the firm's competitive position. Ideally, the firm should be strong enough to withstand downside risks such as a drop in sales or a decrease in profit margins.

At times it is possible to reconsider the structure of a loan so as to permit it to "cash flow." That is, the term of the loan might be extended or the amortization pattern changed. Often a bank will grant a loan with the expectation that it will be continually renewed, thus becoming a permanent part of the firm's financial structure (labeled an "evergreen" loan). In that case the loan will still be written as if it is due within the short term, and the bank must assure itself of a viable "exit strategy." However, the firm would be expected to service the loan by simply covering interest payments.

Step 4: Assemble the Detailed Loan Structure, Including Loan Covenants

If the analysis thus far indicates that a loan is in order, the final step is to assemble the detailed structure. Having previously determined the type of loan and repayment schedule, the focus shifts to the loan covenants and pricing.

Writing Loan Covenants

Loan covenants specify mutual expectations of the borrower and lender by specifying actions the borrower will and will not take. Covenants generally fall into three categories: (1) those that require certain actions such as regular provision of financial statements; (2) those that preclude certain actions such as undertaking an acquisition without the permission of the lender; and (3) those that require maintenance of certain financial ratios. Loan covenants must strike a balance between protecting the interests of the lender and providing the flexibility management needs to run the business. The covenants represent a mechanism for ensuring that the business will remain as strong as the two parties anticipated at the time the loan was granted.

The principal covenants that govern the management of the firm include restrictions on other borrowing, pledging assets to other lenders, selling substantial assets, engaging in mergers or acquisitions, and paying of dividends. The financial covenants should seek to address the significant risks identified in the financial analysis, or to at least provide early warning that such risks are surfacing. Some commonly used financial covenants follow:

- *Maintenance of minimum net worth.* This covenant assures that the firm will maintain an "equity cushion" to protect the lender. Covenants typically require a level of net worth rather than a particular level of income. In the final analysis, the lender may not care whether that net worth is maintained by generating income, cutting dividends, or issuing new equity. Tying the covenant to net worth offers the firm the flexibility to use any of these avenues to avoid default.
- *Minimum coverage ratio.* Especially in the case of a long-term loan, such as a term loan, the lender may want to supplement a net worth covenant with one based on coverage of interest or total debt service. The funds flow coverage ratio presented above would be an example. Maintenance of some minimum coverage helps ensure that the ability of the firm to generate funds internally is strong enough to justify the long-term nature of the loan.
- *Maximum ratio of total liabilities to net worth.* This ratio constrains the risk of high leverage and prevents growth without either retaining earnings or infusing equity.
- *Minimum net working capital balance or current ratio.* Constraints on this ratio force a firm to maintain its liquidity by using cash generated from operations to retire current liabilities (as opposed to acquiring long-lived assets).
- *Maximum ratio of capital expenditures to earnings before depreciation.* Constraints on this ratio help prevent the firm from investing in growth (including the illiquid assets necessary to support growth) unless such growth can be financed internally, with some margin remaining for debt service.

Required financial ratios are typically based on the levels that existed at the time that the agreement was executed, perhaps with some allowance for deterioration but often with some expected improvement over time. Violation of a covenant represents an event of default that could cause immediate acceleration of the debt payment, but in most cases the lender uses the default as an opportunity to re-examine the situation and either waive the violation or renegotiate the loan.

Covenants are included not only in private lending agreements but also in public debt agreements. However, public debt agreements tend to have less restrictive covenants for two reasons. First, since negotiations resulting from a violation of public debt covenants are costly (possibly involving not just the trustee, but bondholders as well), the covenants are written to be triggered only in serious circumstances. Second, public debt is usually issued by stronger, more credit-worthy firms, though there is a large market for high-yield debt. For the most financially healthy firms with strong debt ratings, very few covenants will be used, generally only those necessary to limit dramatic changes in the firm's operations, such as a major merger or acquisition.

Loan Pricing

A detailed discussion of loan pricing falls outside the scope of this text. The essence of pricing is to assure that the yield on the loan is sufficient to cover (1) the lender's cost of borrowed funds; (2) the lender's costs of administering and servicing the loan; (3) a premium for exposure to default risk; and (4) at least a normal return on the equity capital necessary to support the lending operation. The price is often stated in terms of a deviation from the bank's prime rate (the rate charged to stronger borrowers). For example, a loan might be granted at prime plus $1\frac{1}{2}$ percent. An alternative base is LIBOR, or the London Interbank Offer Rate, the rate at which large banks from various nations lend blocks of funds to each other.

Banks compete actively for commercial lending business, and it is rare that a yield includes more than 2 percentage points to cover the cost of default risk. If the spread to cover default risk is, say, 1 percent, and the bank recovers only 50 percent of amounts due on loans that turn out bad, then the bank can afford only 2 percent of their loans to fall into that category. This underscores how important it is for banks to conduct a thorough analysis and to contain the riskiness of their loan portfolio.

FINANCIAL STATEMENT ANALYSIS AND PUBLIC DEBT

Fundamentally, the issues involved in analysis of public debt are no different from those of bank loans and other private debt issues. Institutionally, however, the contexts are different. Bankers can maintain very close relations with clients so as to form an initial assessment of their credit risk and monitor their activities during the loan period. In the case of public debt, the investors are distanced from the issuer. To a large extent, they must depend on professional debt analysts, including debt raters, to assess the riskiness of the debt and monitor the firm's ongoing activities. Such analysts and debt raters thus serve an important function in closing the information gap between issuers and investors.

The Meaning of Debt Ratings

A firm's debt rating influences the yield that must be offered to sell the debt instruments. After the debt issue, the rating agencies continue to monitor the firm's financial condition. Changes in the rating are associated with fluctuation in the price of the securities. The two major debt rating agencies in the U.S. are Moody's and Standard and Poor's. Other rating agencies include Fitch Ratings, A.M. Best, and Dun & Bradstreet.

Using the Standard and Poor's labeling system, the highest possible rating is AAA. Proceeding downward from AAA, the ratings are AA, A, BBB, BB, B, CCC, CC, C, and D, where D indicates debt in default. Table 10-2 presents examples of firms in rating categories AAA through D, as well as average yields across all firms in each category. Less than 1 percent of the public nonfinancial companies rated by Standard & Poor's have the financial strength to merit a AAA rating. Among the few are General Electric, Johnson & Johnson, and Toyota—all among the largest, most profitable firms in the world. AA firms are also very strong and include Microsoft and Wal-Mart. Firms rated AAA and AA have the lowest costs of debt financing; at year-end 2005, their average yields were less than a quarter of a percent over the 12-month LIBOR rate.

To be considered investment grade, a firm must achieve a rating of BBB or higher, which is an important threshold as many funds are precluded by their charters from investing in any bonds below that grade. Even to achieve a grade of BBB is difficult. Daimler Chrysler, the automobile manufacturer and owner of Mercedes Benz, one of the world's most recognizable brands, was rated BBB, or barely investment grade in May 2006. Its large U.S. rivals, Ford and General Motors, were rated BB and B, respectively, at the same time. Some of the world's largest airlines, including British Airways and American Airlines, are also rated below investment grade.

Table 10-2 shows that the cost of debt financing rises markedly once firms' debt falls below investment grade. For example, at year-end 2005, yields for BBB rated debt issues were less than 1 percent over the 12 month LIBOR rate whereas yields for B rated issues were more than 3 percent above LIBOR rates. Yields for firms with CCC rated debt, which were close to bankruptcy, were more than 7 percent over LIBOR, and the debt securities of a few firms in default that were still traded yielded between 30 percent and 40 percent over the benchmark.

Table 10-3 shows median financial ratios for firms by debt rating category. Firms with AAA and AA ratings have very strong earnings and cash flow performance as

TABLE 10-2	Debt Ratings: Example Firms and Average Yields by Category		
S&P debt rating	**Example firms in 2006**	**Percentage of public industrials given same rating by S&P**	**Average yield, year-end 2005**	**Average spread over 12 month LIBOR rate**
AAA	General Electric Johnson & Johnson Toyota Motor Corporation	0.7%	4.92%	0.08%
AA	Home Depot Inc. GlaxoSmithKline Wal-Mart Stores, Inc.	2.4%	5.06%	0.22%
A	Coca-Cola Enterprises McDonald's Corp. Target Corporation	15.4%	5.21%	0.37%
BBB	Daimler Chrysler AG Best Buy Co. Duke Energy Corp.	25.4%	5.75%	0.91%
BB	Ford Motor Company Amazon.com British Airways	27.3%	7.60%	2.76%
B	General Motors Lucent Technologies American Airlines (AMR)	24.6%	7.88%	3.04%
CCC	XM Satellite Radio Silicon Graphics	3.3%	12.00%	7.16%
CC	Fedders Corporation	0.2%	16.81%[a]	11.97%
D	Northwest Airlines Calpine Corporation	0.8%	39.91%[a]	35.07%

a. Representative yields as most securities not actively traded.

Source: Standard and Poor's Compustat 2006.

well as minimal leverage. AAA rated firms often have large surpluses of cash such that net debt is negative. Firms in the BBB class are only moderately leveraged, with about 32 percent of net capitalization coming from net debt. Earnings tend to be relatively strong, as indicated by a pretax interest coverage (EBIT/interest) of 5.5 and a cash flow debt coverage (cash flow from operations/total debt) of nearly 38 percent. Firms at the bottom of the ratings spectrum, however, face significant risks: They typically report losses, have high leverage, and have interest coverage ratios less than 1.

| TABLE 10-3 | Debt Ratings: Median Financial Ratios by Category |

Median ratios for overall category in January 2006
(excludes financial firms)

S&P debt rating	Earnings before interest and taxes to net capital	Pretax interest coverage	Cash flow from operations to total debt	Net debt to net capital
AAA	25.3%	31.4	118%	−3%
AA	32.2	16.7	85	14
A	20.2	9.2	52	27
BBB	16.5	5.5	38	32
BB	15.1	3.9	26	40
B	10.6	1.4	12	65
CCC	2.9	0.2	1	116
CC	−6.9	−1.2	−5	100
D	−18.1	−0.4	15	93

Source: Standard and Poor's Compustat 2006.

Factors That Drive Debt Ratings

Research using quantitative models of debt ratings demonstrates that some of the variation in ratings can be explained by selected financial statement ratios. Some debt rating agencies rely heavily on these types of quantitative models and they are also commonly used by insurance companies, banks, and others to assist in the evaluation of the riskiness of debt issues for which a public rating is not available.

Table 10-4 lists the factors used by three different firms in their quantitative debt-rating models. The firms include one insurance company and one bank, which use the models in their private placement activities, and an investment research firm, which employs the model in evaluating its own debt purchases and holdings. In each case, profitability and leverage play an important role in the rating. One firm also uses size as an indicator, with larger size associated with higher ratings.

Several researchers have developed quantitative models of debt ratings. Two of these models, both by Kaplan and Urwitz and shown in Table 10-5, highlight the relative importance of the different factors.[3] Model 1 has a greater ability to explain variation in bond ratings. However, it includes some factors based on stock

TABLE 10-4	Factors Used in Quantitative Models of Debt Ratings		
	Firm 1	**Firm 2**	**Firm 3**
Profitability measures	Return on long-term capital	Return on long-term capital	Return on long-term capital
Leverage measures	Long-term debt to capitalization	Long-term debt to capitalization Total debt to total capital	Long-term debt to capitalization
Profitability and leverage	Interest coverage Cash flow to long-term debt	Interest coverage Cash flow to long-term debt	Fixed charge coverage Coverage of short-term debt and fixed charges
Firm size	Sales	Total assets	
Other		Standard deviation of return Subordination status	

market data, which are not available for all firms. Model 2 is based solely on financial statement data.

The factors in Table 10-5 are listed in the order of their statistical significance in Model 1. An interesting feature is that the most important factor explaining debt ratings is not a financial ratio at all—it is simply firm size! Large firms tend to get better ratings than small firms. Whether the debt is subordinated or unsubordinated is next most important, followed by a leverage indicator. Profitability appears less important, but in part that reflects the presence in the model of multiple factors (ROA and interest coverage) that capture profitability. The explanatory power of profitability is then divided between these two variables.

When applied to a sample of bonds that were not used in the estimation process, the Kaplan-Urwitz Model 1 predicted the rating category correctly in 44 of 64 cases, or 63 percent of the time. Where it erred, the model was never off by more than one category, and in about half of those cases its prediction was more consistent with the market yield on the debt than was the actual debt rating. The discrepancies between actual ratings and those estimated using the Kaplan-Urwitz model indicate that rating agencies incorporate factors other than financial ratios in their analysis. These are likely to include the types of strategic, accounting, and prospective analyses discussed throughout this book.

Although debt ratings can be explained reasonably well in terms of a handful of financial ratios based on publicly available data, ratings changes have an important signaling effect. Debt rating downgrades are greeted with drops in both bond and stock prices,[4] even though the capital markets anticipate much of the information reflected in rating changes. This is due to the fact that changes often represent reactions to recent known events and the rating agencies typically indicate in advance that a change is being considered.

		Coefficients	
Firm or debt characteristic	**Variable reflecting characteristic**	**Model 1**	**Model 2**
	Model intercept	5.67	4.41
Firm size	Total assets[a]	.0010	.0013
Subordination status of debt	1 = subordinated; 0 = unsubordinated	−2.36	−2.56
Leverage	Long-term debt to total assets	−2.85	−2.72
Systematic risk	Market model beta, indicating sensitivity of stock price to market-wide movements (1 = average)[b]	−.87	—
Profitability	Net income to total assets	5.13	6.40
Unsystematic risk	Standard deviation of residual from market model (average = .10)[b]	−2.90	—
Riskiness of profit stream	Coefficient of variation in net income over five years (standard deviation/mean)	—	−.53
Interest coverage	Pretax funds flow before interest to interest expense	.007	.006

TABLE 10-5   Kaplan-Urwitz Models of Debt Ratings

The score from the model is converted to a bond rating as follows:
If score > 6.76, predict AAA
   score > 5.19, predict AA
   score > 3.28, predict A
   score > 1.57, predict BBB
   score < 0.00, predict BB

a. *The coefficient in the Kaplan-Urwitz model was estimated at .005 (Model 1) and .006 (Model 2). Its scale has been adjusted to reflect that the estimates were based on assets measured in dollars from the early 1970s. Given that $1 from 1972 is approximately equivalent to $4.79 in 2006, the original coefficient estimate has been divided by 4.79.*

b. *Market model is estimated by regressing stock returns on the market index, using monthly data for the prior 5 years.*

PREDICTION OF DISTRESS AND TURNAROUND

The key task in credit analysis is assessing the probability that a firm will face financial distress and fail to repay a loan. A related analysis, relevant once a firm begins to face distress, involves considering whether it can be turned around. In this section, we consider evidence on the predictability of these states.

   The prediction of either distress or turnaround is a complex, difficult, and subjective task that involves all of the steps of analysis discussed throughout this book: business strategy analysis, accounting analysis, financial analysis, and prospective analysis. Purely quantitative models of the process can rarely serve as substitutes for the hard work the analysis involves. However, research on such models does offer some insight into which financial indicators are most useful in the task. Moreover, there are some settings where extensive credit checks are too costly to justify, and where quantitative distress prediction models are useful.

Models for Distress Prediction

Several distress prediction models have been developed over the years.[5] They are similar to the debt rating models, but instead of predicting ratings, they predict whether a firm will face some state of distress, typically defined as bankruptcy, within a specified period such as one year. One study suggests that the factors most useful (on a stand-alone basis) in predicting bankruptcy one year in advance are the firm's level of profitability, the volatility of that profitability (as measured by the standard deviation of ROE), and its leverage.[6] Interestingly, liquidity measures turn out to be much less important. Current liquidity won't save an unhealthy firm if it is losing money at a fast pace.

A number of more robust, multifactor models have also been designed to predict financial distress. One such model, the Altman Z-score model, weights five variables to compute a bankruptcy score.[7] For public companies the model is as follows[8]:

$$Z = 1.2(X_1) + 1.4(X_2) + 3.3(X_3) + 0.6(X_4) + 1.0(X_5)$$

where

X_1 = net working capital/total assets (measure of liquidity)
X_2 = retained earnings/total assets (measure of cumulative profitability)
X_3 = EBIT/total assets (measure of return on assets)
X_4 = market value of equity/book value of total liabilities (measure of market leverage)
X_5 = sales/total assets (measure of sales generating potential of assets)

The model predicts bankruptcy when $Z < 1.81$. The range between 1.81 and 2.67 is labeled the "gray area."

The following table presents calculations for two companies, Wal-Mart and General Motors (GM), at the end of their respective 2005 fiscal years:

	Model Coefficient	Wal-Mart January 2006		General Motors December 2005	
		Ratios	Score	Ratios	Score
Net working capital/Total assets	1.2	−0.036	−0.04	−0.042	−0.05
Retained earnings/Total assets	1.4	0.363	0.51	−0.002	0.00
EBIT/Total assets	3.3	0.111	0.37	−0.023	−0.08
Market value of equity/Book value of total liabilities	0.6	2.299	1.38	0.027	0.02
Sales/Total assets	1.0	2.260	2.26	0.430	0.43
			4.47		0.32

The table shows the wide performance gap between two of America's most well known firms. Wal-Mart's Z score demonstrates its financial strength and reflects its AA rating.

Wal-Mart has delivered steady sales and earnings growth over the past ten years, and its liabilities are only 43 percent of its market capitalization, indicating relatively low financial leverage. GM's Z score, on the other hand, highlights its poor performance and is emblematic of the fragile state of the U.S. auto industry. GM's net income has declined steadily since 2003, with the losses in 2005 wiping out the firm's retained earnings. Even before servicing its debt, GM posted a loss in 2005. Finally, GM's liabilities are 37 times larger than its market capitalization, an indication of its precarious financial state. As a result, GM's debt was downgraded to B at the end of 2005.

Such models have some ability to predict failing and surviving firms. Altman reports that when the model was applied to a holdout sample containing 33 failed and 33 non-failed firms (the same proportion used to estimate the model), it correctly predicted the outcome in 63 of 66 cases. However, the performance of the model would degrade substantially if applied to a holdout sample where the proportion of failed and non-failed firms was not forced to be the same as that used to estimate the model.

The commercially available ZETA model, also developed by Altman, improves on the predictive power and accuracy of the Z-score model. The ZETA model incorporates seven variables and includes measures of the stability of earnings, debt service coverage, and firm size.[9] While distress prediction models cannot serve as a replacement for in-depth analysis of the kind discussed throughout this book, they do provide a useful reminder of the power of financial statement data to summarize important dimensions of a firm's performance. In addition, they can be useful for screening large numbers of firms prior to more in-depth analysis of corporate strategy, management expertise, market position, and financial ratio performance. The ZETA model, for instance, is used by some manufacturers and other firms to assess the creditworthiness of their customers.

Investment Opportunities in Distressed Companies

The debt securities of firms in financial distress trade at steep discounts to par value. Some hedge fund managers and investment advisors specialize in investing in these securities—even purchasing the debt of firms operating under bankruptcy protection. Investors in these securities can earn attractive returns if the firm recovers from its cash flow difficulties.[10]

Distressed debt investors assess whether the firm is likely to overcome its immediate cash flow problems and whether it has a viable long-run future. Two elements of the framework laid out in Part 2 of this book are particularly relevant to analyzing distressed opportunities. The first is a thorough analysis of the firm's industry and competitive positioning and an assessment of its business risks. This is followed by the construction of well reasoned forecasts of its future cash flow and earnings performance in light of the business analysis.

SUMMARY

Debt financing is attractive to firms with high marginal tax rates and few non-interest tax shields, making interest tax shields from debt valuable. Debt can can also help create value by deterring management of firms with high, stable income/cash flows and few new investment opportunities from over-investing in unprofitable new ventures.

However, debt financing also creates the risk of financial distress, which is likely to be particularly severe for firms with volatile earnings and cash flows, and intangible assets that are easily destroyed by financial distress.

Prospective providers of debt use credit analysis to evaluate the risks of financial distress for a firm. Credit analysis is important to a wide variety of economic agents—not only bankers and other financial intermediaries but also public debt analysts, industrial companies, service companies, and others.

At the heart of credit analysis lie the same techniques described in Chapters 2 through 8: business strategy analysis, accounting analysis, financial analysis, and portions of prospective analysis. The purpose of credit analysis in private debt markets goes beyond the assessment of the likelihood that a potential borrower will fail to repay the loan. It also serves to identify the nature of the main risks involved, and to guide how the loan might be structured to mitigate or control those risks. A well structured loan provides the lender with a viable "exit strategy," even in the case of default. Properly designed accounting-based covenants are essential to this structure.

Fundamentally, the issues involved in analysis of public debt are no different from those involved in evaluating bank loans or other private debt. Institutionally, however, the contexts are different. Investors in public debt are usually not close to the borrower and must rely on other agents, including debt raters and other analysts, to assess creditworthiness. Debt ratings, which depend heavily on firm size and financial measures of performance, have an important influence on the market yields that must be offered to issue debt.

The primary task in credit analysis is assessment of the probability of default. The task is complex, difficult, and to some extent, subjective. A few financial ratios can help predict financial distress with some accuracy. The most important indicators for this purpose are profitability, volatility of profits, and leverage. While there are a number of models that predict distress based on financial indicators, they cannot replace the in-depth forms of analysis discussed in this book.

DISCUSSION QUESTIONS

1. Financial analysts typically measure financial leverage as the ratio of debt to equity. However, there is less agreement on how to measure debt, or even equity. How would you treat the following items in computing this ratio? Justify your answers.
   - Revolving credit agreement with bank
   - Cash and marketable securities
   - Operating leases
   - Unrecorded pension commitments
   - Deferred tax liabilities
   - Preferred stock
   - Convertible debt

2. U.S. public companies with "low" leverage have an interest-bearing net debt-to-equity ratio of 0 percent or less, firms with "medium" leverage have a ratio between 1 and 62 percent, and "high" leverage firms have a ratio of 63 percent or more. Given these data, how would you classify the following firms in terms of their optimal debt-to-equity ratio (high, medium, or low)?
   - a successful pharmaceutical company
   - an electric utility
   - a manufacturer of consumer durables
   - a commercial bank
   - a start-up software company

3. What are the critical performance dimensions for (a) a retailer and (b) a financial services company that should be considered in credit analysis? What ratios would you suggest looking at for each of these dimensions?

4. Why would a company pay to have its public debt rated by a major rating agency (such as Moody's or Standard and Poor's)? Why might a firm decide not to have its debt rated?

5. Some have argued that the market for original-issue junk bonds developed in the late 1970s as a result of a failure in the rating process. Proponents of this argument suggest that rating agencies rated companies too harshly at the low end of the rating scale, denying investment grade status to some deserving companies. What are proponents of this argument effectively assuming were the incentives of rating agencies? What economic forces could give rise to this incentive?

6. Many debt agreements require borrowers to obtain the permission of the lender before undertaking a major acquisition or asset sale. Why would the lender want to include this type of restriction?

7. Betty Li, the CFO of a company applying for a new loan, states, "I will never agree to a debt covenant that restricts my ability to pay dividends to my shareholders because it reduces shareholder wealth." Do you agree with this argument?

8. Cambridge Construction Company follows the percentage-of-completion method for reporting long-term contract revenues. The percentage-of-completion is based on the cost of materials shipped to the project site as a percentage of total expected material costs. Cambridge's major debt agreement includes restrictions on net worth, interest coverage, and minimum working capital requirements. A leading analyst claims that "the company is buying its way out of these covenants by spending cash and buying materials, even when they are not needed." Explain how this might be possible.

9. Can Cambridge improve its Z score by behaving as the analyst claims in Question 8? Is this change consistent with economic reality?

10. A banker asserts, "I avoid lending to companies with negative cash from operations because they are too risky." Is this a sensible lending policy?

11. A leading retailer finds itself in a financial bind. It doesn't have sufficient cash flow from operations to finance its growth, and it is close to violating the maximum debt-to-assets ratio allowed by its covenants. The Vice-President for Marketing suggests, "We can raise cash for our growth by selling the existing stores and leasing them back. This source of financing is cheap since it avoids violating either the debt-to-assets or interest-coverage ratios in our covenants." Do you agree with his analysis? Why or why not? As the firm's banker, how would you view this arrangement?

NOTES

1. The same is true of preferred dividends. However, when preferred stock is cumulative, any dividends missed must be paid later, when and if the firm returns to profitability.

2. Other relevant coverage ratios are discussed in Chapter 5.

3. R. Kaplan and G. Urwitz, "Statistical Models of Bond Ratings: A Methodological Inquiry," *Journal of Business* (April 1979): 231–61.

4. See R. Holthausen and R. Leftwich, "The Effect of Bond Rating Changes on Common Stock Prices," *Journal of Financial Economics* (September 1986): 57–90, and J. Hand, R. Holthausen, and R. Leftwich, "The Effect of Bond Rating Announcements on Bond and Stock Prices," *Journal of Finance* (June 1992): 733–52.

5. See E. Altman, "Financial Ratios, Discriminant Analysis, and the Prediction of Corporate Bankruptcy," *Journal of Finance* (September 1968): 589–609; E. Altman, *Corporate Financial Distress* (New York: John Wiley, 1993); W. Beaver, "Financial Ratios as Predictors of Distress," *Journal of Accounting Research*, Supplement (1966): 71–111; J. Ohlson, "Financial Ratios and the Probabilistic Prediction of Bankruptcy," *Journal of Accounting Research* (Spring 1980): 109–131; and M. Zmijewski, "Predicting Corporate Bankruptcy: An Empirical Comparison of the Extant Financial Distress Models" (working paper, SUNY at Buffalo, 1983).

6. Zmijewski, op. cit.

7. Altman, *Corporate Financial Distress*, op. cit.

8. For private firms, Altman, ibid., adjusts the public model by changing the numerator for the variable X_4 from the market value of equity to the book value. The revised model follows:

$$Z = .717(X_1) + .847(X_2) + 3.11(X_3) + 0.420(X_4) + .998(X_5)$$

where
    X_1 = net working capital/total assets
    X_2 = retained earnings/total assets
    X_3 = EBIT/total assets
    X_4 = book value of equity/book value of total liabilities
    X_5 = sales/total assets

The model predicts bankruptcy when $Z < 1.23$. The range between 1.23 and 2.90 is labeled the "gray area."

9. See Altman, *Corporate Financial Distress*, op. cit.

10. In the period from January 1994 through April 30, 2006, distressed investing outperformed 10 out of 11 other strategies that were tracked by the Credit Suisse/Tremont Hedge Fund Index. The average annual return over that period was 13.60 percent versus a return of 11.3185 percent for the S&P 500 index (assuming dividends were reinvested in the index).

Chapter 11

Mergers and Acquisitions

M ergers and acquisitions have long been a popular form of corporate investment, particularly in countries with Anglo-American forms of capital markets. There is no question that these transactions provide a healthy return to target stockholders. However, their value to acquiring shareholders is less understood. Many skeptics point out that given the hefty premiums paid to target stockholders, acquisitions tend to be negative-valued investments for acquiring stockholders.[1]

A number of questions can be examined using financial analysis for mergers and acquisitions:

- Securities analysts can ask: Does a proposed acquisition create value for the acquiring firm's stockholders?
- Risk arbitrageurs can ask: What is the likelihood that a hostile takeover offer will ultimately succeed, and are there other potential acquirers likely to enter the bidding?
- Acquiring management can ask: Does this target fit our business strategy? If so, what is it worth to us and how can we make an offer that can be successful?
- Target management can ask: Is the acquirer's offer a reasonable one for our stockholders? Are there other potential acquirers that would value our company more than the current bidder?
- Investment bankers can ask: How can we identify potential targets that are likely to be a good match for our clients? And how should we value target firms when we are asked to issue fairness opinions?

In this chapter we focus primarily on the use of financial statement data and analysis directed at evaluating whether a merger creates value for the acquiring firm's stockholders. However, our discussion can also be applied to these other merger analysis contexts. The topic of whether acquisitions create value for acquirers focuses on evaluating the (1) motivations for acquisitions, (2) pricing of offers, (3) forms of payment, and (4) likelihood that an offer will be successful. Throughout the chapter we use Exxon's merger with Mobil in 1999 to illustrate how financial analysis can be used in a merger context.[2]

MOTIVATION FOR MERGER OR ACQUISITION

There are a variety of reasons that firms merge or acquire other firms. Some acquiring managers may want to increase their own power and prestige. Others, however, realize that business combinations provide an opportunity to create new economic value for their stockholders. New value can be created in the following ways:

1. *Taking advantage of economies of scale.* Mergers are often justified as a means of providing the two participating firms with increased economies of scale. Economies of scale arise when one large firm can perform a function more

efficiently than two smaller firms. For example, Exxon and Mobil are both major oil firms with considerable overlap in production and administrative facilities. The merger was expected to provide operating synergies from eliminating duplicate facilities and excess capacity, and from reducing general and administrative costs.

2. *Improving target management.* Another common motivation for acquisition is to improve target management. A firm is likely to be a target if it has systematically underperformed its industry. Historical poor performance could be due to bad luck, but it could also be due to the firm's managers making poor investment and operating decisions, or deliberately pursuing goals which increase their personal power but cost stockholders.

3. *Combining complementary resources.* Firms may decide that a merger will create value by combining complementary resources of the two partners. For example, a firm with a strong research and development unit could benefit from merging with a firm that has a strong distribution unit.

4. *Capturing tax benefits.* In the U.S. the 1986 Tax Reform Act eliminated many of the tax benefits from mergers and acquisitions. However, several merger tax benefits remain. The major benefit is the acquisition of operating tax losses. If a firm does not expect to earn sufficient profits to fully utilize operating tax loss carryforward benefits, it may decide to buy another firm which is earning profits. The operating losses and loss carryforwards of the acquirer can then be offset against the target's taxable income.[3] A second tax benefit often attributed to mergers is the tax shield that comes from increasing leverage for the target firm. This was particularly relevant for leveraged buyouts in the 1980s.[4]

5. *Providing low-cost financing to a financially constrained target.* If capital markets are imperfect, perhaps because of information asymmetries between management and outside investors, firms can face capital constraints. Information problems are likely to be especially severe for newly formed, high-growth firms. These firms can be difficult for outside investors to value since they have short track records and their financial statements provide little insight into the value of their growth opportunities. Further, since they typically have to rely on external funds to finance their growth, capital market constraints for high-growth firms are likely to affect their ability to undertake profitable new projects. Public capital markets are therefore likely to be costly sources of funds for these types of firms. An acquirer that understands the business and is willing to provide a steady source of finance may therefore be able to add value.[5]

6. *Creating value through restructuring and break-ups.* Acquisitions are often pursued by financial investors such as leveraged buy-out firms that expect to create value by breaking up the firm. The break-up value is expected to be larger than the aggregate worth of the entire firm. Often, a consortium of financial investors will acquire a firm with a view of unlocking value from various components of the firm's asset base. For example, two private equity firms, Kohlberg, Kravis and Roberts and Bain Capital, partnered with real estate company Vornado Realty Trust, to purchase the retailer Toys "R" Us. The consortium was widely expected to close down numerous retail locations to monetize the value of the real estate.

7. *Penetrating new geographies.* Cross-border acquisitions are pursued by firms to expand product markets, to capitalize on new technologies, and to capture labor cost advantages which presumably could not have been achieved through joint ventures or supplier contracts. In the 25-year period between 1981 and 2005, over 10 percent of all acquisitions in the U.S. were led by foreign buyers, with close to 1,500 such deals announced in 2005 alone.[6]

8. *Increasing product-market rents.* Firms can also have incentives to merge to increase product-market rents. By merging and becoming a dominant firm in the industry, two smaller firms can collude to restrict their output and raise prices, thereby increasing their profits. This circumvents problems that arise in

cartels of independent firms, where firms have incentives to cheat on the cartel and increase their output.

While product-market rents make sense for firms as a motive for merging, the two partners are unlikely to announce their intentions when they explain the merger to their investors, since most countries have antitrust laws which regulate mergers between two firms in the same industry. For example, in the U.S. there are three major antitrust statutes—The Sherman Act of 1890, The Clayton Act of 1914, and The Hart Scott Rodino Act of 1976.

Anti-competitive concerns were significant for the Exxon-Mobil merger since Exxon and Mobil were the largest and second largest U.S. oil producers, respectively. Merger approval was required by both the U.S. Federal Trade Commission (FTC) and the European Commission. Both did eventually approve the merger but required the new firm to sell assets in certain businesses and regions to preserve competition.

While many of the motivations for acquisitions are likely to create new economic value for shareholders, some are not. Firms that are flush with cash but have few new profitable investment opportunities are particularly prone to using their surplus cash to make acquisitions. Stockholders of these firms would probably prefer that managers pay out any surplus cash flows as dividends, or use the funds to repurchase the firm's stock. However, these options reduce the size of the firm and the assets under management's control. Management may therefore prefer to invest the free cash flows to buy new companies, even if they do not create value for stockholders. Of course, managers will never announce that they are buying a firm because they are reluctant to pay out funds to stockholders. They may explain the merger using one of the motivations discussed above, or they may argue that they are buying the target at a bargain price.

Another motivation for mergers that is valued by managers but not stockholders is diversification. Diversification was a popular motivation for acquisitions in the 1960s and early 1970s. Acquirers sought to dampen their earnings volatility by buying firms in unrelated businesses. Diversification as a motive for acquisitions has since been widely discredited. Modern finance theorists point out that in a well functioning capital market, investors can diversify for themselves and do not need managers to do so for them. In addition, diversification has been criticized when leading firms lose sight of their major competitive strengths and expand into businesses where they do not have expertise.[7] These firms eventually recognize that diversification-motivated acquisitions do not create value, leading to divestitures of business units. Divestitures have been the source of over a third of all acquisitions over the past 25 years, and in 2005 alone, close to 3,600 deals were a result of corporate divestitures.[8]

Key Analysis Questions

In evaluating a proposed merger, analysts are interested in determining whether the merger creates new wealth for acquiring and target stockholders, or whether it is motivated by managers' desires to increase their own power and prestige. Key questions for financial analysis are likely to include:

- *What is the motivation(s) for an acquisition and the anticipated benefits disclosed by acquirers or targets?*
- *What are the industries of the target and acquirer?* Are the firms related horizontally or vertically? How close are the business relations between

them? If the businesses are unrelated, is the acquirer cash-rich and reluctant to return free cash flows to stockholders?

- *What are the key operational strengths of the target and the acquirer?* Are these strengths complementary? For example, does one firm have a renowned research group and the other a strong distribution network?
- *Is the acquisition a friendly one, supported by target management, or hostile?* In the case of a hostile takeover, which is more likely to occur for targets with poor-performing management, will the transaction go through despite the opposition of management who will want to preserve its jobs? Will the hostile acquirer have sufficient access to information to mitigate the risk of overpayment?
- *What is the premerger performance of the two firms?* Performance metrics are likely to include ROE, gross margins, general and administrative expenses to sales, and working capital management ratios. On the basis of these measures, is the target a poor performer in its industry, implying that there are opportunities for improved management? Is the acquirer in a declining industry and searching for new directions?
- *What is the tax position of both firms?* What are the average and marginal current tax rates for the target and the acquirer? Does the acquirer have operating loss carryforwards and the target taxable profits?

This analysis should help the analyst understand what specific benefits, if any, the merger is likely to generate.

Motivation for the Exxon-Mobil Merger

Several industry factors influenced Exxon and Mobil to merge. Since the OPEC oil embargo of 1973, the oil industry had been subjected to wide price fluctuations that increased exploration risks. For example, real prices per barrel increased from $11.83 in 1973 to $50.94 in 1981 and then declined precipitously to $16.61 per barrel in 1986. Between 1987 and 1998, prices continued to fluctuate wildly, with a low of $10.53 in 1998 and a high of $23.15 in 1990. In addition to pricing risks, oil companies faced significant political risks in exploration since much of their reserves were located in politically volatile countries, where private property rights were subject to change.

The industry responded to these challenges by adopting cost reduction programs. From 1980 to 1992, employment at eight major oil companies declined by 63 percent, from 800,000 to 300,000. Headquarters staff at six of the largest firms declined from 3,000 to 800 in the period 1988 to 1992. In addition, companies sought to increase flexibility by leasing rather than owning tankers. But as prices continued to plummet in the late 1990s, oil companies sought other ways to increase efficiency.

The outcome was a series of large mergers and acquisitions that transformed the industry: BP merged with Amoco in 1998 and acquired Arco the following year; Total, a French oil firm, acquired the large Belgian oil firm Petrofina in late 1998 and subsequently purchased Elf Aquitaine in a $49 billion hostile takeover; Texaco was acquired by Chevron in 2000; and Phillips Petroleum acquired Tosco in early 2001, and late during the same year agreed to merge with Conoco.

The management of Exxon and Mobil argued that a merger would provide the new company with three significant benefits. First, the merger would facilitate efficiency improvements such as streamlining administrative overhead, eliminating excess capacity and duplicate facilities, using purchasing power to reduce raw material costs, and coordinating exploration in regions where the two firms operated separately. At the time of the merger, management estimated that it would save $730 million by cutting roughly 9,000 jobs and closing offices, an additional $1.2 billion by trimming business overlap, and another $780 million by sharing exploration, procurement budgets, and technology. All told, management stated that it could realize cost savings of about $2.8 billion per year through the merger. These savings were expected to be fully realized by the third year after the merger. Second, management noted that the two companies had complementary strengths and assets that would help increase productivity. While Exxon was financially conservative and had been growing its oil reserves only modestly, with an average five-year reserve replacement ratio of only 102 percent, Mobil was touted as one of the leading exploration firms, with a five-year reserve replacement ratio of 147 percent. Exxon was a leader in deepwater exploration in West Africa, which complemented Mobil's production and exploration activities in Nigeria and Equatorial Guinea. In the Caspian, Exxon's presence in Azerbaijan complemented Mobil's strength in Kazakhstan, including a significant interest in the Tengiz field and its presence in Turkmenistan. Complementary exploration and production operations also existed in South America, Russia, and Eastern Canada. Finally, management argued that the merger provided the company with the scale required to manage the risks associated with very sizeable investments involved in new exploration projects.

Analysts and the financial media concurred with management's assessments of the economic benefits that potentially would be derived from the merger. Some analysts nevertheless expressed concern that differences in the cultures of the two companies might make it difficult for them to actually achieve these synergies. Exxon had a reputation for being "tight-lipped and conservative" whereas Mobil was viewed as "more open, both to the public and to new ideas."[9]

ACQUISITION PRICING

A well thought-out economic motivation for a merger or acquisition is a necessary but not sufficient condition for it to create value for acquiring stockholders. The acquirer must be careful to avoid overpaying for the target. Overpayment makes the transaction highly desirable and profitable for target stockholders, but it diminishes the value of the deal to acquiring stockholders. A financial analyst can use the following methods to assess whether the acquiring firm is overpaying for the target.

Analyzing Premium Offered to Target Stockholders

One popular way to assess whether the acquirer is overpaying for a target is to compare the premium offered to target stockholders to premiums offered in similar transactions. If the acquirer offers a relatively high premium, the analyst is typically led to conclude that the transaction is less likely to create value for acquiring stockholders.

Premiums differ significantly for friendly and hostile acquisitions. Premiums tend to be about 30 percent higher for hostile deals than for friendly offers, implying that hostile acquirers are more likely to overpay for a target.[10] There are several reasons for this. First, a friendly acquirer has access to the internal records of the target, improving the accuracy in valuing the target and making it less likely that it will be surprised by hidden liabilities or problems once it has completed the deal. In contrast, a hostile acquirer does not have this advantage in valuing the target during negotiations and is more likely to overpay. Second, the delays that typically accompany a hostile acquisition often provide opportunities for competing bidders to make an offer for the target, leading to a bidding war.

Comparing a target's premium to values for similar types of transactions is straightforward, but has several practical problems. First, it is not obvious how to define a comparable transaction. Figure 11-1 shows the mean and median premiums paid for U.S. targets over a 25-year period between 1981 and 2005. Average premiums rose from around 40 percent through the mid-1990s to between 50 and 60 percent in 1999–2001. Median premiums also increased during this period, from around 30 percent to 40 percent. Despite the increase in M&A activity in 2004 and 2005, median premiums dropped significantly from the highs of 1999–2001 to only 23 to 24 percent. However, mean and median premiums have to be interpreted with caution since there is considerable variation across transactions, making it difficult to use these estimates as a benchmark.

A second problem in using premiums offered to target stockholders to assess whether an acquirer overpaid is that measured premiums can be misleading if an offer is anticipated by investors. The stock price run-up for the target will then tend to make estimates of the premium appear relatively low. This limitation can be partially offset by using target stock prices one month prior to the acquisition offer as the basis for calculating premiums. However, in some cases offers may have been anticipated for even longer than one month.

| FIGURE 11-1 | Merger Activity and Premium Paid: 1981–2005 |

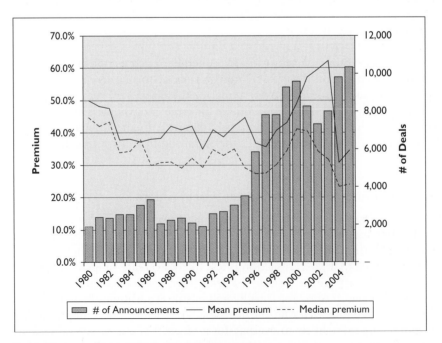

Source: Mergerstat Review 2006 (FactSet Mergerstat, LLC).

Finally, using target premiums to assess whether an acquirer overpaid ignores the value of the target to the acquirer after the acquisition. The acquirer expects to benefit from the merger by improving the target firm's operating performance through a combination of economies of scale, improved management, tax benefits, and spillover effects derived from the acquisition. Clearly, acquirers will be willing to pay higher premiums for targets that are expected to generate higher merger benefits. Thus, examining the premium alone cannot determine whether the acquisition creates value for acquiring stockholders.

Analyzing Value of the Target to the Acquirer

A second and more reliable way of assessing whether the acquirer has overpaid for the target is to compare the offer price to the estimated value of the target to the acquirer. This latter value can be computed using the valuation techniques discussed in Chapters 7 and 8. The most popular methods of valuation used for mergers and acquisitions are earnings multiples and discounted cash flows. Since a comprehensive discussion of these techniques is provided earlier in the book, we focus here on implementation issues that arise for valuing targets in mergers and acquisitions.

We recommend first computing the value of the target as an independent firm. This provides a way of checking whether the valuation assumptions are reasonable, since for publicly listed targets we can compare our estimate with premerger market prices. It also provides a useful benchmark for thinking about how the target's performance, and hence its value, is likely to change once it is acquired.

Earnings Multiples

To estimate the value of a target to an acquirer using earnings multiples, we have to forecast earnings for the target and decide on an appropriate earnings multiple, as follows:

Step 1: Forecasting earnings Earnings forecasts are usually made by first forecasting next year's net income for the target assuming no acquisition. Historical sales growth rates, gross margins, and average tax rates are useful in building a pro forma income model. Once we have forecasted the income for the target as an independent firm, we can incorporate into the pro forma model any improvements in earnings performance that we expect to result from the acquisition. Performance improvements can be modeled on numerous dimensions including

- Higher operating margins through economies of scale in purchasing, or increased market power;
- Reductions in expenses as a result of consolidating research and development staffs, sales forces, and/or administration; or
- Lower average tax rates from taking advantage of operating tax loss carryforwards.

Step 2: Determining the price-earnings multiple How do we determine the earnings multiple to be applied to our earnings forecasts? If the target firm is listed, it may be tempting to use the preacquisition price-earnings multiple to value postmerger earnings. However, there are several limitations to this approach. First, for many targets, earnings growth expectations are likely to change after a merger, implying that there will be a difference between the pre- and postmerger price-earnings multiples. Postmerger earnings should then be valued using a multiple for firms with comparable growth and risk characteristics. (See discussion in Chapter 7.) A second problem is that premerger price-earnings multiples are unavailable for unlisted targets. Once again it becomes necessary to decide which types of listed firms are likely to be good comparables. In addition, since the earnings being valued are the projected earnings for the next 12 months or the next full fiscal year, the appropriate benchmark ratio should be a *forward* price-earnings ratio. Finally, if a premerger price-earnings multiple is appropriate for valuing postmerger earnings, care is required to ensure that the multiple is calculated prior to any acquisition announcement since the price will increase in anticipation of the premium to be paid to target stockholders.

The following table summarizes how price-earnings multiples are used to value a target firm before an acquisition (assuming it will remain an independent entity) and to estimate the value of a target to a potential acquirer:

Summary of Price-Earnings Valuation for Targets

Value of target as an independent firm	Target earnings forecast for the next year, assuming no change in ownership, multiplied by its *premerger* forward PE multiple.
Value of target to potential acquirer	Target *revised* earnings forecast for the next year, incorporating the effect of any operational changes made by the acquirer, multiplied by its *postmerger* forward PE multiple.

Limitations of Price-Earnings Valuation   As explained in Chapter 7, there are serious limitations to using earnings multiples for valuation. In addition to these limitations, the method has two more that are specific to merger valuations:

1. PE multiples assume that merger performance improvements come either from an immediate increase in earnings or from an increase in earnings growth (and hence an increase in the postmerger PE ratio). In reality, improvements and savings can come in many forms—gradual increases in earnings from implementing new operating policies, eliminating overinvestment, managing working capital better, or paying out excess cash to stockholders. These types of improvements are not naturally reflected in PE multiples.
2. PE models do not easily incorporate any spillover benefits from an acquisition for the acquirer since they focus on valuing the earnings of the target.

Discounted Abnormal Earnings or Cash Flows

As discussed in Chapters 7 and 8, we can also value a company using the discounted abnormal earnings and discounted free cash flow methods. These require us to first forecast the abnormal earnings or free cash flows for the firm and then discount them at the cost of capital, as follows.

Step 1: Forecasting abnormal earnings/free cash flows   A pro forma model of expected future income and cash flows for the firm provides the basis for forecasting abnormal earnings/free cash flows. As a starting point, the model should be constructed under the assumption that the target remains an independent firm. The model should reflect the best estimates of future sales growth, cost structures, working capital needs, investment and research and development needs, and cash requirements for known debt retirements, developed from a financial analysis of the target. The abnormal earnings method requires that we forecast abnormal earnings or net operating profit after tax (NOPAT) for as long as the firm expects new investment projects to earn more than their cost of capital. Under the free cash flow approach, the pro forma model will forecast free cash flows to either the firm or to equity, typically for a period of five to ten years. Once we have a model of the abnormal earnings or free cash flows, we can incorporate any improvements in earnings/free cash flows that we expect to result from the acquisition. These will include the cost savings, cash received from asset sales, benefits from eliminating overinvestment, improved working capital management, and excess cash paid out to stockholders.

Step 2: Compute the discount rate   If we are valuing the target's postacquisition abnormal NOPAT or cash flows to the firm, the appropriate discount rate is the weighted average cost of capital (WACC) for the target, using its expected *postacquisition* capital structure. Alternatively, if the target's equity cash flows are being valued directly or if we are valuing abnormal earnings, the appropriate discount rate is the target's *postacquisition cost of equity* rather than its WACC. Two common mistakes are to use the acquirer's cost of capital or the target's *preacquisition* cost of capital to value the postmerger abnormal earnings/cash flows from the target.

The computation of the target's postacquisition cost of capital can be complicated if the acquirer plans to make a change to the target's capital structure after the acquisition, since the target's costs of debt and equity will change. As discussed in Chapter 8, this involves estimating the asset beta for the target, calculating the new equity and debt betas under the modified capital structure, and finally computing the revised cost of equity capital or WACC. As a practical matter, the effect of these changes on the WACC is likely to be quite small unless the revision in leverage has a significant effect on the target's interest tax shields or its likelihood of financial distress.

The following table summarizes how the discounted abnormal earnings/cash flow methods can be used to value a target before an acquisition (assuming it will remain an independent entity) and to estimate the value of a target firm to a potential acquirer.

Summary of Discounted Abnormal Earnings/Cash Flow Valuation for Targets

Value of target as an independent firm	(a) Present value of abnormal earnings/free cash flows to target equity assuming no acquisition, discounted at *premerger* cost of equity, or (b) Present value of abnormal NOPAT/free cash flows to target debt and equity assuming no acquisition, discounted at *premerger* WACC, less value of debt.
Value of target to potential acquirer	(a) Present value of abnormal earnings/free cash flows to target equity, *including benefits from merger,* discounted at *postmerger* cost of equity, or (b) Present value of abnormal NOPAT/free cash flows to target debt and equity, *including benefits from merger,* discounted at *postmerger* WACC, less value of debt.

Step 3: Analyze sensitivity   Once we have estimated the expected value of a target, we will want to examine the sensitivity of our estimate to changes in the model assumptions. For example, answering the following questions can help the analyst assess the risks associated with an acquisition:

- What happens to the value of the target if it takes longer than expected for the benefits of the acquisition to materialize?
- What happens to the value of the target if the acquisition prompts its primary competitors to respond by also making an acquisition? Will potential changes in industry dynamics affect the firm's plans and estimates?

Key Analysis Questions

To analyze the pricing of an acquisition, the analyst is interested in assessing the value of the acquisition benefits to be generated by the acquirer relative to the price paid to target stockholders. Analysts are therefore likely to be interested in answers to the following questions:

- What is the premium that the acquirer paid for the target's stock? What does this premium imply for the acquirer in terms of future performance improvements to justify the premium?
- What are the likely performance improvements that management expects to generate from the acquisition? For example, are there likely to be increases in the revenues for the merged firm from new products, increased prices, or better distribution of existing products? Alternatively, are there cost savings as a result of taking advantage of economies of scale, improved efficiency, or a lower cost of capital for the target?
- What is the value of any performance improvements? Values can be estimated using multiples or discounted abnormal earnings/cash flow methods.

Exxon's Pricing of Mobil

Exxon's $74.2 billion price for Mobil represented a 26.4 percent premium to target stockholders over the market value on November 20, 1998, when rumors of a merger first reached Wall Street. This was below the mean and median premiums reported for all acquisitions during that year (41 percent and 30 percent, respectively). However, it was toward the high end of estimates made by J. P. Morgan, Exxon's financial advisor, who reviewed 38 large comparable acquisitions and concluded that a 15–25 percent premium was justified. In comparison, BP had paid a 35 percent premium for Amoco during the same period.

In terms of traditional multiples-based forms of valuation, Exxon's pricing of Mobil appears to be reasonable. For example, at the time of the announcement of Exxon's offer, the PE multiple for other firms in the oil industry that were comparable to Mobil ranged from 19.3 to 23.8. Exxon's offer valued Mobil at 22.7 times current earnings.

The market reaction to the acquisition announcement suggests that analysts initially believed that the deal was marginal for Exxon's stockholders—Exxon's stock price dropped by 1.5 percent (adjusted for market-wide changes), or $2.6 billion, during the 11 days prior to the announcement through to the actual announcement day. However, by the tenth trading day after the announcement, Exxon's stock was up 3.6 percent (also adjusted for market-wide changes), or $6.3 billion. Given the $15.5 billion premium that Exxon paid for Mobil, investors believed that the merger would create value of $21.8 billion.

Subsequent short-term financial results for Exxon-Mobil support the market's optimism about the merger synergies. In August 2000, Exxon-Mobil announced that merger synergies had reached $4.6 billion, far ahead of projections at the time of the merger. Analysts projected that they would reach $7.0 billion by 2002.

ACQUISITION FINANCING AND FORM OF PAYMENT

Even if an acquisition is undertaken to create new economic value and is priced judiciously, it may still destroy shareholder value if it is inappropriately financed. Several financing options are available to acquirers, including issuing stock or warrants to target stockholders, or acquiring target stock using surplus cash or proceeds from new debt. The trade-offs between these alternatives from the standpoint of target stockholders usually hinge on their tax and transaction cost implications. For acquirers, they can affect the firm's capital structure and provide new information to investors.

As we discuss below, the financing preferences of acquiring and target stockholders can diverge. Financing arrangements can therefore increase or reduce the attractiveness of an acquisition from the standpoint of acquiring stockholders. As a result, a complete analysis of an acquisition will include an examination of the implications of the financing arrangements for the acquirer.

Effect of Form of Payment on Acquiring Stockholders

From the perspective of the acquirer, the form of payment is essentially a financing decision. As discussed in Chapter 10, in the long term firms choose whether to use debt or equity financing to balance the tax and incentive benefits of debt against the risks of financial distress. For acquiring stockholders, the costs and benefits of different financing alternatives therefore usually depend on three factors described below: how the offer affects their firm's capital structure, any information effects associated with different forms of financing, and control issues arising from the form of payment.

Capital Structure Effects of Form of Financing

In acquisitions where debt financing or surplus cash are the primary form of consideration for target shares, the acquisition increases the net financial leverage of the acquirer. This increase in leverage may be part of the acquisition strategy, since one way an acquirer can add value to an inefficient firm is to lower its taxes by increasing interest tax shields. However, in many acquisitions an increase in postacquisition leverage is a side effect of the method of financing and not part of a deliberate tax-minimizing strategy. Demands by target shareholders for consideration in cash could lead the acquirer to have a postacquisition capital structure that can potentially reduce shareholder value for the acquirer by increasing the risk of financial distress.

To assess whether an acquisition leads an acquirer to have too much leverage, financial analysts can assess the acquirer's financial risk following the proposed acquisition by these methods:

- Analyze the business risks and the volatility of the combined, postacquisition cash flows against the level of debt in the new capital structure, and the implications for possible financial distress.
- Assess the pro forma financial risks for the acquirer under the proposed financing plan. Popular measures of financial risk include debt-to-equity and interest-coverage ratios, as well as projections of cash flows available to meet debt repayments. The ratios can be compared to similar performance metrics for the acquiring and target firms' industries to determine whether postmerger ratios indicate that the firm's probability of financial distress has increased significantly.
- Examine whether there are important off-balance-sheet liabilities for the target and/or acquirer that are not included in the pro forma ratio and cash flow analysis of postacquisition financial risk.

- Determine whether the pro forma assets for the acquirer are largely intangible and therefore sensitive to financial distress. Measures of intangible assets include such ratios as market to book equity and tangible assets to the market value of equity.

Information Problems and the Form of Financing

In the short term, information asymmetries between managers and external investors can make managers reluctant to raise equity to finance new projects. Managers' reluctance arises from their fear that investors will interpret the decision as an indication that the firm's stock is overvalued. In the short term, this effect can lead managers to deviate from the firm's long-term optimal mix of debt and equity. As a result, acquirers are likely to prefer to use internal funds or debt to finance an acquisition since these forms of consideration are less likely to be interpreted negatively by investors.[11]

The information effects imply that firms forced to use stock financing are likely to face a stock price decline when investors learn of the method of financing.[12] From the viewpoint of financial analysts, the financing announcement may, therefore, provide valuable news about the acquiring managers' views of their own company's value prior to the acquisition. On the other hand, it should have no implications for analysis of whether the acquisition creates value for acquiring shareholders since the news reflected in the financing announcement is about the *preacquisition* value of the acquirer and not about the *postacquisition* value of the target to the acquirer.

A second information problem arises if the acquiring management does not have good information about the target. Stock financing then provides a way for acquiring stockholders to share the information risks with target shareholders. If the acquirer finds out after the acquisition that the value of the target is less than previously anticipated, the accompanying decline in the acquirer's equity price will be partially borne by target stockholders who continue to hold the acquirer's stock. In contrast, if the target's shares were acquired in a cash offer, any postacquisition loss would be fully borne by the acquirer's original stockholders. The risk-sharing benefits from using stock financing appears to be widely recognized for acquisitions of private companies, where public information on the target is largely unavailable.[13] In practice it appears to be considered less important for acquisitions of large public corporations.

Control and the Form of Payment

There is a significant difference between the use of cash and stock in terms of its impact on the voting control of the combined firm postacquisition. Financing an acquisition with cash allows the acquirer to retain the structure and composition of its equity ownership. On the other hand, depending on the size of the target firm relative to the acquirer, an acquisition financed with stock could have a significant impact on the ownership and control of the firm postacquisition. This could be particularly relevant to a family-controlled acquirer. Therefore, the effects of control need to be balanced against the other costs and benefits when determining the form of payment.

Over the last 25 years, offers that are 100 percent cash have comprised 42 percent of all acquisitions, exceeding all-stock offers (30 percent) and mixed stock and cash offers (28 percent). The popularity of all-cash offers has increased since 2000, rising to 54 percent of all deals in 2005 whereas the use of all-stock offers has declined to only 21 percent.

Effect of Form of Payment on Target Stockholders

The key payment considerations for target stockholders are the tax and transaction cost implications of the acquirer's offer.

Tax Effects of Different Forms of Consideration

Target stockholders care about the after-tax value of any offer they receive for their shares. In the U.S., whenever target stockholders receive cash for their shares, they are required to pay capital gains tax on the difference between the takeover offer price and their original purchase price. Alternatively, if they receive shares in the acquirer as consideration and the acquisition is undertaken as a tax-free reorganization, they can defer any taxes on the capital gain until they sell the new shares.

As a result, U.S. tax laws appear to cause target stockholders to prefer a stock offer to a cash one. This is certainly likely to be the case for a target founder who still has a significant stake in the company. If the company's stock price has appreciated over its life, the founder will face a substantial capital gains tax on a cash offer and will therefore probably prefer to receive stock in the acquiring firm. However, cash and stock offers can be tax-neutral for some groups of stockholders. For example, consider the tax implications for risk arbitrageurs, who take a short-term position in a company that is a takeover candidate in the hope that other bidders will emerge and increase the takeover price. They have no intention of holding stock in the acquirer once the takeover is completed and will pay ordinary income tax on any short-term trading gain. Cash and stock offers therefore have identical after-tax values for risk arbitrageurs. Similarly, tax-exempt institutions are likely to be indifferent to whether an offer is in cash or stock.

Transaction Costs and the Form of Payment

Transaction costs are another factor related to the form of payment that can be relevant to target stockholders. Transaction costs are incurred when target stockholders sell any stock received as consideration for their shares in the target. These costs will not be faced by target stockholders if the bidder offers them cash. Transaction costs are unlikely to be significant for investors who intend to hold the acquirer's stock following a stock acquisition. However, they may be relevant for investors who intend to sell, such as risk arbitrageurs.

Key Analysis Questions

For an analyst focused on the acquiring firm, it is important to assess how the method of financing affects the acquirer's capital structure and its risks of financial distress by asking the following questions:

- What is the leverage for the newly created firm? How does this compare to leverage for comparable firms in the industry?
- What are the projected future cash flows for the merged firm? Are these sufficient to meet the firm's debt commitments? How much of a cushion does the firm have if future cash flows are lower than expected? Is the firm's debt level likely to impair its ability to finance profitable future investments if future cash flows are below expectations?

Exxon's Financing of Mobil

Exxon offered Mobil shareholders 1.32 Exxon shares for each Mobil share. Given Mobil's 780 million shares outstanding, Exxon issued 1,030 million shares, which at $72 per share implied a total offer of $74.2 billion. While the premerger equity value of Exxon represented 75 percent of the combined market value, the premium paid for Mobil's shares caused the postmerger proportion of ownership to drop to about 70 percent for Exxon and rise to 30 percent for Mobil.

The merger was structured as a "tax-free reorganization" for federal income tax purposes. This implied that Mobil shareholders would not recognize any gain or loss for federal income tax purposes from exchanging their Mobil stock for Exxon-Mobil stock in the merger.

By using stock to finance the acquisition, Exxon actually reduced its financial leverage. Initially the market reacted negatively to the offer, lowering Exxon's stock price by 1.5 percent (adjusting for marketwide returns) on the announcement date (December 1, 1998). This reaction could have occurred because investors interpreted Exxon's stock offer as indicating that its own managers considered its stock to be overvalued. Yet in the following ten days, Exxon's stock staged a recovery, increasing by 3.6 percent.

ACQUISITION OUTCOME

The final question of interest to the analyst evaluating a potential acquisition is whether it will indeed be completed. If an acquisition has a clear value-based motive, the target is priced appropriately, and its proposed financing does not create unnecessary financial risks for the acquirer, it may still fail because the target receives a higher competing bid, there is opposition from entrenched target management, or the transaction fails to receive necessary regulatory approval. Therefore, to evaluate the likelihood that an offer will be accepted, the financial analyst has to understand whether there are potential competing bidders who could pay an even higher premium to target stockholders than is currently offered. They also have to consider whether target managers are entrenched and likely to oppose an offer to protect their jobs, as well as the political and regulatory environment in which the target and the acquirer operate.

Other Potential Acquirers

If there are other potential bidders for a target, especially ones who place a higher value on the target, there is a strong possibility that the bidder in question will be unsuccessful. Target management and stockholders have an incentive to delay accepting the initial offer to give potential competitors time to also submit a bid. From the perspective of the initial bidder, this means that the offer could potentially reduce stockholder value by the cost of making the offer (including substantial investment banking and legal fees). In practice, a losing bidder can usually recoup these losses and sometimes even make healthy profits from selling to the successful acquirer any shares it has accumulated in the target.

On some occasions, the original bidder includes a break-up fee in the acquisition contract which is payable should the target company choose to be acquired by a different partner. For example, in late 2005 Johnson & Johnson signed an agreement to acquire Guidant Corporation for about $21 billion. A takeover battle for Guidant resulted when Boston Scientific made a higher offer. Over the ensuing seven weeks (from December 2005 to January 2006), both Johnson & Johnson and Boston Scientific increased their bids on multiple occasions. Eventually, Boston Scientific won with a $27 billion offer. However, in addition to the purchase price, Boston Scientific had to reimburse Guidant the termination fee of $705 million payable to Johnson & Johnson.

Key Analysis Questions

The financial analyst can determine whether there are other potential acquirers for a target and how they value the target by asking the following questions:

- Who are the acquirer's major competitors? Could any of these firms provide an even better fit for the target?
- Are there other firms that could also implement the initial bidder's acquisition strategy? For example, if this strategy relies on developing benefits from complementary assets, look for potential bidders who also have assets complementary to the target. If the goal of the acquisition is to replace inefficient management, what other firms in the target's industry could provide management expertise?

Target Management Entrenchment

If target managers are entrenched and fearful for their jobs, it is likely that they will oppose a bidder's offer. Some firms have implemented "golden parachutes" for top managers to allay their concerns about job security at the time of an offer. Golden parachutes provide top managers of a target firm with attractive compensation rewards should the firm get taken over.[14] However, many firms do not have such schemes, and opposition to an offer from entrenched management is a very real possibility.

More generally, there are a variety of structural impediments know as takeover defense mechanisms that provide a disincentive to acquiring firms. Many such defenses were used during the turbulent 1980s, when hostile acquisitions were at their peak. Some of the most widely adopted include poison pills, staggered boards, super-majority rules, dual-class recapitalizations, fair-price provisions, ESOP plans, and changes in states of incorporation to states with more restrictive anti-takeover laws. While the existence of takeover defenses for a target indicates that its management is likely to fight a bidding firm's offer, defenses have typically not prevented an acquisition from taking place. Instead, they tend to cause delays, which increase the likelihood that there will be competing offers made for the target, including offers by friendly parties solicited by target management, called "white knights." Takeover defenses, therefore, increase the likelihood that the bidder in question will be outbid for the target, or that it will have to increase its offer significantly to win a bidding contest. Given these risks, some have argued that acquirers are now less likely to embark on a potentially hostile acquisition.

Key Analysis Questions

To assess whether the target firm's management is entrenched and therefore likely to oppose an acquisition, analysts can ask the following questions:

- Does the target firm have takeover defenses designed to protect management?

- Has the target been a poor performer relative to other firms in its industry? If so, management's job security is likely to be threatened by a takeover, leading it to oppose any offers.
- Is there a golden parachute plan in place for target management? Golden parachutes provide attractive compensation for management in order to deter opposition to a takeover for job security reasons.

Antitrust and Security Issues

Regulators such as the Federal Trade Commission in the U.S. and the European Competition Commission assess the effects of an acquisition on the competitive dynamics of the industry in which the firms operate. The objective is to ensure that no one firm, through mergers and acquisitions, creates a dominant position that can impede effective competition in specific geographies or product markets. For instance, in July 2001 the European Competition Commission rejected GE's proposed $41 billion purchase of Honeywell International on the grounds that the merger would have severely reduced competition in the aerospace industry and resulted in higher prices for customers, particularly airlines.

In addition, political concerns around firms that have an impact on the national and economic security of a country come under the scrutiny of local lawmakers, whose opposition can often derail cross-border acquisition efforts. The U.S., for instance, has a specific inter-agency committee that vets foreign takeovers of U.S. assets on national security grounds. Two recent high profile cases—China's CNOOC oil company's proposed acquisition of California-based Unocal in mid-2005 and Dubai Ports World's acquisition of U.S. port terminals in March 2006—underscore the importance of assessing this risk. Chevron, another interested bidder for Unocal, used CNOOC's links to the Chinese government to generate political opposition to the CNOOC bid, which eventually led CNOOC to drop its offer. Similarly, political opposition based on the United Arab Emirates government's control of Dubai Ports World and the national security concerns over port infrastructure forced the company to sell the U.S. operations as part of its acquisition of British port operator P&O.

Key Analysis Questions

To assess whether the regulators and/or government is likely to oppose an acquisition, analysts can ask the following questions:

- What proportion of industry sales do the two firms control? Is this likely to be of concern to regulators in countries in which the firms operate? Are the combined firms likely to be able to reduce regulatory opposition by selling certain business units?
- Is the target firm or the industry in which it operates of strategic importance or in the national interest of the country in which it is located? Is the ownership structure of the acquirer likely to create political opposition to the deal?

Analysis of Outcome of Exxon's Offer for Mobil

Analysts covering Mobil had little reason to question whether Mobil would be sold to Exxon. The offer was a friendly one that had received the approval of Mobil's management and board of directors. There probably was some risk of another major oil company entering the bidding for Mobil. For example, BP had shown an appetite for making major acquisitions with its purchase of Amoco in August 1998. In early 1999 BP also acquired Arco in a second mega-deal. Chevron was also rumored to be open to an acquisition, and in October 2000 it acquired Texaco. In the end, none of these competitors made a bid for Mobil.

Despite the spate of mergers in the petroleum industry starting in 1997, the concentration level in the overall industry was well below the threshold at which the U.S. regulatory agencies would raise antitrust concerns. While this test applied to the global exploration and production markets, the refining and distribution markets were more segmented. Consequently, regulators required Exxon-Mobil to divest its wholesale distribution facilities. The European Commission, after a series of probes of the merger, mandated the sale of numerous assets and business lines as a pre-requisite of its approval for the merger. The acquisition was completed on December 1, 1999, twelve months after announcement of the initial agreement.

SUMMARY

This chapter summarizes how financial statement data and analysis can be used by financial analysts interested in evaluating whether an acquisition creates value for an acquiring firm's stockholders. Obviously, much of this discussion is also likely to be relevant to other merger participants, including target and acquiring management and their investment banks.

For the external analyst, the first task is to identify the acquirer's acquisition strategy. We discuss a number of strategies. Some of these are consistent with maximizing acquirer value, including acquisitions to take advantage of economies of scale, improve target management, combine complementary resources, capture tax benefits, provide low-cost financing to financially constrained targets, and increase product-market rents.

Other strategies appear to benefit managers more than stockholders. For example, some unprofitable acquisitions are made because managers are reluctant to return free cash flows to shareholders, or because managers want to lower the firm's earnings volatility by diversifying into unrelated businesses.

The financial analyst's second task is to assess whether the acquirer is offering a reasonable price for the target. Even if the acquirer's strategy is based on increasing shareholder value, it can overpay for the target. Target stockholders will then be well rewarded but at the expense of acquiring stockholders. We show how the ratio analysis, forecasting, and valuation techniques discussed earlier in the book can all be used to assess the worth of the target to the acquirer.

The method of financing an offer is also relevant to a financial analyst's review of an acquisition proposal. If a proposed acquisition is financed with surplus cash or new debt, it increases the acquirer's financial risk. Financial analysts can use ratio analysis of the acquirer's postacquisition balance sheet and pro forma estimates of cash flow volatility and interest coverage to assess whether demands by target stockholders for consideration in cash lead the acquirer to increase its risk of financial distress.

Finally, the financial analyst is interested in assessing whether a merger is likely to be completed once the initial offer is made, and at what price. This requires the analyst to determine whether there are other potential bidders, whether target management is entrenched and likely to oppose a bidder's offer, or whether the deal could fail due to antitrust or security concerns.

DISCUSSION QUESTIONS

1. Since the year 2000, there has been a noticeable increase in mergers and acquisitions between firms in different countries (termed cross-border acquisitions). What factors could explain this increase? What special issues can arise in executing a cross-border acquisition and in ultimately meeting your objectives for a successful combination?

2. Private equity firms have become an important player in the acquisition market. These private investment groups offer to buy a target firm, often with the cooperation of management, and then take the firm private. Private equity buyouts rose from just 2 percent of U.S. merger and acquisition activity in 2000 to 15 percent as of December 2005. Private equity buyers tend to finance a significant portion of the acquisition with debt.

   a. What types of firms would make ideal candidates for a private equity buyout? Why?

   b. How might the buyout firm add sufficient value to the target to justify a high buyout premium?

3. Kim Silverman, CFO of the First Public Bank Company, notes, "We are fortunate to have a cost of capital of only 10 percent. We want to leverage this advantage by acquiring other banks that have a higher cost of funds. I believe that we can add significant value to these banks by using our lower cost financing." Do you agree with Silverman's analysis? Why or why not?

4. The Boston Tea Company plans to acquire Hi Flavor Soda Co. for $60 per share, a 50 percent premium over current market price. John E. Grey, the CFO of Boston Tea, argues that this valuation can easily be justified using a price-earnings analysis: "Boston Tea has a price-earnings ratio of 15, and we expect that we will be able to generate long-term earnings for Hi Flavor Soda of $5 per share. This implies that Hi Flavor is worth $75 to us, well below our $60 offer price." Do you agree with this analysis? What are Grey's key assumptions?

5. You have been hired by GT Investment Bank to work in the merger department. The analysis required for all potential acquisitions includes an examination of the target for any off-balance-sheet assets or liabilities that have to be factored into the valuation. Prepare a checklist for your examination.

6. A target company is currently valued at $50 in the market. A potential acquirer believes that it can add value in two ways: $15 of value can be added through better working capital management, and an additional $10 of value can be generated by making available a unique technology to expand the target's new product offerings. In a competitive bidding contest, how much of this additional value will the acquirer have to pay out to the target's shareholders to emerge as the winner?

7. In 1995 Disney acquired ABC television at a significant premium. Disney's management justified much of this premium by arguing that the acquisition would guarantee access for Disney's programs on ABC's television stations. Evaluate the economic merits of this claim.

8. A leading oil exploration company decides to acquire an Internet company at a 50 percent premium. The acquirer argues that this move creates value for its own stockholders because it can use its excess cash flows from the oil business to help finance growth in the new Internet segment. Evaluate the economic merits of this claim.

9. Under current U.S. accounting standards, acquirers are required to capitalize goodwill and report any subsequent declines in value as an impairment charge. What performance metrics would you use to judge whether goodwill is impaired?

10. As an external adviser to the U.S. Government's interagency committee that vets foreign takeovers, you have been asked to provide expert testimony on the proposed takeover of a major U.S. airport by a Dutch airport management services company. Would you recommend that the acquisition be granted regulatory approval? What are the different issues you will examine and present to the committee?

NOTES

1. In a review of studies of merger returns, Michael Jensen and Richard Ruback conclude that target shareholders earn positive returns from takeovers, but that acquiring shareholders only break even. See M. Jensen and R. Ruback, "The Market for Corporate Control: The Scientific Evidence," *Journal of Financial Economics* 11 (April 1983): 5–50.

2. Much of our discussion is based on the analysis of the acquisition presented by F. Weston, "The Exxon-Mobil Merger: An Archetype," *Journal of Applied Finance* 12, no. 1, Spring/ Summer 2002.

3. Of course, another possibility is for the profitable firm to acquire the unprofitable one. However, in the U.S. the IRS will disallow the use of tax loss carryforwards by an acquirer if it appears that an acquisition was tax-motivated.

4. See S. Kaplan, "Management Buyouts: Evidence on Taxes as a Source of Value," *Journal of Finance* 44 (1989): 611–632.

5. K. Palepu, "Predicting Takeover Targets: A Methodological and Empirical Analysis," *Journal of Accounting and Economics* 8 (March 1986): 3–36.

6. FactSet Mergerstat, LLC, *Mergerstat Review 2006* (Santa Monica, CA, 2006), pp. 248–249.

7. Chapter 2 discusses the pros and cons of corporate diversification and evidence on its implications for firm performance.

8. FactSet Mergerstat, LLC, *Mergerstat Review 2006* (Santa Monica, CA, 2006), pp. 248–249.

9. See S. Liesman and A. Sullivan, "Tight-Lipped Exxon, Outspoken Mobil Face Major Image, Cultural Differences," *Wall Street Journal*, December 2, 1998.

10. See P. Healy, K. Palepu, and R. Ruback, "Which Mergers Are Profitable—Strategic or Financial?," *Sloan Management Review* 38, no. 4 (Summer 1997): 45–58.

11. See S. Myers and N. Majluf, "Corporate Financing and Investment Decisions When Firms Have Information That Investors Do Not," *Journal of Financial Economics* (June 1984): 187–221.

12. For evidence see N. Travlos, "Corporate Takeover Bids, Methods of Payments, and Bidding Firms' Stock Returns," *Journal of Finance* 42 (1987): 943–963.

13. See S. Datar, R. Frankel, and M. Wolfson, "Earnouts: The Effects of Adverse Selection and Agency Costs on Acquisition Techniques," *Journal of Law, Economics, and Organization* 17 (2001): 201–238.

14. H. Singh and F. Harianto, "Management–Board Relationships, Takeover Risk, and the Adoption of Golden Parachutes," *Academy of Management Journal* 32 (1989): 7–24, find that entrenched managers create golden parachute contracts to avoid the disciplinary effect of corporate takeovers. J. Machlin, H. Choe, and J. Miles, "The Effects of Golden Parachutes on Takeover Activity," *Journal of Law and Economics* 36 (1993): 861–876, find that golden parachutes increase the likelihood of an acquisition.

Chapter 12
Communication and Governance

Corporate governance has become an increasingly important issue in capital markets throughout the world following financial market meltdowns in Asia and the U.S. These market collapses exposed problems of accounting misstatements and lack of corporate transparency, as well as governance problems and conflicts of interest among the intermediaries charged with monitoring management and corporate disclosures.

The breakdowns have increased the challenge for managers in communicating credibly with skeptical outside investors, making it more difficult for new (and in some cases even established) firms to raise capital. Financial reports, the traditional platform for management to communicate with investors, were viewed with increased skepticism following a number of widely publicized audit failures and the demise of Arthur Andersen.

The market crashes have also raised questions about improving the quality of governance by information and financial intermediaries. New regulations, such as the Sarbanes-Oxley Act in the U.S., attempt to increase accountability and financial competence for audit committees and external auditors, who are charged with reviewing the financial reporting and disclosure process, and accountability for the CEO and CFO who are required to certify the validity of both financial statements and internal controls.

This chapter discusses how many of the financial analysis tools developed in Chapters 2 through 8 can be used by managers to develop a coherent disclosure strategy, and by corporate board members and external auditors to improve the quality of their work. The following types of questions are dealt with:

- Managers ask: Is our current communication policy effective in helping investors understand the firm's business strategy and expected future performance, thereby ensuring that our stock price is not seriously over- or undervalued?
- Audit committee members ask: What are the firm's key business risks? Are they reflected appropriately in the financial statements? How is management communicating on important risks that cannot be reflected in the financial statements? Is information on the firm's performance as presented to the board consistent with that provided to investors in the financial report and firm disclosures?
- External auditors ask: What are the firm's key business risks, and how are they reflected in the financial statements? Where should we focus our audit tests? Is our assessment of the firm's performance consistent with that of external investors and analysts? If not, are we overlooking something, or is management misrepresenting the firm's true performance in disclosures?

Throughout this book we have focused primarily on showing how financial statement data can be helpful for analysts and outside investors in making a variety of decisions. In this chapter we change our emphasis and focus primarily on management and governance agents. Of course an understanding of the management communication process and corporate governance is also important for security analysts and investors. The approach taken here, however, is more germane to insiders since most of the types of analyses we discuss are not available to outsiders.

GOVERNANCE OVERVIEW

As we discuss throughout this book, outside investors require access to reliable information on firm performance, both to value their debt and equity claims and to monitor the performance of management. When investors agree to provide capital to the firm, they require that managers provide information on their company's performance and future plans.

However, left to their own devices, managers are likely to paint a rosy picture of the firm's performance in their disclosures. There are three reasons for manager optimism in reporting. First, most managers are genuinely positive about their firms' prospects, leading them to unwittingly emphasize the positive and downplay the negative.

A second reason for management optimism in reporting arises because firm disclosures play an important role in mitigating "agency" problems between managers and investors.[1] Investors use firm disclosures to judge whether managers have either run the firm in investors' best interests or abused their authority and control over firm resources. Reporting consistently poor earnings increases the likelihood that top management will be replaced, either by the board of directors or by an acquirer who takes over the firm to improve its management.[2] Of course, managers are aware of this and have incentives to show positive performance.

Finally, managers are also likely to make optimistic disclosures prior to issuing new equity. Recent evidence indicates that entrepreneurs tend to take their firms public after disclosure of strong reported, but frequently unsustainable, earnings performance. Also, seasoned equity offers typically follow strong, but again unsustainable, stock and earnings performance. The strong earnings performance prior to IPOs and seasoned offers appears to be at least partially due to earnings management.[3] Rational outside investors recognize management's incentives to manage earnings and inflate expectations prior to a new issue. They respond by discounting the stock, demanding a hefty new issue discount, and in extreme cases refusing to purchase the new stock. This raises the cost of capital and potentially leaves some of the best new ventures and projects unfunded.[4]

As discussed in Chapter 1, financial and information intermediaries help reduce agency and information problems faced by outside investors. These intermediaries evaluate the quality of management representation in the firm's disclosures, provide their own analysis of firms' (and managers') performance, and make investment recommendations and decisions on behalf of investors. As presented in Figure 12-1, these intermediaries include internal governance agents, assurance professionals, information analyzers, and professional investors. The importance of these intermediaries is underscored by the magnitude of the fees that they collectively receive from investors and entrepreneurs.

Internal governance agents, such as corporate boards, are responsible for monitoring a firm's management. Their functions include reviewing business strategy, evaluating and rewarding top management, and assuring the flow of credible information to external parties. Assurance professionals, such as external auditors, enhance the credibility of financial information prepared by managers. Information analyzers, such as financial analysts and ratings agencies, are responsible for gathering and analyzing

FIGURE 12-1   The Intermediation Chain Between Managers and Investors

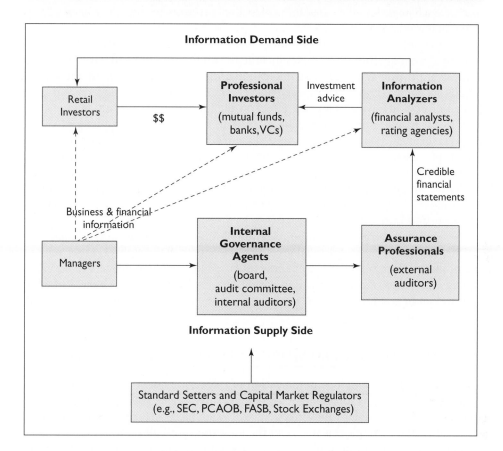

information to provide performance forecasts and investment recommendations to both professional and retail individual investors. Finally, professional investors (such as banks, investment advisors, private equity firms, hedge funds, mutual funds, insurance companies, and venture capital firms) make investment decisions on behalf of dispersed investors. They are therefore responsible for valuing and selecting investment opportunities in the economy.

In this framework, management, internal governance agents, and assurance professionals are charged with supplying information. The demand for information comes from individual and professional investors and information analyzers. Both the supply and demand sides are governed by a variety of regulatory institutions. These include public regulators, such as the Securities and Exchange Commission (SEC), the Public Company Accounting Oversight Board (PCAOB), and bank regulators, as well as private sector bodies such as the Financial Accounting Standards Board (FASB), the American Institute of Certified Public Accountants (AICPA), and stock exchanges.

The level and quality of information and residual information and agency problems in capital markets are determined by the organizational design of these intermediaries and regulatory institutions. Key organizational design questions include: What are the optimal incentive schemes for rewarding top managers? What should be the composition and charter of corporate boards? Should auditors assure that financial reports comply with accounting standards or represent a firm's underlying economics? Should there be detailed accounting standards or a few broad accounting principles? What should be the organizational form and business scope of auditors and analysts? What incentive schemes should be used for professional investors to align their interests with individual investors?

A variety of economic and institutional factors are likely to influence the answers to these design questions. Examples include the ability to write and enforce optimal contracts, proprietary costs that might make disclosure costly for investors, and regulatory imperfections. The spectacular rise and fall of Enron suggests that these limitations could have a first-order effect on the functioning of capital markets.

While it is interesting to speculate on how to improve the functioning of capital markets through changes in organizational design, that issue goes beyond the scope of this chapter. Instead, we discuss how the financial analysis tools developed in Chapters 2 through 8 can be used to improve the performance of some of the information intermediaries who have been widely criticized following revelations of financial reporting fraud and misstatements at companies such as Enron, WorldCom, Tyco, Xerox, Global Crossing, and Lucent.[5]

We have already discussed the application of financial analysis tools to equity and credit analysts and to professional investors in Chapters 9 through 11. In the remainder of this chapter, we discuss how these tools can be used by managers to develop a strategy for effective communication with investors, by members of boards of directors and audit committees in overseeing management and the audit process, and by audit professionals.

MANAGEMENT COMMUNICATION WITH INVESTORS

Some managers argue that communication problems are not worth worrying about. They maintain that as long as managers make investment and operating decisions that enhance shareholder value, investors will value their performance and the firm's stock accordingly. While this is true in the long run, since all information is eventually public, it may not hold in the short or even medium term. If investors do not have access to the same information as management, they will probably find it difficult to value new and innovative investments. In an efficient capital market, they will not consistently over- or undervalue these new investments, but their valuations will tend to be noisy. This can make stock prices relatively noisy, leading management at various times to consider their firms to be either seriously over- or undervalued.

Does it matter if a firm's stock is over- or undervalued for a period? Most managers would prefer to not have their stock undervalued, since it makes it more costly to raise new financing. They may also worry that undervaluation is likely to increase the chance of a takeover by a hostile acquirer, with an accompanying reduction in their job security. Managers of firms that are overvalued may also be concerned about the market's assessment, since they are legally liable for failing to disclose information relevant to investors.[6] They may therefore not wish to see their stock seriously overvalued, even though overvaluation provides opportunities to issue new equity at favorable rates.

A Word of Caution

As noted above, it is natural that many managers believe that firms are undervalued by the capital market. This frequently occurs because it is difficult for managers to be objective about their company's future performance. After all, it is part of their job to sell the company to new employees, customers, suppliers, and investors. In addition, forecasting the firm's future performance objectively requires them to judge their own capabilities as managers. Thus, many managers may argue that investors are uninformed and that their firm is undervalued. Only some can back that up with solid evidence.

If management decides that the firm does face a genuine information problem, it can begin to consider whether and how this could be redressed. Is the problem potentially serious enough that it is worth doing something to alter investors' perceptions? Or is the problem likely to resolve itself within a short period? Does the firm have plans to raise new equity or to use equity to acquire another company? Is management's job security threatened? As we discuss below, management has a wide range of options in this situation.

Key Analysis Questions

We recommend that before jumping to the conclusion that their firms are undervalued, managers should analyze their firms' performance and compare their own forecasts of future performance with those of analysts, using the following approach:

- *Is there a significant difference between internal management forecasts of future earnings and cash flows and those of outside analysts?*
- *Do any differences between managers' and analysts' forecasts arise because of different expectations about economy-wide performance?* Managers may understand their own businesses better than analysts, but they may not be any better at forecasting macroeconomic conditions.
- *Can managers identify any factors that might explain a difference between analysts' and managers' forecasts of future performance?* For example, are analysts unaware of positive new R&D results, do they have different information about customer responses to new products and marketing campaigns, etc.? These types of differences could indicate that the firm faces an information problem.

Example: Communication Issues for FPIC Insurance Group

In 1999 FPIC Insurance Group Inc. was the largest provider of liability insurance for doctors and hospitals in Florida. In the period 1996 to 1998, FPIC reported stable returns on equity of 17 percent, average growth in revenues, net income, and book equity of 25 percent. On December 31, 1998, the firm had a book value per share of $15.85, a price-to-book value of 2.23, a price to earnings multiple of 15.9, and an equity beta of 1.57.

In August 1999, the firm's stock price declined from $45.25 to $14.25. The stock decline began on August 10, the day the company reported a 48 percent jump in second-quarter profits to $7.4 million. The earnings increase was in part attributable to FPIC's Florida Physicians unit releasing $8.1 million in reserves it had set aside against future claims, compared with $4 million in the year-ago quarter. In addition, the company reported higher-than-expected claims in a health insurance plan offered to Florida Dental Association members.

Reuters reported that the stock price decline reflected investors' concern about the quality of the firm's earnings. In response, FPIC spokeswoman Amy D. Ryan stated, "As far as we're concerned, we had a great quarter." The company's chief operating officer, John Byers, argued that the company's decision to release the unit's reserves was normal business practice and based on its expectations of future claims. In response to the higher than expected dental claims, the company announced that it had increased its rates for this insurance.

The sharp decline in its price raises questions about the valuation of the company's stock. On September 9, 1999, the price-to-book ratio was less than 1, and the price-to-earnings multiple was 6.0. The market, therefore, expected that the company would generate a return on equity somewhat lower than its cost of capital. FPIC's management appeared to be puzzled by the sharp drop in price and argued that the market was undervaluing the firm. However, before reaching this conclusion, a number of questions need to be answered:

- Was the firm previously overvalued? If so, what forces were behind the market's high valuation of the company? Had management been painting too rosy a picture for the company's future in its meetings with analysts?
- What events explain the company's sudden drop in stock value? As noted above, the primary question for analysts was the quality of the firm's earnings. However, management needed to have a deeper understanding of these issues.
- If management believed that the firm was actually undervalued, what options were available to correct the market's view of the company?

COMMUNICATION THROUGH FINANCIAL REPORTING

Financial reports are the most popular format for management communication. Below we discuss the role of financial reporting as a means of investor communication, the institutions that make accounting information credible, and the situations in which the reporting is likely to be ineffective.

Accounting as a Means of Management Communication

As we discussed in Chapters 3 and 4, financial reports are an important medium for management communication with external investors. Reports provide investors with an explanation of how their money has been invested, a summary of the performance of those investments, and a discussion of how current performance fits within the firm's overall philosophy and strategy.

Accounting reports not only provide a record of past transactions but also reflect management estimates and forecasts of the future. For example, they include estimates of bad debts, forecasts of the lives of tangible assets, and implicit forecasts that outlays will generate future cash flow benefits that exceed their cost. Since management is likely to be in a position to make forecasts of these future events that are more accurate than those of external investors, financial reports are a potentially useful way of communicating with investors. However, as discussed, investors are also likely to be skeptical of reports prepared by management. The Sarbanes-Oxley Act requires the CEO and CFO to certify that the financials fairly represent the financial performance of the company and that internal controls are adequate to support those financial statements. This requirement increases the accountability of senior management and mitigates some of the investors' skepticism.

Factors That Increase the Credibility of Accounting Communication

A number of mechanisms mitigate conflicts of interest in financial reporting and increase the credibility of accounting information that is communicated to stockholders. These include accounting standards, auditing, monitoring of management by financial analysts, and management reputation.

Accounting Standards and Auditing

Accounting standards, such as those promulgated by the FASB and the SEC in the U.S., provide guidelines for managers on how to make accounting decisions and provide outside investors with a way of interpreting these decisions. Uniform accounting standards attempt to reduce managers' ability to record similar economic transactions in different ways, either over time or across firms. Compliance with these standards is enforced by external auditors who attempt to ensure that managers' estimates are reasonable. Auditors, therefore, reduce the likelihood of earnings management.

Monitoring by Financial Analysts

Financial intermediaries such as analysts also limit management's ability to manage earnings. Financial analysts specialize in developing firm- and industry-specific knowledge, enabling them to assess the quality of a firm's reported numbers and to make any necessary adjustments. Analysts evaluate the appropriateness of management's forecasts implicit in accounting method choices and reported accruals. This requires a thorough understanding of the firm's business and the relevant accounting rules used in the preparation of its financial reports. Superior analysts adjust reported accrual numbers, if necessary, to reflect economic reality, perhaps by using the cash flow statement and the footnote disclosures.

Analysts' business and technical expertise as well as their legal liability and incentives differ from those of auditors. Consequently, analyst reports can provide information to investors on whether the firm's accounting decisions are appropriate or whether managers are overstating the firm's economic performance to protect their jobs.[7]

Management Reputation

A third factor that can counteract external investors' natural skepticism about financial reporting is management reputation. Managers that expect to have an ongoing relation with external investors and financial intermediaries may be able to build a track record for unbiased financial reporting. By making accounting estimates and judgments that are supported by subsequent performance, managers can demonstrate their competence and reliability to investors and analysts. As a result, managers' future judgments and accounting estimates are more likely to be viewed as credible.

Limitations of Financial Reporting for Investor Communication

While accounting standards, auditing, monitoring of management by financial analysts, and management concerns about its reputation increase the credibility and informativeness of financial reports, these mechanisms are far from perfect. Consequently, there are times when financial reporting breaks down as a means for management to communicate with external investors. These breakdowns can arise when (1) there are no accounting rules to guide practice or the existing rules do not distinguish between poor and successful performers, (2) auditors and analysts do not have the expertise to judge new products or business opportunities, or (3) management faces credibility problems.

Accounting Rule Limitations

Despite the rapid increase in new accounting standards, accounting rules frequently do not distinguish between good and poor performers. For example, current accounting rules do not permit managers to show on their balance sheets in a timely fashion the benefits of investments in quality improvements, human resource development programs, research and development (with the exception of software development costs), and customer service.

Some of the problems with accounting standards arise because it takes time for standard setters to develop appropriate standards for many new types of economic transactions. Other difficulties arise because standards are the result of compromises between different interest groups (e.g., auditors, investors, corporate managers, and regulators).

Auditor and Analyst Limitations

While auditors and analysts have access to proprietary information, they do not have the same understanding of the firm's business as managers. The discrepancy between managers' and auditors'/analysts' business assessments is likely to be most severe for firms with distinctive business strategies, or firms that operate in emerging industries. In addition, auditors' decisions in these circumstances are likely to be dominated by concerns about legal liability, hampering management's ability to use financial reports to communicate effectively with investors.

Finally, conflicts of interest faced by auditors and analysts make their analysis imperfect. Conflicts can potentially induce auditors to side with management to retain the firm as an audit client. They can also arise for analysts who provide favorable ratings and research on companies to increase their firm's investment banking business and trading volume among less informed investors. New regulations that increase oversight of audit firms by the Public Company Accounting Oversight Board, and limit the impact of investment banking on financial analysts' incentives, have been put in place to reduce auditor and analyst conflicts of interest.

Management Credibility Problems

There is limited evidence on when management is likely to face credibility problems with investors. However, managers of new firms, firms with volatile earnings, firms in financial distress, and firms with poor track records in communicating with investors should expect to find it difficult to be seen as credible reporters.

If management has a credibility problem, financial reports are likely to be viewed with considerable skepticism. Investors will view financial reporting estimates that increase income as evidence that management is padding earnings. This makes it very difficult for management to use financial reports to communicate positive news about current or future performance.

Example: Accounting Communication for FPIC Insurance Group

FPIC Insurance Group's key financial reporting estimates are for loss reserves for insurance claims using actuarial analyses of its own and other insurers' claims histories. At the end of fiscal year 1998, FPIC reported a loss reserve of $242.3 million. In its 10-K, management warned that "the uncertainties inherent in estimating ultimate losses on the basis of past experience have grown significantly in recent years, principally as a result of judicial expansion of liability standards and expansive interpretations of insurance contracts. These uncertainties may be further affected by, among other factors, changes in the rate of inflation and changes in the propensities of individuals to file claims. The inherent uncertainty of establishing reserves is relatively greater for companies writing long-tail casualty insurance."

To help investors assess its track record in making loss estimates, FPIC is required to provide a detailed breakdown of changes in loss estimates from prior years given actual claim losses. These data indicate that FPIC has actually been quite conservative in prior years' forecasts and has historically incurred fewer losses than it had initially predicted.

It is interesting to note that the area that raised questions for investors about FPIC's record was precisely its conservative estimation of loss reserves and their subsequent reversal. By being conservative, management may have raised questions about its ability to forecast losses reliably in the future, or given investors the impression that it had been managing earnings.

Key Analysis Questions

For management interested in understanding how effectively the firm's financial reports help it communicate with outside investors, the following questions are likely to provide a useful starting point:

- What are the primary business risks that have to be managed effectively? What processes and controls are in place to manage the business risks? How are these risks reflected in the financial statements? For example, credit risks are reflected in the bad debt allowance, and product quality risks are reflected in allowances for product returns and the method of revenue recognition. For these types of risks, what message is the firm sending on the management of these risks through its estimates or choices of accounting methods? Has the firm been unable to deliver on the forecasts underlying these choices? Alternatively, does the market seem to be ignoring the message underlying the firm's financial reporting choices, indicating a lack of credibility?
- How does the firm communicate about important risks that cannot be reflected in accounting estimates or methods? For example, a company's management of its technological innovation risk through research and development is difficult to reflect in its financial statements, and investors will still have questions about this business issue.

COMMUNICATION THROUGH FINANCIAL POLICIES

Managers can also use financing policies to communicate effectively with external investors. One important difference between this type of communication and additional disclosure is that the firm does not provide potentially proprietary information to competitors. Financial policies that are useful in this respect include dividend payouts, stock repurchases, financing choices, and hedging strategies.

Dividend Payout Policies

A firm's dividend payout decisions can provide information to investors on managers' assessments of the firm's future prospects. Dividend payout, defined as cash dividends as a percentage of income available to common shareholders, reflects the extent to which a company pays out profits or retains them for reinvestment. Because paying dividends reduces financial slack and is thus costly, a firm's dividend policy can help management communicate effectively with external investors. Investors recognize that managers will only increase their firm's dividend rate if they anticipate that the payout will not have a serious effect on the firm's future financing options. Thus, the decision to increase dividends can help investors appreciate management's optimism about the firm's future performance and ability to finance growth. This arises because dividend payouts tend to be sticky as managers are reluctant to cut dividend payouts. Managers will only increase dividends when they are confident that they will be able to sustain the increased payout rate in future years. Consequently, investors interpret dividend increases as signals of managers' confidence in the quality of current and future earnings.[8]

As a result, managers in high-growth firms tend to set low dividend payout policies and retain their internally generated funds for reinvestment to minimize any costs from capital market constraints on financing growth options. On the other hand, firms with high and stable operating cash flows and few investment opportunities have high dividend payouts to reduce managers' incentives to reinvest free cash flows in unprofitable ventures.

Stock Repurchases

In some countries, such as the U.S. and the U.K., managers can use stock repurchases to communicate with external investors. Under a stock repurchase, the firm buys back its own stock, either through a purchase on the open market, through a tender offer, or through a negotiated purchase with a large stockholder. Of course a stock repurchase, particularly a tender offer repurchase, is an expensive way for management to communicate with outside investors that they believe that the firm is undervalued. Firms typically pay a hefty premium to acquire their shares in tender offer repurchases, potentially diluting the value of the shares that are not tendered or not accepted for tender. In addition, the fees to investment banks and lawyers, and for share solicitation, are not trivial. Given these costs, it is not surprising that research findings indicate that stock repurchases are effective signals to investors about the level and risk of future earnings performance.[9] Research findings also suggest that firms that use stock repurchases to communicate with investors have accounting assets that are less reflective of firm value and have high general information asymmetry.[10]

Financing Choices

Firms that have problems communicating with external investors may be able to use financing choices to reduce them. For example, a firm that is unwilling to provide proprietary information to help dispersed public investors value it appropriately may be willing to provide such information to a knowledgeable private investor, which can become a large stockholder/creditor, or to a bank that agrees to provide the company with a significant new loan. A firm with credibility problems in financial reporting can also sell stock or issue debt to an informed private investor such as a large customer who has superior information about the quality of its product or service.

Such changes in financing and ownership can mitigate communication problems in two ways. First, the terms of the new financing arrangement and the credibility of the new lender or stockholder can provide investors with information to reassess the value of the firm. Second, the accompanying increased concentration of ownership and the role of large block holders in corporate governance can have a positive effect on valuation. If investors are concerned about management's incentives to increase shareholder value, the presence of a new block shareholder or significant creditor on the board can be reassuring. This type of monitoring arises in leveraged buyouts, start-ups backed by venture capital firms, and firms with equity partnership investments. In Japanese and German corporations, it may also arise because large banks own both debt and equity and have close working relationships with firms' managers.

Of course, in the extreme, management can decide that the best option for a firm is to no longer operate as a public company. This can be accomplished by a management buyout, where a buyout group (including management) leverages its own investment (using bank or public debt finance), buys the firm, and takes it private. The buyout group hopes to run the firm for several years and then take the company public again, hopefully with a track record of improved performance that enables investors to value the firm more effectively.

Hedging

An important source of mispricing arises if investors are unable to distinguish between unexpected changes in reported earnings due to management performance and transitory shocks that are beyond managers' control (e.g., foreign currency translation gains and losses). Managers can counteract these effects by hedging such "accounting" risks. Even though hedging may be costly, it is valuable if it reduces information problems that potentially lead to misvaluation.

Example: Stock Buybacks at FPIC Insurance Group

On August 12, 1999, FPIC Insurance Group announced that it would immediately begin purchasing shares of its common stock. As many as 429,000 shares were to be repurchased under the program. The company argued that the dramatic drop in its stock price was unwarranted and that its stock was now greatly undervalued. William R. Russell, president and chief executive officer of FPIC stated:

> We believe the recent drop in our stock price may be linked to certain changes in our reserving policy that were described in our earnings release. We believe that our reserving policy is now and has always been appropriate. We believe that the market has overreacted and that FPIC continues to be an excellent long-term investment. Our repurchases . . . reflect our commitment to enhance shareholder value. (Reuters, August 12, 1999)

The repurchase temporarily arrested FPIC's stock price slide. The price recovered from $21 to around $26 during the period surrounding the announcement. However this effect was temporary, and the price subsequently fell further to $14.25. On November 9, 1999, with the stock trading at $15.75, the Board of Directors approved an additional stock buyback program, authorizing the repurchase of an additional 500,000 shares. The announcement, which came in conjunction with the release of third quarter earnings, received a favorable market reaction, and the stock closed the day at $17.31, a gain of almost 10 percent.

Key Analysis Questions

For management considering whether to use financing policies to communicate more effectively with investors, the following questions are likely to provide a useful starting point for analysis:

- Have other potentially less costly actions, such as expanded disclosure or accounting communication, been considered? If not, would these alternatives provide a lower cost means of communication? Alternatively, if management is concerned about providing proprietary

> information to competitors, or has low credibility, these options may not be effective.
> - Does the firm have sufficient free cash flow to be able to implement a share repurchase program or to increase dividends? If the firm has excess cash available today but expects to be constrained in the future, a stock repurchase may be more effective. Alternatively, if management expects to have some excess cash available each year, a dividend increase may be in order.
> - Is the firm cash constrained and unable to increase disclosure for proprietary reasons? If so, management may want to consider changing the mix of owners as a way of indicating to investors that another informed outsider is bullish on the company. Of course, another possibility is for management itself to increase its stake in the company.

ALTERNATE FORMS OF INVESTOR COMMUNICATION

Given the limitations of accounting standards, auditing, and monitoring by financial analysts, as well as the reporting credibility problems faced by management, firms that wish to communicate effectively with external investors are often forced to use alternative methods. We discuss two additional ways that managers can communicate with external investors and analysts below.

Analyst Meetings

One popular way for managers to help mitigate communication problems is to meet regularly with financial analysts that follow the firm. At these meetings, management will field questions about the firm's current financial performance and discuss its future business plans. In addition to holding analyst meetings, many firms appoint a director of public relations, who provides further regular contact with analysts seeking more information on the firm.

In the last ten years, conference calls have become a popular forum for management to communicate with financial analysts. Recent research finds that firms are more likely to host calls if they are in industries where financial statement data fail to capture key business fundamentals on a timely basis.[11] In addition, conference calls themselves appear to provide new information to analysts about a firm's performance and future prospects.[12] Smaller and less heavily traded firms in particular benefit from initiating investor conference calls.[13]

While firms continue to meet with analysts, new SEC rules, called Regulation Fair Disclosure (or Reg FD), have changed the nature of these interactions. Under these new rules, which became effective in the U.S. in October 2000, firms that provide material nonpublic information to security analysts or professional investors must simultaneously (or promptly thereafter) disclose the information to the public. While Reg FD has reduced the information that managers disclose in private meetings, recent research shows that the regulation has enhanced the conference call's ability to improve analyst forecast accuracy and consensus by eliminating selective disclosure.[14]

Voluntary Disclosure

Another way for managers to improve the credibility of their financial reporting is through voluntary disclosure. Accounting rules usually prescribe minimum disclosure requirements, but they do not restrict managers from voluntarily providing additional information. These could include an articulation of the company's long-term strategy, specification of nonfinancial leading indicators that are useful in judging the effectiveness of the strategy implementation, explanation of the relation between the leading indicators and future profits, and forecasts of future performance. Voluntary disclosures can be reported in the firm's annual report, in brochures created to describe the firm to investors, in management meetings with analysts, or in investor relations responses to information requests.[15]

One constraint on expanded disclosure is the competitive dynamics in product markets. Disclosure of proprietary information on strategies and their expected economic consequences may hurt the firm's competitive position. Managers then face a trade-off between providing information that is useful to investors in assessing the firm's economic performance and withholding information to maximize the firm's product market advantage.

A second constraint in providing voluntary disclosure is management's legal liability. Forecasts and voluntary disclosures can potentially be used by dissatisfied shareholders to bring civil action against management for providing misleading information. This seems ironic, since voluntary disclosures should provide investors with additional information. Unfortunately, it can be difficult for courts to decide whether managers' disclosures were good-faith estimates of uncertain future events which later did not materialize, or whether management manipulated the market. Consequently many corporate legal departments recommend against management providing much voluntary disclosure. One aspect of voluntary disclosure, earnings guidance, has been particularly controversial. There is growing evidence that the guidance provided by management plays an important role in leading analysts' expectations towards achievable earnings targets, and that management guidance is more likely when analysts' initial forecasts are overly optimistic.[16]

Finally, management credibility can limit a firm's incentives to provide voluntary disclosures. If management faces a credibility problem in financial reporting, any voluntary disclosure it provides is also likely to be viewed skeptically. In particular, investors may be concerned about what management is not telling them, particularly since such disclosures are not audited.

Example: Other Forms of Communication at FPIC Insurance Group

In the months subsequent to the earnings announcement and the precipitous drop in stock price, the board and management of FPIC Insurance Group made a series of moves to regain investor confidence. On August 23, 1999, in a high level management shake-up, the company's chief financial officer and the president of FPIC's Physicians Insurance subsidiary were fired. According to a statement by FPIC Chairman Robert Baratta, ". . . the board of directors felt the company could benefit from changes at this time in its senior management structure." (Reuters, August 24, 1999)

In addition, over the three-month period from August through October 1999, insiders were active buyers of the stock. During that time, nine different insiders purchased additional shares in contrast to no sellers. This sent a strong signal to investors that those people with a close understanding of the firm were believers in its business prospects and confident that the stock performance would eventually reflect that.

In a move to address investor concerns regarding its reserve policy, the company commissioned a reserve study by a nationally recognized independent actuarial adviser that performed no other services for FPIC. The study analyzed the net loss and allocated loss adjustment expense reserves as of June 30, 1999. According to CEO Russell, "We are happy to report that this study confirms our belief that our reserves with respect to this business are adequate. This study should eliminate the concerns that have been raised." However, the voluntary study and added disclosure did not do much to address investors' concerns, and the stock price lost 12 percent in the two days following the announcement. FPIC was hit by the general economic downturn from 2000 to 2002. In the fourth quarter of 2000, the company increased its loss reserves dramatically in response to unfavorable trends in claims data. In 2000, it barely broke even and in 2001 it reported a sizable loss. Performance improved in 2002, and by 2004 it earned a 14.4% ROE and had 19% sales growth. The stock price steadily recovered and in May 2007 was $44.50.

THE ROLE OF THE AUDITOR

In the U.S. the auditor is responsible for providing investors with assurance that the financial statements are prepared in accordance with Generally Accepted Accounting Principles, or GAAP. This requires the auditor to evaluate whether transactions are recorded in a way that is consistent with the rules produced by regulators (including the FASB, PCAOB, and SEC) and whether management estimates reflected in the financial statements are reasonable. The results of the audit are disclosed in the audit report, which is part of the financial statements. The auditor issues an unqualified report if (a) the firm's financial statements conform to GAAP, (b) the accounting methods are applied consistently throughout the prior three years, (c) the internal controls are adequate, and (d) there is no substantial doubt about the firm's ability to survive. If the financials do not conform to GAAP, the auditor is required to issue a qualified or an adverse report that provides information to investors on the discrepancies. If the auditor is uncertain about whether the firm can survive during the coming year, a going concern report is issued that points out the firm's survival risks.

In contrast, in the U.K. and countries that have adopted the U.K. system, such as Australia, New Zealand, Singapore, Hong Kong, and India, auditors undertake a broader review than their U.S. counterparts. U.K. audits are required to not only assess whether the financial statements are prepared in accordance with U.K. GAAP, but also to judge whether they fairly reflect the client's underlying economic performance. This additional assurance requires more judgment on the part of the auditor and increases the value of the audit to outside investors.

The essential procedures involved in a typical audit include (1) understand the client's business and industry to identify key risks for the audit, (2) evaluate the firm's internal control system to assess whether it is likely to produce reliable information, (3) perform preliminary analytic procedures to identify unusual events and possible errors, and (4) collect specific evidence on controls, transactions, and account balance details to form the basis for the auditor's opinion. In most cases client management is willing to respond to issues raised by the audit to ensure that the company receives an unqualified audit opinion. Once the audit is completed, the auditor presents a summary of audit scope and findings to the Audit Committee of the firm's board of directors.

It is worth noting that in both the U.S. and U.K. systems, the audit is not intended to detect fraud. Of course in some cases it may do so, but that is not its purpose. The detection of fraud is the domain of the internal audit department of the firm itself.

Challenges Facing Audit Industry

To understand the current problems facing the audit industry, it is necessary to go back to the mid-1970s, when two critical events created pressures on audit firms to cut costs and seek other revenue sources. The first of these was a decision by the Federal Trade Commission, concerned with a potential oligopoly by the large audit firms, to pressure the major firms to compete aggressively with each other for clients. The second was a shift in legal standards that enabled investors of companies with accounting problems to seek legal redress against the auditor without having to show that they had specifically relied on questionable accounting information in making their investment decisions. Instead, they could assert that they had relied on the stock price itself, which was affected by the misleading disclosures. This change, along with increasing litigiousness, dramatically increased the lawsuit risk for auditors.

Audit firms responded to the new business environment in several ways. They lobbied for mechanical accounting and auditing standards and developed standard operating procedures to reduce the variability in audits. This approach reduced the cost of audits and provided a defense in the case of litigation. But it also meant that auditors were more likely to view their role narrowly rather than exercise broader business judgment.

Furthermore, while mechanical standards make auditing easier, they do not necessarily increase corporate transparency.[17] Audit firms decided that profit margins would be thin in a world of mechanized, standardized audits, and they responded in two ways. One way was by aggressively pursuing a high volume strategy, and so audit partner compensation and promotion became more closely linked to a cordial relationship with top management that attracted new audit clients and retained existing clients. This made it difficult for partners to be effective watchdogs. The large audit firms also responded to challenges to their core business by developing new consulting services, which were higher margin and higher growth. This diversification strategy deflected top management energy and partner talent from the audit side of the business to the more profitable consulting part.

The Enron debacle dramatically illustrated many of the problems facing the industry.[18] The use of mechanical, standardized audits encouraged Enron's auditors to take a narrow perspective on their role as financial report watchdogs. Even though they may have believed that Enron's reports met GAAP, they failed to ask big-picture questions about their client's strategy, core risks, and the company's overall transparency. Mechanical standards made it easier for Enron's unscrupulous managers not only to meet the letter of GAAP (although in the end they did not even do that) but also to skirt their spirit, concealing important obligations and overstating profits. Finally, the pressure on Enron's auditors to retain their clients and to grow their firms' consulting businesses reduced their independence, leading them to approve questionable accounting decisions and to work closely with management to meet Enron's financial reporting objectives.

The Sarbanes-Oxley Act was designed to correct some of the structural problems facing the industry. The Act has banned audit firms from providing certain types of consulting services to their audit clients and mandates that the audit partner be rotated every five years. The Act requires the Audit Committee of the Board of Directors to become more active in appointing the auditor and reviewing the audit. While these actions are widely expected to improve governance and the audit process, they have been a boon to audit firm profitability, with the added costs becoming a point of controversy in the business community.

Role of Financial Analysis Tools in Auditing

How can the financial analysis tools discussed in this book be used by audit professionals? The relevance to the audit of the four steps in financial analysis—strategy analysis, accounting analysis, financial analysis, and prospective analysis—is discussed briefly below.

Strategy Analysis Strategy analysis is critical to the first stage of the audit, understanding the client's business and industry. It is important that the auditor develop the expertise to be able to identify the chief risks facing its client. Given the sheer volume of activity, it is impossible to review all the transactions of the firm during the audit. Time and attention should be focused on the areas that investors need in order to evaluate the firm's value proposition and how well it is managing key success factors. These are also likely to be the areas worth further testing and analysis by the auditor, to assess their impact on the financial statements.

Accounting Analysis For the auditor, accounting analysis involves two steps. First, the auditor must understand how the key success factors and risks are reflected in the financial statements. The second step in accounting analysis is for the auditor to evaluate management judgment reflected in the critical financial statements items.

Financial Analysis Financial ratios help auditors judge whether there are any unusual performance changes for their client, either relative to past performance or relative to their competitors. Any such changes merit further investigation to ensure that the reasons for the change can be fully explained and to determine what additional tests are required to satisfy the auditor that the reported changes in performance are justified. Careful ratio analysis can also reveal whether clients are facing business problems that might induce management to conceal losses or keep significant obligations off the balance sheet. Such information should alert auditors that extra care and additional detailed tests are likely to be required to reach a conclusion on the client's financial statements.

Prospective Analysis Auditors use prospective analysis to assess whether estimates and forecasts made by management are consistent with the firm's economic position. In addition, the market's perception of a client's future performance provides a useful benchmark for affirming or questioning the auditor's assessment of the client's prospects. If the auditor concludes that the market is either overly optimistic or pessimistic about a client, he or she can determine whether additional disclosure will help investors develop a more realistic view of the company's prospects.

Key Analysis Questions

The following questions are likely to provide a useful starting point for auditors in their analysis of a client's financial statements:

- What are the chief business risks facing the firm? How well are these risks managed?
- What are the accounting policies and estimates that reflect the firm's principal risks? What tests and evidence are required to evaluate management judgment that is reflected in these accounting decisions?
- Do the critical ratios indicate any unusual changes in client performance? What tests and evidence are required to understand the causes of such changes?
- Has firm performance deteriorated, creating pressure on management to manage earnings or record off-balance-sheet transactions? If so, what additional tests and evidence are required to provide assurance that the financial statements are consistent with GAAP?
- How is the market assessing the client's prospects? If different from the auditor, what is the reason for the difference? If the market is overly optimistic or pessimistic, are there implications for client disclosure or accounting estimates?

Example: Auditing FPIC Insurance Group

For FPIC Insurance Group, how well the company manages claim risk is its most critical success factor. Not surprisingly, the stock price volatility appears to be largely driven by changing perceptions of this risk. In the financial statements, claim risk is reflected in the reserves set aside for future claims. This should be a principal focus of the audit.

Questions for the auditor include the following:

- Why did the company change its reserve policy this period? Does the change reflect a change in its business model, such as an attempt to reduce insurance sales to more risky customers? If so, is there evidence of a change in customer demographics and claim patterns?
- Does the change reflect excessive over-reserving by the client in earlier periods? If so, why did the auditors approve this earlier policy? Why did management select this year to release those reserves?
- Is the change in reserve policy justifiable, or is management simply responding to pressure to meet unrealistic market expectations?
- What information is available about a representative sample of outstanding claims? Are estimates of the cost of settling these claims realistic given prior settlements and experiences for other firms in the same industry?
- If the change in claim reserves appears to be reasonable, what additional information can the firm provide to investors to address their concerns? Will this information need to be audited?

THE ROLE OF THE AUDIT COMMITTEE

Audit committees are responsible for overseeing the work of the auditor, for ensuring that the financial statements are properly prepared, and for reviewing the internal controls at the company. Audit committees, which are mandated by many stock exchanges and by the SEC, typically comprise three to four outside directors who meet regularly before or after the full board meetings.

In the last few years, requirements for audit committee have been expanded and formalized. In December 1999, the SEC, the national stock exchange(s), and the Auditing Standards Board issued new audit committee rules based largely on recommendations of the Blue Ribbon Committee (BRC) on Improving the Effectiveness of Corporate Audit Committees. The new rules defined best practices for judging audit committee members' independence and qualifications.

Following the collapse of Enron, additional audit committee requirements were created under the Sarbanes-Oxley Act. The Act requires that audit committees take formal responsibility for appointing, overseeing, and negotiating fees with external auditors. Audit committee members are required to be independent directors with no consulting or other potentially compromising relation to management. It is recommended that at least one member of the committee have financial expertise, such as being a CFO, CEO, or retired audit partner.

The audit committee is expected to be independent of management and to take an active role in reviewing the propriety of the firm's financial statements. Committee members are expected to question management and the auditors about the quality of the firm's financial reporting, the scope and findings of the external audit, and the quality of internal controls.

In reality, however, the audit committee has to rely extensively on information from management as well as internal and external auditors. Given the ground that it has to cover, its limited available time, and the technical nature of accounting standards, audit committees are not in a position to catch management fraud or auditors' failures on a timely basis.

How then can the audit committee add value?[19] We believe that many of the financial analysis tools discussed in this book can provide a useful way for audit committees to approach their tasks. Many of the applications of the financial analysis steps discussed for auditors also apply for audit committees.

In its scrutiny of financial statements, the committee should use the 80–20 rule, devoting most of its time to assessing the effectiveness of those *few* policies and decisions that have the *most* impact on investors' perceptions of the company's critical performance indicators. This should not require any additional work for committee members, since they should already have a good understanding of the firm's key success factors and risks from discussions of the full board.

Audit committee members should also have sufficient financial background to identify where in the financial statements the important risks are reflected. Their discussions with management and external auditors should focus on these risks. How well are they being managed? How are the auditors planning their work to focus on these areas? What evidence have they gathered to judge the adequacy of the financial statement estimates?

The audit committee also receives regular reviews of company performance from management as part of their board duties. Committee members should be especially proactive in requesting information that helps them evaluate how the firm is managing its key risks, since this information can also help them judge the quality of the financial statements. Audit committee members need to ask: Is information on company performance we are receiving in our regular board meetings consistent with the picture portrayed in the financial statements? If not, what is missing? Are additional disclosures required to ensure that investors are well informed about the firm's operations and performance?

Finally, audit committees need to focus on capital market expectations, not just statutory financial reports. In today's capital markets, the game begins when companies set expectations via analyst meetings, press releases, and other forms of investor communications. Indeed, the pressure to manage earnings is often a direct consequence of Wall Street's unrealistic expectations, either deliberately created by management or sustained by their inaction. Thus, it is also important for audit committees to oversee the firm's investor relations strategy and ensure that management sets realistic expectations for both the short and long term.

Key Analysis Questions

The following questions are likely to provide a useful starting point for audit committees in their discussions with management and auditors about the firm's financial statements:

- How are the critical business risks facing the firm being managed?
- How are these risks reflected by accounting policies and estimates in the financial statements? What was the basis for the external auditor's assessment of these items?
- Is information on the critical value drivers and firm performance presented to the full board consistent with the picture of the firm reflected in the financial statements and MD&A?
- What expectations is management creating in the capital market? Are these likely to cause undue pressure to manage earnings?

SUMMARY

This chapter discussed how many of the financial analysis tools developed in Chapters 2 through 8 can be used by managers to develop a coherent disclosure strategy, and by corporate board members and external auditors to improve the quality of their work.

By communicating effectively with investors, management can potentially reduce information problems for outside investors, lowering the likelihood that the stock will be mispriced or unnecessarily volatile. This can be important for firms that wish to raise new capital or avoid takeovers, or whose management is concerned that its true job performance is not reflected in the firm's stock price.

The typical way for firms to communicate with investors is through financial reporting. Accounting standards and auditing make the reporting process a way for managers to not only provide information about the firm's current performance but also indicate, through accounting estimates, where they believe the firm is headed in the future. However, financial reports are not always able to convey the type of forward-looking information that investors need. Accounting standards often do not permit firms to capitalize outlays, such as R&D, that provide significant future benefits to the firm.

A second way that management can communicate with investors is through non-accounting means. We discussed several such mechanisms, including using financial policies (such as stock repurchases, dividend increases, and hedging) to help signal management's optimism about the firm's future performance; meeting with financial analysts to explain the firm's strategy, current performance, and outlook; and disclosing additional information, both quantitative and qualitative, to provide investors with similar information as management has.

In this chapter we have stressed the importance of communicating effectively with investors. But firms also have to communicate with other stakeholders, including employees, customers, suppliers, and regulatory bodies. Many of the same principles discussed here can also be applied to management communication with these other stakeholders.

Finally, we examined the capital market role of governance agents, such as external auditors and audit committees. Both have recently faced considerable public scrutiny following a spate of financial reporting meltdowns in the U.S. Much has been done to improve the governance and independence of these intermediaries. We focus on how the financial analysis tools developed in the book can be used to improve the quality of audit and audit committee work. The tools of strategy analysis, accounting analysis, financial analysis, and prospective analysis can help auditors and audit committee members to identify the key issues in the financial statements to focus on and provide commonsense ways of assessing whether there are potential reporting problems that merit additional testing and analysis.

DISCUSSION QUESTIONS

1. Apple's inventory increased from $1 billion on December 29, 1994, to $1.95 billion one year later. In contrast, sales for the fourth quarter in each of these years increased from $2 billion to $2.6 billion. What is the implied annualized inventory turnover for Apple for these years? What different interpretations about future performance could a financial analyst infer from this change? What information could Apple's management provide to investors to clarify the change in inventory turnover? What are the costs and benefits to Apple from disclosing this information?

What issues does this change raise for the auditor? What additional tests would you want to conduct as Apple's auditor?

2. a. What are likely to be the long-term critical success factors for the following types of firms?
   - a high technology company such as Microsoft
   - a large low-cost retailer such as Wal-Mart

   b. How useful is financial accounting data for evaluating how well these two companies are managing their critical success factors? What other types of information would be useful in your evaluation? What are the costs and benefits to these companies from disclosing this type of information to investors?

3. Management frequently objects to disclosing additional information on the grounds that it is proprietary. For instance, when the FASB proposed to expand disclosures on (a) accounting for stock-based employee compensation (issued in December 2002) and (b) business segment performance (issued in June 1997), many corporate managers expressed strong opposition to both proposals. What are the potential proprietary costs from expanded disclosures in each of these areas? If you conclude that proprietary costs are relatively low for either, what alternative explanations do you have for management's opposition?

4. Financial reporting rules in many countries outside the U.S. (e.g., the U.K., Australia, New Zealand, and France) permit management to revalue fixed assets (and in some cases even intangible assets) which have increased in value. Revaluations are typically based on estimates of realizable value made by management or independent valuers. Do you expect that these accounting standards will make earnings and book values more or less useful to investors? Explain why or why not. How can management make these types of disclosures more credible?

5. Under a management buyout, the top management of a firm offers to buy the company from its stockholders, usually at a premium over its current stock price. The management team puts up its own capital to finance the acquisition, with additional financing typically coming from a private buyout firm and private debt. If management is interested in making such an offer for its firm in the near future, what are its financial reporting incentives? How do these differ from the incentives of management that are not interested in a buyout? How would you respond to a proposed management buyout if you were the firm's auditor? What about if you were a member of the audit committee?

6. You are approached by the management of a small start-up company that is planning to go public. The founders are unsure about how aggressive they should be in their accounting decisions as they come to the market. John Smith, the CEO, asserts, "We might as well take full advantage of any discretion offered by accounting rules, since the market will be expecting us to do so." What are the pros and cons of this strategy? As the partner of a major audit firm, what type of analysis would you perform before deciding to take on a start-up that is planning to go public?

7. Two years after a successful public offering, the CEO of a biotechnology company is concerned about stock market uncertainty surrounding the potential of new drugs in the development pipeline. In his discussion with you, the CEO notes that even though they have recently made significant progress in their internal R&D efforts, the stock has

performed poorly. What options does he have to help convince investors of the value of the new products? Which of these alternatives are likely to be feasible?

8. Why might the CEO of the biotechnology firm discussed in Question 7 be concerned about the firm being undervalued? Would the CEO be equally concerned if the stock were overvalued? Do you believe that the CEO would attempt to correct the market's perception in this overvaluation case? How would you react to company concern about market under- or overvaluation if you were the firm's auditor? Or if you were a member of the audit committee?

9. When companies decide to shift from private to public financing by making an initial public offering for their stock, they are likely to face increased costs of investor communications. Given this additional cost, why would firms opt to go public?

10. German firms are traditionally financed by banks, which have representatives on the companies' boards. How would communication challenges differ for these firms relative to U.S. firms, which rely more on public financing?

NOTES

1. M. Jensen and W. Meckling, "Theory of the Firm: Managerial Behavior, Agency Costs, and Capital Structure," *Journal of Financial Economics* 3 (October 1976): 305–360, analyzed agency problems between managers and outside investors. Subsequent work by Bengt Holmstrom and others examined how contracts between managers and outside investors could mitigate the agency problem.

2. K. Murphy and J. Zimmerman, "Financial Performance Surrounding CEO Turnover," *Journal of Accounting and Economics* 16 (January/April/July 1993): 273–315, find a strong relation between CEO turnover and earnings-based performance.

3. See S. Teoh, I. Welch, and T. Wong, "Earnings Management and the Long-Run Market Performance of Initial Public Offerings," *The Journal of Finance* 63 (December 1998): 1935–1974, and S. Teoh, I. Welch, and T. Wong, "Earnings Management and the Underperformance of Seasoned Equity Offerings," *Journal of Financial Economics* 50 (October 1998): 63–99.

4. This market imperfection often referred to as a "lemons" or "information" problem, is also discussed in Chapter 1. It was first studied by George Akerlof in relation to the used car market in "The Market for 'Lemons': Quality Uncertainty and the Market Mechanism," *Quarterly Journal of Economics* 90 (1970): 629–650.

5. Of course improved analysis alone is unlikely to be sufficient to improve market intermediation if the structural reforms implemented by the Sarbanes-Oxley Act and the stock exchanges fail to correct the serious conflicts of interest for intermediaries that we have witnessed in the last few years.

6. D. Skinner, "Earnings Disclosures and Stockholder Lawsuits," *Journal of Accounting and Economics* (November 1997): 249–283, finds that firms with bad earnings news tend to predisclose this information, perhaps to reduce the cost of litigation that inevitably follows bad news quarters.

7. For example, G. Foster, "Briloff and the Capital Market," *Journal of Accounting Research* 17, no. 1 (Spring 1979): 262–274, finds firms that are criticized for their accounting by Abraham J. Briloff in *Barron's* on average suffer an 8 percent decline in their stock price around the article publication date. H. Desai and P. Jain, "Long-Run Stock Returns Following Briloff's Analyses," *Financial Analysts Journal* 60, no. 2 (March/April 2004): 47–56, find significant declines in one- and two-year performance of the firms that Briloff criticized.

8. Findings by P. Healy and K. Palepu in "Earnings Information Conveyed by Dividend Initiations and Omissions," *Journal of Financial Economics* 21 (September 1988): 149–175, indicate that investors interpret announcements of dividends initiations and omissions as managers' forecasts of future earnings performance.

9. See L. Dann, R. Masulis, and D. Mayers, "Repurchase Tender Offers and Earnings Information," *Journal of Accounting and Economics* (September 1991): 217–252, and M. Hertzel and P. Jain, "Earnings and Risk Changes Around Stock Repurchases," *Journal of Accounting and Economics* (September 1991): 253–276.

10. See M. Barth and R. Kasznik, "Share Repurchases and Intangible Assets," *Journal of Accounting and Economics* 28 (December 1999): 211–241.

11. See S. Tasker, "Bridging the Information Gap: Quarterly Conference Calls as a Medium for Voluntary Disclosure." *Review of Accounting Studies* 3, no. 1–2 (1998): 137–167.

12. See R. Frankel, M. Johnson, and D. Skinner, "An Empirical Examination of Conference Calls as a Voluntary Disclosure Medium," *Journal of Accounting Research* 37, no. 1 (Spring 1999): 133–150.

13. See M. Kimbrough, "The Effect of Conference Calls on Analyst and Market Underreaction to Earnings Announcements," *The Accounting Review* 80, no. 1 (January 2005): 189–219.

14. See A. Irani, "The Effect of Regulation Fair Disclosure on the Relevance of Conference Calls to Financial Analysts," *Review of Quantitative Finance and Accounting* 22, no. 1 (January 2004): 15–28.

15. Recent research on voluntary disclosure includes M. Lang and R. Lundholm, "Cross-Sectional Determinants of Analysts' Ratings of Corporate Disclosures," *Journal of Accounting Research* 31 (Autumn 1993): 246–271; M. Lang and R. Lundholm, "Corporate Disclosure Policy and Analysts," *The Accounting Review* 71 (October 1996): 467–492; M. Welker, "Disclosure Policy, Information Asymmetry and Liquidity in Equity Markets," *Contemporary Accounting Research* (Spring 1995): 801–827; C. Botosan, "The Impact of Annual Report Disclosure Level on Investor Base and the Cost of Capital," *The Accounting Review* (July 1997): 323–350; and P. Healy, A. Hutton, and K. Palepu, "Stock Performance and Intermediation Changes Surrounding Sustained Increases in Disclosure," *Contemporary Accounting Research* 16, no. 3 (Fall 1999): 485–521. This research finds that firms are more likely to provide high levels of disclosure if they have strong earnings performance, issue securities, have more analyst following, and have less dispersion in analyst forecasts. In addition, firms with high levels of disclosure policies tend to have a lower cost of capital and bid–ask spread. Finally, firms that increase disclosure

have accompanying increases in stock returns, institutional ownership, analyst following, and stock liquidity. In addition, in "The Role of Supplementary Statements with Management Earnings Forecasts," *Journal of Accounting Research* 41 (December 2003): 867–890, A. Hutton, G. Miller, and D. Skinner examine the market response to management earnings forecasts and find that bad news forecasts are always informative but that good news forecasts are informative only when they are supported by verifiable forward-looking statements.

16. See J. Cotter, I. Tuna, and P. Wysocki, "Expectations Management and Beatable Targets: How do Analysts React to Explicit Earnings Guidance?" *Contemporary Accounting Research* 23, no. 3 (Autumn 2006): 593–628.

17. For example, M. Nelson, J. Elliott, and R. Tarpley, in "Evidence from Auditors About Managers' and Auditors' Earnings Management Decisions," *The Accounting Review* 77 (2002 Supplement): 175–202, show that mechanical accounting rules for structured finance transactions lead to more earnings management.

18. See P. Healy and K. Palepu, "The Fall of Enron," *Journal of Economic Perspectives* 17, no. 2 (Spring 2003): 3–26, and P. Healy and K. Palepu, "How the Quest for Efficiency Undermined the Market," *Harvard Business Review* (July 2003): 76–85.

19. See P. Healy and K. Palepu, "Audit the Audit Committees: After Enron Boards Must Change the Focus and Provide Greater Financial Transparency," *Financial Times*, June 10, 2002, p. 14.

INDEX

Note: In each entry, the first number is the chapter number; the numbers following the hyphen (-) are the range of pages on which the entry appears. Bold type is used to indicate the numbers of rules. Italic type indicates the page numbers of charts and tables. An "n" after a page number indicates that the entry is an author's note.

AUTHOR INDEX